HUMAN RESOURCE MANAGEMENT IN HOSPITALITY

MALAY BISWAS

Indian Institute of Management
Rohtak

OXFORD
UNIVERSITY PRESS

OXFORD
UNIVERSITY PRESS

Oxford University Press is a department of the University of Oxford.
It furthers the University's objective of excellence in research, scholarship,
and education by publishing worldwide. Oxford is a registered trade mark of
Oxford University Press in the UK and in certain other countries.

Published in India by
Oxford University Press
YMCA Library Building, 1 Jai Singh Road, New Delhi 110001, India

ISBN-13: 978-0-19-806985-0
ISBN-10: 0-19-806985-5

Typeset in Baskerville
by Laserwords Private Limited, Chennai

To my chemistry teacher at Don Bosco School, Krishnanagar
Shri Sujeet Biswas
who generously introduced me to the wonderful world of calculus

And to my mother
Smt. Devi Biswas
who silently taught me the meaning of patience through her life

And also to my father-in-law
Shri Shambhu Ghosh
who has always provided timely guidance in my life's journey

Preface

The hospitality industry in India has recently emerged as one of the foremost contributors to the services sector, and may well help the country transition from a manufacturing sector-driven economy to a services sector-driven economy. Despite tumultuous market conditions, the services sector has recorded a steady growth and the economy has witnessed an upswing in the number and range of international hotel chains that have begun operations in India. Leading Indian hospitality brands such as Taj Hotels, Resorts and Palaces are expanding their operations in select international tourism markets in the US and in Africa. Thus, the whole dynamics of the hospitality business is changing at a furiously rapid pace.

To sustain this growth in the hospitality industry, it is crucial to source a talented man-power, and for doing so, human resource management (HRM) in the hospitality industry plays an important role for many compelling reasons. First, efficient employee management provides strategic and cost leadership. Second, trained and talented manpower can provide a hospitality organization durable competitive advantage over rivals. Third, manpower cost is one of the prime factors for the production of hospitality services. Fourth, hospitality employees are in great demand in other service sectors too, such as airlines, retail, BPOs/KPOs/call centres, and banks. Thus, having manpower specifically trained for hospitality industry needs is a prime requirement.

The situation has been complicated with the advent of the new-generation employees. These employees are differently talented and join the work with different sets of ambitions and aspirations. Media-savvy, they enjoy broadcasting their current experiences through social media sites such as Facebook and Twitter, with multiple friends in dispersed loca-tions, who join in and add more colour to the shared experience. Managing this young and dynamically different manpower poses critical challenges for HR professionals. The biggest challenge being that authority is no longer a valid instrument of management and is to be routinely questioned.

Ordinary rules of management may not necessarily work for the new generation. We need to decode them, find suitable generalizations, and then develop appropriate strate-gies, which may work for some time. Management techniques, which worked with earlier generations, may fall short while dealing with the new-generation employees. Therefore, HRM practices are on the verge of developing new language, new architecture, and new vocabulary.

ABOUT THE BOOK

Voluminous research works are continuously unfolding in the field of HRM. Accommo-dating them in a textbook predominantly targeted at the undergraduate level of education is indeed a difficult task. This book, however, with its simplified presentation of the HRM practices followed in the Indian hospitality industry, attempts to introduce the reader to the beautiful world of human endeavour, individually and collectively co-created by employees, to deliver ultimate customer delight in a delicate hospitality environment. The book also provides the rationale behind certain HRM practices by integrating the discourse with recent findings from the behavioural sciences, without compromising on simplicity. Curious students will find it a valuable resource for further advancement of their knowledge. Most of the case studies in the book have been tried and tested in the class environment.

Over years of teaching hospitality management students, I have acutely felt the need for having a book specific to HRM in the Indian hospitality industry. Referring to books predominantly written for American and European audiences often invites a number of problems, as the practice of HRM in a country is deeply and intimately linked with the legal framework specific to that country. Referring to such books creates confusion in the minds of students, as they often mix US laws with Indian laws, without knowing the distinctions. It is equally true that the Indian workspace is distinctly different because of its social, cultural, and political orientation. This book focuses on India-specific stories, discussions, and practices, which will provide typical insights into the Indian hospitality business.

The reader will gain deeper insights into the prevalent HRM practices, as the human side of the organization is no longer the exclusive domain reserved for HR professionals. Individuals, whether they operate as an executive chef, executive housekeeper, front office manager, or general manager of the hotel, play an important role in the management of the human dimension in the hospitality business. Irrespective of the career choice a student makes on completing a hotel management programme, the acquisition of man management skills is a must. This book will go a long way in serving this purpose.

KEY FEATURES

The key features of the book are
- guidelines on the practical aspects of HRM in the hospitality industry,
- numerous examples, figures, tables, templates, and diagrams,
- a holistic view of the subject by taking into account all aspects of organizational behaviour,
- specific laws related to the hospitality industry, and
- appendices on abusive supervision and counterproductive behaviour.

Pedagogical Features

The book includes the following pedagogical features.

Indian hospitality-centric discussion A dedicated discourse on HRM with special reference to the Indian hospitality industry has been presented. This will enable the reader to comprehend the issues and relate to them with a high degree of comfort.

Integrated behavioural dynamics with HRM discourse The HRM function has been explained with adequate theoretical frameworks, sourced from the behavioural sciences. This enables the reader to develop a solid understanding of the issues.

Mini cases and examples The content of each chapter has been explained using examples and mini cases to make it relevant and meaningful to the reader.

Illustrations, figures, flow diagrams, and diagrams Wherever possible, a number of diagrams, illustrations, figures, and flow diagrams have been added to present a coherent view of specific issues.

User-friendly but content rich Each chapter has been written in a user-friendly style, without compromising on the content.

In this book, teachers will find numerous stories that are interesting and appropriate for introducing topics. I particularly encourage professional colleagues to utilise the case studies to deliver a stimulating classroom experience.

COVERAGE AND STRUCTURE

The book has been divided into the following fourteen chapters.

Chapter 1—Introduction to Human Resource Management—begins with a discussion on the inherent characteristics of the service industry, especially the hospitality industry. A brief outline has been presented showcasing how human resource functions acquire new dimensions and meanings in the hospitality industry. The discussion then moves on to map the various challenges faced by HR professionals in the Indian hospitality industry. The debate over the effectiveness of the human resource function and organization performance has been presented. The chapter ends with the various competencies required by today's HR professionals to deal with the emerging business concerns.

Chapter 2—Manpower Planning—highlights the meaning and importance of manpower planning in a hospitality organization. It provides an introductory discussion on the manpower planning process, charting out the various decision points. A rudimentary discussion has been presented to provide a glimpse of the various forecasting methods deployed for manpower planning. The chapter closes with a discussion on the various managerial actions required for dealing with the excess or shortfall of manpower, derived out of the manpower planning process.

Chapter 3—Recruitment—presents an introductory discussion on employee recruitment, one of the important managerial functions for a human resource manager. Discussion on recruitment starts with the importance of the recruitment process. It also highlights the managerial dilemma: whether to recruit employees from within the organization or to source it from the outside labour market, as each case inherits a diverse range of benefits and limitations, requiring managerial discretion to handle it carefully for organizational effectiveness. Subsequently, the discussion moves on to recruitment policy and its characteristics and closes with a brief sketch of the interview process.

Chapter 4—Training and Development—presents a brief sketch of the training and development function in a hospitality organization. It starts with a discussion on the importance of the training function, especially in a hospitality organization, and moves on to training needs identification process. An introductory discussion has been presented on the various training methods used to deliver a training programme. The chapter closes with a brief discussion on the various qualities required for being an effective trainer.

Chapter 5—Performance Appraisal—presents a concise discussion on performance appraisal. The chapter begins with a discussion on the prime importance of management of the performance management system in a hospitality organization, highlighting reasons that explain why the performance appraisal system fails. The discussion moves on to the balanced scorecard architecture embedded in many hospitality organizations for management of employee performance. The benefits of using the 360-degree feedback framework have been outlined in brief. The chapter closes with a few suggestions for strengthening the employee performance management framework in Indian hospitality organizations.

Chapter 6—Employee Motivation—discusses the theoretical underpinnings on employees' motivation. The reader is introduced to various drivers of employees' motivation. The discussion then moves on to the various theoretical frameworks developed by behavioural scientists for explaining employee motivation. Managerial action with reference to employee motivation is often linked to its measurement. Therefore, the discussion on measuring employee motivation is particularly important and interesting for the reader. The chapter ends with a short note on the strategies deployed by human resource professionals to motivate employees.

Chapter 7—Compensation and Benefit Management—deals with one of the most important functions of the human resource manager. The chapter begins with a discussion on the dynamic business environment and its impact on the compensation policy of a hospitality organization. A brief discussion on the various components of a compensation policy has been presented for its relevance and organizational effectiveness. Compensation policies are deeply linked to labour laws, human psychology, and labour economics. This integral relationship has been explored. The chapter ends with the current practices in executive compensation in the hospitality industry.

Chapter 8—Job Satisfaction—reviews the current practices of enlightened organizations that design a range of activities to enhance employees' job satisfaction. The chapter begins with an explanation of the term 'job satisfaction' as accepted by behavioural scientists. The importance of job satisfaction among employees working in the hospitality sector is covered, along with the determinants of job satisfaction. Next is presented the various measurement practices followed to assess the current state of employee satisfaction. The chapter ends with the results of job satisfaction.

Chapter 9—Organizational Culture—discusses one of the most important fabrics in a hospitality organization. The chapter presents the meaning and functions of organizational culture. It examines the role of organizational cultures for delivering strategic competence. Organizational culture has been construed in multiple frameworks. Selective frameworks, such as the cultural web model, OCTAPACE model, and competing value framework model, have been highlighted. This will enable the reader to have a stronger grip on the invisible fabric of organizational culture of any hospitality organization. The chapter next turns to the various diagnostic arrangements embedded in an organization to capture the basic tenets of organizational culture. Managerial implications include how organizations transmit cultural components among its employees. Therefore, the chapter ends with a short discussion on the role of top leadership in creating and sustaining various elements of organizational culture in a hospitality organization.

Chapter 10—Organizational Conflict and Collective Bargaining—begins with a definition of organization conflict and brings out the extent of harm that dysfunctional conflicts can have on a hospitality organization. Using a theoretical framework developed by Thomas Kilmann, an introductory discussion has been presented on the conflict resolution techniques that potentially resolve organizational conflict. The chapter then moves on to the strategies followed by HR managers to eliminate the effects of organizational conflicts. It ends with a short note on collective bargaining, which is an essential and legal arrangement in the Indian labour management system.

Chapter 11—Indian Labour Laws in the Indian Hospitality Industry—presents a brief sketch on the Indian labour laws that are applicable in the Indian hospitality business context. The chapter begins with a summary on the legal frameworks available to address labour problems. The chapter next deals with special cases such as employee compensation and the relevant legal provisions pertaining to it. Subsequently, the chapter explicates the various legal infrastructures installed by the Government of India to maintain industrial peace and harmony. The chapter ends with a critical appreciation of the state of the Indian legal framework for the management of workers and presents a set of recommendations for improvement.

Chapter 12—Disciplinary Action—examines the role of the disciplinary action undertaken by HR professionals to maintain and develop a strong administrative and disciplined work architecture. It highlights the legal provisions and principles that are required to be adhered to while dealing with delinquent employees. The chapter provides a substantial discussion on employee discipline, using various legal provisions. Employee communication (in the form of charge sheet) with reference to employee discipline has been highlighted at the end of the chapter.

Chapter 13—Human Resource Information System—presents a brief review of various modules integrated under human resource information architecture to provide timely and transparent employee support for organizational effectiveness.

Chapter 14—International Human Resource Management—examines the HRM function in a global context. It begins with a short discussion on the need for advancing our knowledge about HR management in the context of international hospitality business. It also highlights the various strategies adopted by Indian multinationals to grow internationally. The discussion on cultural nuances and influences on employees' behaviour is particularly significant, especially for the reader who aspires to work in the international arena in the near future. A brief discussion has been presented about the global manpower planning and staffing practices followed in international HR management. The chapter moves on to highlight the varied type of training imparted to expatriate employees for better organizational effectiveness. The discussion has also been enriched with theoretical dynamics that capture the expatriates' psychological adjustment process, usually experienced in an international workspace. The discussion also highlights the critical issues pertaining to compensation and benefit management for expatriate employees.

ACKNOWLEDGEMENTS

During my tenure in the hospitality industry as a human resource professional and subsequently as an academician, I have been fortunate to have come across a number of accomplished people who have extended their support to me in my professional and academic endeavours. I sincerely acknowledge the valuable lessons I learned from them. From the available knowledge base, but within the limited mandate of an undergraduate textbook, I have attempted to provide a brief sketch on human resource management dynamics. I sincerely believe that professional colleagues engaged in imparting hospitality education throughout India will find the book useful to help bring the human dimension of the business into the class environment.

I have written this book at a time when I was undergoing a unique experience in my life. This experience and the associated stress affected many things in my life, including this book. So, what otherwise could have been completed in six months has taken about two years.

I express my sincere gratitude for the patience, professionalism, and diligent work by the editorial team at Oxford University Press India, without whose support this book could not have been completed.

Though I have exercised due care, extreme work pressure, career commitment, and lack of time might have resulted in a few errors creeping in. All errors of facts and interpretation are my own.

I eagerly look forward to receiving your valuable comments and suggestions for further improvements at malay.biswas@gmail.com.

Malay Biswas

Contents

Preface v

1. INTRODUCTION TO HUMAN RESOURCE MANAGEMENT 1

Introduction 1
Human Resource Management—In Search of Definition 1
Brief Outline of the Indian Labour Movement 2
Growth Drivers for the Indian Service Sector 5
Why Managing Human Resources Is Gaining More Importance 9
Hospitality Industry Characteristics 12
Implications of the Characteristics 15
Human Resource Roles 16
Exploring the Relationship between Human Resource and
    Organizational/Firm Performance 18
Human Resource Challenges 18
Functions of Human Resource Managers 22
Competency of HR Managers 25
Case Study: A Road to Travel 30

2. MANPOWER PLANNING 33

Introduction 33
Importance of Manpower Planning 34
Factors to Be Considered for Effective Manpower Planning 36
Manpower Planning Process 40
Managing Workforce Surplus and Shortfall 41
    Strategies for Dealing with Workforce Surplus 42
    Strategies for Dealing with Shortfall in Workforce 42
What Should Manpower Planning Offer? 43
Human Resource Information System and Manpower Planning 45
Case Study: Ram Mohan's Dilemma 46

3. RECRUITMENT 49

Introduction 49
Introduction to Recruitment 49
Sources of Recruitment 50
    Internal Recruitment 50
    External Recruitment 52
What to Look for in Prospective Candidates 54
    Successful Employees 54
    Employee Competency 55
When to Recruit 56
Recruitment Policy 56
Company Brand and Recruitment 57
    Initial Screening and Shortlisting 57
    Communication with Shortlisted Candidates 58
    Employment Tests 60
    Group Discussion 60
    Personal Interview 61
How to Prepare for the Interview 63
Legality and Recruitment 64
Case Study: Manpower Problem for Spa Business 65

4. TRAINING AND DEVELOPMENT 67

Introduction 67
Importance of Training 67
Training Function and Size of the Hotel 69
Training Need Identification Process 70
Hospitality Industry Relevant Training in India 72
Training Cycle 73
Training Evaluation 75
Training Methods 75
Trainers' Qualification and Experience 77
Training—Cost or Investment? 78
Organizational Culture and Training 79
Case Study: Strategy for China 82

5. PERFORMANCE APPRAISAL 85

Introduction 85
Purpose of Performance Appraisal System 85
Appraising What—Employee, Process, or Performance? 87

Performance Appraisal Process   87
Usage of Performance Appraisal   88
   Administrative Purpose   88
   Developmental Purpose   88
Difficulties Associated with the Performance Appraisal Process   88
Why Does the Performance Appraisal System Fail?   91
Management by Objectives   92
Underlying Theories   94
Balanced Scorecard   95
Difficulties Associated with Balanced Scorecard Administration   97
The 360-degree Feedback System   99
   Individual Benefit   99
   Organizational Benefit   101
   Prerequisites for Successful Implementation of the 360-degree Feedback System   101
   The 360-degree Feedback System and Its Content   102
Feedback Partners   104
Managing Employee Performance   105
   Theoretical Underpinning   106
Effective Performance Appraisal System   108
Case Collectives   113

6. EMPLOYEE MOTIVATION

115

Introduction   115
Motivation   115
Motivated Employees—Key to Gaining Competitive Edge   116
Various Motivation Theories   117
   Maslow's Theory   117
   Herzberg's Two-factor Theory   118
   Adams' Equity Theory   119
   B.F. Skinner's Reinforcement Theory   120
Measurement of Employee Motivation   120
   Employee Satisfaction Survey   121
   Turnover Rate   121
   Walk the Talk   121
   Incidence of Counterproductive Behaviour   121
Goal-Setting Theory   121
   Creative Tension   122
   Management by Objectives   122
How to Motivate Employees   123
Group Motivation   130
Benchmarking   130
Case Study I: Victim by Design   133
Case Study II: Checkmate   133

7. COMPENSATION AND BENEFIT MANAGEMENT   135

Introduction   135
Components of a Compensation Policy   135
Objectives of a Good Compensation System   138
Determinants of an Effective Compensation Policy   139
Psychological Theories and Remuneration   143
Equity and Compensation Management   144
Business Strategy and Compensation   145
   Compensation Strategy during Recession   145
   Compensation Strategy during Business Boom   145
Compensation and Diverse Philosophical Underpinnings   146
Executive Compensation in India   148
Employee Stock Option Plan   151
Executive Benefit Management   152
The Practice of Tipping   154
Compensation Policy and Its Limitations   154
Case Study: Employee Satisfaction Survey   156

8. JOB SATISFACTION   159

Introduction   159
Theories of Motivation   160
   Maslow's Theory   160
   Herzberg's Theory of Motivation   161
Correlates of Job Satisfaction   161
Importance of Job Satisfaction   165
Measurement of Job Satisfaction   167
   Job Descriptive Index   168
How Employees Express Their Dissatisfaction   169
Administrative and Managerial Implications of Job Satisfaction   170
Case Study I: Hemant's Dilemma   174
Case Study II: Ram Murthy's Challenges   175
Case Study III: Jojo and His Boss   176

9. ORGANIZATIONAL CULTURE   177

Introduction   177
Observable Aspect of Organizational Culture   178
Functions of Organizational Culture   179
Is Culture a Strategic Resource or Shadow Liability?   180
Cultural Models   184

Cultural Web   184
OCTAPACE Model   186
Competing Value Framework   192
Diagnosing Organizational Culture   194
Positive or Negative Culture   198
How Organizations Transmit Their Culture   201
How Leaders Nurture, Embed, and Communicate Culture   202
Managing and Changing Culture   205
Case Study: Organization of 'Sirs'   210

10. ORGANIZATIONAL CONFLICT AND COLLECTIVE BARGAINING   211

Introduction   211
What Is Organizational Conflict?   211
Organizational Conflict: Is It Desirable?   211
Types of Conflict   213
Labour Laws and Organizational Conflict   214
Conflict Resolution   214
Various Measures Undertaken to Minimize Organizational Conflict   217
Collective Bargaining and Negotiation   218
Collective Bargaining Process   219
Case Study: Power Web   221

11. INDIAN LABOUR LAWS IN THE HOSPITALITY INDUSTRY   223

Introduction   223
Labour Legislations Impacting Hospitality   226
    Payment of Gratuity Act, 1972   226
    Workmen Compensation Act, 1923   228
    Trade Union Act, 1926   230
    Industrial Dispute Act, 1947   235
    Employees Provident Fund and Miscellaneous Provision Act, 1951   237
    Employees State Insurance Act, 1948   237
    Payment of Bonus Act, 1965   239
    Shops and Establishment Act   239
Contract Workers and Labour Laws   240
    Growth in Numbers of Contract Workers   241
    Reason for Deployment of Contract Workers   241
    Contract Labour (Regulation and Abolitions) Act, 1971   242
    Minimum Wages Act, 1948   243
    Payment of Wages Act, 1936   244
    Equal Remuneration Act, 1976   245
    Sexual Harassment at Workplace Bill, 2010   245
Labour Law—Artefact of the Past? Is It Time for Healthy Dialogues?   246
Case Collectives   252

12. DISCIPLINARY ACTION

255

Introduction 255
Principles of Natural Justice 257
Positive Discipline—Counselling 258
Factors to Consider When Disciplining 258
Disciplinary Guidelines 260
Bringing More Transparency into the Process 261
Disciplinary Process 261
Essential Features of a Charge Sheet 263
Case Study I: The Plight of Rana Kumar 267
Case Study II: The Curious Case of the 'King of Good Times' 269

13. HUMAN RESOURCE INFORMATION SYSTEM

275

Introduction 275
Modules of Human Resource Information System 278
E-service and Human Resource Information System 286
Case Study I: No Taker 289
Case Study II: System Migration 289

14. INTERNATIONAL HUMAN RESOURCE MANAGEMENT

291

Introduction 291
Need for International Human Resource Management 291
Characteristics of Indian Multinationals 293
Role of National Culture 294
Recruitment Practice in the Global Market 299
Global Manpower Planning 301
Training and Development in International HR Management 303
Types of Training for Expatriates 306
Five-stage Process of International Adjustment 308
Component of Performance in the Global Context 311
Compensation Management in the Global Context 312
Closing Thoughts 314
Case Study: Expat Repatriation 316

Appendix A: Counterproductive Behaviour 319
Appendix B: Abusive Supervision 327
Index 337

1 Introduction to Human Resource Management

INTRODUCTION

The management of human resources (HR) plays an important role in the service industry, especially in the hospitality business. The involvement of employees in the production of services is relatively high in the hospitality industry and service is co-produced through close participation between employees and the consumers. Thus, employees play one of the most significant roles in the hospitality industry. In this chapter, the subject of human resource management (HRM) has been introduced. Then, the various features of the service industry where HRM plays a role have been discussed. The various challenges an HR manager faces in today's business environment have been outlined. And finally, the various competencies required in HR executives in the service industry have been elaborated.

HUMAN RESOURCE MANAGEMENT—IN SEARCH OF DEFINITION

'Human resource management is defined as a strategic and coherent approach to the management of an organization's most valued asset—the people working there who individually and collectively contribute to the achievement of its objectives' (Armstrong 2008). As per the definition, HRM

1. is a strategic and coherent management approach;
2. deals with the most valuable asset, human resource;
3. is for individual and collective contribution; and
4. is to achieve the organizational goal.

However, this definition is relatively simple and a clearer articulation is required. The definition states that the function of HRM is only focused on the achievement of the organizational goal. However, as per present-day industry practices, in many cases, the HR department also undertakes various steps to fulfil the aspiration of the individual employees within the framework of organizational objectives.

LEARNING OBJECTIVES

After reading this chapter, you will be able to:

- identify characteristics of the service industry, especially the hospitality industry
- examine human resource management (HRM) in the context of the hospitality industry
- map the various challenges faced by human resource professionals in the Indian hospitality industry
- appreciate the relationship between HRM and organizational performance
- develop an understanding of the various competencies required by today's HR professionals to deal with the emerging business concerns

Today, HR functions have moved beyond preparing policy statements for implementation. HRM is defined as holding human resources in meaningful logical and relational networks, organized effectively to achieve organizational and individual objectives collectively. This definition makes a marked departure from the earlier definition on several counts:

1. HR professionals engage human beings, converged under one organizational umbrella;
2. they are in a meaningful relational network of interactions;
3. they consider human beings as a resource;
4. they are deployed to achieve organizational goals and individual goals collectively.

The HR team develops a network of relationships among the employees, and allows it to grow in such a way that each individual can have a meaningful experience individually and collectively. Disconnected individuals in organizational workspace are a leading cause of problems for HR managers. For example, restaurant stewarding staff work in isolation for long hours and little remuneration. They are always on the look-out for better opportunities. Therefore, employee turnover is very high among them. They may share a wrong perception about the HR function as a department that fills up forms and warning letters.

To connect individual employees with the collective organizational goals poses a realistic challenge for the HR team. An important addition in the definition is that HR executives strive to achieve organizational as well as individual goals. The HR department tries to ensure the achievement of these individual goals by adopting various strategies. For example, at the job interview, applicants' suitability is checked against the organizational objectives. The HR team also helps individuals achieve their career objectives. By fulfilling career objectives, they achieve the organization's growing demand for talents. Thus, investing in individual growth results in organizational growth. Therefore, an individual's aspirations and dreams are a part of the organizational goal. Therefore, it can be concluded that fulfilling individual employee's aspirations, in turn, nourishes the organizational goal, which is in fact the stated goal of every HR manager.

BRIEF OUTLINE OF THE INDIAN LABOUR MOVEMENT

In India, HRM has come a long way. Before industrialization, the Indian industry was always centred around the skilled craftsmen, who worked in a small workspace attached to their residence. This situation changed relatively when royal patronage was available, especially to manufacture various types of sophisticated weapons for war requirements. However, it was always under the autocratic regime controlled by the whims of the chief master craftsman. Under the British regime, this continued for quite sometime. As sentiments for freedom from the British regime became stronger, many Indian entrepreneurs took the initiative, under the support of the Swadeshi movement, to start a large-scale manufacturing business unit. For example, Tata Iron and Steel Company Ltd (TISCO) started to operate in the year 1910–1911. However, industrialization got its momentum only after India got freedom from British rule. Pandit Jawaharlal Nehru, with his first five-year programme, emphasized the need for heavy industries. Till the 1980s, a similar pattern was seen. Nevertheless, similar to any other industrialization process, this phase was marked by the tussle between entrepreneurs and trade unions. The industrial workspace became the battleground between these two powerful parties and was often marked by bloodbath. The trade union movement got patronage from the various political parties and they formed their own labour wing. This was often complicated by multiple trade unions in the workplace. Recognition of one party often led to labour agitations by the other parties. The organizational workspace became a venue for demonstrating political power rather than addressing employees' interests. Thus, it is debatable that the true contribution of trade unions was to safeguard the interest of the employees. Entrepreneurs and labour often used lockouts and strikes to demonstrate their respective strengths. Although, with the passing of time, a dozen labour laws were passed for maintaining the overall well-being of the employees, social security measures often became a matter of manipulation. In spite of having an inherent mechanism embedded in the legal framework, industrial unrest was common and failed to produce discernible results to a large extent. The labour department of various states were flooded with labour cases, which generated another lengthy saga of its own.

With the recent growth in the Indian economy, this tussle has been greatly reduced. Personnel management and industrial relations management concepts have transformed into human resource management. Scarcity of trained staff, which was one of the problems seen during the last few years when the Indian economy was making long strides, with around 9 per cent growth of the economy, has been overcome. These days, labour is considered a precious resource, required to be respected, cajoled, and given share partnership in the ESOPs (employee stock option plan) programme. Thus, in the truest sense, human resource management has travelled a long way before graduating to this level. Although the old pattern of the trade unions still lingers on, their influence has reduced quite drastically—and so has their union membership. Table 1.1 suggests a gradual erosion of the trade union membership since 1990, especially among male employees. However, this trend is reversed in the case of female employees. Over time, the union membership among female employees has gone up, from 9.7 per cent in the year 1990 to 26.8 per cent in the year 2002. The growth in numbers among female employees could be explained by the higher number of women who are gainfully employed in economic activities during the current years as compared to earlier times. Growth in the service sector has created employment opportunities for the Indian workforce, and more educated female employees prefer to participate in the economic activities than ever before.

Table 1.1 Union membership over the years

Year	No. of registered trade unions	No. of unions submitting returns	Membership of unions submitting returns							
			Men		Women		Total membership (in thousands)	Average membership per union
			Number (in thousands)	Percentage to total	Number (in thousands)	Percentage to total		
1991	53,535	8418	5507	90.3	594	9.7	6100	725
1992	55,680	9165	5148	89.6	598	10.4	5746	627
1993	55,784	6806	2636	84.1	498	15.9	3134	460
1994	56,872	6277	3239	79.1	856	20.9	4095	652
1995	57,952	8162	5675	86.8	863	13.2	6538	801
1996	58,988	7242	4250	75.9	1351	24.1	5601	773
1997	60,660	8872	6504	87.8	905	12.2	7409	835
1998	61,992	7403	6104	84.2	1145	15.8	7249	979
1999	64,817	8152	5190	81	1218	19	6407	786
2000	66,056	7253	4510	83.2	910	16.8	5420	747
2001	66,624	6531	4392	74.8	1481	25.2	5873	900
2002	68,544	7812	5102	73.2	1871	26.8	6973	893

Source: http://industrialrelations.naukrihub.com/figures.html accessed on 22 March 2011.

GROWTH DRIVERS FOR THE INDIAN SERVICE SECTOR

Over the years, the contribution of the service sector to the national GDP of India has increased substantially. For example, in the period 1951–1980, the contribution of the service sector to national GDP was 4.5 per cent per annum. This rate increased substantially to 6.6 per cent in the year 1981–1990 and reached 7.5 per cent during the period 1991–2000 (Table 1.2).

The service sector has become one of the leading contributors in employment generation for the country although this growth in the service sector is incomparable with employment growth. For example, in 1965–1966, the service industry contributed 18.1 per cent of the employment, which reached 23.5 per cent in 1999–2000 (Table 1.3).

Among the fast-growing business subsectors of the service segment are IT services, communication services, financial services, hotels and restaurants, community services, and trade (distribution) services. Some of the subsectors of the service industry that grew as per the trends are real estate, legal services, transport, storage, personal services, and public administration and defence.

The hospitality industry has grown significantly over the years. It contributed 4.8 per cent in the 1980s, which subsequently grew to 6.5 per cent in the 1990s and

Table 1.2 Economic growth rate across different sectors

	Average growth rate (in per cent per annum)		
	1951–1980	1981–1990	1991–2000
Agriculture	2.1	4.4	3.1
Industry	5.3	6.8	5.8
Services	4.5	6.6	7.5
GDP	3.5	5.8	5.8

Source: Central Statistical Organization (CSO).

Table 1.3 Real GDP growth

Years	Employment	Gross capital formation
1965–1966	18.1	46.1
1970–1971	20	43.7
1980–1981	18.9	44
1990–1991	24.4	41.2
1999–2000	23.5	39.6

Source: Central Statistical Organization.

to 9.3 per cent (almost 1 per cent of GDP) in 2000. This is a significant development (Gordon and Gupta 2003). According to Rath and Raj (2006), the industrial sector and the service sector growth were complementary. They also reported that the service sector has made jobless growth (growth in Indian service industry did not accompany equivalent growth in employment numbers); however, it has provided a new dimension of stability to India's GDP growth. Agricultural production is often dependent on the Indian monsoon. It is one of the factors that contribute significantly to India's GDP growth.

During the last few years, India witnessed an unprecedented economic growth. During the financial year 2007–2008, the Indian economic growth rate was seen hovering around 9 per cent. The Indian growth story is unique and controversial. It is unique because it has given a jobless economic growth. It is controversial because no unanimous agreement has emerged as to what drives the economic growth in India. Recent recession the world over did not make much dent on Indian economic growth, which continued to achieve about 8 per cent annual growth.

In spite of several threats to the economy, such as the skyrocketing oil prices and the recent fear of depression in the US, Kamath (2007) observed that 'the Indian growth story is based on multiple cylinders—consumption, investment, domestic demand, global competitiveness, knowledge-based businesses, industrial growth. Cyclical downturns in any one sector can occur but it is the combination of all factors that will keep the economy running at the rates that we are now seeing. In addition, there is ample scope to do much better, be it in the agriculture sector or in terms of infrastructure development. There are a lot of growth stories waiting to happen.'

Economic growth is often associated with the enhanced immediate role of the service sector and its contribution to the GDP, employment, and investment. It is equally true for the Indian economy too. In India, the service sector contributes about 54 per cent of the GDP. The Indian service sector has grown at an annual growth rate of over 7.5 per cent, while the manufacturing sector has grown at around 6 per cent since 1990. With the advent of this growth, the service industry requires huge but quality manpower. At present, it deploys about 28 per cent of the total workforce. Surprisingly, employment creation in the service sector is still lagging behind. This is quite unprecedented as the jobless growth experienced by the service sector in India is unlike that of other countries. Thakral (2008) observed that the Indian hospitality industry has grown to ₹604.32 billion in the financial year 2006–2007, which is 21.27 per cent over that in the previous financial year. In another assessment of the World Travel and Tourism Council's 2006 Travel and Tourism Economic Research report, the industry is expected to grow by 8 per cent per annum, in real terms, between 2007 and 2016.

Cost advantage, responsive customer service architecture, huge middle-class market, strategic location in the south-east Asian region, English-speaking educated employees, availability of 'frugal engineering' architecture, stable democratic political set-up, global economic boom, and so on have, in fact, facilitated this growth story to unfold. A detailed discussion on all the factors follows.

Cost advantage   Relative cost advantage for production and delivery of service in India is playing a significant role in shifting business from the US, Canada, and Europe to BRIC countries (Brazil, Russia, India, and China). Most of the western companies are trying to achieve competitive advantage over others by migrating to low-cost countries. This will provide added advantage and a better level of latitude in managing their strategic competence as well. This is unleashing a new life to many of these western companies. Thus, India, along with other BRIC countries, is a strong contender for attracting business from western companies.

Responsive customer service architecture   The Indian youth constitute the new labour economy. They avail most of the business opportunities visible in the economy and form the backbone of the new customer-responsive architecture. This provides a unique opportunity for western companies to utilize this customer-responsive architecture to service their worldwide customers, which gives ample push to the Indian economy.

Huge middle-class market   India's middle-class market is one of the attractive points for western companies to migrate to India. The intention of their strategic action is to bring business closer to the customers. The huge middle class market powers the domestic demand—this provides good protection from the international dynamic market conditions and provides quite a stable and predictable demand pattern. Thus, India's is, in fact, a domestic consumption led growth story. This constellation of demand from this domestic market works as an attractive factor for shifting business from the farthest corner of the earth to India. It brings economies of operation and scale into business and provides a competitive base to these companies.

Geographical proximity to other growing economies   World economies are growing; however, most of the growth is unfolding in the Asian regions. India's geographical proximity to other Asian powerhouses such Indonesia, Laos, Malaysia, Myanmar, Vietnam, Singapore, Philippines, Thailand (all member nations of Association of Southeast Asian Nations, ASEAN), and China also makes it an attractive option (Table 1.4).

The growth prospect in India remained undiminished in spite of the economic downturn observed throughout the world in the years 2008–2011. Although it has reduced the growth level to a large extent, India remained one of the few markets besides China where growth remained attractive in comparison to the other developed and emerging economies (Table 1.5).

English-speaking employees   One of the legacies of the 200 years of British rule is that it has given India one critical advantage over other nations—an

Table 1.4 Real GDP growth—Sector wise

Sector	Q1 (April–June)		Q2 (July–September)		Q3 (October–December)		April–December (Q1 + Q2 + Q3)/3	
	2007–2008	2008–2009	2007–2008	2008–2009	2007–2008	2008–2009	2007–2008	2008–2009
Agriculture	4.4	3	4.4	2.7	6.9	−2.2	5.5	0.6
Industry	8.5	5.2	7.5	4.7	7.6	0.8	7.9	3.5
Services	10.7	10.2	10.7	9.6	10.1	9.5	10.5	9.7
Overall	9.1	7.9	9.1	7.6	8.9	5.3	9	6.9

Source: Central Statistical Organization.

English-speaking population. English is now the linking language across cultures and nations. In India, the education system provides a good supply of English-speaking students. Thus, the availability of English-speaking employees has made India one of the attractive places for relocating western business ventures.

Presence of frugal engineering Frugal engineering signifies an Indian system of production that inherits qualities of frugality in its philosophy and approach towards the production of products and services. Cheap labour, lean production systems suitable for tropical environment, and innovative and economical practices for cost reduction are a few characteristics of frugal engineering.

Booming market conditions World economy grew quite substantially during the last decade, especially in the BRIC nations. This made India an engine for growth. Indian companies contributed to providing support to the world's economic growth, especially software service companies such as Tata Consultancy Services (TCS), Infosys, and Wipro. Indian companies are even attempting to acquire reputed brands from the international market, wherever they are found to be strategic fits.

Stable democratic political set-up Post independence, India's political environment has been marked by stability and democracy, unlike its neighbouring countries. The democratic set-up prevents uncertainty in the management of economy. It ensures the legal process in the country. Adherence to basic human rights, strong economic development, growing consumptions, developing educational infrastructure, and stable relationship with other countries are a few democratic dividends that India has enjoyed since independence. Democratic set-up indicates limited political risks unlike countries under dictatorial regime. Low political risks attract more investments into the countries and thus promote overall growth and development.

Table 1.5 Real GDP growth—year-on-year per cent change

		2007	2008	2009
Asia		**7.6**	**6**	**4.9**
Industrial Asia		**2.4**	**0.8**	**0.1**
	Japan	2.1	0.5	−0.2
	Australia	4.4	2.4	1.8
	New Zealand	3.2	0.7	1.5
Emerging Asia		**9.5**	**7.7**	**8.5**
Newly industrialized economies		**5.6**	**3.9**	**2.1**
	Hong Kong SAR	6.4	3.7	2
	Korea	5	4.1	2
	Singapore	7.7	2.7	2
	Taiwan POC	5.7	3.8	2.2
	China	11.9	9.7	8.5
	India	9.3	7.8	6.3
ASEAN 5		**6.3**	**5.4**	**4.2**
	Indonesia	6.3	6	4.5
	Malaysia	6.3	5.7	3.8
	Philippines	7.2	4.4	3.5
	Thailand	4.8	4.5	4
	Vietnam	8.5	6.3	5.5
Emerging Asia excluding China		**7.3**	**5.9**	**4.4**
Emerging Asia excluding China and India		**5.9**	**4.6**	**3.1**

Note: Entries in bold indicate aggregation of nations.
Source: Regional Economic Outlook: Asia and Pacific, November 2008, published by International Monetary Fund, Washington.

WHY MANAGING HUMAN RESOURCES IS GAINING MORE IMPORTANCE

Dealing with the new generation, rapid technological changes, rising inflation, and so on make managing human resources very important.

Dealing with the new generation A subtle change is underway in the workforce composition. A brand new generation of employees is taking over the reign of the

Indian industries. The new generation is different by virtue of its attitude, amount of patience, and preference. It appears that this generation gives more importance to the present consumption rather than postponing it for future gain. Job hopping is usual business for them. They prefer to live for today than for tomorrow. The earlier generation always compromised with the entry-level low salary, considering a lifelong employment and future benefits. The dynamic operations of the HR department are required to be innovative enough to suit the requirement of this generation. They should adopt new approaches to attract the young generation—it almost requires reinventing itself.

Rapid technological changes Recently, the world has witnessed unprecedented and rapid technological changes, which poses a lot of problems. With increased computing power, companies are learning to do business in a newer format, making it much easier than earlier. E-service under an integrated data management platform provides a rich experience to the employees. With technological advancement, a scalable system creates a huge problem. Available knowledge and competency suddenly become redundant and the organization requires replenishing the total knowledge power by introducing training and development or by bringing fresh talent into the organization. Software is evolving every year with new editions and innovations. Hardware configuration and network capability are also rapidly changing. As a result, the whole world is renewing itself with a complete new configuration.

Rising inflation Inflation is a global problem; however, in a growing economy, it is a serious problem as it often brings its spiral effect on the living standard of employees. Rising costs and inflation rates make it difficult for the common citizen to live within the means of his or her earning. This makes many compensation packages redundant. The real power of money gets reduced with every successive year, and this generates considerable widespread labour dissatisfaction. Subsequently, this dissatisfaction may graduate to industrial unrest, leading to strike and lockout. To avoid this kind of difficulty, it is required to fine-tune the compensation packages with the market conditions (Table 1.6).

Globalization Globalized economy facilitates easier movement of wealth, fund, product, and services. It helps to move towards a boundaryless world. With this globalization process, the world economy is becoming more interdependent. The problem in one country easily influences the global economy as a whole. With time, the workplace becomes more diverse, filled with people from different nationalities. Some international workspaces such as hotels located in the Middle Eastern countries are highly multicultural, filled with employees from India, Pakistan, Bangladesh, Sri Lanka, Philippines, Egypt, and China.

Limited supply of highly skilled manpower Although there are thousands of hospitality business schools and institutes awarding business management degrees, the

Table 1.6 Annual inflation rate

Wholesale price index (WPI)	29 March 2008 (y-o-y)	28 March 2009 (y-o-y)
All commodities	7.75	0.26
Primary articles	9.68	3.46
Food articles	6.54	6.31
Fuel group	6.78	−6.11
Manufactured products	7.34	1.42
Manufactured food products	9.4	7.51
Excluding fuel	8.01	2.01
Excluding food articles and fuel	8.38	0.95
Consumer price index (CPI)	8 February (y-o-y)	9 February (y-o-y)
Industrial workers	5.47	9.63
Agricultural labourers	6.38	10.79
Rural labourers	6.11	10.79
Urban non-manual employees[#a]	4.84	10.38

[#a]Pertains to January.
Source: RBI: http://www.rbi.org.in/scripts/notificationuser.aspx?id=4936&mode=0#T1 accessed on March, 2011.

shortage of skilled manpower is still a critical problem. At times, it is very difficult to place students from these schools in suitable jobs. Hence, an elaborate training programme is designed to acclimatize them to an organization. For example, hotel groups such as Taj and Oberoi take in fresh graduates and provide intensive training before absorbing them for active work duty. This socialization process plays a critical role in enhancing knowledge, skill set, and the attitude of the employees.

Frequent changes in business conditions of world economy Frequent changes in the economic conditions of the world influence the magnitude of the business. An economic boom provides opportunity for good business, and the HR manager makes immediate adjustments in the recruitment, training, appraisal, and compensation package administration. A sudden free fall into a depression often requires immediate adjustment in all HR functions and modalities. Thus, the HR department is required to engineer flexible organizational structures and processes, which could be tuned with the amount of business. For example, many HR managers deploy a contingent workforce to handle the extra business load in the organization.

During a weak business position, it is believed that removal of the contingent work-force is relatively less painful for the organization.

Old government rules and regulations   Although the government introduces new rules and regulations now and then, some of the existing regulations were drafted a few decades ago, when business conditions in India were radically different from now. Old legislations impose certain duties and responsibilities. Each piece of legis-lation directs the maintenance of records using specific formats. This appears to be almost impossible to adhere to as all these books of records are in a specific format. New business context and technological development demand a complete overhaul of the management of industrial peace and harmony.

HOSPITALITY INDUSTRY CHARACTERISTICS

Before a cricket match begins, each captain makes a close observation about the pitch quality. An experienced captain makes an assessment of the behaviour of the pitch, for example, the amount of bounce, swing, and so on. Similarly, as a manager responsible for human resources, one should have a deeper understand-ing about this industry and how it behaves. This knowledge helps the managers perform their work effectively. Thus, knowledge of the service industry, especially the hospitality industry, is very important.

The service industry, especially the hospitality industry, differs significantly from the manufacturing environment. For example, if an employee in a car manufactur-ing factory was unhappy while assembling the engine, the customer buying it will not know about his unhappiness at all. In a hotel, the customer will easily know of an employee's unhappiness. The participation of an employee is so intense in the production of services that it colours the service production and service deliv-ery. Employee satisfaction is deeply linked with customer satisfaction. A happy employee will be motivated to go beyond the design of the service delivery system and deliver better solutions, accurately in line with the requirement of the ever-changing customers. Thus, the organization undertakes a wide range of efforts to make employees happy.

The emotional status of each employee (happy, depressed, feeling good, etc.) is easily communicable within the service production infrastructure in a hospitality organization and can easily influence other members with whom the employee interacts. In behavioural science, this is called *emotional contagion*. Emotional con-tagion signifies transference of emotion among interacting individuals. In other words, individual employees bring in their individual mood and feeling to the organization. Thus, depressed employees have the potential to negatively influence whoever interacts with them. Multiple interactions unfold every moment in an organization. Therefore, the HR executives need to be careful about this.

The service industry possesses unique characteristics unlike the manufactur-ing environment. Service is co-produced during interactions with employees and customers and thus it cannot be stored. In any hotel, the most perishable product is not fish or vegetable; rather it is the service, which is not produced in the absence of customers.

The hospitality industry possesses the following characteristics.

Glamorous industry   One of the critical features of this industry is that it is considered a glamorous industry. Service is co-produced in an aesthetically rich decorative environment. A big and beautiful lobby; well-groomed, well-spoken, and caring staff members—all these attempt to communicate glamour. This glamorous part of the industry generates interest and attraction as part of the industry. However, it is important to note that behind this glamorous lifestyle are hidden the disciplined and well-synchronized efforts of the staff members. This glamorous industry status is achieved by the consistent efforts of a proper dress code, efficient housekeeping, and the deployment of aesthetically rich employees.

Intangibility and low monitoring   The service industry produces services that are intangible. It finds embodiment only when it is consumed in close participation by the customer and employees. In other words, it becomes tangible only when it is consumed. By being intangible, it poses a number of problems, which hospitality managers must consider. Monitoring of the service production in the hospitality industry is difficult as it unfolds all around, even where supervisors are not present. An example is that the performance of drivers, working for a travel agency, is difficult to monitor.

Aesthetic discrimination   A silent transformation is underway for the Indian labour force—a subtle but radical change in terms of the quality of manpower requirement for the service sector. In the service sector, especially in the retail and hospitality segments, the employee plays a crucial role. An employee, with his or her personal qualities such as accent, body language, skin colour, gender, and 'stylized presentation of self', adds value to the service composition. Employees enriched with these aesthetic qualities (such as looking good, sounding right) facilitate to unfold the desired service encounter (Nickson et al. 2001). These are considered as absolute necessary ingredients for production of service. Service is composed and co-produced with intimate interaction of physical elements of servicescape and employees. This aesthetic expression in the organizational context is known as *aesthetic labour*. Therefore, aesthetically rich individuals might get preferred treatment.

Labour intensive   The production of services predominantly signifies relatively more labour components. India is an overpopulated country, second only to China. As per the 2011 census preliminary report, the Indian population has reached 1.21 billion (*Economic Times*, March 2011). Thus, India is uniquely positioned to utilize its human talent for the service of the world economy. Utilization of labour-intensive service components in hotels is considered a luxury, for example, the butler service. Under this service, a dedicated butler is allocated to a specific guest.

Invariability   Service production is a very delicate business as co-production of any service requires customer and employee. Most interestingly, the multitude of services produced in a hospitality organization is with the help of employees located at different levels of the hierarchy. An employee works for a limited period called a *shift*. On completion of the shift, another employee replaces him or her and continues to produce the service for consumption by the customer. Constant changing of employees affects the service quality. Although each employee is chained to the strict process regime, an employee adds additional spice to the service quality, which makes the service so unique and memorable. This poses considerable amount of difficulty for the organization to maintain consistency in the service production. Most of the hospitality organizations have intensive training programmes, wherein they attempt to instil service orientation among new recruits to limit variability.

Renewed role of self   The role of individual labour participation in the service environment is relatively restricted and scripted and offers limited manoeuvrability. Each employee's behaviour is bound by the limited service delivery obligations, and often, they need to address guests with 'Good morning sir!', 'May I assist you, madam?' when a guest approaches them. The linguistic expression varies across hotel chains. An employee has to learn such scripts and jargon as per the organization's requirement, philosophy, and practice. Thus, tutoring self, before deployment in any organization, is required.

Inseparability   Service cannot be separated from the service providers. An intimate relationship with the service providers makes employees so important in the hospitality workspace. This intimate relationship will force the HR manager to select aesthetically rich employees. An aesthetic attribute constitutes important service production components and adds value to the service experience. Although with the advent of self-service arrangement the elimination of employees from the service production is technologically possible, it could not be extended to every sphere of the hospitality business, especially in five-star hotel environments. This is not possible for Indian five-star hotels because this industry, by its very nature, is a high-involvement industry. Employees thus become the essential ingredient for production of services.

Perishability   Service is perishable, which means that if not consumed within a specific period, it will cause considerable revenue loss. For example, service in the restaurant should be consumed before 11 o'clock at night or a seat on a plane should be occupied during the flight. The placement of employees at the restaurant or the flight does not guarantee that guests will avail of these facilities and services. This embeds a good degree of uncertainty in the service composition and service-generating capability. Service that is not consumed during a specified period is lost forever. Service production capabilities should be properly utilized, that is, the right number of employees should be deployed, keeping in mind the ever-changing business load. Therefore, it requires a rightful estimation of business. While deployment of excess manpower capability causes companies' considerable manpower cost in terms of salary and wages, lack of manpower will negatively influence the service production capacity—thus potentially generating considerable service complaints.

Low monitoring environment Managing employees in the low monitoring service environment is relatively challenging. Human beings deployed in an organization are considered as a resource as each individual in the service environment brings into the organization his or her knowledge, expertise, skills, and so on. However, having such quality in individual employees is no guarantee that it will be deployed in an organization. Therefore, it requires a lot of managerial skill to harness this human potential into a reality.

IMPLICATIONS OF THE CHARACTERISTICS

The question we address in this section is simple—how do all these features influence HR functions. Indeed, the service industry characteristic influences and complicates the functions of the HR department in many ways.

Glamorous industry The service industry, especially the hospitality industry, carries a glamorous workspace. Many youngsters are attracted to this industry because of its inherent characteristics. They expect seeing well-groomed people, dealing with the who's who of society—from movie stars to sport stars to corporate icons—and working in a beautifully organized workspace. These initial perceptions, in many cases, get shattered when they start working. They realize that though it is nice to see such well-organized workspaces, it is difficult to maintain them. They realize that to remain well-groomed individuals, each employee is required to follow a strict regime of diet, lifestyle, and hygiene schedule. Thus, the HR manager must provide a realistic job preview before anybody joins the organization. Job preview means realistic representation of the nature of job before awarding employment to prospective candidates. This job preview facilitates managing employees' expectations from the job also.

Invariability and inseparability These features of the hospitality industry signify that service production and experience will vary according to knowledge, skill, and motivational and other dispositional conditions of the employee, despite installing elaborate service processes. A simple example to make this point clear is that the 'smile of each employee is different'. The HR department, thus, maintains elaborately designed service processes to bring uniformity in the production of services. Managing guest history in a digital format using tailor-made software is very important. This will enable each employee to access the official version of the guest's requirements and will be able to fulfil their requirements, irrespective of which employee is serving the guest. All these efforts are directed to reduce the variability of service production due to different sets of employees serving the guests across different shifts.

Emotional labour Employees working in this industry are mostly emotionally disconnected. Individual employees carry various dispositions in line with life stages, age, immediate environment, and so on. However, it is expected that these varieties of genuine human experience should not be brought about. An employee should present only a 'happy kind of persona', which will add value to the service composition of the organization. It is indeed legitimate for the employers to demand a positive persona during a service production episode; however, these emotional deprivations cause apparent disconnection with the employees' true feelings and self. Long exposure to this kind of service production environment can potentially cause psychological harm. Employees lose control over their emotional experience and learn to repress it. Therefore, the HR team needs to have a supporting environment to assist employees to overcome emotional difficulties, if they arise at all.

Emotional intelligence Service production in a hospitality organization is filled with unpredictability. Different customers have different preferences and to accommodate this diverse range of preferences, employees working in the service industry need to put in extra efforts. It is not necessary that employees, in spite of their wholehearted efforts, be able to satisfy all the customers and their supervisors. Therefore, employees may get emotionally disturbed because of an ill-mannered customer's misbehaviour. Employees need to have emotional literacy to deal with emotional disturbances caused by rude customers and supervisory misbehaviours. Therefore, emotional intelligence is an important asset, which is to be sharpened to survive in service industry environment.

HUMAN RESOURCE ROLES

The HR department plays a significant role in the hospitality business. This role ranges from internal conscience to managing strategic roles.

Internal conscience HR managers carry the implied responsibility of managing the ethical framework of the organization. They are the internal conscience and it is expected that they enforce ethical and other organizational standards to avoid any deviation. Their role is to maintain ethical behaviour among employees and in their dealings with the external world. HR heads play a significant role in designing, managing, and enforcing the code of ethical conduct in an organization, which are broad guidelines on ethical behavioural standards applicable to an organization. In the case of deviation and deficiency, the HR executives are required to intervene and steer the situation to an ethical conclusion. Maintaining high ethical standards in the organization is one of the prime roles that an HR head is expected to play. An HR executive ensures maintenance of the ethical infrastructure inside the organization by embedding the processes and procedures to uphold the ethical code of conduct. This is expected to work as a deterrent and self-check correction in case of unethical behaviour expressed inside the organization.

Guidance and counsellor role HR managers provide guidance in employee-related issues, and they possess specific expertise in dealing with human-related issues. Managing the human dimension inside an organization often presents significant challenges. Many mergers and acquisitions fail not because they were not a financially prudent deals or because the marketers failed to sell the newly acquired product range, but because they did not take into account and address employee-related issues adequately.

Strategist role The hospitality industry is a labour-intensive industry, and the HR department can play a significant role in developing strategies for synergetic contribution in generating excellent service quality. By using various labour configurations, HR executives exercise a significant role in providing strategic impetus to the organizational development.

Innovation and change agent role Innovation is the prime requirement for any business to survive as the market condition is always changing. The market condition constitutes the customer's preferences, the competitor's ever-changing strategies, technological advancement, new product in the market, and so on. To survive in this kind of fluctuating market conditions, the organization requires innovation in the way they produce the product and in the way they access their market or the places where it could be produced. This whole range of activities requires constant reconfiguration of the organization structure, location of service production, and the way they deal with employees. HR managers play a significant role in orchestrating and maintaining relational and structural infrastructure conducive to innovation. Various organizational processes, which could be introduced by the HR department, can significantly influence the organizational innovation capacity.

Mentoring role The HR team is required to play an internal consultant's role. They have to introduce new changes in process, facilitate the dissemination process, and help others to adopt the new changed processes. This role has to be fulfilled with diplomacy, sincerity, and openness. Without this, acceptability across the board gets reduced. Legitimacy of the internal consultancy role is always a matter of concern, and this affects effectiveness and acceptability of the HR executives in an internal consultant's role.

Internal communicator role HR managers are the communicators for an internal audience, that is, employees and the management. For production of service, employees are the most crucial factor. Internal communication highlights organizational achievement, new work processes, internal gala events, and so on. Thus, communication provides multiple benefits—it helps garner ongoing support for various organizational activities. Regular internal communication, packaged well with attractive presentations, generates automatic subscription among employees for important events and issues. Needless to say, the disbursement of information at regular intervals gives a feeling to each employee that they are all important.

Administrator role Members of the HR department are seen as administrators in the organizational context, who uphold organizational ethical values, maintain discipline in the organization, facilitate the organizational members to arrive at some degree of agreement, and punish the deviant or delinquent employees.

EXPLORING THE RELATIONSHIP BETWEEN HUMAN RESOURCE AND ORGANIZATIONAL/FIRM PERFORMANCE

It appears to be common sense knowledge that robust HR practices will potentially contribute significantly to achieve the organizational objectives. HR managers organize human resources in different configurations for effective performance. These configurations motivate employees by remunerating good performers and supporting weak performers, and hold them together for fulfilment of the collective aspirations of individual and organizational growth. On the other hand, badly managed human resources will allocate more attention on in-fighting to fulfil individual objectives rather than collective organizational goals. This will create conflict among employees; poorly supported employees will find other avenues for fulfilling individual goals. This also will become fertile ground for counterproductive behaviour, such as theft from the organization, sabotage of organizational processes, and ultimately taking the law into their hands rather than relying on the organizational justice system. Recent research indicates that proper management of HR functions significantly influence the organizational performance. For example, Gooderham, Parry, and Ringdal (2008) found that the overall impact of HR on a firm's performance is relatively modest. However, the intensity of the relationship varies according to the various HR configurations. Similarly, Read, Srinivasan, and Doty (2009) reported that social capital and HR capital significantly contribute to organizational performance. Thus, it could be safely said that appropriate HR configurations could leverage for extraordinary organizational performance indeed.

HUMAN RESOURCE CHALLENGES

HR manager and strategic partners The HR department deals with one of the most important resources of the organization—human resource. They have the expertise to deal with human idiosyncrasy. In line with organizational strategy, an HR executive contributes by steering scarce talents inside the organization. Considerable human process knowledge provides unique support to the organizational infrastructure in order to achieve the organizational objectives. Their contribution helps the organization link HR strategies with the overall business organization. A robust partnership and representation of HR team members in the board provides the requisite support. However, the power of the HR members in the board is relatively less, and they appear to play a secondary role in comparison to other members of the board owing to erosion of trust. In terms of producing results, general confidence in the HR professionals is gradually weakening; it is believed that predominantly marketing/sales and finance employees overshadow HR professionals in such strategic situations.

In order to become full strategic partners, HR professionals must play a significant role. HR executives are drastically failing to provide adequate support to the employees across hierarchy. At times, the aspirations and dreams of employees cannot be nourished by organizational life. In most of the hospitality organizations, employees work for more than 14 h, well beyond the provisions of the law. The HR department is drastically failing to inspire the workforce to unite and contribute, and generally, HR is the least preferred profession among MBAs. Helpless employees submit to the will of the organization to maintain their job, and workplace stress is on the rise. At times, HR executives are not able to take a call even in their own department. For example, the forceful consumption of earned leave from the organization is engineered more out of financial concern rather than the well-being of employees. The HR department is just becoming the executioner of decisions of other corporate board members. This kind of silent role will trigger the question of legitimacy of the profession. The HR profession is not able to represent the aspiration of certain sections of the employees for which the HR team is recruited. 'A regime which provides human being no deep reason to care about one another cannot long preserve its legitimacy' (Sennett 1998, p.1).

Enhancing the line managers' competency with HR skills   Research reports indicate that line managers are being entrusted with more responsibilities in managing their local employee-related issues rather than accessing their HR functions. The HR manager may not have deeper insight about the working situation in a department that is affecting employees. Line managers are exposed to and are responsible for the well-being of their immediate employees, and this provides ample opportunities to provide a customized solution within the broad framework of the employment policy to suit the local requirement. For example, an executive chef in a five-star hotel understands the problem of his or her kitchen staff more than others, as they work in close proximity to the staff and thus are better equipped to provide unique solutions. This guarantees generation of solutions that are appropriate, timely, and relevant for the local employment problem. Devolution of responsibilities for managing human resources to the local line managers provides ample opportunities for the HR manager to engage or to become involved in more strategic activities. However, a general concern is that these line managers may not have adequate competency and training to provide employee solutions. Thus, this provides considerable challenges to the HR professionals to transfer the knowledge, skill, and attitude to the line managers so that they can handle sensitive employee issues. A management historian highlights that when work was centred on skills and organized under a craft system, handling the human resource aspect of the business was always under the master craftsmen.

Nimble HR organizational architecture Business in an organization is deeply related to the level of the business cycle. During boom time, organizations struggle to maintain adequate manpower resources; organizations gear up to face the manpower crunch by enhancing the pay structure, moderating other compensation and remuneration arrangements. As business sentiments move from boom to depression-type situations, business goes down and so does the requirement of manpower. With the new business conditions, suddenly the manpower crunch changes to manpower surplus. Manpower rationalization appears to be an urgent need of the hour. Many companies are attempting to deploy contingent workers to meet the additional requirement of the business. Most of the hospitality companies are now relying heavily on contingent workforce. Although it is indeed affecting quality service production, it provides adequate legal sanction to reduce manpower in the shortest possible time. Thus, organizational architecture and its processes are required to be nimble and flexible enough so that swift action could be implemented without affecting the overall business opportunity.

Coping and leading change inside the hospitality organization The waves of change are strong, consistent, and touching every organization. The world suddenly appears to be shrinking in terms of access and exposure. New generations of this new era are entering the job market. This generation values a framework of reference that is different from that of the earlier generation. All this poses a unique readjustment problem for an organization. Readjustment could be revising the compensation and reward package in tune with the new generation. Reconfiguration in the work format such as working from home is not unusual anymore, as broadband makes it possible to transfer huge amounts of data without much effort, although data security could be an issue. Many hospitality trained members are providing services from home without taking up a regular job. Change process always generates disruptive political dynamism inside the organization. Leading change always generates a group of losers and winners—HR managers need to be efficient change masters so that they can create and sustain winning organizations.

Keeping up with expanding form of knowledge The domain of HR practice is not clearly demarcated. At the same time, it is not a set of definitive knowledge, as what works for one hospitality company may not work for another. It is expanding everyday. Localization of global solution and practice is widespread. In other words, although most HR executives remain restrained within a set of activities, the way these activities are performed is different and often requires fine-tuning according to the organizational culture. Installing the best practice from other organizations is a delicate job as it demands refinement to the tune of local requirement. On the demise of old theories, new theories emerge. HR managers attempt to incorporate some of the selective theories in their human infrastructure. Small innovations happen in the organization all the time, some of which are reported and some not. The HR department should utilize some of these developments in their work culture.

Fine-tuning the profession   Since HR as a profession is still evolving, it is relatively difficult to articulate the domain and depth of the profession. Uncertainty in human behaviour, be it individual or group, often colours the true outcome. Thus, HR intervention is a relatively evolving profession, often fine-tuned with specific organizational requirement.

Learning to manage a multicultural set-up   A multicultural set-up is where employees from different countries converge under one organizational umbrella. For example, cruise liners provide an organizational set-up where Indians, Pakistanis, Philipinos, Sri Lankans, Bangladeshis, Egyptians, and so on work in the same workspace with their own preferences. Managing this kind of set-up is a real challenge. Another set-up could be multinational organizations, where business operations are scattered across nations and they are required to interact to deliver value to the customer. Either way, it poses a unique challenge to the HR team. Understanding multicultural sentiments is crucial in an organizational set-up.

Sourcing talent for organizational effectiveness   One of the leading challenges is to source scarce talent for organizational effectiveness. The organizational workspace is becoming a constellation of individuals possessing very specific and rare talents. This specific talent with renewed technological advancement can become outdated in no time. New specific domain skill set suddenly becomes an urgent requirement for the survival of the organization.

Creative synergy in diverse talent   The biggest challenge for the HR head is to put diverse talents to organizational effectiveness. Diverse talents bring their idiosyncrasies such as an uncompromising attitude, a glorified past and hype of achievement, stubbornness in attitude, unbending ego, and so on. This generates considerable amount of heat, leading to other incidental problems such as high employee turnover. This constant change in a group formation generates further relational conflict. Thus, the organization always stays in a flux and fails to reach performing stage. Dedicated HR efforts are required to be embedded inside the organization to produce discernible human infrastructure capable of producing durable and sustainable results.

Struggle to remain relevant   It is important to note that HR executives are continuously struggling to remain relevant within the industry context. Kochan (2004) argued that HR executives are currently facing a 'crisis of trust and a loss of legitimacy in the eyes of its major stakeholders'. It is important that to remain relevant in the fast-changing hospitality business environment, HR executives need to rediscover the profession by being useful in the organizational life of the employees. Lack of trust in human resource professionals for the delivery of business results is also a major concern. Thus, the HR department needs to be innovative, genuine, and result oriented.

FUNCTIONS OF HUMAN RESOURCE MANAGERS

HR managers have various roles to perform. Some of their functions are discussed here.

Human resource planning HR planning is an important function that ensures long-term management of manpower, their demand and supply situation, sourcing points, and deployment. This framework of functions mostly deals with macro business situations. The HR head makes long-term manpower predictions and devises durable strategies to overcome any manpower-supply related issues.

Organizational design and development Devising proper organizational structure suitable for a specific business requirement is a very crucial function. The structure should be nimble and flexible enough to respond to challenges associated with the different phases of the business cycle and other moments of organizational crisis.

Budgeting, controlling, and measurement An HR function does not earn anything directly by its operation and operates within the strict limits of its budget. Installing a proper metric system in every organizational hierarchy is a prerequisite for business. Proper budgeting provides execution of HR functions effectively during a specified period. This requires proper manpower planning, an effective control system, and a culture of evidence-based management.

Motivation Motivating the workforce to achieve higher levels of performance is one of the key functions of HR managers. They endeavour to create conducive human infrastructure, adequately embedded in the organizational architecture, which potentially motivates various role incumbents. Some elements that potentially motivate an employee towards a job include identity of the work, importance of the work, variety of work clubbed under one job, freedom embedded in job execution, and amount of feedback and acknowledgement given by the supervisor. The HR manager attempts to embed these elements in the job so that any incumbent, assigned to this role, is motivated and attracted to the job.

Leadership HR professionals play a significant role, touching every sphere of organizational life. They initiate, lead, and maintain the role wherever employees are concerned. In a reciprocally networked world, where leaders and subordinates are connected with each other for symbiotic survival, HR managers can practice servant leadership (i.e., leaders have multiple opportunities for serving others better). This could generate miraculous energy inside the human infrastructure; thus, it will significantly affect the achievement of the organizational objectives. Each organization attempts to achieve its organizational objectives—but by practicing servant leadership, it adds a human touch to the affairs of human pursuits.

Quality and performance management An HR executive provides a fair workspace, where employees can produce quality performance. Developing a key metric system on which each employee's performance will be assessed, communicating it effectively throughout the organization, and subsequently evaluating the employees' performance using the same metric system against the employees' actual performance are crucial. Many companies have migrated from the traditional performance management system to the balance scorecard based performance appraisal system, supplemented by a 360 degree feedback system. These functions are crucial because proper execution of performance management is always linked with remuneration and compensation management. Good performance is to be acknowledged by remuneration, average performance to be encouraged to excel, and below average performance should be given adequate support and training. Thus, this function entails a whole range of activities. Any hospitality organization that fails to perform this function finds it difficult to retain its employees.

Employee involvement generation function   An HR executive effectively organizes various activities intended to generate higher involvement of the employees in organizational activities. Various activities to cheer the employees are initiated, as it would create joy at the workplace and generate higher employee satisfaction. This subsequently generates customer satisfaction and eventually corporate profit.

Maintaining ethical infrastructure   Developing an ethical backbone in an organizational context is a key function, and the HR department develops an employee code of conduct. This is communicated through various strategies. In the case of a violation, the HR manager plays a significant role in disbursing appropriate punishments and actions, including termination in case of a grave deviance from the code. Corporate wrongdoing is on the rise and scandals such as Enron and Satyam frequently remind us about the importance of the ethical landscape. Thus, the HR department is required to install and sustain a broad corporate culture, where transparency and candid exchange of opinions are possible. A friendly policy for whistle-blowers is required to be incorporated rather than blaming or prosecuting them. Internal disclosure works relatively as a safety valve before it reaches unmanageable proportions. Research indicates that most of the whistle-blowers are given severe punishments including termination of services and other related treatment in the workplace. HR department has a great responsibility to maintain a robust backbone of ethical infrastructure that is more strategic in nature.

Legal adherence and compliance   Adhering to legal regulations is a crucial function as non-adherence invites criminal and civil punishment. Thus, HR professionals must use the highest degree of restraint before executing any HR overhaul inside the organization. They are required to manage employees within regulatory frameworks.

Job analysis   Job analysis functions include information about the job execution process and the kind of skill sets required to perform at the desired stage. Job analysis consists of two distinct functions:

Job description   This entails answering questions such as what is the nature of the job, what kind of job one needs to do, who occupies certain role or position as employee?

Job specification   This lists out the qualification and experience sets required to do the job. These two functions are very important as they bring role clarity about the kind of job each individual is required to do.

Recruitment   In line with manpower planning, recruitment is one of the processes to increase headcount inside the organization. Recruiting in appropriate numbers within a specific period from the appropriate sources is crucial. This function maintains fresh blood in the system and ensures adequate manpower in the organization.

Career planning and development   The HR department is responsible for managing the career of each individual working for their organization. Ineffective handling may generate a huge amount of grudges and employee dissatisfaction. In the era of high turnover, some may doubt the installation of the career planning and development process, but it is important to have one. This should be done systematically and should have an all-inclusive approach.

Training and development   Training and development includes identifying training needs and vendors/trainers and delivery of training and evaluation of post-training performance. It is a crucial function of the HR manager, especially in the era of technological advancements. Proper training infrastructure in the organization provides constant supply of well-groomed manpower to face tomorrow's challenges. Ready-made trained staff members are difficult to source. Given the fact that staff turnover rate is relatively very high, training provides important support.

Compensation and benefit management   Management of compensation and benefits is another key function of HR managers. A good compensation and benefit package attracts a good number of applicants. In addition, the existing employees will be interested to stay with the company, which leads to relatively less expenses on training and development of new employees. Compensation should be calculated on the basis of market conditions, competition offerings, industry practices, organizational capability, legal sanction, local business situation, and so on. This function demands considerable skills of the HR manager to perform the job.

Labour relations management   Managing labour relationship signifies maintaining a smooth relationship with employees, representatives of employees, and trade union leaders. Trade unions get legalized sanction to form a union, which represents the employees' demand and aspiration. In India, there has been a long history of troubled relationship between trade union leaders and management. Economic growth in India made jobs more easily available than in the past; hence, labour unions have recently lost their sheen. However, the labour union can flourish once again if the Indian economy stagnates for a long period in the coming years. Most national political parties also have labour wings, which effectively organize action inside the organization. In the past, Indian organizations have witnessed bloodbaths because of failure to maintain a smooth relationship with the labour unions. Thus, managing labour relationship is a crucial function for every HR manager.

Health and safety Maintaining the health and safety of employees is important, and there are specific legal provisions that the HR department is required to adhere to. Accidents are mostly seen in kitchens and the hotels' engineering department. Training staff on how to handle the various machines and appliances, safety precautions, and reinforcement of safety regulations are some important issues. Fire accidents are another danger that the hotel management should always be ready to handle. Regular training, practice runs, and so on keep everyone prepared to handle such situations. Employee health is also very important, especially in the hospitality industry. To prevent any transfer of germs, viruses, and contagious diseases to the valued guests of a hotel, regular medical fitness tests are crucial. Besides, there are some occupational hazards frequently seen in the hospitality industry. For example, a higher incidence of backache has been seen among room boys working in the housekeeping department. HR executives are required to institute a regular training regime, which will enhance the employees' internal strength to handle the rigour involved with each specific type of job.

Discipline Discipline among employees is an important issue and should be done in accordance with labour regulations. The misconduct of one employee cannot be ignored as it has a potential risk of other employees trying to imitate the act. Thus, maintaining discipline inside the service industry is crucial. Initially the HR department should follow behavioural modification tactics to reverse some of the bad behavioural expressions among employees. Disciplinary action should be initiated only when other avenues are closed or have failed to produce discernable positive results.

COMPETENCY OF HR MANAGERS

HR managers should have the following competencies.

Analytical competency HR managers must have critical analytical skills as this is required to understand complex business situations. Complex analytical power includes business sense and understanding of numbers and figures in various governmental, industrial, and organizational reports. Readings on individual and group behaviour and their finer expression in the organizational context is a prerequisite for HR managers.

Communication competency Communication is one of the most important competencies for HR professionals. Mixing it with diplomacy and political correctness, HR professionals cut across the boundaries of hierarchy and are effective. Frequent changes in the business scenario pose considerable challenges to introduce suitable changes in the organization. To communicate these changes, HR managers must use the most appropriate language and mode of communication, at the appropriate time. Any lapse will unnecessarily invite labour relations problem.

Persuasion competency As HR managers are predominantly dealing with human beings in various relational contexts, persuasion is the very essence of HR function. Persuading employees to follow the rules and regulations of the company and persuading employees to join community work are some examples. With good communication skills and persuasion competency, HR professionals become effective in achieving the organizational goals.

Strategic competency Understanding the business dynamism in the changing business scenario is a very important competency. Most organizations are undergoing constant transformation that includes mergers, acquisitions, joint ventures, and other interorganizational set-up. With renewed business situations, HR managers must learn to do business in a new way. Organizing reenergized human effort to achieve the organizational objectives requires intensive HR efforts.

For example, a few states in India carry a bad reputation for trade union problems. Years ago, when one of the leading hotel companies wanted to start a hotel in one of these states, they faced an acute dilemma. HR directors deployed a unique strategy to overcome the trade-union-related problem by bringing in specially trained staff from their Mumbai, Bangalore, and Delhi hotel properties. These employees were specially recruited six months before the inauguration and subsequently transferred. They took employees from the local market, but the majority were from other states. This gave the local hotel HR managers enough breathing space for them to develop suitable strategies for the subsequent years.

Lack of strategic understanding and non-action can potentially generate devastating results. One hospitality company aspired to play the leading role in the Indian hospitality market. In their investors' relation presentation, they did not hesitate to state where new hotel properties were going to be acquired. However, action equivalent to the aspiration of the company was not seen from the HR professionals. For example, within one year, that hotel bought one hotel company in the Asia Pacific region. A few staff members were deployed from the flagship companies to this newly acquired property. However, this attempt failed drastically. Most of them came back to India. They faced great difficulties in adjusting with the new organizational and national culture. The HR department should have developed long-term strategies to handle this type of manpower requirements.

Ethical competency HR managers deal with human beings and give attention to their development and growth to enhance the quality of relational exchanges. Having trust and faith in this relational exchange is crucial for smooth organizational functions. Besides, an ethical workspace works as a deterrent for counterproductive employee behaviours such as theft and sabotage of companies' products and processes. An ethical workspace provides a fair and just environment with equal opportunity to grow. Ethical erosion in the corporate world is a matter of grave concern. HR managers can play a significant role in instituting sincerity, transparency, and fair system and processes, which will allow ethical behaviour to flourish. Some of the control mechanisms instituted by the HR department are potentially capable of generating a wrong perception among employees. Alliance with wrongful actions inside the organization is often implicated.

Behavioural knowledge competency Behavioural knowledge does not stand for speculated knowledge, relevance of which has not been examined or evaluated. HR managers engage everyday to manage the network of relational web. They are required to have intense knowledge about individual and group behavioural dynamics. They need to know how an individual forms his or her perception about others, how the individual will behave in a group set-up, how groups will behave over a period of time, and so on.

Legal competency HR managers should have an in-depth understanding about the various labour legislations and its implications. They need to know how to undertake disciplinary action, what kind of deduction could be made from the salary, what is the maximum permissible limit for disbursing salaries, how to deal with trade unions, and so on. A hospitality organization comes under various labour legislations such as The Payment of Wages Acts, The Payment of Bonus Act, 1965, The Employees State Insurance Act, 1948, The Employees Provident Fund and other Miscellaneous Act, The Trade Union Act 1926, The Workmen Compensation Act, 1923, The Industrial Dispute Act, and so on. Not understanding these acts may create monumental problems. Each piece of legislation places the responsibility on the management of the hospitality organization to fulfil its requirements within a specified time limit; else, this will invite penalty and imprisonment. Thus, exposure to legal procedures is quite important.

SUMMARY

The basic essence of human resource management (HRM) function is to manage workforce. HRM is all the more important in the services and hospitality industry, where the employee is a key asset, the production of services happens in the vicinity of the guest, and most of the service delivery encounters cannot be measured.

The HR function involves a number of activities such as recruiting the right kind of employees, providing them training, managing employee performance by rewarding high performers, dealing with other performance issues, adherence to legal provisions applicable to workforce management, and so on. The purview of HR functions has changed substantially over time. Personnel management is transformed into human resource development functions. Today, HRM function is not carried out in isolation. It is an integral part of the strategic intent of the company. Thus, HR functions play a crucial role for the success of any hospitality organization.

KEY TERMS

Aesthetic discrimination   It signifies differentiation on the basis of physical attractiveness, attractive voice modulation, and culturally desirable body features (such as height) practiced by the management while selecting, remunerating, and terminating services of employees.

Analytical competency   Competency to collect, analyse, and present relevant data for decisions.

Communication competency   Competency to communicate management-related information to its audience.

Emotional literacy   Emotional literacy indicates possession of qualities that help individuals read their emotions and the emotions of other people and thus, effectively deal with their own emotions and the emotions of others.

HR competency   Relevant competencies required to successfully practice human resource management.

Human resource management   Human resource management is defined as holding human resource in meaningful relational networks, organized effectively to achieve organizational and individual objectives collectively.

Line manager   Line managers are those who are directly connected with the production of services, such as front office manager and food and beverage manager.

Staff managers   Staff managers such as human resource managers and finance managers are those who provide support and expert advice on certain issues to the line managers.

EXERCISES

Concept Review Questions

1. Define the human resource management function with special reference to service, more specifically, hospitality industry.
2. Map the various challenges that HR executives face while working in hospitality organizations.
3. Elucidate the various competencies required for HR managers working in hospitality and service organizations.
4. Examine the relationship between HR functions and organizational effectiveness.

Critical Thinking Questions

1. Why do we need managers? Can we manage our business without them?
2. 'HR professional competency is inadequate in relations to the challenge they face in the hospitality industry'. To what extent, do you agree with statement? Provide adequate rationale for your answer.

3. 'HR professionals are losing their legitimate right to represent employees' concern'. Critically examine the statement about its claims.

Assignment

Browse through web pages and locate a few advertisements given to recruit HR professionals for the Indian hospitality industry. Identify the commonality and differences among all these advertisements.

REFERENCES

Armstrong, M., *Strategic Human Resource Management: A Guide to Action*, 4th edition, Kogan Page, London, 2008.

Gordon & Gupta, *Understanding India's Service Sector Revolution*, IMF Working Paper, WP/04/171, Asia Pacific Department, September, 2004.

Gooderham, P., Parry, E., and Ringdal, K., 'The impact of bundles of strategic human resource management practices on the performance of European firms', *The International Journal of Human Resource Management*, Volume 19, Issue 11, 2008, p. 2041–2056.

Kochan, T.A. , 'Restoring Trust in the Human Resource Management Profession', WPC 0013, MIT Institute of Work and Employment Research, The MIT Workplace Centre, available at Sennett, R., *The Corrosion of Character*, WW Norton, New York, 2004, p.1.

Kamath, K.V., 'The India Growth Party Has Just Only Started', 2007, http://economictimes.indiatimes.com/articleshow/2656987.cms, accessed on 12 May 2011

Nickson, D., Warhurst, C., Witz A., and Cullen, A., 'The Importance of Being Aesthetic: Work, Employment and Service Organization', in Sturdy, A., Grugulis, I., and Willmott, H., (eds), *Customer Service: Empowerment and Entrapment*, Palgrave, Houndmills, 2001, p.170–190.

Rath, D.B., and Raj, R., 'Analytics and Implications of Services Sector Growth in Indian Economy', *The Journal of Income and Wealth*, Volume 28, No.1, January–June 2006.

Read, K., Srinivasan, N., and Doty, D.H., 'Adapting Human and Social Capital to Impact Performance: Some Empirical Findings from the U.S. Personal Banking Sector', *Journal of Managerial Issues*, Volume 21, Issue 1, 2009, p.36–57.

Sennett, R., *The Corrosion of Character*, WW Norton, New York, 1998, p. 1.

Thakral, T., 'Hotel industry is poised for a new growth phase', *The Financial Express*, March 20, 2008, http://www.financialexpress.com/news/hotel-industry-is-poised-for-a-new-growth-phase/286542/2, accessed on 12 May 2011

The Economic Times, Census of India 2011: India's population rises to 1.21 billion; sex ratio lowest since Independence, March 31, 2011 accessed available at http://articles.economictimes.indiatimes.com/2011-03-31/news/29366018_1_world-population-percentage-decadal-growth-census-commissioner, accessed on 02 April 2011

A ROAD TO TRAVEL

Two roads diverged in a yellow wood,
And sorry I could not travel both
And be one traveller, long I stood
And looked down one as far as I could
To where it bent in the undergrowth;
....
Two roads diverged in a wood, and
I—I took the one less travelled by,
And that has made all the difference.

Robert Frost *(1874–1963), – Mountain Interval*

Andrew William has been the general manager of the SAT Group of Hotels for the last 10 years. He is from Germany, but his family has settled in India since a long time. He has seen a lot of ups and downs in the hospitality industry. He is called 'old fashioned' by the new generation, and his employees perceive him as a 'tough guy'.

Xuan Zo Kue, sales manager, is an MBA from a well-known management institute from China. He has been recruited last year to acclimatize himself to the Indian style of operations and will ultimately be part of the China expansion plan, which is likely to be launched soon by the group. Xuan (pronounced as *Jouan*) has a lot of Chinese relatives in Kolkata and had studied in St. Xavier's School, Kolkata, for seven years, before his family resettled in China. He speaks Hindi, Marathi, Bengali, and English fluently.

It was 5.00 p.m. After the day's sales call and other itineraries, Xuan was having a conversation with Anita, a fresh pass-out from a management institute, working as a sales executive. Anita was finding it difficult to adjust between her work and family pressure, and thus, it was affecting her sales performance.

A call came from the general manager's office. Xuan reluctantly left the conversation with Anita midway with a promise to continue the discussion in the next few days.

'I am sorry to call you at such short notice. But I think it is important', Andrew started warmly.

'Oh that's fine,' Xuan replied.

'I am just concerned about our last quarter sales figures—it is going down—something needs to be done. A report suggests that Oberoi, Taj, and Marriott have all achieved spectacular performance results during the last quarter.'

'It is a temporary phase—we will get over it.'

'No… No doubt about that. I have no question about your sincerity. What worries me is your style of operation. I feel you should extract more from your sales people, rather than going soft with them.'

Xuan listened carefully.

'You are here for results. But the results are not impressive, I am afraid. You are required to control your sales people more and tell them to plan their daily activities. Their productivity is damn low if you check.'

'Mr William, I feel I am helping them achieve what we want. I motivate them, give them pep talks, crack jokes, and somehow this makes the workload easier to carry. I also call their families if they are ill and on their birthdays,' Xuan continued.

This seems more in line with the Guanxi school of thought, Andrew thought and continued to listen.

'If I do not do that I will find deadwoods. Most of these employees have been locked here for the last 10 years with only a slight salary hike over the years. We do not pay them enough and have lost many good sales guys to competition. And moreover, as a manager, I have some responsibility to look after them.'

'See Xuan, I think you have to come out of whatever you have got as cultural inheritance or burden. Whatever you call it—Guanxi or Kankei or Kwankye. When we operate on a global level, we are required to remember the bottom line, and the bottom line is money—how much money we are making at the end of the day. I think as a manager you are required to control your sales people more.'

'But Sir, I believe that control kills their spirit. I am trying to just inspire and motivate them to achieve. And I would like to reassure you that I think we will achieve our annual target. Many new ideas are coming from them—which is rare for this hotel, and we will round up a few of them and launch a new campaign. I assure you that they are working hard and most days they are working up to 10 p.m.'

'All that is fine. But I still feel that you need to change ….'

The next phase of the conversation on this topic did not go well. Xuan came out of the meeting feeling absolutely tired and exhausted. He looked around in his office and saw sincere people, working, full of *joie de vivre*. He sat down in front of his computer and opened the internet browser and typed 'naukri.com'. Perhaps he was looking for change. After all, he was tired now.

Discussion Questions

Read the case carefully. Find the meaning of the words Guanxi, Kankei, and Kwankye. When you come for class, you are required to have your own views about their actions and also attempt to provide answers to the following questions.

1. As the general manager of the hotel, was it wise of William to tell his subordinates what needed to be done to solve their problems? Is this the right approach to deal with the situation in the case study?
2. Do you think Xuan is competent to deal with William? Do you think Xuan needs to develop persuasive capacity to deal with William?
3. Who is right in the above case? Which road to travel—William's or Xuan's and why? Being an HR manager, do you think you can do something?

2 Manpower Planning

INTRODUCTION

Planning is an essential ingredient for any managerial function, whether it is for sales, operations, or human resources. Planning eliminates a lot of inefficiencies, duplicity of efforts, and adhocism in the system. This chapter deals with one of the most important functions of HR managers: manpower planning.

Manpower planning becomes all the more critical for HR managers in the hospitality industry as it involves the most valuable asset of the service industry, human beings. Any kind of inefficiency or incorrect planning will cause considerable damage to the motivation of the employees, and this, in turn, will affect their dealing with guests, resulting in lower customer satisfaction, and therefore, might lead to lower business results. Thus, manpower planning is sensitive, important, and essential for the growth of the business. This chapter highlights the processes, needs, and other associated questions involved with manpower planning.

Manpower planning is indeed an important task and is the result of coordinated actions across different departments and hotels. It is highly synchronized with the strategic actions that a company wants to achieve in the coming years. This work becomes more complicated when the HR team needs to plan for deployment of personnel on a global scale. The global dream of many Indian multinational hospitality companies to play a bigger game around the world is gaining ground. The wave of 'going global' has also arrived in India. Indian multinationals invested about 56.7 billion dollars (comprising inbound deals for 24.8 billions and outbound deals for 31.9 billions) in 948 deals world over during the first nine months of 2010 (*Economic Times* 2010). This is a significant departure from the past, where India has always been known to be the recipient of large foreign investment, and this new development has led India to achieve the tenth position in the global takeover bid. This implies that many Indian multinationals are gaining

LEARNING OBJECTIVES

After reading this chapter, you will be able to understand

- the meaning and importance of manpower planning in a hospitality organization
- the manpower planning process
- the various forecasting methods deployed for manpower planning
- the methods to deal with excess manpower as well as shortfall in manpower

ground in foreign lands to manufacture and provide services. To have trained manpower across domestic and international hotel properties, manpower planning indeed could play a significant role.

The question is, 'what is the implication of this development on HR practices?' This raises a number of issues: How many employees will be required to manage these foreign acquisitions? What kind of people would be able to manage these newly acquired businesses effectively? Should Indian or foreign nationals be given the responsibility of managing this newly acquired business? When do we require additional manpower to manage these businesses? Do we have the required skill set within the organization to handle these foreign acquisitions? How do we deal with downturn in the business? How many executives will be required to run the domestic operation? This chapter attempts to answer these crucial questions and develop an understanding about the importance of planning.

Definition Manpower planning signifies those aspects of managerial functions that allow assessing the current as well as future manpower requirements for an organization. In other words, manpower planning is an assessment, which helps to deploy the right number of employees at the right place, at the right time, for the achievement of the organizational goal. Growing organizations need to have an adequate supply of talented employees to support the business. At the same time, during a recession, the organization needs to shed some manpower in line with the business demand, and therefore, the organization needs to be prepared for every eventuality. Manpower planning allows the HR department to develop a blueprint for the management of human resources, which will provide support for every eventuality for the next two to five years.

IMPORTANCE OF MANPOWER PLANNING

Manpower planning is an important function carried out by the HR department. It provides a unique opportunity to the HR executives to go beyond the issues of the current financial year and to develop flexible, nimble, and appropriate work-force strength for organizational success in the long run. A big challenge to the HR manager is finding the right kind of people at the budgeted cost when a vacancy arises. Manpower planning provides a long-term view to the HR executives and prevents them from being short-sighted. While delivering solutions to problems arising out of HR operations during a current year, HR professionals do not lose focus from the long-term goal of the organization, and provide better linkage for delivery of sustainable solutions.

Manpower planning helps an organization in the following ways.

It brings discipline to the system Manpower planning is the process of methodically forecasting the future demand and supply requirement of manpower. For example, it maps out the average number of employees who usually leave the organization in a year, the number of employees who are due to retire, and so on. It also decides whether the current workforce composition is suitable for the achievement of the organizational goal. While examining the workforce in terms of skill set and capacity, manpower planning clearly highlights actionable strategy. This gives the organization ample time and scope to devise ways to fill the gap, if any, in the workforce in a disciplined manner. Thus, the departure of a significant individual should not become a panic situation, as through manpower planning, the HR manager would have anticipated such eventualities and would have planned how to fill the gaps.

It brings predictability   To have relatively accurate prediction about future earning, one needs to plan for expenses. Labour expense plan helps to understand the cost structure and thus enables relatively accurate predictability. It is common to find companies giving revenue-earning guidance to its investors quarter by quarter, stretching to the year-end figure. All these guidelines declared by the companies require adequate data support. Any rosy picture about the share earning will eventually have implications in the stock market. Many Indian multinationals are becoming members of stock exchanges in the United States. In the United States, the Sarbanes–Oxley Act (a law pertaining to corporate governance) is applicable, which prescribes a number of rules and regulations for the maintenance of data support for any kind of earning guidance and recommends severe punishment in case of violation of any clause. Thus, the Indian multinationals fall under various legal sanctions and compliance is essentially mandatory with certain exceptions. Manpower planning provides adequate support for the management of payroll expenses. In some industries, such as hospitality and information technology sector, payroll expense has a major influence on corporate earning. Manpower planning provides a clear picture in this regard, and the management of organizational affairs becomes more predictable, and thereby, manageable too.

It helps to devise proper recruitment function   Manpower planning helps to have relatively tentative headcounts, which in turn trigger recruitment or retrenchment activities and provides detailed guidance about the number of employees required for any business in the coming years. This manpower requirement plan helps to guide the HR department in developing a recruitment plan. Different types of functions require different types of sourcing as highlighted in Table 2.1.

For recruitment of a steward or any other entry-level job, the HR manager needs to focus on hotel management institutes and industrial training institutes (ITI). In order to fill the gap at the middle management level, internal promotion could be one of the effective options; in case a suitable candidate is not available, they can look into competition hotels for the requisite recruitment.

Table 2.1 Sources of recruitment

Types of manpower	Functions	Sources of recruitment
Entry-level staff	Steward	Hotel management institutes/ industrial training institutes
	Receptionist	
	Trainee	
Entry-level executives	Trainee executives	Hotel management institutes
	Junior managers	Internal promotions/competition hotels
	Assistant managers	Internal promotions/competition hotels
Middle-level executives	Departmental heads	Internal promotions/competition hotels
	Unit head	Internal promotions/competition hotels
Senior-level executives	Divisional head	Internal promotions/related business
	Strategic business unit head	Internal promotions/related business
Top-level management	Managing directors/CEO, etc.	Internal promotions/international recruitment drive

FACTORS TO BE CONSIDERED FOR EFFECTIVE MANPOWER PLANNING

Manpower planning is about planning the deployment of employees in various organizational hierarchies. This deployment could be effective if good-quality manpower is placed in right quantities at the right time. However, as it is difficult to predict the future, it is all the more difficult to imagine the business situation in the next two to three years. For example, during the recession (2007–2010), many employees were laid off and some hotel organizations had to resort to closing their overseas offices to cut costs. Thus, the country's economic, social, and political conditions also play a key role in the development of effective planning.

Health of other industries　The hospitality industry is dependent on the success of other industries. When the other industries in a country do well economically, they generate additional business in the form of conferences and movement of business travellers. An affluent economy, nourished by industrial growth, often takes the liberty to indulge in spending more money on the consumption of luxurious experiences. When the stock market does well, it puts an additional fund in the pocket of individual consumers. In such situations, more human resources are required at the hospitality organizations to support the spurt in travel and tourism activities. Therefore, it is important to review business conditions and growth rates of other industries while developing manpower planning templates.

Economic growth of the country Economic growth is a key indicator for gauging the condition of the hospitality business. As India registers high economic growth, it also generates a considerable amount of growth for the hospitality industry. Therefore, GDP (gross domestic product) growth provides considerable guidance about the health of the hospitality industry. In general, the hospitality industry players pay low salaries. However, when economic growth creates abundant jobs in the market, the hospitality industry is likely to lose its good-quality manpower to higher paying jobs from other service industry players. This will create tremendous pressure on the payroll budget and on the HR department to locate good-quality manpower for their organization. Thus, while developing an effective manpower plan, the HR manager needs to develop a framework that will operate at the time of high economic growth as well as economic downturn.

Table 2.2 highlights that trade hotels and restaurants achieved almost 12.4 per cent growth in the year 2005–2006. The growth rate slowed down to 11.2 per cent in the year 2006–2007, then went down to 9.5 per cent in 2007–2008, and further dipped to 5.3 per cent during the economic downturn in the year 2008–2009. However, in the year 2009–2010, it started recovering and reached 8.3 per cent. It is interesting to note that when economic development has been observed in all

Table 2.2 Rate of growth at factor cost during 2005–2010

	2005–2006	2006–2007	2007–2008	2008–2009	2009–2010
Agriculture, forestry, and fishing	5.2	3.7	4.7	1.6	−0.2
Mining and quarrying	1.3	8.7	3.9	1.6	8.7
Manufacturing	9.6	14.9	10.3	3.2	8.9
Electricity, gas, and water supply	6.6	10.0	8.5	3.9	8.2
Construction	12.4	10.6	10.0	5.9	6.5
Trade, hotels, and restaurants	12.4	11.2	9.5	5.3	8.3*
Transport, storage, and communication	11.5	12.6	13.0	11.6	–
Financing, insurance, real estate, and business services	12.8	14.5	13.2	10.1	9.9
Community, social, and personal services	7.6	2.6	6.7	13.9	8.2
GDP at factor cost	9.5	9.7	9.2	6.7	7.2

Source: CSO; Economic Survey of India, 2010 downloaded from *indiabudget.nic.in* accessed on March, 2011; *Transport and communication included for 2009–2010 in trade, hotels, and restaurants.

other industries, trade, hotel, and restaurants have also demonstrated spectacular growth. As highlighted in Table 2.2, the economic development in a country is deeply related to the growth in the hospitality industry. The hospitality industry needs to make considerable adjustments while dealing with different growth levels. Manpower planning thus plays a crucial role in enabling HR managers to have a dynamic workforce.

Political stability   Political stability contributes greatly to the success of the hospitality business. For instance, in any country, political dictatorship brings political uncertainty and travellers hesitate to visit that country, and this negatively impacts business there. HR professionals need to take this into consideration, and it becomes critical for them to deploy appropriate manpower.

Organizational growth plan   While developing a manpower plan, it is essential that the HR team should be given a clear picture about the strategic growth the company wants to achieve. This will enable the HR department to plan for sourcing and budgeting the payroll expenses. For example, if a hotel chain wants to simultaneously start 3 hotels in China, 2 in Malaysia, 5 in the Middle East, and 10 in various European countries, this will pose many difficulties for the HR department. This is because all these cultural environments would pose considerable challenge and the working environment in each hotel would be different, and it would be challenging to operate in various regions of the world. These challenges are also accentuated if language and cultural differences between the two working environments are high. While undertaking manpower planning, the department needs to decide on whether to recruit employees from the local market. It needs to address the following questions:

1. Can the local markets provide adequate support for all these hotels?
2. What are the local labour rules?
3. How many employees can be recruited from outside the country?
4. How can the organizational culture of the company be built in all those hotels?

Examination of organizational resource   For manpower planning to be effective, the HR department needs to review the current strength of the manpower and how it will grow inside and also how the aspirations of the current employees will be fulfilled. Thus, the HR executives should have the following information: a replacement chart, promotion chart, skill inventory, succession planning, retirement schedule, employee turnover details, and so on. As some employees would retire either on reaching retirement age or by taking voluntary retirement each year, the HR manager needs to look into this aspect very seriously. As these employees possess good experience, their departure should not create a vacuum or deficiencies in service delivery. The promotion chart indicates the growth plan for the deployed employees. The aspirations of these employees should be able to accommodate the growth of the company. The skill inventory indicates the skill set available inside the organization to support the future growth of the company. Any deficiencies in the skill set should be fulfilled by recruiting skilled individuals and by developing the required manpower through internal growth and training and development.

Forecasting methods The HR manager needs to develop a robust forecasting model for sound manpower planning (Fig. 2.1). The various methods available are discussed in the following subsections.

Rule of thumb or guess work The HR team could carry out manpower planning using past experience and past successful protocol. An experienced HR manager relies on past experience to develop a manpower plan. Although these plans could be developed intuitively, nonetheless it is linked with the past. However, as many hospitality organizations are growing at a faster rate, past history is not that relevant. Thus, rule of thumb requires supplementary support from other methods.

Expert opinion The HR manager could rely on experts providing consultancy services to various hospitality organizations and having considerable knowledge of the industry. Owing to their continuous exposure, they are more familiar with the inner core of many organizations and are equipped to provide better support. Multi-organizational experience makes them develop apparently correct estimations about the type and quality of manpower required for the coming years.

Scenario planning Scenario planning is a scientific technique where several faces of the future are imagined and articulated with the help of a diverse expert group. Each group consists of people with intense knowledge in diverse subjects such as sociology, technology, economics, statistics, industrial knowledge, anthropology, and other social sciences. Owing to their diverse background, experts contribute and envisage

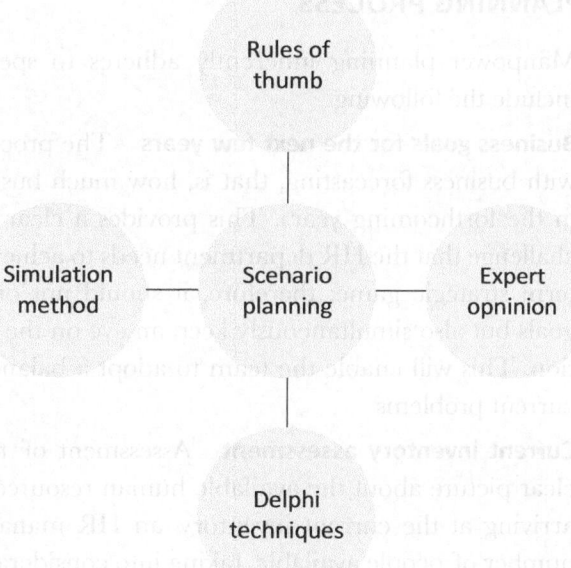

Figure 2.1 Forecasting methods

the future according to their perception. Intense interaction among the members of the group provides the opportunity to have a synthesized view of the future. Likewise, a number of groups are formed and each one of these groups provides alternative viewpoints about the future. These alternative interpretations about the future and the implications give an insight to the HR team about the way they should prepare and the action they should take to effectively meet the future challenges.

Delphi technique   The Delphi technique is a method of probing and arriving at some degree of conclusion using a group of experts. It is a method of group decision making and forecasting that involves successively collating the judgements of experts. It is a structured way of coming to a common agreement on issues, especially when accumulated knowledge in that area is relatively less. It involves administering a structured questionnaire several times among subject experts, and each time an attempt is made to develop the focused issues. This technique provides a slice of insight from the experts on the subject.

Simulation modelling   Most of the estimations follow the point estimate method, that is, most of the worksheet is prepared in Microsoft Excel using specific figures while estimating tentative results. However, through common sense, we know that the figures used to arrive at a specific tentative result could be erroneous because some of the estimated and associated assumptions used for the calculation may not be exactly correct. In such a situation, simulation methods accommodate a tentative data range instead of fixed point estimates and allow us to run the simulation analysis a thousand times. This result provides more trustworthy figures than point estimates.

MANPOWER PLANNING PROCESS

Manpower planning inherently adheres to specific processes (Fig. 2.2), which include the following.

Business goals for the next few years   The process of manpower planning starts with business forecasting, that is, how much business is estimated to be achieved in the forthcoming years. This provides a clear picture about the nature of the challenge that the HR department needs to achieve. Manpower planning is a long-term strategic game; therefore, it should not only examine immediate business goals but also simultaneously keep an eye on the long-term goals of the organization. This will enable the team to adopt a balanced approach while dealing with current problems.

Current inventory assessment   Assessment of the current inventory provides a clear picture about the available human resources within the organization. While arriving at the current inventory, an HR manager must have clarity about the number of people available, taking into consideration retirement, natural turnover ratio, internal promotion, and so on. This current inventory assessment provides a clear picture of the available human resources.

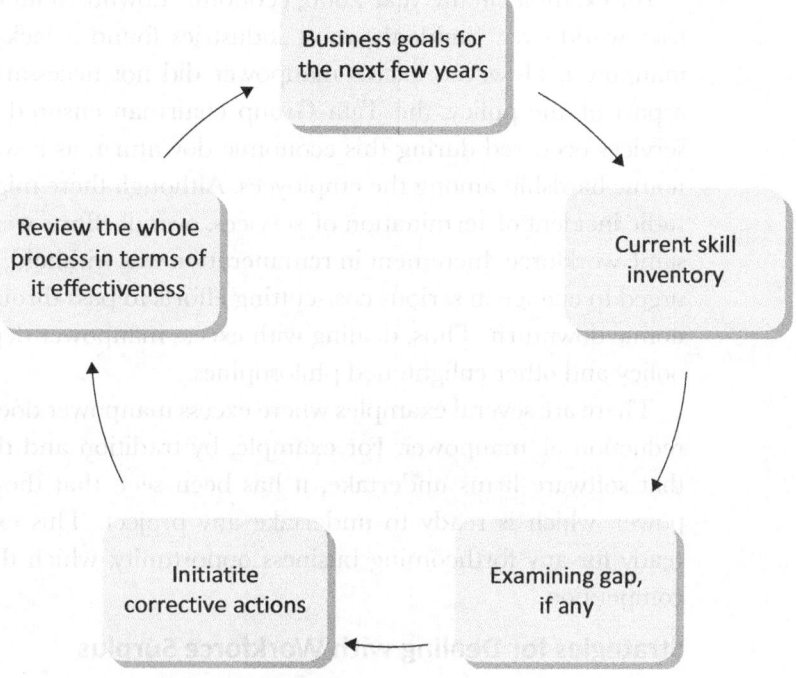

Figure 2.2 Manpower planning process

Comparison The current inventory is compared with the manpower requirement estimation that is arrived at after assessing the business goals set for the next few years. Out of this comparison, the workforce strength that needs reinforcement and recruitment is assessed, and the HR department charts out exhaustive plans for the source of manpower. In case the organization finds that they have excess manpower, they could redeploy the excess employees in other business organizations, send them on a transfer or for further studies or training, or offer voluntary retirement schemes for the reduction of manpower. In case of shortfall in manpower, the department should devise suitable plans to fill the gap.

MANAGING WORKFORCE SURPLUS AND SHORTFALL

A number of options are available for a manager in any organization to deal with surplus or shortfall of manpower. However, this work should be done in line with the legal framework applicable in the country, and also, all such decisions should be examined on appropriate humanitarian grounds. The question of reduction in manpower is very sensitive, and adequate safeguard should be exercised. Some of the measures undertaken to reduce manpower is less painful, such as employee transfer. Some of the measures bring untold misery to the employees, such as termination or retrenchment of services. Therefore, it should be done carefully, keeping in mind the human implications.

For example, in the year 2008, economic downturn influenced almost all industries world over. Suddenly, most industries found a lack of business and excess manpower. However, excess manpower did not necessarily need any action. As a part of the policy, the Tata Group chairman ensured that no termination of services occurred during this economic downturn, as it would create further economic hardship among the employees. Although there might have been some sporadic incident of termination of services, overall efforts were made to maintain the same workforce. Increment in remuneration was withheld, and the employees were urged to engage in serious cost-cutting efforts to pass through this impromptu economic downturn. Thus, dealing with excess manpower depends on the company's policy and other enlightened philosophies.

There are several examples where excess manpower does not necessarily require reduction of manpower. For example, by tradition and the unique type of work that software firms undertake, it has been seen that they maintain excess manpower, which is ready to undertake any project. This excess manpower is kept ready for any forthcoming business opportunity, which they would win from the competition.

Strategies for Dealing with Workforce Surplus

Freeze on recruitment The hospitality industry often experiences a business cycle more intimately than any other industry because of its relationship with all other industries. Thus, whenever the hospitality industry experiences a downturn in business, one of the most effective strategies followed is to freeze new recruitment. This is less painful to the existing workforce.

Voluntary retirement The HR department could launch a scheme among existing employees for voluntary retirement and can announce the qualifying criteria for the scheme. For example, employees who have been working for 10 or more years with the company are usually allowed to opt for voluntary retirement scheme. This provides a lump sum retirement and termination benefits amount to the employees and also helps them find alternative and perhaps more lucrative professional options.

Lay-off The HR manager could lay off some employees, after adhering to the provisions highlighted in Chapter V-B of the Industrial Dispute Act. In India, lay-off signifies temporary cessation of work due to shortage of coal, power, and so on. It is not a permanent termination of the relationship between employees and employers, and there are certain provisions that need to be complied with.

Strategies for Dealing with Shortfall in Workforce

Recruitment Shortfall in the workforce strength should be replenished with new talent. Depending on the requirement as dictated by organizational goals and current inventory assessment, the HR team should make plans for the recruitment of adequate number of employees.

Transfer   In case a hospitality organization has several units, perhaps operating in different countries, the HR department could examine the possibility of finding suitable employees from other units. For example, a travel service company that operates in a multilocation multicountry format can manage its shortfall in one country either by local recruitment or by internal transfer across units.

Outsourcing   Outsourcing is an attempt to redraw the boundary of the organization where some unproductive and unprofitable activities of the organization are discontinued and given to outside party to conduct. It helps decide the work that would be undertaken by the organization and the non-essential part of the business that could be given to an outside agency to execute. For example, a lot of multinational companies have shifted their service delivery unit/manufacturing unit from the United States and Europe (which attracts high wage cost) to relatively low wage countries (such as India, Philippines, and Bangladesh). Outsourcing is a strategic tool to have a flexible workforce inside the organization, and although initially this outsourcing drive was due to cost advantage, currently, there are other factors also that are guiding the outsourcing decision. Outsourcing is taking one closer to the customer. Economic development is sweeping the BRIC nations (Brazil, Russia, India, and China) and South Africa, and consumption in the world is getting refocused on all these regions. Much of the outsourcing is done to achieve closer proximity to the customer. Thus, outsourcing is an effective method to manage a flexible workforce, but it should be done cautiously. A proper metric system of evaluation should be developed before awarding a specific function under this method.

WHAT SHOULD MANPOWER PLANNING OFFER?

Manpower planning unites a diverse range of human resource functions such as recruitment, training, and performance appraisal and helps present a comprehensive picture of employee deployment, their effectiveness, scope for development, and so on. Manpower planning thus shares an intimate relationship with corporate strategic objectives. Connecting diverse range of human resource functions provides unique opportunity to HR executives to play the role of a strategic partner. Unleashing diverse range of actions, HR managers contribute meaningfully to organizational effectiveness and strengthen its base for future actions (Fig. 2.3).

Effective manpower planning by the HR department would do the following.

Support current recruitment plan   Effective manpower planning should provide robust support to the recruitment activities. It should guide the timing of recruitment, type of recruitment, kind of recruitment, and so on. Manpower planning provides a clear picture about the type of skilled manpower required.

Support training plan   Manpower planning should highlight the gross deficit in terms of skills in the organization. This provides guidance to the kind of training that needs to be imparted to employees for enhancement of their skills to face the

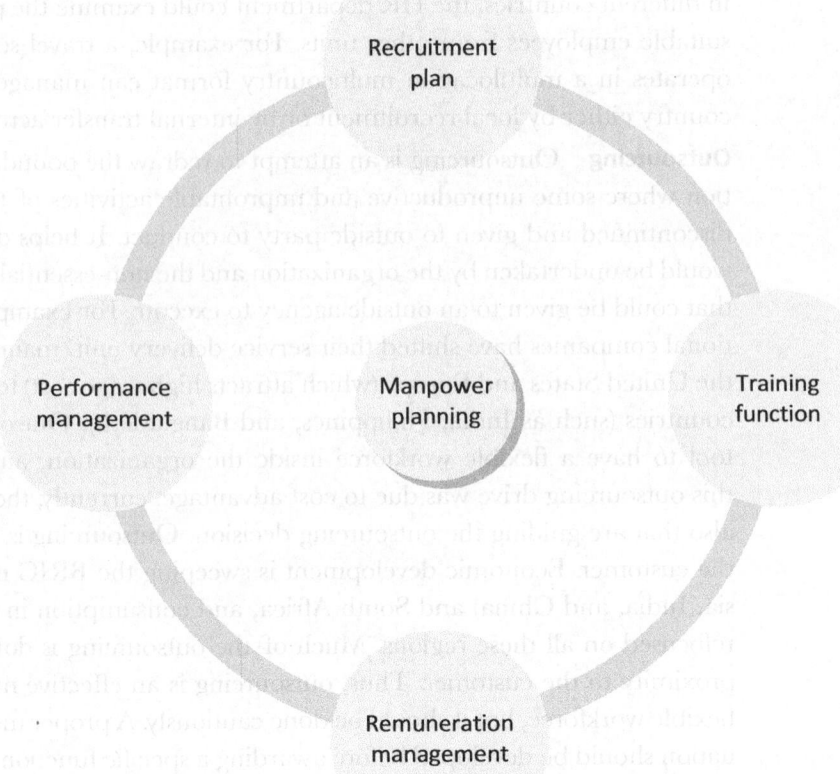

Figure 2.3 Linking manpower planning with other HR functions

current business challenges. A training plan is therefore intimately linked with the manpower planning process.

Support performance linkage Manpower planning should provide information about the adequacy of the present level of employee performance with reference to the business goals set by the organization. In case of any gap, the HR team could undertake steps to reset the performance standard to achieve the overall business goals.

Support remuneration linkage The manpower planning process provides a broad spectrum view of the current industry status and the reasons for the current short-fall of manpower. This helps the HR team to revise their remuneration package in tune with the current market practices. A gross economic review provides the relevant picture of growth in the industry. This works as information backbone for making suitable changes in the remuneration package.

HUMAN RESOURCE INFORMATION SYSTEM AND MANPOWER PLANNING

Human resource information system (HRIS) is a software framework where employee-related information is stored, processed, and utilized in decision making with reference to career planning, promotion, transfer, and so on. While planning manpower, HRIS provides timely support by preparing a user-friendly report that allows the HR manager to take data-driven decisions. Proprietary software is available to execute HRIS. For example, Oracle has an HRIS, which is being used by many hospitality organizations in India and abroad.

Analysis   The HR department prepares various types of analysis to review the current manpower capacity and the required manpower. Some of the reports could be the following.

Age-wise review   An age-wise review examines employees as per their age and current position. This report provides a panoramic picture about the number of employees on the verge of retirement, the effect of their retirement on the various functions, and the requisite actions to fill the gap in the skill inventory.

Skill inventory   The HR team could prepare an inventory of current skill availability in the organization. This will provide an up-to-date assessment about the current skill inventory. Comparing this with the business goals, the department could review the adequacy of manpower requirement.

SUMMARY

Manpower planning is focused on the long-term manpower requirement of an organization. Manpower planning is one of the crucial functions undertaken by the HR team to predict correctly the exact level of manpower requirement. This process provides a clear picture about the manpower requirement for the next few years. In the hospitality business, manpower plays a significant role and could effectively decide success or failure. It is a prime function because the result of manpower functions ushers a broad range of actions; for example, shortfall of trained manpower for new acquisitions triggers renewed vigour in the recruitment functions. It also triggers training functions to develop adequate manpower for overcoming shortfall in manpower.

KEY TERMS

Delphi method   Delphi method is a method of probing and arriving at some degree of conclusion using a group of experts.

Manpower planning   Manpower planning is a managerial planning process conducted by the HR team to predict the manpower requirement over the next few years and plan necessary action to respond to the manpower requirement so that the organization can achieve the right type of manpower at the right time at the right number.

Outsourcing Outsourcing is an attempt to redraw the boundary of the organization where some of the organizational unproductive and unprofitable activities are discontinued and given to outside party to conduct.

Scenario planning Scenario planning is building multiple future business scenarios using a diverse group of experts.

EXERCISES

Concept Review Questions

1. Critically examine the need for manpower planning. How does it relate to other human resource functions?
2. Review the manpower planning process usually followed in a hospitality organization.

Critical Thinking Questions

1. Review the current manpower requirement in the light of current economic, political, and social context. Which are the factors that should be given due consideration while evaluating all these factors?
2. Explore the relationship between manpower planning function and other human resource functions.

Assignment

Did you see any evidence of manpower planning in the hospitality organization where you got the opportunity to undergo industrial training? How could manpower planning be useful for that organization? Share your ideas.

REFERENCES

Economic Times, http://articles.economictimes.indiatimes.com/2010-10-04/news/27605654_1_m-a-volume-merger-and-acquisition-volume-largest-indian-outbound-deal accessed on 15 May 2011.

CASE STUDY

RAM MOHAN'S DILEMMA

Ram Mohan has been working as an HR director for the last 10 years for a travel service company that operates only in India. Their sales offices are located in Delhi, Mumbai, Chennai, Bangalore, Kolkata, Ahmedabad, and Pune. However, recently, this company made a strategic alliance with an internationally reputed travel agency operating in four regions of the world—Beijing, Dubai, Brussels, and California. Presently, offices in all these regions are well staffed.

However, the managing director of the company has presented an aggressive growth plan after this new acquisition of the international agency. Mohan has visited all the offices and spoken with the local HR managers located in all these offices. An important concern is that although all these international offices are financially connected they are very different in terms of work culture. He also believes that not everything in their work culture is conducive to achieving the multiple growth that his company wants to achieve.

Ram Mohan strongly believes that some employees from these offices should come to India to work on a rotation, and this will develop better synergy with the parent unit. Besides, business from China is growing at about 25 per cent, and to maintain this unusual growth, he believes that an aggressive recruitment drive needs to be undertaken without fail. One HR manager has suggested transferring some employees from India to all these foreign locations to develop synergy.

Discussion Questions

1. Should Ram Mohan send employees who are at present posted at different Indian cities on international posting to achieve better integration of manpower? Provide your rationale.
2. Should Ram Mohan invite employees who are at present posted at different international offices to India? Provide your rationale.
3. Can manpower planning solve the problem of Ram Mohan? What other information do you need to provide support to Ram Mohan?
4. As an advisor, you are required to provide realistic suggestion to Ram Mohan. What suggestion would you like to give him?

3 Recruitment

INTRODUCTION

Recruitment is a very important function that is executed by the HR department. In the service industry, especially the hospitality business, it is very important to recruit the right kind of employees. Suitable recruitment ensures the supply of the right type of human resources for the ongoing operations of the hospitality business. In case the appropriate people are not hired, the hospitality organization would not be able to meet customer requirements and create customer delight.

In this chapter, we examine the role of the recruitment function for organizational success, various sources of recruitment, and alternatives to recruitment. It is imperative to examine the recruitment process and review the merit of these processes and also examine how the recent geopolitical developments in India have changed some of these processes.

INTRODUCTION TO RECRUITMENT

Recruitment is the process of identifying and hiring the best qualified candidate (from within or outside an organization) for an actual or anticipated job vacancy in a most timely and cost-effective manner. This function helps acquire the right kind of employees for the organizational workforce and has undergone substantial changes over the years. Earlier India, with limited economic growth, had inherited unemployment problem, and the supply side of the workforce was always found to be heavier than the demand for manpower. In new India, having an economic growth level hovering over 8 per cent, the industry experienced shortage of skilled and well-groomed staff for their workforce. Higher economic growth has created multiple opportunities for career growth. Technology has also undergone tremendous change and now enables the prospective employee and employer to interact through various communication modes (web portals such as monster.com, naukri.com, video conference, email, and chat).

Recruitment function is very crucial, especially for the service industry, as the production and delivery of services is done with the help of employees. The central and key role of employees in the service industry has made the recruitment function important and also a time-consuming process. Proper recruitment ensures the production of services as per the blueprint of the service design; however, wrong recruitment may jeopardize the whole service delivery. Some industry analysts speculate the growth of industry from the recruitment rate. This has been seen especially for the IT sector and its allied information service industries. When the economic growth in the country remains unstunted in spite of recent economic downturn, it is difficult to find the right kind of trained staff for hospitality organizations, as employees opt for relatively high paid jobs in other related service sectors such as call centres, banks, insurance, IT, and sales. A very important factor is the timely acquisition of talents. However, it becomes difficult to recruit employees within a short period, as the recruitment process is time consuming.

SOURCES OF RECRUITMENT

In general, there are two sources of recruitment—internal and external.

Internal Recruitment

Internal recruitment means the acquisition of employees from inside the organization, and this often involves promotion or transfer across locations or between departments or through employee referral. When vacancies arise, the HR department circulates internal advertisement in their web portal or through the company's internal email services. Existing employees, who are interested in this new position within the company, send their applications to the corporate human resource department. Subsequently, this department examines the suitability of the candidates, at present working for the organization in lower ranks. If the candidates are found suitable, the HR department prefers internal recruitment as it potentially generates positive work environment, is relatively less expensive, and quickens the recruitment process. It also leads to low employee turnover rates and high productivity. However, it could change the internal political atmosphere and trigger a number of resignations.

Advantages There are various advantages of recruiting from within the organization. These include the following:

1. Generation of positive work environment: Internal recruitment generates hope for promotion, but it should be based on merit only and should be an objective process. This will generate a positive feeling among employees. Employees' morale will be high, as internal recruitment indicates accommodation of internal talent for upcoming opportunities, and each employee may find accommodation of his or her career objective within the company.

2. Speed: Internal recruitment quickens the whole recruitment process. Timely recruitment of talent is very important, and external sourcing of talent often involves a time-consuming recruitment process, which slows the timely recruitment objective. However, in the case of internal recruitment, it shortens the timely process.

3. Avalability of past performance data: Past performance data pertaining to the employees is instantly available to the recruitment authority, which is not necessarily possible in the case of external recruitment. Research indicates that most of the biodata/resumes presented to recruitment authorities include some degree of exaggeration and misstatement of facts, which is not verifiable, and it is difficult to know the exactness of the facts. Recruitment process, mostly undertaken under huge time constraints, does not give provisions to examine every detail presented in the biodata.

4. Performance: Employees, currently employed in the organization, are already familiar with the rules, regulations, and cultural nuances, and they may not require additional training before occupying the new position. Therefore, it takes them less time to join and settle in the new position. Employees recruited from outside often require some transitory time for adjustment within the cultural web of the organization, and thus, it takes them some additional time before becoming a full-fledged employee. Besides, there is no guarantee that the employee recruited from outside the organization will be able to get accustomed to the specific cultural context. Thus, recruitment from external market often involves risk.

Disadvantages There are some disadvantages of internal recruitment. These include the following:

1. Lack of fresh ideas: Internal recruitment promotes individuals who performed well inside the organization and thereby the legacy of their past continues. This deprives the organization of fresh ideas, and the organization becomes myopic in its approach and attitude. External recruitment provides an opportunity for bringing in new benchmark ideas that have been successful in other organizations.

2. Political dynamics: Promoting one individual to a higher position often generates a high degree of political drama among the other prospective candidates. It may generate hopelessness among the non-promoted candidates and may demotivate them, and some of them may subsequently leave the organization. Thus, recruitment of one individual can often trigger mass departure of employees, and this would magnify the recruitment problem.

Methods of internal recruitment

Some of the methods of internal recruitment are discussed here.

HR information system (HRIS) Most enlightened HR departments maintain employee-related data in an organized manner in the human resources information system (HRIS). This system maintains all the employee particulars in a software database, which is very user-friendly and searchable. In case of specific requirement, the HR manager can easily identify and find a list of employees who are suitable for the vacant position. This easily searchable employee data is a great asset, especially for large organizations. From these shortlisted candidates, the concerned authority can easily select the employee who best meets the requirements for the post.

Job posting   Most companies have developed internet-based medium to communicate with their employees about important events, development, and so on. This platform can also be used for job posting. Each employee has his or her own email id and often regularly receives details pertaining to vacancies within the company. It depends on whether the candidates will be interested in a specific posting. This process makes the recruitment process fair and objective, and each employee gets an equal opportunity to apply for a specific job.

External Recruitment

External recruitment concerns recruitment from outside the organization. This facilitates the entry of new people and ideas into the organization. However, the acceptance of and reaction to a new entrant is sometimes sceptical and may have a negative impact on group cohesion and morale.

Methods of external recruitment

Methods available for external recruitment include the following:

Advertisement   Whenever vacancies arise inside the organization, the company gives advertisements in national daily newspapers and accesses a wider pool of prospective candidates. These advertisements often involve details of the company, the basic qualifications required, job location, job content, job specifications, compensation, and so on.

Campus recruitment   Campus recruitment is used to recruit recently passed graduates for entry-level jobs. With the growth of academic institutions, campus recruitment is actively promoted by these institutions as it is a relatively inexpensive recruitment method. It begins with formal communication between recruiting companies and representatives from the academic institution. After arriving at a mutual agreement about salary package, date of the interview, and so on, the campus interview begins, mostly with a presentation by the recruiting company. Each company attempts to make an interesting presentation regarding the job opportunity, growth of the company, and so on. The campus recruitment process involves paper-and-pencil tests, group discussions, and interviews. A number of variations are possible; for example, those who are aspiring to join the kitchen of a five-star hotel are often subjected to food trial. Similarly, those who are aspiring to join a software firm might be subjected to additional tests such as programming skill evaluation phase, where each candidate is examined in terms of his or her programming capabilities.

Direct application   With the advent of technology, most organizations have their own web sites. This web portal also works as a database master by giving a provision to prospective candidates to apply for suitable jobs. The HR manager can manage this data by developing a suitable database and then preparing a list of suitable candidates and utilizing this accumulated data while recruiting employees. This method of data acquisition is the most common and least expensive source of external recruitment. The disadvantage of this type of recruitment is that there is a time lag between the time the applicants send their application and the time they are called. When the applicants finally receive a call for interview, they may have joined elsewhere and may no longer be interested in the job for which they had applied.

Employment agencies   Employment agencies provide assistance in finding suitable candidates for hospitality organizations. They encourage prospective candidates to register and upload their biodata with them. These are most effective when the particular skill or expertise is scarce in the market or the organization has difficulty in searching for a potential candidate. When their service is sought, they provide shortlisted candidates from their databank, and at the end of the placement, charge either the employer or the candidate or both.

Job portals   A number of job portals have come up, such as monster.com and naukri.com, which help prospective employees and employers get connected. The web portals charge the hospitality organization for hosting an advertisement on its behalf and also host the applicant's data. The prospective candidate may apply to the hospitality company by sending an email. The applicant can register on the web portal and upload the biodata, through which prospective employers can find suitable applicants. Passive support from these job portals helps find suitable candidates at shorter notice. The job portal charges varying amount of fees depending on the depth of the relationship with the organization.

Referral   Referral by existing employees is considered to be the most friendly selection process. Whenever the structure and composition of a team changes owing to exit/recruitment, the team undergoes stress as a new member attempts to find his or her space in the group. Referral reduces stress among the new recruits as they have their friends working for the company. This process of group formation has been explained by Tuckman with his group development model, which suggests that newly recruited employees initially engage in conflict but subsequently get settled. However, employees selected from friends circle will be less likely to adopt a conflict approach and would take less time to settle. The initial process of team formation potentially generates conflict while interacting with each other for performance and may influence the new recruits badly. There is a possibility that the newly recruited employees may not be comfortable in dealing with the stress that originated from the initial interactions with the existing group, and decide to leave. When a known person recommends a candidate, this stress may get reduced. This is an effective recruitment tool, especially during the time of economic boom.

WHAT TO LOOK FOR IN PROSPECTIVE CANDIDATES

This is one of the most important aspects that an HR manager should pay attention to. Mostly, it is done using past success records, past experience of the recruiters, and so on. However, it is possible to recruit employees by adhering to some scientific methods that are devised using organizational databank. For ready reference, we highlight only a few of them.

Successful Employees

HR managers could look at the employees who are highly successful in the organization and devise certain psychometric assessments that derive some traits commonly present among these successful employees for a specific job. By identifying these traits and qualities, the HR manager can develop a repertoire of skill sets for a specific job. Subsequently, it is relatively easy to develop suitable methods to assess specific traits and qualities (Table 3.1) by psychometric tests, interview questions, group discussions, skill tests, and so on. For example, for certain jobs in the hospitality business, being a team player is an essential quality for any successful employee. However, it is relatively difficult to ascertain during recruitment whether the applicant is a team player or not. The recruiting authority could devise simulated activities or psychological games to ascertain how the applicant in question is behaving, which could provide certain clues about the candidate.

Recruitment is an important function with reference to its success. Thus, deployment of scientific process provides assurance of successful recruitment function. This kind of cause-and-effect relationship in the recruitment function provides clear guidelines on what to look for in a candidate and makes the system more transparent, systematic, and effective.

Table 3.1 Sample criteria and its measurement method

Skill set required	Method of evaluation
Team player	Group task
Positive mind frame	Interview question
Achievement oriented	Past record/interview question
Market knowledge	Interview question
Extrovert	Psychometric test
Pleasing personality	Interview question
Self-management	Interview question
Job knowledge	Tests

Employee Competency

The interview panel conducts an intense review of the competency of individual applicants who are interested in joining the company. But what is job competency? (See Exhibit 3.1.) A number of definitions are available:

- A job competency is 'an underlying characteristic of a person which results in effective and/or superior performance in a job' (Klemp 1980).
- 'A competency is a reliably measurable, relatively enduring characteristic (or combination of characteristics) of a person, team or organization, which causes and statistically predicts a criterion level of performance' (Spencer 2003).
- A competency is defined 'as an underlying characteristic of a manager causally related to superior performance on the job' (Everts 1988 p. 50).
- All these definitions emphasize the 'underlying characteristic' of individuals capable of producing superior performance.

Exhibit 3.1   Hospitality Takes on a Different Challenge

Café Coffee Day (CCD) employs 50 speech- and hearing-impaired people at various outlets; Costa Coffee outlet in Greater Kailash, Delhi, is run by 18 such employees. Hotels, too, are proactively employing differently abled people. Take the case of hospitality major, ITC Maurya, which recruits differently abled people in back-end operations and database management. "We have been recruiting differently abled people for some time," says ITC Hotels' vice-president Deepak Haksar. "Our Bangalore property is a fine example where differently abled people are employed and recognised for the same." Similarly, JW Marriott employs intellectually disabled school pass-outs at its Mumbai property.

While some have begun by tying up with NGOs, the JW Marriott Hotel in Mumbai recruits intellectually disabled and dyslexic pass-outs from a special school 'Dilkhush'. "We have five such employees at present. They are trained for three months and then assigned housekeeping, laundry, or back-office tasks in restaurants. For us, it is a CSR (corporate social responsibility) initiative aimed at providing equal opportunity to this segment of the society," explains Mielle Batliwala, HR manager, JW Marriott.

Lemon Tree Hotels has three such employees working for its Gurgaon hotel. The hotel chain intends to recruit 100 differently abled employees in the next 4 years. While it may be a great CSR initiative, it also offers the hospitality industry, which is facing talent crunch and high attrition rate, an alternate talent pool for back-office operations. With infrastructure for differently abled as mandated by the government for all three-, four-, and five-star hotels, it becomes easier to employ such people, says Rahul Pandit, vice-president of operations and people, Lemon Tree Hotels. 'Since a hotel already has infrastructure for differently abled people, it becomes easier to hire them. Also there are many job positions in a hotel that are not very technical and do not require specific skills'.

As far as salaries are concerned, they are at par with other employees, say industry heads. At Costa Coffee, they earn the same average salary of ₹5500 as other employees. Marriott also claims to pay equal salaries.

Source: Adapted from: http://economictimes.indiatimes.com/news/news-by-company/corporate-trends/Hospitality-takes-on-a-different-challenge/articleshow/2539487.cms accessed on May 2010.

WHEN TO RECRUIT

When to recruit is often a strategic question. Cost benefit of recruitment of one employee clearly established as productivity per employee is an important criterion for the recruitment of employees. Thus, to maintain the relative meaning of productivity in the hospitality organization, the concept of sanctioned manpower has been established. It is a collective exercise where the senior management decides about the positioning of manpower at different levels in the organization. Once this level is decided, the HR manager attempts to find suitable candidates. For example, in housekeeping, the number of employees is on average decided on the basis of the number of rooms. Room to employee ratio is approximately 1:2. In restaurants, seating cover to employee ratio decides the number of employees to be deployed. Each industry has developed some crude yardstick that often provides some kind of guidance to the HR executives. Whenever the headcounts fall below this yardstick, the HR team should initiate recruitment function. An impending business opportunity also could trigger the recruitment process.

RECRUITMENT POLICY

It is important to put in place a sound recruitment policy, which outlines the basic framework to be fulfilled during the recruitment process. A robust recruitment policy clearly highlights the basic principles and ethical tenets that the HR department should adhere to. The recruitment policy should be clear, simple, pragmatic, and flexible (Fig. 3.1).

Clear   Policy statement is the guideline for managers to implement. A clear policy with clarity in expression will not provide any space for speculation, subjective interpretation, and confusion. For example, the recruitment policy should give

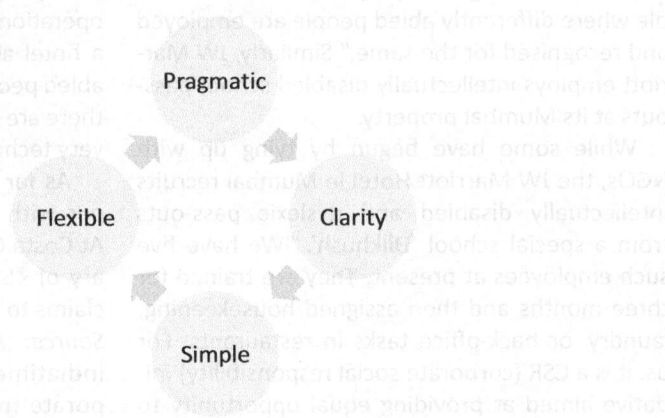

Figure 3.1   Essential characteristics of recruitment plan

clear guidelines regarding internal or external recruitment or enumerate the broad conditions on where to follow what type of recruitment.

Simple Policy statement should be simple and should not be a mammoth document that is difficult to implement. Simplicity will bring speed and facilitate smooth implementation.

Practical Recruitment policy should be pragmatic and be deeply connected with the changing scenario of the socio-economic conditions of the country. A grand policy without a touch of pragmatism or realism will cause difficulties while implementing the policy.

Flexible Recruitment policy should be flexible to incorporate the requisite changes relevant to the changing situations. It should have a flexible approach that allows the HR department to implement it easily.

COMPANY BRAND AND RECRUITMENT

A company's brand image is what differentiates a company and its services from others. Reputed brands/companies always lure prospective candidates. As the candidate is already familiar with the brand, the HR person does not need to explain much and it gives him or her an upper hand at the time of negotiation. A good brand image is a positive perception that is carried by individuals and is a great resource that could be intelligently deployed to attract good-quality candidates. The reputation of Taj Hotels Resorts and Palaces generates a huge amount of interest among prospective candidates. The Taj People Philosophy (Exhibit 3.2) clearly outlines what the company is and what they believe in.

Initial Screening and Shortlisting

With the advent of email facilities, HR departments regularly receive a lot of job applications for the entry level, but the number goes down with higher levels of

Exhibit 3.2 Taj People Philosophy

The Taj People Philosophy displays our commitment to and belief in our people.

We see Talent Management as the most important sustainable competitive advantage in the future.

You are an important member of the Taj family.

We endeavour to select, retain, and compensate the best talent in the industry.

We reward and recognize quality customer care based on individual and team performance.

We commit to providing you with opportunities for continuous learning and development.

We abide by fair and just policies that ensure your well-being and that of your family, the community, and the environment.

We commit to regular and formal channels of communication, which nurture openness and transparency.

We strongly believe that you are the Taj.

Source: Adapted from: http://www.tajhotels.com/About-Taj/Careers/taj-promises.html.

hierarchy. Reputed business houses regularly get even more number of unsolicited applications. Therefore, the HR department should have a disciplined approach to categorize and update the records for future use. In the absence of sophisticated and systematic practices, the HR department will be deprived of utilization for competitive advantage.

All applications received by any HR department are not necessarily suitable for the organization. The application may have a shortfall in terms of experience, educational qualifications, industry exposure, and so on. For example, for junior executive position in a tour and travel company, a master's degree in travel and tourism and an active experience in a reputed travel agency could be crucial. Similarly, in the case of a reputed hotel chain, a diploma or degree in hotel management is an important criterion. Thus, only candidates who fulfil the basic criteria in terms of educational qualification and adequate training in the specified field are called for the next round of the selection process (Fig. 3.2).

Communication with Shortlisted Candidates

Written communication—either email or letter sent through courier—is preferably used to communicate with a prospective candidate. Each letter should have the following information (Exhibit 3.3):

- Interview venue and time
- Person to be contacted
- Documents to be brought along

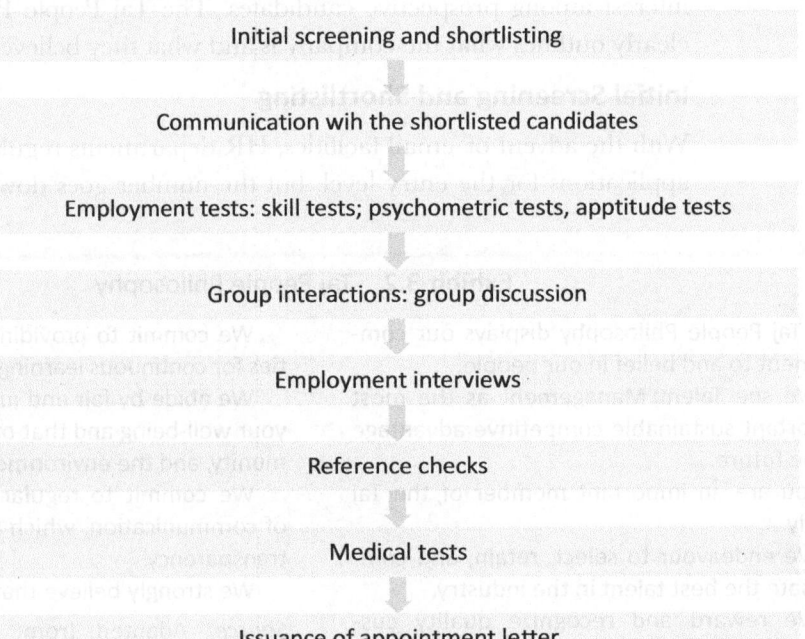

Initial screening and shortlisting

Communication wih the shortlisted candidates

Employment tests: skill tests; psychometric tests, apptitude tests

Group interactions: group discussion

Employment interviews

Reference checks

Medical tests

Issuance of appointment letter

Figure 3.2 Selection process

Exhibit 3.3 Sample Interview Call Letter

SWH/Fac Rect/HRFB/2011 31 October 2011
Anthony D'Cruz
A-9, High Street East,
New Land Corner,
Mumbai

Dear Mr D'Cruz,

With reference to your application for the position of food & beverage manager in our hotel, we are pleased to invite you for a personal interview.

We request you to report at 11.00 a.m. on 15 November at the Starwood Blue Hotel, Navi Mumbai, and you may be required to stay till late evening. You are required to submit copies of documents such as evidence of work experience and qualifications as mentioned in your application.

Kindly confirm your participation in the process.

As per our policy, we reimburse travel expenses by first class non-AC or by second class AC train for the shortest route and local conveyance upto Rs 1000 in the case of an outstation candidate.

Looking forward to hearing from you.

Sincerely,

Robert Hamfrey
Human Resource Manager
Starwood Blue Hotel
SeaSide Road (East)
Mumbai

- Provision of accommodation to outstation candidates: Some hospitality organizations provide accommodation during the selection process if the candidate comes from a remote destination.
- Travel reimbursement policy: Some hospitality organizations reimburse second AC rail fare for executive positions and economy class airfare for senior executive/managerial positions. At the time of communicating with the prospective candidates, this useful information can be shared.
- Time required for the interview process: In some cases, interview timing stretches beyond normal office hours. This information would help the candidates not to book their return journey on the same day.
- Time lag: Adequate time cushion should be given to the candidates to organize for the interview, such as getting leave from their present organization and arranging train tickets. Thus, the interview date and the issuance of call letter should have adequate time gap between them.

Employment Tests

Employment tests are conducted at the beginning of the selection process. They vary across organizations. A simple and basic framework is that these tests consist of aptitude tests, psychometric tests, and skill tests.

Aptitude test

It is a structured test used to measure the aptitude of the candidate. Using this test, the candidate would be evaluated in terms of knowledge, acquisition skill, intelligence, and so on. While confronted with multiple choices in the organization, an individual with the right degree of aptitude will be able to tide over the challenges smoothly. These tests should be developed carefully by the organization.

Psychometric test

This test consists of psychometric evaluation of prospective candidates using criteria such as introversion, extroversion, and so on. It provides a privilege view of the candidates' management of psychological energy to the selection panel. It is a privilege view because the result of the psychometric test provides an insight into how psychological energy is managed by the applicants. A huge number of dedicated psychometric tests have been developed with the intent to measure specific issues. For example, 16 PF (a type of psychometric test) provides the personality profile of a candidate. One important thing to remember is that most of these tests require dedicated training for interpretation of the result. Without specific knowledge of the psychometric instrument, administration of psychometric scale is dangerous and likely to be misinterpreted and misused. Most of the instruments are quite robust and have been reinforced for detecting lies. The candidate needs to fill up the instruments as honestly as possible—this enhances the likelihood of selection. It is also important to remember that the candidates should fill up the instrument as what they are as of now, and not what they aspire to be. The candidate should refrain from speculating or guessing about the right answer expected by the company.

Skill test

This is a special phase where the skill and knowledge of the candidate is being examined. As discussed earlier, this phase is generally seen in software firms and the hospitality industry. Software engineers are usually given a problem to solve within a specific period. Candidates appearing for the hotel's kitchen, that is, food production, also undergo trade test where they are required to prepare a number of dishes within a limited time and resources. This gives a clear idea about the competency of the candidates. Candidates not found suitable in this phase are usually eliminated from the next phase of the selection process.

Group Discussion

Candidates who have qualified in all the phases discussed earlier are sent for the group-discussion (GD) phase. GD provides general understanding about the candidates' team work, assertiveness, proficiency in language, and diction. In this phase, 8–12 candidates are called into a room where they sit in a circular mode and are given a topic to discuss for about 10–15 min. Group discussion is not about how much the candidates speak but how they present their thoughts—in a clear and argumentative manner, building, agreeing, or refuting the earlier arguments in such a way that the candidates' argumentative position could be clearly understood. It is important that the level of interaction should follow the general decorum of discussion. The interviewer is interested to know the following:

- How does a candidate speak?
- When the candidate speaks, is it nourished with logical arguments? Do these arguments build over the arguments already presented by other candidates?
- How are the facts and figures presented to develop coherent viewpoints? This phase also provides clues regarding the candidate's presentation skills and knowledge.

In the hospitality industry, communication is a key dimension of the product. Therefore, candidates who fail to effectively communicate with others are usually eliminated in this round.

Personal Interview

Personal interview is one of the most important phases where the applicant and the selection committee members interact with each other face to face. The objective of the personal interview is to gain more knowledge about the candidate, and this provides useful insights about the candidate's behaviour, for example, dealing with stress—this subsequently plays a deciding role in the selection decision of the candidates.

Some of the favourite interview questions are as follows:

How long will you work with us, because by selecting you, we will be making a lot of investment to groom you for the industry?

Why should I select you for the job?

Why are you not joining other companies?

The applicant needs to start preparing for the interview at the time of drafting the application for the job itself. All particulars in the application letter should be accurate; otherwise, during interview, the trained and experienced interviewer can easily identify the discrepancy. During interview, the candidate is required to manage his or her nerve and attempt to answer questions to the best of his or her knowledge. Recently, interviewers have started using behavioural event interview (BEI) techniques wherein it is believed that one's past behaviour is an important predictor for future behaviour. Using this technique, the interviewer asks structured questions pertaining to the behaviour of the individual in the past. Some of the sample questions are as follows:

Give me a specific example of a time when you convinced your supervisor of the merit of your idea.

Using this question, the interviewer wants to know about your assertiveness.

Tell me about a time when you came up with an innovative solution to a challenge your company was facing.

Using this question, the interviewer wants to know about your creativity and imaginative strength.

An applicant is required to adhere to certain protocols termed STAR while answering this type of questions (Fig. 3.3). STAR stands for situation, task, actions, and results.

Situation   The candidate needs to talk about a situation—how bad or how challenging the situation was. This gives a clear idea about the magnitude of the challenge the candidate has surpassed. For example, when the interviewer asks a question:'Tell me, at a time when all members in your team were uncooperative to resolve the organizational crisis, how did you overcome it?' This kind of question is usually asked when the job applicant has claimed to have persuasive skills and mentioned it in the biodata. The candidate is required to explain the true nature of the problem. Critical assessment of the situation by the interviewer will enable him or her to understand the situation well.

Task   The candidate needs to talk about the nature of the task. What options did he or she have? Extending the example stated under 'Situation', the interviewee needs to tell the options he or she thought of to bring about a solution to the problem. This will highlight the applicant's level of maturity and is an excellent way of understanding the candidate. The candidate can say, 'I had three options. First was to resign and go. Second option was to change my view and ally with my other colleagues even though I knew it was not the appropriate way to bring about a solution. The final option was to engage with the group members and create a space for my line of arguments and sell my ideas to them and work hard with each individual to see if he or she can find the merit of my arguments'.

Actions   Out of multiple options, which one did they choose? Why did they choose that particular solution? What did they do? Extending the example described earlier, presume that the candidate chose one option to bring about a solution. The candidate can say, 'I opted for the last option. I engaged with each team member one-to-one and explained the merit of my solution. I argued the reasons why their solution would ultimately fail to produce any durable results. I showed my research data that highlighted that whoever opted for their solutions have ultimately failed. I think it worked well.'

Figure 3.3   The STAR process

Results Highlight how the particular solution brought about results and how it had been appreciated. The candidate can say, 'Gradually, I garnered enough support to persuade all members to opt for my solution. And it worked very well. We achieved 2 per cent additional business growth.'

HOW TO PREPARE FOR THE INTERVIEW

The following points need to be kept in mind while preparing for an interview:

1. Research about the company: It is important for the candidate to be familiar with the products and services of the company. Information pertaining to the relative position of the competition and any significant changes in the organization would be of enormous use to the candidate. As a part of this process, the candidate should browse the company web site, read the policy statement, and so on.

2. Review your biodata: Review your biodata and examine how your skill set could help the organization to achieve its stated goals.

3. Revise your knowledge: Revise your knowledge in the field you have applied for, as the interviewers would ask technical questions regarding your field of study and the position you have applied for.

4. Positive mindset: Maintain a positive mind set and demonstrate high level of energy.

5. Sleep well: Get a good night's sleep the night before the interview so that you are fresh and rested.

6. Eye contact: During the interview, maintain eye contact with each member of the interview panel. This would reflect your confidence level to the panel.

7. Stress management: Manage your stress before and during the interview.

Once the candidate clears the various rounds such as GD and personal interview and is found suitable for the job, he or she will undergo the rest of the selection phase.

Reference checks and recommendations With the growing scare of terror attacks and corporate espionage, the HR department makes sure that they double check the references given by the candidates. This reaffirms credibility of the candidate and eliminates the possibility of selecting candidates with wrong intentions or doubtful backgrounds. Any particulars given in the biodata, especially past experience details, are verified with past employers.

Medical tests It is an important phase where the selected candidate's medical fitness is examined. In this phase, a number of tests are conducted to examine the general health of the candidate, which highlight health-related problems, if any.

Issuance of appointment letter On successful completion of this process, appointment letter is issued. It should give clarification regarding the job title, date of joining, name of the person to be contacted, salary details, any other benefits, and all other terms of employment.

LEGALITY AND RECRUITMENT

While recruiting employees, HR executives should examine the Indian legal contexts and should adhere to the current policy of the government. While working for a government institution, the HR department will be subject to a different quota system promulgated by the Indian government and judiciary bodies. In a private business organization, it is not yet mandatory to follow different quota systems based on caste, creed, and so on. However, while fixing the salary of the new candidate, the HR team needs to give special attention to various provisions of the labour laws such as The Equal Remuneration Act, The Payment of Bonus Act, The Employees State Insurance Act, and The Payment of Wages Act.

SUMMARY

Recruitment is an important function exercised by HR managers who acquire potential candidates from the market. With the economic growth, a number of job options are available to potential employees, and the company should develop a robust compensation policy to attract the right kind of candidates. Recruitment of employees is a recurring function; hence, HR managers should develop coherent processes for the management of smooth operation, which contributes to the brand image of the organization. Rejected candidates should not get a wrong impression about the company. In addition, the HR managers should adhere to the legal requirements while selecting employees.

KEY TERMS

Behavioural event interview technique   It is a type of interviewing technique where past performance of the prospective candidate is used to judge for future performance.

Psychometric test   Psychometric test signifies a whole range of tests that are used to assess the psychological orientation of the candidates.

Recruitment   It is the process of identifying and hiring the best qualified candidate (from within or outside an organization) for an actual or anticipated job vacancy in a most timely and cost-effective manner.

STAR   It is a standardized answer format required to be followed by the job applicants while answering situational questions. The term STAR is an abbreviation where S stands for situation, T for task, A for actions, and R for results.

EXERCISES

Concept Review Questions

1. Critically examine the role of recruitment function for a hospitality business organization.
2. Review the employee selection process of a hospitality organization and recommend relevant improvement.

3. What are behavioural event interview techniques? Highlight the relevant steps required to adhere to while appearing for interview under this process.

Critical Thinking Questions

1. Examine the relevance of Indian labour laws while recruiting employees for a hospitality organization.
2. Is it fair to select candidates on the basis of their looks? Provide rationale for your opinion. What are the repercussions on the employees, organization, and business as a whole?

Assignment

Conduct a survey among students in your hotel management institute selected in campus recruitment. Focus on their preparation before job interview, interview day, actual interview, and coping with positive and negative interview results. Close the report with key learning points for you.

REFERENCES

Everts, H., 'The Competency Programme Of the American Management Association', *Journal of Management Development*, Volume 7, Issue 6, 48–56, 1988.

Klemp, G.O., *The Assessment of Occupational Competence*, Washington, DC: Report to the National Institute of Education, 1980.

Spencer, L.M., *The Talent Management Handbook*. McGraw-Hill, New York, 2003.

CASE STUDY

MANPOWER PROBLEM FOR SPA BUSINESS

Ramnath Dev works as a senior vice-president in a leading hospitality chain. Recently, a lot of reputed hospitality chains have identified health-related experiential services (spa business) as a new stream of revenue. Most of them have started the spa business. However, it is very difficult to find trained manpower for the profession. Besides, this industry inherits a good amount of stigma. For example, finding female employees for the spa department becomes a very difficult task.

Dev is thinking of advertising in the newspaper. However, he doubts whether it will generate a good number of applications, and he wants to approach schools where students come from the economically backward section of society. He is exploring the idea of recruiting students from this backward area. He thinks that in the absence of trained manpower, he needs to start a training centre, which will provide skill sets that would be adequate for the industry. He is considering how to implement his idea. However, he is not sure whether his idea will work.

Discussion Questions

1. Should Dev give advertisement in newspapers to find suitable employees for the spa business?
2. Should Dev poach employees from the competition? What would be the various implications of this type of decision?
3. You are required to give suitable recommendations to Dev.

4 Training and Development

INTRODUCTION

In Chapters 2 and 3, we learnt about manpower planning and the process of recruitment. An individual brings various resources in terms of intelligence, personality, knowledge, skills, and attitude to the organization. These diverse resources are crucial to bring forth innovation and in the production of services. However, in many cases, these resources are not adequate to the requirements of the hospitality industry. Thus, training that attempts to equip employees with the requisite skills and knowledge is required. In this chapter, we learn about the process of training and development. Training is closely related to learning and is not limited to the acquisition of knowledge and skill; it also signifies that newly learned behaviour should make a lasting change in behaviour. To have a lasting change in behaviour, the organization makes consistent and sincere efforts by providing an environment that is conducive to learning and transfer of learning in organizational workspace.

IMPORTANCE OF TRAINING

Training plays a very significant role in an organization, as it enables an organization to remain relevant in the changing world of business. Technology, lifestyles, and political and economical dynamics play significant roles in changing the landscape of the organization. Training facilitates the existing workforce to learn new skill sets and remain relevant in the organization and to acquire improved level of understanding that helps an organization grow. Training is important because of the following reasons (Fig. 4.1):

New culture   Each hotel has its own culture, that is, 'way of doing business' as it identifies and articulates in a unique way. It is relatively difficult for an outsider to acclimatize to the new organizational culture. This also potentially increases the possibility of cultural clash when an outsider joins the organization. Therefore, when employees

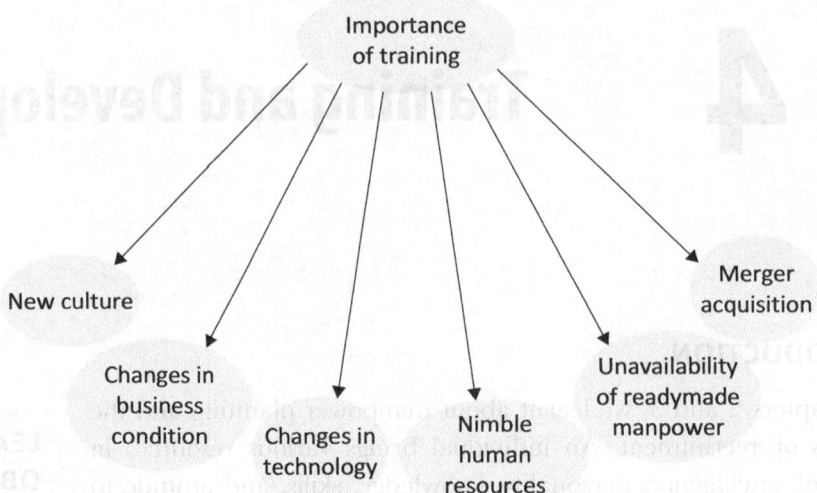

Figure 4.1 Importance of training

join any hotel, they are required to undergo a specific process to acclimatize themselves to the business environment. They are given detailed briefing on the typical organizational processes, the meaning of the company's mission and vision statement, organizational life, and so on. In terms of time invested by the organization, this training process, called *socialization process*, could range from a period of one day to a few months, depending on the business responsibility of the new recruits. Usually, the training department provides the introductory inputs, which are given during this socialization process.

Changes in business conditions   Business dynamics is always a product of various external and internal elements. External elements could be changes in position in a business cycle (boom, depression, stagnated depression, etc.), changes in political dynamics, changes in the preference of the customers, and changes in government rules and regulations; changes in lifestyle of customers and employees often cause considerable disability in the business environment. Internal changes could be changes in ownership or/and changes in financial conditions of the business that often potentially cause considerable changes in the dynamic condition of the organization. Business organizations are required to take corrective action in tune with the magnitude of the challenges presented to the stakeholders. Customer preference is always changing, and each hotel attempts to provide services that are in tune with the customers' needs. In case a hotel fails to adjust according to customer requirement, the future of the business will be bleak. Each hotel needs to incorporate changes in the business processes to better service the changing nature of the guests, and these changes should be informed to the employees.

Changes in technology Technology is always changing, and with this change, it destabilizes and disrupts the business environment. With the growth of the popularity and usage of the Internet, each individual employee needs to have a basic understanding of the Internet and know how to use it for acquiring knowledge to resolve work-related problems.

Nimble human resource Human resources consist of employees who are located in different hierarchies and in different positions with their own distinct individualities. Each has his or her responsibilities; most of the work an individual does is a learned behaviour. With consistent effort, an individual learns how to do the business. However, as all individuals are not equally talented, it is important that each employee receives due care and mentoring from trained professionals.

Unavailability of ready-made manpower Manpower in a ready-to-use format is not available. Most of the hospitality management training institutes provide basic skill training to the students. However, the syllabi of some of the educational programmes are already a few decades old and the world has changed so much since then. Therefore, before being able to utilize their skills in real business context, the newcomers require a wide range of inputs. For example, Oberoi Group of Hotels has its OCLD programme, whereas Taj Hotels Resorts and Palaces has TMTP programme. They take fresh talents from the market and put them through a rigorous training process.

Mergers and acquisitions Mergers and acquisitions (M&As) bring two distinct organizations together with their distinct history and heritage. Training professionals utilize various holistic training approaches to bring the two organizations together, to develop understanding about each other, and to refocus their efforts to achieve collective goals. It has been found that in most cases, M&As fail because of the misfit between two organizational cultures. Therefore, during these kinds of dramatic changes, training is essential for smoothening the relationship among distinct entities.

TRAINING FUNCTION AND SIZE OF THE HOTEL

Although in this chapter the nature of the training function has been described for chain hotels or five-star hotels, this training function in smaller hotels acquires considerable new meaning and format; in some cases, training is non-existent. In most cases, the management of small hotels considers formal training as less effective and more of a cost centre. Individuals trained with appropriate skills are rather problematic as it may trigger large-scale resignations for better opportunity in five-star properties/hotels located overseas. Individuals with appropriate skills are also a misfit to the requirement of the small hotels service standard. Small hotels operate at a lower price range, and hence, less demanding customers avail of the almost non-existent service standard of the hotel. Besides, whenever only vague service standards exist, employees often take short cut approaches to produce services, as they are not provided with adequate resources. Therefore, formal knowledge about service standard is almost none and often requires a high degree of compromise. There are some recent exceptions in the industry. For example, although Ginger Hotels could be classified as small, it differs significantly in its composition of products and services. Employees of Ginger Hotels are well trained to operate within a limited service range. In general, small hotels, driven by the owner of the properties (not a part of reputed hotel chain; absence of brand value), may give training functions relatively lower priority.

TRAINING NEED IDENTIFICATION PROCESS

Before embarking upon training activities, it is important to know the various needs of the employees and where they require assistance. This training need identification process (Fig. 4.2) requires an integrated approach to collectively make meaning of diverse data pertaining to employees' performance.

Individual analysis   Each individual employee has a unique psychological orientation (traits, personalities, value system) and different knowledge and experience. These apparent resources could be a great resource for the organization, provided it develops a synthesis process that is capable of combining divergent qualities of individuals into productive purposes. Otherwise, the divergent resources that each individual employee brings with him or her could be the source of tremendous conflict and anarchy. Thus, each individual should be evaluated with respect to the job assigned to him or her and the kind of cultural heritage each individual brings in with reference to the existing organizational culture. In case of a negative gap, the individual should be subjected to training. Individual analysis includes the following.

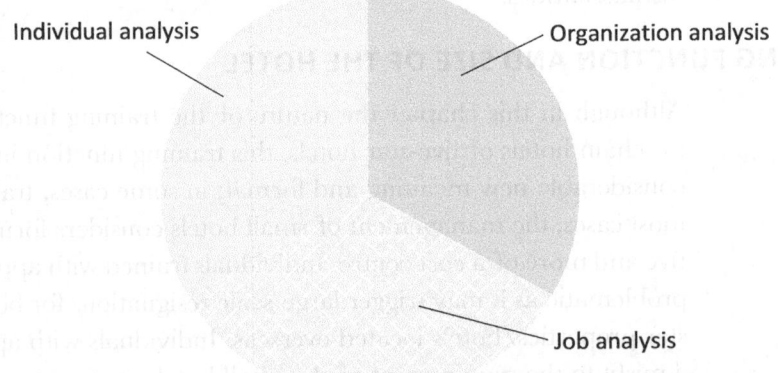

Figure 4.2   Three types of analysis required for the identification of training needs

Performance management Most of the professionally managed hotel companies have performance appraisal framework. Performance of the employees is appraised monthly, quarterly, half-yearly, and yearly. This appraisal generates two important data: first, about the performance level or score; second, about the weakness of the employees, which hinders them from achieving excellent results. This information of employees is collected, summarized, and examined. Training professionals organize suitable training programmes to remove all these deficiencies in order to enhance the quality of employees' performance.

Customers' Complaint Customer complaint and feedback are a great source of information. The customer is the ultimate consumer of hotels' services; they are in the right position to estimate the deficiencies in the service production process. Therefore, recurring complaints about the quality of services could provide clues about the stagnant problem pertaining to process and employees. Customer feedback provides a realistic and more accurate picture about the quality of services that is produced by hotels' employees. Training professionals could initiate a remedial process to improve the situation.

Exit interview Exit interview is one of the important sources for identifying the training needs. Exit interview is an interview with an employee who has resigned from the hotel, which could be conducted in a formal or informal format. The formal format usually captures information pertaining to the reason for the employee's resignation. This captures the overall nature of the experience of working for the organization. It is believed that when an employee is leaving an organization, he or she is relieved from any kind of pressure—hence, less distortion of information and more likelihood of getting a fair assessment about the organization is possible. The data generated out of multiple exit interviews is summarized and examined for the identification of problems. Subsequently, the HR manager could organize initiatives for the introduction of suitable changes. This exit interview data potentially highlights various training needs. For example, quarterly assessment of exit interview data suggests that a good number of staff have resigned because they were not happy about their restaurant manager. An overall assessment of complaints suggests that the restaurant manager has reportedly behaved harshly with his staff members. In some cases, his rudeness has created a lot of panic in the department. This clearly indicates the existence of a problem. Training is one of the options to generate sensitivity towards the staff. The training department could intervene by providing training, which enhances the supervisory capacity of the restaurant manager.

Job analysis Job analysis provides highly informative guidance, which could be used to devise/launch training initiatives. Job analysis highlights the range of current talents in terms of quality in comparison with the requirement of service productions standard in hotels; any deficiencies observed are predominantly addressed with the help of training initiatives. For example, with the introduction of a new property management system (i.e., Fidelio), employees, who were comfortable in the older system, will experience great difficulties. Hence, employees are required to be trained in the new operating system. Hence, these deficiencies will also indicate what each employee needs to learn, who should receive the training, and so on.

Organizational analysis Organizational analysis involves reviewing organizational processes actively pursued throughout the organization to identify inherent weaknesses and to find a solution in terms of tomorrow's requirement. This process provides a gap analysis between the skill sets available/deployed and the skill requirements for tomorrow. This gap analysis provides insightful guidance on what needs to be done with the skill gap. Subsequently, this data is utilized for devising a suitable training programme if it is decided to develop that skill set inside the organization.

Briefly, on successful completion of organizational, job, and individual analyses, the HR department should have the answers they need to know to the following questions to start the training programme:

- Who needs the programme?
- What kind of training programme is required?
- What is the frequency of the programme?
- Should the programme content be developed or sourced from outside agencies?
- Should employees be trained or those who possess these skills be recruited?

HOSPITALITY INDUSTRY RELEVANT TRAINING IN INDIA

Relevant training is required for the hospitality industry in India. These are discussed in the following subsections.

Source for pre-employment training Source for pre-employment training for Indian hospitality sector is available from various government-run institutions such as Institute of Hotel Management, Catering Technology and Applied Nutrition (IHMCTAN). Over a long period, they were the only source of qualified and trained manpower for the Indian hospitality industry. They run diploma/degree level programmes and postgraduate programmes. With the advent of liberalized education policy, a number of private institutions have come up. Some of these institutions have entered into agreement with foreign universities for brand and academic support. However, the quality of training imparted by these institutions requires fresh appraisal. Under Industrial Training Institutes (ITI), they run apprenticeship programmes with the active support of five-star hotels. The range of the programmes varies quite widely. Besides, Indian Institute of Travel and Tourism Management (IITTM) also runs several postgraduate programmes for travel-related services.

In-house programme Some of the reputed hotel chains in India have developed their in-house training department, as the requirements of each of these reputed hotels are so unique to their own organization that training is not easily available outside. These in-house training departments predominantly engage in operational training, cultural indoctrination training, new process education training, and so on. They operate at a lower platform end of training workspace. Specialized training is often outsourced from small training firms.

Small training firms In India, small training firms have grown rapidly. They operate in a specific area of management training. They are specialists in some of the human development processes, and some reputed hotel chains avail of their services from time to time.

Management development programme Most of the reputed management institutes run management development programmes. Academic professionals from these institutes impart training on various issues such as negotiation skill, revenue management, data-driven marketing management, and sales training. These programmes are relatively costly, and only selected employees from reputed hotel chains attend such programmes.

TRAINING CYCLE

Training should not be construed as training session only. It should be considered as a cyclic process (Fig. 4.3), which begins with training need identification and ends with training evaluation.

Training need identification process Training need identification is the first step that highlights the existence of various deficiencies and loopholes in the system. To survive in today's competitive world, hotels need to eradicate deficiency and enhance competency among employees. This process involves linking a wide range of HR processes to have a comprehensive view of the system and is an essential step for the effective operation of the training department.

Formulation of training plan Once the training needs of an organization have been identified, the training department needs to devise a specific plan of action. Wide diverse needs should get different types of treatment. For example, attitudinal problems should get behavioural training, process problems need process-related training, lack of knowledge on how to serve food should get skill-based training, and so on. The training department needs to make a training plan for all the various needs that have been identified.

Assessment of capabilities of the training department The training department must assess its capabilities with respect to the demand of the organization. The training department in most of the hotels are capable of handling general training; however, in case any individual requires specific training for which no training

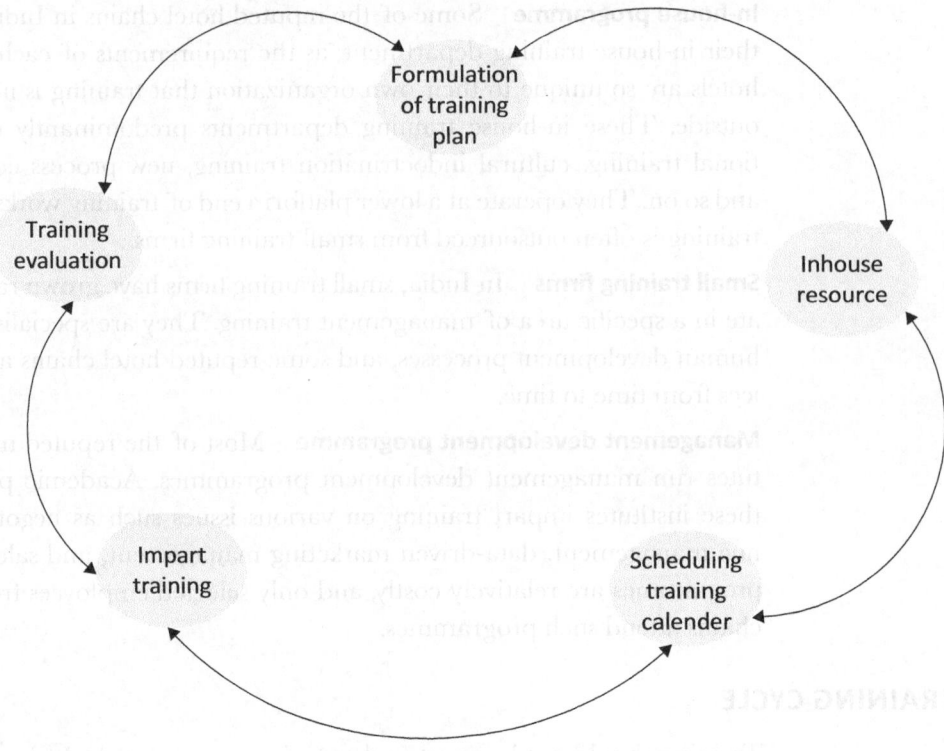

Figure 4.3 Training cycle

resource is available, an outside agency that conducts training should be contacted. For example, individual employees who require attitudinal training should be referred to a T-group trainer.

Scheduling training calendar Preparing the training calendar is an important task of the training department. Training calendar provides vital information regarding training date, venue, eligibility, and so on. While devising the training calendar, a list of important facts is required to be kept in mind. For example, the training calendar should consider the off season and heavy season of business. In India, predominantly, September to March is considered busy business season. Therefore, most of the training should be organized during this time unless situations warrant otherwise. For example, if a training programme is organized by an outside agency such as IIMs, there is no option but to schedule it as per the outside agency's timing.

Impart training Training should be imparted in a most conducive environment, where the learner can acquire skills without much interruption. Proper food, lodging, and transportation facilities should be organized. In short, learning should be a pleasurable experience.

TRAINING EVALUATION

On completion of training, it is important to know whether the learner, who acquired new skills during the training programme, has been successful in translating it into his behaviour and results. Training involves a huge cost. Hence, in order to consider the training cost as an investment, it should make positive business sense when it produces long-term business results. Kirkpatrick (1994) provided a four-step model for the evaluation of training outcomes:

Reaction The goal of this phase is to develop an understanding about the trainee's immediate reaction after attending the training programme. This provides multiple inputs to the trainers about the level of knowledge, skills, and ability acquired during the programme. Through this feedback, the trainers can also come to know how the training content can be enhanced in the future.

Learning The goal of this phase is to examine the first display of knowledge, skills, and abilities acquired during a training programme. The trainee attempts to execute the task with the help of the newly learned skills. This could be assessed using performance test, attitude questionnaire, and so on.

Behaviour The goal of this phase is to assess the changes in behaviour arising out of the training programme. Trainees, exposed to real business situations, attempt to implement the task with the help of their newly acquired skills. This is one of the most critical parts of a training evaluation process.

Results The actual impact of the training potentially makes a lasting result on the organizational performance. The impact of trainees' enhanced activities acquired during the training programme is studied, as to whether it has influenced improved organizational performance such as higher productivity, reduction of employee turnover, and increased sales.

TRAINING METHODS

A wide range of training methods are available; which method will be ultimately utilized depends on a number of factors: availability of in-house knowledge, time required, number of participants, cost of the training, feasibility of getting all trainees under one umbrella, and so on. A few of the widely used training methods, often suitable for Indian hospitality industry, are discussed here.

Classroom training Classroom instruction is widely used to impart training in the hotel industry. Classroom instruction is suitable where knowledge is required to be imparted in a controlled environment. With the advent of technological development, classroom instruction is supported by a projector, and one can access the outside world through video conferencing. One of the disadvantages of classroom training is that it does not replace the actual working environment. However, classroom training prevents trainees from getting distracted, as it is carried out in a closed and controlled environment.

On-the-job training   On-the-job training is also widely used in the hotel industry. As classroom training miserably fails to provide actual working experience, on-the-job training format allows trainees to acquire new skills in the actual workspace. Most of the hotel management institutes organize this training with the support of operational five-star hotels where the trainees get a closer look at the actual working environment and realistically develop skills that will be highly useful to them. One of the difficulties with on-the-job training is that the trainees do not get a holistic training of a job; they only get exposure to the lower end of job experience. In many cases, trainees spend the entire training period wiping plates and never get an opportunity to interact with the guests. Most hotels consider trainees as cheap alternatives to contract employees. Thus, instead of providing training, the hotel management becomes more concerned with the extraction of work. It is important that the hotel management institute should negotiate with the hotels about the learning outcome of the on-the-job training. This will ensure that the trainees acquire the requisite skills.

Business games and case studies   In some cases, rather than having on-the-job experience, business games are used to develop multidimensional learning experience. Business games describe business plans, mission, current situations, and a few business dilemmas. It is expected that trainees develop a few alternative solutions. In a classroom environment, each participant tries to test the merit of the answer; thus, collectively, the participants develop an interesting and deeper level of understanding on any issue. It is highly effective as the learning becomes the responsibility of the learner. Collective wisdom is deployed to find any solution; hence, it appears that it provides a unique opportunity to develop a deeper level of understanding about business issues that otherwise could not have been created. Case study discussion format is widely used in business schools.

Outdoor training   Outdoor training implies that the training programme is conducted outside the periphery of the working environment. This kind of training provides a unique non-work environment where the learning from any specific task could be transferred in the workplace. Participation in outdoor training, including mountain climbing, white water rafting, and other outdoor activities, often provides unique learning experience, which is believed to be transferred in the workplace. During this training programme participants experience various degrees of difficulties to execute tasks. Participants, individually or in group, develop various strategies to overcome these difficulties. This experience works as a valuable gift, and the insight developed during this programme could be used subsequently in the workplace.

Job rotation   Job rotation is an effective method of developing deeper level of knowledge on any job. An employee gets the opportunity to move from one part of a big job to others. On completion of training, the employee develops holistic and insightful understanding of the nitty-gritty of the job. For example, a front-office executive could be moved to housekeeping for a week and then to restaurant for a week to gain knowledge about the working of those departments. Job rotation works as an excellent platform to broaden the horizon of the individual employee's work experience.

TRAINERS' QUALIFICATION AND EXPERIENCE

Trainers in the corporate world engage in adult education and need to have a deeper level of understanding about the human learning process. In most of the hotels, trainers are individuals who have professionally worked in hotel's operation area and have subsequently become interested in adult education. Trainers' experience in the operational areas provides a deeper level of grounding and conviction in their presentation. Therefore, the trainers' exposure to working environment is crucial. However, a trainer is expected to have the following qualities:

1. Deeper level of knowledge in the business organization: Deeper level of business knowledge provides strength to the presentation. Because of the depth in the level of knowledge, a trainer can make presentations in clearer terms and in the language and jargon of the trainees.

2. Good presentation skills: Good presentation skill is very important. To retain the attention of the trainees, the trainer needs to present the content effectively. Maintaining interest in the content of the presentation is a prerequisite for successful learning and implementation of the training.

3. Good understanding of human psychology: Good understanding of human psychology will help the trainer at the time of designing the training content and its delivery and achieve the overall objective of the training. To engage the human psyche in an active learning process, the presenter should make the presentation interesting with the inputs and activities in the right sequence so that the trainee finds it interesting and learnable. For example, in the post-lunch session, participants are vulnerable to sleep and not be able to maintain attention. Good understanding of human psychology will enable the trainer to design the programme in such a manner that the session will have more of activities and games, as this energizes the participants and helps them maintain steady attention on the content of the programme.

4. Presentable personalities: A trainer is expected to have a presentable personality. This enhances the capacity to retain the attention of the trainees and also generate their trust.

5. Presence of mind: All training sessions could be planned and rehearsed; however, each training session is expected to be different. Participants have the potential to change the temperament of the session and may ask questions that the presenter did not rehearse. Presence of mind is necessary to overcome any awkwardness that may arise during the training programme.

6. Technology savvy: Trainers in today's age are required to be technology savvy. Technology provides a wide range of possibilities to source and present important issues that are relevant to the content of the programme.

7. Knowledge of content development protocol: Knowledge about the course design is crucial. Designing the training content intelligently is crucial for the success of any programme. Participants' knowledge and experience as well as life issues need to be kept in mind while designing the content.

TRAINING—COST OR INVESTMENT?

'Economies of training' is always debatable. Training activities in the hospitality sector are often directed to improve service quality and eventually achieve customer satisfaction and customer delight. Benefits of training include reduction in error and its associated cost, increase in quality of service, new capabilities, less amount of supervision, fault-free services, increase in employee motivation, possibilities for career advancements, competitive advantages, and so on. However, the relationship between service improvements and training activities is difficult to substantiate with adequate evidence because this relationship is not linear and straightforward. The effect of training is often distant and unquantifiable, and linking it with improved services is difficult to prove. Therefore, it is convenient to consider training as expenses.

Training employees is also a risky business as there is no guarantee that the trained employees will ultimately stay with the company. Training activities are mostly encouraged during good times when the companies are making considerable amount of profit. However, during recession or economic downturn, training function becomes an avoidable cost overhead and gets axed first from the HR budget. However, if the training function is managed well in association with other HR functions, it could provide discernible improvement in customer service, employee attitude, and service production environment. In some cases, training function fails because it does not get the requisite support from other organizational infrastructure.

For example, a five-star hotel recently revamped its spa business. It is financially successful and economically rewarding; however, it has one typical problem—finding trained staff to manage this labour-intensive business. There is no training institute that could provide trained manpower. Hence, the management of the hotel decided to revamp its in-house training function. The training department made evidence-based spa treatment procedure and processes. One of the difficulties was to source manpower that could be trained. General interest among local communities is relatively less. The societal system presents unique problems: in this business, female employees provide massage and other body engagement to male and female customers, which many conservative societies will not permit. After considerable effort, this five-star hotel chain found a good number of employees who were given three-month intensive training. During this time, they were provided wholesome food, accommodation, and full salaries. On successful completion of training, they were assigned to various five-star properties at different locations. However, in most cases, the trained employees resigned from the company within six months of assignment as the competition hotels in India and abroad were ready to pay much higher salaries. Thus, the training department of the hotel is always busy preparing fresh batch of supplies for replacement of employees. Although training function by itself was successful, in the absence of a responsive human resource infrastructure and policy, the training function remained in the loop of constant business.

Training cost includes the trainee's salary, replacement cost, trainer's cost, venue cost, equipment cost, transportation cost, course material cost, and so on, whereas the relevant benefits as discussed earlier include reduction in error and its associated cost, increase in the quality of service, fault-free services, increase in employee motivation, competitive advantages, and so on. To consider training as an investment, an HR manager must strive to achieve more gain from the training. If benefits exceed the nominal cost, then it is truly an investment.

ORGANIZATIONAL CULTURE AND TRAINING

Training by itself is not an end; it is rather the beginning of a new journey. A trainee learns new process knowledge, new way of performing the job, new way of looking at relations, new way of interpreting cultural heritage, and so on. However, without adequate organizational support, such training will hardly produce discernible results. An employee may learn to do the job in different ways; however, before sceptic supervisors, the employee may not feel safe to practice the newly acquired skills. Therefore, it could be said that for smooth transfer of training, appropriate organizational culture is necessary. Some of these are discussed in the following subsections.

Opportunity to practice An employee acquires new process knowledge, but to make a lasting change, the employee should be given appropriate opportunity to practice. In the absence of organizational space for practice, the employee may easily forget these newly acquired skills and go back to the old way of being. For example, students learn new techniques for opening and serving a champagne bottle to guests; however, without adequate opportunities to do so during their industrial training at different hotels, they may easily forget and lose confidence in executing this simple task.

Climate for transfer Learning organizations encourage each of its members, irrespective of their position or designation, to subscribe to the practice of continued learning. This collective aspiration of continued learning and improvement of service delivery makes a unique cultural space where newly learned skills can easily get absorbed with the existing ones. Thus, learning organization environment is suitable for transfer of learning.

Supervisory support   Employees equipped with newly learned knowledge do not get the opportunity and courage to practice in the presence of dominating sceptic supervisors. Derogatory outlooks towards subordinates' newly acquired skills actively prevent its practice. Thus, supervisory support is essential in reaping the fruits of the training process.

Self-confidence   Individuals with their newly acquired skills may not be confident to practice it immediately; their self-doubt, disbelief, and lack of confidence prevent them from practicing the newly acquired skills. Active encouragement from the organizational culture and individual determination could substantially improve the confidence level among employees and trigger them to practice their skills.

Peer support   As important as it is to have supervisory support to practice newly acquired skills, so is peer support. In a hierarchical organizational set-up, where corporate rat race governs and overwhelms relational exchanges, peer support is difficult to achieve. Peers consider each other as competitors; anybody showcasing extraordinary talents becomes winner for the next promotion. Thus, when peer support becomes radically absent from organizational life, an employee with newly acquired skills fails to practice. As they spend most of their time among these peer groups, their nature of exchange among relational members decides whether an individual will find courage to practice it in an organizational context.

Limitations of training   In some cases, when training is wrongly used, organized, or designed, it harms individuals and the organization. For example, out of five catering assistants, one is selected for a training programme to be held at an IIM. It is indeed highly motivating for him or her; however, the other catering assistants get highly discouraged by this action of the management and interpret it that they are not important or may question the legitimacy of the selection criteria. In brief, this will generate motivation for one but demotivation for more number of employees. The predominant focus of training is learning; however, many corporate bodies consider training as a corporate gift to visit attractive tourist spots, and learning becomes secondary. Employees not selected for the training programme find it unacceptable and demotivating. In many cases, the training function ends with the training programme itself, and there is no monitoring infrastructure to ascertain the employees' progress. This reduces the impact of the training on employees. Thus, training, although theoretically designed to help employees learn new techniques, might also cause a number of harms. Hence, the HR team should be careful.

SUMMARY

Training is an important function of the HR department. This function is gradually getting higher importance as employee turnover is relatively high in the hospitality industry. The skill sets required to generate performance are also not readily available. Although a good number of hotel management institutes have sprung up throughout India, it is difficult to utilize the students directly in hotels. Specific training is required to be imparted as per the requirement of the hotel. Hence, training occupies a significant role in hospitality industry. Training should be considered as investment and should be encouraged in every department. The trainer should be well versed in the industry practice. Training function does not end by its delivery, and adequate mechanism should be developed to review trainees' development. This will provide useful data, which will help design even better programmes for the trainees, understand what is and is not working well with the programme, and thus indicate the changes that are required in the programme.

KEY TERMS

Case study   It is a description of phenomena or event, usually used to stimulate discussion. This discussion creates opportunity to understand one phenomena or event from multiple perspectives.

Classroom training   It is the training imparted in a classroom environment.

Outdoor training   It is the training conducted outside of the class with the help of games, activities, and challenges.

Qualities of the trainers   Bare minimum qualities or competencies considered to be required for the successful delivery of knowledge, skill, and experience.

Training need identifications   These are diverse learning needs required to be identified before imparting training to the employees.

EXERCISES

Concept Review Questions

1. Describe training need identification process.
2. Argue that training is an important function in the changing business situation.
3. Describe trainers' qualities for being successful in the organization.
4. Explain the limitations of training.

Critical Thinking Questions

1. To what extent do you believe that training in various business schools truly prepares you for the challenges that exist in Indian hotel industry?
2. During campus interview, you have been selected for the Taj Management Training Programme. What kind of training should you expect from this programme so that you could become general manager of a hotel within the next five years? Review your individual answer with other students to examine your level of understanding.

Assignment

Prepare a report about your industrial training experience: What you liked, what you did not like, and what could have been done to improve your learning experience. How could the learning have been more profound? Could the training manager of the hotel where you have undergone training have done more to improve your learning experience? Do you think that there is something you could have avoided altogether during the training?

REFERENCES

Kirkpatrick, D.L., *Implementing the Four Levels—A Practical Guide for Effective Evaluation of Training Programs* 3/e, Berrett–Koehler Publishers, San Francisco, 1994.

CASE STUDY

STRATEGY FOR CHINA

SAT hotels are one of the leading players in Indian hospitality sector and presently looking forward to expand their hotel business in China, Middle East, and South East Asian market. The challenge before SAT hotels appears to be overwhelming. For a long time, the SAT group of hotels has been a key domestic player in India, and suddenly it realizes the importance of expanding its business in foreign soil. Foreign hotel chains, with huge brand names, marketing potential, and budgets have already entered Indian market. SAT group of hotels does not stand a chance to confront the potential challenge from these international hotel chains in the next 20 years. Therefore, the decision to expand is almost a compulsion.

K.N. Satpure, the senior vice-president, HRD, prepares draft war plans to face the coming level of competition. His strategy is to train and motivate manpower not only for the existing hotels but also for the newly acquired hotels. His greatest difficulty is to provide manpower support for the hotels acquired in China. This presents considerable difficulties as China is significantly different in its culture, language, and way of life. Satpure forms a committee to investigate this matter. This committee consists of several members from sales, operations, and human resource department. This committee proposes a wide range of recommendations:

1. Recruitment of Chinese-speaking people—In India, this poses considerable difficulties as there are very limited suitable candidates who can speak Chinese. They recommended recruiting Chinese-speaking employees from Kolkata.
2. Provision of operational and management skills by imparting classroom training.

3. Provision of good salaries.

Satpure has been reading the recommendations from the committee. However, he appears to be unhappy with the report. He now refers the case to you—a leading expert from the hotel industry—for your viewpoints. Your responsibility is to provide adequate advice so that he finally can take appropriate decision.

Discussion Questions

1. Is there any way SAT hotels could develop recruitment and training that will ensure constant supply of manpower for their imminent acquisition of hotels in China?
2. What strategies do the Indian companies that are expanding their business in China follow? Find a few examples from web research.
3. Should SAT hotels recruit local Chinese employees for hotels in China or should they be sent from India? Which is the best strategy? Argue.

5 Performance Appraisal

INTRODUCTION

Performance appraisal system plays a significant role in the hospitality organization. When hotels fail to manage employees' performance, hotels will fail to sustain customer services infrastructure. The appraisal system provides a data-based ground for remunerating and promoting employees. It also helps identify weak employees, who require special assistance and training. However, performance appraisal often generates misunderstanding and stress among employees. Thus, it is important that the whole process is transparent to the parties involved, and an open culture of transparency is essential for the success. This performance appraisal process is usually done on a half-yearly and yearly basis. Half-yearly assessment of performance is intended to provide interim feedback to the employees about their performance.

It is always important to tell the employees what the management expects from them in terms of performance. Performance objectives should be clear, measurable, achievable, and executable through a fair process. In case of ambiguity, the employees will get confused and may not be able to provide the desired results. Managing employees' performance is a crucial task for the HR department and is deeply related to other functions such as training and development, compensation and benefits management, discipline management, and strategic decision management.

PURPOSE OF PERFORMANCE APPRAISAL SYSTEM

Development and maintenance of an effective performance appraisal system in hospitality organizations is very essential. An effective system of performance appraisal consists of deployment of effective methods for assessing an employee's performance and communicating the result of the appraisal to the employee for initiating corrective actions, if any. When such a system is deeply integrated with various

LEARNING OBJECTIVES

After reading this chapter, you will be able to
- identify the prime importance of management of performance management system in the hospitality sector
- understand the reasons why performance appraisal system fails
- critically examine the role of balanced scorecard architecture as a performance appraisal system
- review the benefits of using 360-degree feedback framework
- suggest suitable frameworks for the management of employees' performance in Indian hospitality industry

other functions, deriving accurate results from the appraisal system is crucial and non-negotiable. These functions include the following:

1. Strategic support: The appraisal system provides an overall picture of implementation of strategic objectives. Hospitality organizations outline various strategic intents and expect employees located at various hierarchies to implement those within a specific time limit. Thus, the appraisal system provides a clear estimation of the objectives and the extent to which it should be achieved with the collective efforts of individual employees. With the advent of several regulatory restrictions, monitoring and reporting authentic institutional performance to the investors is essential. Thus, performance appraisal is an important event in organizational life, which provides strategic support for the organization.

2. Compensation and benefit management: An effective performance appraisal system provides information about various types of performers, that is, excellent performers, average performers, deadwoods, and so on. This greatly facilitates the management of compensation and benefits among employees. Excellent performance inside the organization requires reinforcement in terms of increment, promotion, and other remunerative avenues. In the absence of such remunerative reinforcements, excellent performers will not have a reason to perform better than others, and this will lead to an overall deterioration of performance. Hence, reinforcing the performance of excellent performers is crucial and requires a balanced approach. Acknowledging the performances of excellent performers may motivate other employees and generate positive impetus throughout the organization.

3. Control mechanism: Performance appraisal empowers the employees and the management to have a control on performance. The management gets privileged access to information about the sources of excellent and deficient performances. This enables the management to have an informed choice of interventions to steer the performance of the organization. Deficiencies can be corrected with little efforts. Similarly, employees gain a sense of control by knowing their present level of performance and can correct it if it appears to be deficient with respect to the target.

4. Training need identification: The performance appraisal system provides insight into the area where employees are not able to perform well. Deficiency in work performance originates because of various reasons: poor knowledge of job, poor skill sets in the changing scenario, bad attitude, and so on. This provides informational assistance about the nature of training that is required to be executed by the organization.

5. Sense of fairness: The performance appraisal system is a great enabler of a sense of fairness among employees. Research indicates that lack of fairness in the system may possibly generate dysfunctional and deviant behaviour among

employees. If employees believe that they are treated fairly in terms of allocation of resources, they will feel motivated. In the absence of this sense of fairness, employees may engage in counterproductive behaviour, and it may result in the organization suffering from high employee turnover. The performance appraisal system helps deploy a fair yardstick to evaluate all employees' performance. Thus, there is high likelihood that the appraisal system will be accepted by the employees and contribute to reducing the sense of unjust experience.

APPRAISING WHAT—EMPLOYEE, PROCESS, OR PERFORMANCE?

Appraising 'what' is one of the crucial questions in an appraising process. It was customary under traditional management to assess employees and not their performance. Employees are exposed to their supervisors' scrutiny. It is important that only performance and not the employee is appraised, and bringing objectivity in the appraisal process is mandatory. Otherwise, employees will not engage during this appraisal process and will find avenues to influence the score not necessarily by performance but by engaging in various non-productive political activities. Hence, it is important to generate faith in the system by providing unbiased performance score for each employee.

PERFORMANCE APPRAISAL PROCESS

An effective performance appraisal process inherits certain definitive steps, which ensure smooth and successful implementation. Any omission or any other shortcut or shortened process may potentially defeat the very objective of the performance appraisal system. The process involves the following:

1. Identification of strategic deliverables as a whole: First, the top management of the company identifies the organizational goals. For example, a hospitality company could set a revenue target of Rs 5500 crores for the next year and 30 per cent growth in the subsequent years, and the addition of 5 hotel properties located in various international locations every year.

2. Identification of performance standards: It involves defining performance standards for each component of the job. Customer satisfaction score is pegged at 4 out of a scale of 5 (with higher score indicating excellence in service experience). Performance standards could be sourced from the job description, unifying them under meaningful clusters.

3. Setting up measurable goals: This refers to providing rating scale for different performance levels. For example, on achievement of target, an individual employee will get a score of 3, and for every 0.06 change in performance level, the performance score will change by 0.03; thus, an individual achieving a customer satisfaction score of 4.06 will achieve a performance score of 3.03.

4. Objective assessment of actual performance: Each employee or group is assessed using the scale as described earlier without any bias and prejudice.

5. Comparative assessment between standards and actual performance: Any difference between the performance target and actual performance could be a source of information about an individual employee's growth and development. Individuals could make focal effort to ensure that the gap between the performance standard and actual performance could be addressed.

6. Providing feedback to the employees: The reviewer could provide the necessary performance feedback on the various improvements required to be made by the employees. The reviewer could help the employee chalk out a plan to improve the actual performance.

7. Initiate corrective actions, if required: The employee, after receiving feedback from the reviewer, could initiate corrective actions, if required.

USAGE OF PERFORMANCE APPRAISAL

Performance appraisal is predominantly used for two distinct purposes: administrative purpose and development purpose.

Administrative Purpose

Administrative purpose signifies utilization of appraisal data for critical decisions such as awarding increments and promotions, dismissal of services, and other relevant organizational processes. A robust performance appraisal process generates data pertaining to an employee's performance during a specific period. This data provides grounds to discriminate among employees pertaining to compensation and benefit management. Performance data enlightens the HR department about who are performing the critical functions well, how effective they are in executing their job, and how to sustain similar or higher level of performance. Thus, performance appraisal potentially generates critical information for the management of the organization.

Developmental Purpose

Performance appraisal is also utilized for employees' development. It generates data pertaining to employees' performance during a specific period, and this data highlights the various sources of deficiencies for employees' performance. This data could be utilized for framing training programmes, which potentially enhances the capabilities of the employees. If this data is utilized for developmental purposes, authenticity comes back in to the system, and employees will be more candid in accepting the appraisal.

DIFFICULTIES ASSOCIATED WITH THE PERFORMANCE APPRAISAL PROCESS

The performance appraisal process is executed by individuals, who are not free from various human deficiencies and biases. Managers who are appraising the performance of their respective supervisors and executives often generate considerable political temperature inside the organization. Sometimes, managers show unnecessary generosity while rating certain individuals; however, everyone is not privileged to have a generous performance rating—some employees become scapegoats and are subjected to extreme critical appraisal. This happens because of various reasons as discussed in the following subsections.

Leniency error You must have noticed that some teachers in your school were generous/lenient, and it was relatively easy to get a good score from them. Some teachers exercised an extremely cautious approach while marking. Thus, leniency error signifies inappropriate rating of performance, which arises because of the rater's own standard irrespective of other available global standards. This leniency error makes comparative evaluation impossible. In the hospitality industry, employees' performance is rated by their managers and supervisors. If a housekeeping executive gives generous rating to all room boys and floor supervisors, but the food and beverage (F&B) manager gives a relatively low rating to all stewards, catering assistants, and restaurant managers, this poses a significant problem for the HR manager to make sense of. A cursory glance at the ratings will present a completely misguided picture. It will appear that all housekeeping staff are performing, whereas employees working in the F&B department are not performing well. This problem could be reduced if each rating is supported by precise explanation as to what it means. In the absence of supporting explanation to each rating, the raters will have ample freedom to figure it out as per their understanding and frame of reference. Thus, it is important that the raters are well versed in the rating scale and exercise the highest degree of discretion before rating a performance.

Halo error Halo error signifies a kind of deficient rating, where one critical factor of the performance has overwhelmingly influenced the overall rating. Deployment of aesthetic attributes in the hospitality environment often blinds the other deficiencies. If a housekeeping supervisor overestimates the role of the hardworking element among his or her subordinates, and thereby gives an overall generous rating, this will create a biased score. Hardworking persona of the employee might be legitimate, but in spite of being hardworking, low productivity could be a serious issue. Overgenerosity in rating will significantly produce an irrational performance appraisal system. Another interesting fact to be noticed is that in a situation where an employee is successful in generating a picture of being hardworking, but with low productivity, two distinct things must be happening. Either the employee is faking and managing the hardworking persona with the help of various impression management techniques or the employee has a 'willing heart' but does not have the requisite skill sets to deliver it. Both cases require urgent interventions. If he or she is using impression management techniques to illustrate his or her range of initiatives inside the organization, honest feedback will potentially contribute to enhance productivity. If he or she is showing a lot of initiatives but failing to improve productivity, he or she immediately requires assistance such as referring him or her for some training programme.

Similarity error Similarity error signifies erroneous rating that originates from the similarity in characteristics between the rater and ratee. Individual employees who demonstrate similar kind of behavioural characteristics as that of the evaluator will be perceived as a performer and vice versa.

Disinterested appraisers When an appraiser is not motivated and considers the appraisal system as an organizational ritual that is required to be performed for the continuance of employment, biased appraisal result may jeopardize the appraisal system. You might have noticed that when you fill up some customer feedback form, you give whatever rating that comes to your mind. You do not have any stake for your rating as you are not interested in filling up those forms; your behaviour in those circumstances resembles the appraiser described here.

Play-safe tendency In some cases, the supervisor wants to play safe with his or her subordinates and does not want to disappoint them by awarding a high or low score and adopts a middle path by rating all employees in the department as average. All subordinates are thereby treated as average, and true performance does not emerge from the performance appraisal system. Instead of appraising the performance, the supervisor's main concern is directed towards managing peaceful political environment.

Displaced performance In many cases, instead of appraising performance, the supervisor may appraise individuals. When the employees are appraised rather than their performance, the supervisor may rely on various shortened approaches. Thus, good rating could be a function of strength of relationship with the supervisor, the kind of information employees bring about other employees, the amount of praise disbursed by the employees, and so on. Once the employees understand that their supervisor is adopting such a shortcut approach, this will engender political behaviour among employees, and they will attempt to score higher by engaging in various internal infighting. This is not at all a welcome sign for any organization. As the supervisor will most probably refer to recent interactional experiences while evaluating employees, the employees will attempt to improve the interactional level a few months before appraisal time, and subsequently after appraisal will withdraw from work. It is important to understand that this is bad for the organization. Attention must be given to employees who are performing consistently over a period of six months to one year; otherwise, they will leave the organization.

Pygmalion effect This suggests that when a supervisor perceives an individual as an excellent performer, with time, he or she really starts getting extraordinary performance from them. What you believe in an individual employee turns out to be his or her actual behaviour. Therefore, extending the logic, it could be suggested that a supervisor sees what he wants to see and what the supervisor finds as performance is nothing but his or her perception.

Attribution theory This theory suggests that the employees' performance or non-performance could be attributed to external control or internal control. When a supervisor perceives that the reason for performance or non-performance is at the disposal of an individual employee (internal control), it is likely to generate lower rating or vice versa. When the performance of a sales manager seems to arise from bad market conditions for which he or she was not responsible (external control), he or she is likely to be appraised in a positive light. However, if poor sales performance could be attributed to individual employees, the concerned employee is likely to get low ratings.

WHY DOES THE PERFORMANCE APPRAISAL SYSTEM FAIL?

Longenecker (1997) reported top 10 reasons why the performance appraisal system fails. In most cases, the reasons were unclear objectives, poor relationship with the boss, lack of information about the job that the subordinate performed, relative absence of continuous feedback, non-conducive political climate, weak performance reward linkage, supervisor's lack of assessing skills, and inconsistent review process.

Unclear objectives Employees, in most cases, do not know what is expected of them. This makes the appraisal process similar to a headless chicken. Clear articulation in metric term in all most possible cases will eliminate this ambiguity.

Poor relationship with superior Instead of assessing the real performance, in most cases, a supervisor assesses the work of a subordinate on the merit of his or her relationship. Inferior relationship with the supervisor will invite low score with abundant plausible logic for rating low. Although performance appraisal is all about appraising the performance, in the real context, it may possibly turn out to be a political one as well.

Lack of information about subordinate's performance With the advent of a flatter organizational structure, where one manager is taking care of more number of employees, the reporting system has been stretched. Thus, the manager may not have adequate knowledge and time to investigate a subordinate's performance. Because of poor knowledge about the employee's actual performance, the managers only guess and assume about the subordinate's performance, and any appraisal that originated out of guess work is bound to be inappropriate and incorrect. This inaccurate appraisal could potentially generate more dissatisfaction among the subordinates.

Lack of continuous feedback Annual review is a one-time yearly affair. Feedback should not be given only at the end of the year. It is doubtful whether the supervisor will use his or her valuable time to review the whole year's performance—it is quite an impossible proposition. To make the feedback process effective, timely disbursement of feedback is crucial so that corrective action could be taken immediately.

Guesswork As a supervisor is remotely located from the actual workplace, he or she may not have the time to review each day's work. Some of the job is very technical and co-created with the true participation of customer and employees, and monitoring each interaction with guests is a very difficult proposition. So, when appraisal time comes, one of the most frequently used methods is guesswork. This makes performance appraisal process and its implementation a mockery and a boring ritual of the HR department. Performance appraisal is a process where the employee finds avenues to progress, and all the parties should be more interested. However, in most cases, everybody involved in the process attempts to do it perfunctorily.

Political climate In most cases, the organizational political climate presents a huge amount of hindrances. Charged political climate prevents frank conversation and drives out transparency from the system. Thus, performance appraisal becomes a means of achieving political goals. Theoretically, the objectives of a fair appraisal system are noble. However, in the hands of untrained HR executives, it is a weapon given to powerful individuals to use it to fulfil their political objectives.

Weak performance and reward linkage Compensation management is deeply linked with performance management as good performance of employees is acknowledged by awarding good remuneration and promotion. However, in many cases, compensation management is considered to be a separate function that is almost disconnected from the performance management of the organization. This apparent disconnection leads employees to believe that performance appraisal is a mere ritual of the HR department, and it makes the whole process meaningless. Instead of performance as a basis of reward, if other considerations and yardstick are deployed, the whole performance appraisal system will collapse similar to a house of cards. If such a situation is created, employees will invent a new definition of performance, which would include engaging in political activities, other initiatives for harming colleagues, and so on.

To overcome many of these difficulties, two distinct developments have been made: 360-degree feedback system and balanced score card system. Before we discuss these two performance appraisal methods, we need to develop our understanding on a few issues such as management by objectives (MBO), goal-setting theory, and creative tension. Understanding these will enable the reader to comprehend the 360-degree feedback system and the balanced score card system better.

MANAGEMENT BY OBJECTIVES

Management by objectives (MBO) philosophy is one of the primary attempts to construe organizational intervention as a global construct, which is one of the first attempts to understand work under an integrated umbrella. This concept is about 60 years old; however, the attraction to MBO philosophy is notable. Peter Drucker articulated this concept in his book *The Practice of Management*, first published in the year 1954. This theory gives a broader understanding of work and potentially connects every individual with the strategic objectives of the company. Each individual employee could clearly see his or her role and how it links with the corporate strategic objectives. These linkages provide meaning to the mundane job done at various levels. MBO is a process where the strategic objectives of the company are cascaded down to every department and every individual of an organization. This brings clarity into the system. Division of labour deprives employees from experiencing a sense of completion and craftsmanship, as each employee executes only a part of the total function required to produce a complete product. MBO provides a clearer picture where each employee is located and how his or her function is connected with the bigger goal of the organization and it brings back the sense of pride into his or her work.

MBO can be executed in two ways:

1. Top-down approach
2. Bottom-up approach

The top-down approach signifies that corporate performance, derived out of the strategic planning process, gets cascaded down across various departments, designations, and employees. The bottom-up approach signifies that lower level managers participate to develop the target, which is integrated to the overall target of the company.

MBO potentially generates involvement and enhances participation inside the organization. When lower level managers are involved in the planning process, it generates interest as they own the solution and it also generates interest among lower level staff as if they are responsible for their own fate. Employees know what they are doing and how their contribution is linked with the overall corporate objectives. This provides a sense of identity and provides the management operation a data-driven approach. Rather than working under the imposed whims of the boss, this enables the lower level staff to have meaning in their world.

As each performance that unfolds at every nook and corner of the organization is integrated with the grand objective of the organization, coordination becomes much easier. This in turn provides feedback to the employees if they are deviating. The goal that is set by the department works as a guiding star and makes the evaluation easier and also aligns individual aspirations and makes it translatable to a real action plan.

MBO provides a robust frame of reference while approaching management of performance, collectively organized in the corporate world. However, similar to any other concept, it is not free from inherent weaknesses. Although as a concept it is intellectually stimulating and believable, organization-wide implementation poses a significant problem. Installing organization-wide goals derived out of participatory activities require careful guidance from organizational development consultants. At the same time, when the organizations attempt to implement, it appears to be time consuming. MBO provides a platform but does not provide clear-cut recommendations on the content, and also, performance is narrowly defined. It lacks substance to clearly guide on the various constituents of performance. However, it is needless to state that MBO has provided one of the most important underlying logics for management of employee performance. In other words, MBO has facilitated the linking of performance appraisal with the strategic goal of the organization and has brought clarity and accountability into the system.

UNDERLYING THEORIES

There are a few theories that attempt to explain the performance appraisal system. We study two important theoretical frameworks, which will help us deepen our understanding of performance appraisal. These underlying theories are discussed in the following subsections.

Goal-setting theory   Goal-setting theory suggests that a goal has inherent qualities to attract performance. A goal generates a concerted effort all across the organization, enables focused efforts to achieve organizational goal, and gives stable guidance to the follower. Multiple advantages of having suitable goals are that it brings synergy and leads to the achievement of performance. However, employees in the department must perceive the goal as achievable and believe that they have the capability to achieve it. In organizational behavioural science, it is called *self-efficacy*, which is a prerequisite for the successful application of goal-setting theory in a hospitality organization. This brings out the important role of the supervisory and executive staff. It is important that they should work on the target by generating a positive environment of possibility. Counselling the staff that the target is achievable is an important task of a manager.

Creative tension   Peter Senge (1990) in his book *The Learning Organization* highlighted the theory of creative tension, which suggests that an individual should be in touch with the current reality and 'articulated vision'. This will generate deep knowledge and inherent unconscious tension in the approach to life, which will generate enough momentum to achieve the objectives. Therefore, a clearer picture of what we have, what we are, and where we want to go will make collective efforts much easier to achieve. Senge highlighted this theory as a theory that explains individual behaviour.

If employees know their truest assessed performance level and aspire to achieve the shared goal within a specific time, then this will generate paradigm shifts in the collective behaviour of the group. As a manager in a hotel, continuous constructive feedback and installing individual and collective goals will be of great help in achieving the goal.

BALANCED SCORECARD

The balanced scorecard is a substantial advancement of the MBO framework. Art Schneiderman, an independent consultant, developed the first balanced scorecard in 1987 at Analog Devices. Subsequently, Kaplan and Norton (1992 and 1993) documented this in their book titled *The Balanced Scorecard*. The balanced scorecard is a framework that is used to measure an employee's performance. While MBO is a philosophy, the balanced scorecard framework provides a robust, pragmatic, and implementable roadmap to assess the performance of the employees. This framework integrates the whole business into numerical expression of targets and objectives. This grand objective or goal is then subsequently allocated and shared at every layer of organization members, which gives clarity to the system. Transparency is the backbone of the balanced scorecard, and each member in the organization knows what is expected of him or her, and this knowledge empowers the organizational members to undertake suitable action. Constant comparison against target could provide continuous feedback about the performance. Under this system, each employee knows where he or she stands in terms of performance and what is needed to enhance the performance. This provides considerable freedom to each employee and brings back accountability into the system (Fig. 5.1).

The balanced scorecard believes in the spirit of MBO, but gives more guidance on the content and framework of the performance. It highlights the need for considering the performance of each employee from four dimensions/perspectives:

1. Customer focus objectives/targets
2. Finance focus objectives/targets
3. Employees' learning and growth
4. Internal process

This broader frame of reference to assess performance provides a robust and comprehensive way of addressing many organizational problems. The traditional

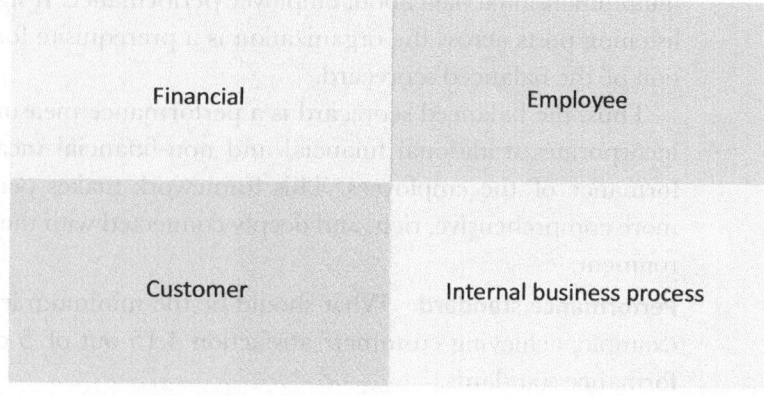

Financial	Employee
Customer	Internal business process

Figure 5.1 Balanced scorecard framework

performance appraisal system acknowledges supervisory power to assess the performance, which has been taken away under the balanced scorecard framework.

Customer   In most cases in real business context, the assessing body is hardly available when the service is being produced, and it is the customer who enjoys the quality of services and knows what is good and what is not. Therefore, the customer is one of the evaluators for organizational performance. As they are located in the closest position in the service production environment, this proximity provides them the legitimate right to assess the craftsmanship of an employee's performance.

Finance   Each step in service production invites cost. Thus, unrestrained expenses to satisfy a customer might lead to the closure of business. Therefore, evaluation of performance should be done in terms of cost and customer satisfaction. Cost is one of the determinants of efficiency in the service production environment.

Employee's learning and growth   The third component of the balanced scorecard is the employee's learning and growth. Employees are consistently attempting to excel in service production and its quality. This investment will make the company sustain their competitive advantage.

Internal process   The fourth component is the internal process improvement.

One of the critical features of the balanced scorecard system of appraisal is in its metric system. The balanced scorecard accommodates only measurable criteria in terms of performance targets and evaluation. Each performance target is expressed in numerical terms (such as sales target for the year of ₹350 crores from food and beverage outlets). Installation of numeric system facilitates objective evaluations, free from the appraiser's bias. Thus, this process promotes transparency, fairness, and justice inside the organization. Installation of the balanced scorecard makes holistic changes in its approach and makes the organization data driven. However, to make it successful, arrangements are required to be made to capture multidimensional data about employee performance. It signifies that installation of listening posts across the organization is a prerequisite for successful implementation of the balanced scorecard.

Thus, the balanced scorecard is a performance measurement approach, which incorporates traditional financial and non-financial measures to assess the performance of the employees. This framework makes performance measurement more comprehensive, rich, and deeply connected with the service production environment.

Performance standard   What should be the minimum level of performance? For example, achieving customer satisfaction 4.15 out of 5 could be one of the performance standards.

Performance rating   For example, a rating of 4.15 will get a score of 3; 10 per cent above 4.15 will get a score of 4; and 20 per cent above this score will get 5.

Table 5.1 KRA template for front office manager (partial view)

Customer focus	Weightage (%)	Scoring method
		Score between 15 and 25 = 1
Satisfaction of the guest	10	Score between 26 and 30 = 2
Repurchase intention	5	Score between 31 and 35 = 3
Courtesy index of front office staff	5	Score between 35 and 40 = 4
Fluency in check out	5	41 and above = 5

Table 5.2 KRA template for general manager (partial view)

Employee focus	Weightage (%)	Scoring method
		Score between 15 and 25 = 1
Employee satisfaction score	15	Score between 26 and 30 = 2
Training man hours	5	Score between 31 and 35 = 3
Retention rate for key employees	5	Score between 35 and 40 = 4
Legal compliance	5	41 and above = 5

Similarly, 10 per cent below 4.15 will get a score of 2 and 20 per cent below the performance standard will get 1. From the example, it is clear that performance appraisal is almost apparently transparent. Individual consideration while awarding any rating has vanished with the advent of metric-based performance system. During your industrial training, you must have seen why most managers are concerned about excellent customer ratings. Employees' performance is now subject to multiple scrutinies for the generation of accurate representation, and it is believed that the company will gain competitive advantage for long-term survival.

Tables 5.1 and 5.2 show samples of balanced scorecard template for managers.

DIFFICULTIES ASSOCIATED WITH BALANCED SCORECARD ADMINISTRATION

The balanced scorecard framework promises to measure employee performance using multiple criteria and with numerical denomination. This facilitates reduction of subjective interpretation of performance, which under the traditional performance appraisal system often causes considerable harm to the credibility of the whole performance appraisal system. However, these promises of sound balanced scorecard system cannot be automatically fulfilled and require robust organizational framework and support to implement it successfully. A few of these limitations should be reckoned with while designing the performance appraisal system.

Sound organizational infrastructure The balanced scorecard relies on various metric systems of macro and micro organizational performances. Therefore, before the introduction of the balanced scorecard system, the organization should be prepared for evidence-based management practices. The balanced scorecard utilizes a range of metrics to measure employee performance. Some of these metrics are customer satisfaction score, customer revisit intention score, employee satisfaction score, employee sense of growth score, process improvement scores, food cost performance, and so on. This signifies that the organization requires to gear up their organizational rules, regulations, and processes.

Time-consuming event Balanced scorecard design and implementation are a time-consuming affair. When most executives are under tremendous pressure for organizational performance, allocation of time for meetings related with designing and devising a metric system for balanced scorecard performance management system is considerably difficult. Without close participation of all departments, this balanced scorecard system is vulnerable to collapse. Budgeting adequate time for the balanced scorecard system, especially at the time of introduction of the system, is a non-negotiable requirement.

Deriving proper metric system Successful implementation of proper metric system relies upon sound and innumerable metric system. Identifying these metric systems and installing them at suitable places in the organizational infrastructure for collection of data are a difficult proposition. Installing the wrong metric system may ruin the whole balanced scorecard system.

Team dynamics Balanced scorecard in its basic constituents suggests that each employee requires achieving the right kind of balance among its four basic parts. Customer satisfaction at the cost of financial damages could be seen easily under the balanced scorecard system. Thus, team dynamics operating in organizational context should be supportive for facilitating balanced scorecard processes. Privileged individuals who have benefited for long under the traditional performance appraisal system may join together to ruin and discredit the balanced scorecard system. Commitment from top management could stop these privileged individuals by restraining their political activities.

Synergy between corporate objectives and individual employee objectives The basic premise is that the balanced scorecard system comprehends corporate goals into numerical orders, which are redistributed among various role incumbents positioned at various organizational hierarchies. Thus, at least the summation of individual employee objectives should represent the aggregative corporate goals. In case the synergy between corporate objectives and employee objectives are not achieved, the balanced scorecard may collapse.

Predominance over quantification of every employee's performance The balanced scorecard accommodates only numerical expression of all performance data. In service work context, it is sometimes difficult to install numeric performance target and evaluation.

THE 360-DEGREE FEEDBACK SYSTEM

It is a system where an employee's performance is assessed by multiple stakeholders, for example, self, peers, supervisors, subordinates, customers, and so on. It is believed that a combination of feedback will provide a better and holistic picture about an individual, which is much superior to one-source appraisal usually carried out by the immediate supervisor. However, before installing the 360-degree feedback system, an organization is required to fully gear up and build adequate human resources infrastructure for successful implementation of this process. For example, implementation of the 360-degree feedback system must have due support and sanction from the top management. Employees are required to be educated about the objective of the 360-degree feedback system, how to give authentic feedback, and so on. This is important because an employee may easily misunderstand the objective of the programme and may assume that the top management is interested to know about his or her faults.

The objective of the 360-degree feedback system is developmental. In most cases, the 360-degree feedback system is managed with the highest degree of confidentiality and never linked with reward or compensation package. The data generated through the 360-degree feedback system are shared with only the employees, and a helping hand is extended to them to enhance the capability of the individuals. Before implementing it, several pilot tests are required to be carried out so that every organization's cultural and other infrastructural peculiarity could be accommodated in the final version of the 360-degree feedback system. However, attempts should be made to improvise the process and content of the 360-degree feedback system at the earliest opportunity (Fig. 5.2).

Individual Benefit

The 360-degree feedback system generates a multidimensional view about an individual. As per the Johari window framework (Fig. 5.3), each individual

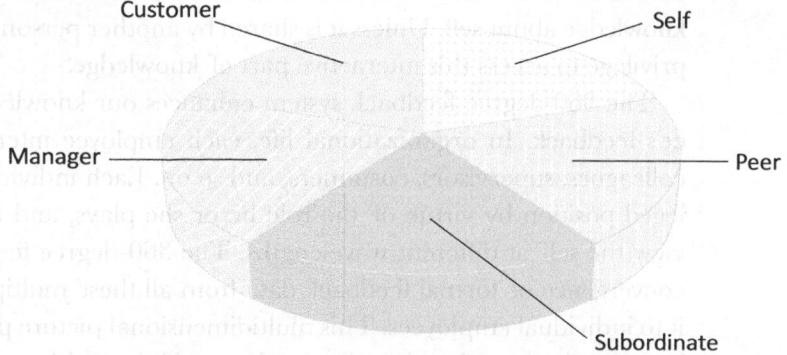

Figure 5.2 Various sources of feedbacks

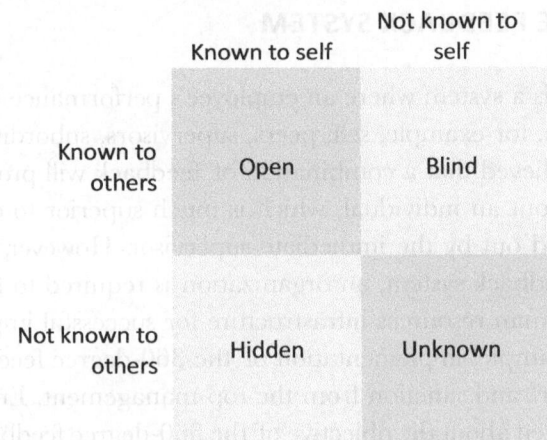

Figure 5.3 Johari window

should generate four types of knowledge. Joseph Luft and Harry Ingham developed this framework in 1955. This gives us an understanding about self, from four dimensions:

1. *Open dimension* signifies all knowledge about self, which is known to self as well as to others.
2. *Blind dimension* signifies all the knowledge about self that is not known to self but is known to others.
3. *Hidden dimension* signifies all the secret knowledge about self, which is only known to self.
4. *Unknown dimension* signifies all the knowledge about self, which is not known to anybody. Even self is not aware of them.

Our available knowledge about self is not adequate, but it appears to be so real that we adopt that knowledge as final. However, some part of self is generated during interaction or while dealing with others. The knowledge generated during these interactions is witnessed by self and the other person, who develops knowledge about self. Unless it is shared by another person, self will never have the privilege to access this interactive part of knowledge.

The 360-degree feedback system enhances our knowledge by introducing other's feedback. In organizational life, each employee interacts with subordinates, colleagues, supervisors, customers, and so on. Each individual is located at a privileged position by virtue of the role he or she plays, and the individual is able to view the self at different wavelengths. The 360-degree feedback system facilitates convergence of formal feedback data from all these multiple sources and presents it to individual employees. This multidimensional picture provides a comparatively better and comprehensive picture about self. As multiparty is involved in the generation of feedback, it has the potential for higher acceptability.

Organizational Benefit

Employee development process

The 360-degree feedback framework accumulates and synthesizes employee data from multiple sources to make a comprehensive picture about an individual's performance. Multiparty participations in the system bring back authenticity and credibility, and acceptability is relatively higher than in other traditional methods. The 360-degree feedback system offers feedback about an individual employee's performance. Thus, it opens up the possibility of continuous learning among employees.

The 360-degree feedback system allocates attention to mapping an employee's capability pertaining to his or her communication skills, leadership qualities, adaptability, strength and quality of relational network, individual productivity, personal development, and so on. It is important to note that these are crucial skill sets that are required for the generation of performance. An employee's communication skill is one of the important prerequisites for executing and relating with the world. Leadership qualities are essential; especially, crisis-inflicted organizational workspaces always look for strong leadership qualities. Adaptability is crucial as organizational workspace is undergoing constant change, and this quality helps individual employees to easily get adjusted to the challenges of the new world order faster than others. Strength and qualities of relational network help them perform, especially when the organizational blueprint of service delivery fails to map extraordinary demands of customers. With the help of this social capital, it is easier to persuade others to go beyond the blueprint and accommodate the special request of the guest. In India, low labour productivity is a major concern as it reduces individual effectiveness drastically. Thus, employee productivity is a major concern. Panoramic feedback about employee's feedback is crucial and could be a leading developmental issue for employees.

Prerequisites for Successful Implementation of the 360-degree Feedback System

To make the 360-degree feedback system effective, the following basic guidelines should be adhered to:

1. Sanction from the top management: The HR department should acquire requisite commitment associated with this process, as this will provide seriousness and credibility to the whole process. In the absence of strong commitment from the top management, this process will potentially generate junk data about employee performance and generate a higher degree of conflict throughout the organization.

2. Feedback competency: Employees should be trained to provide effective feedback, which would help the concerned employee improve performance in the light of the feedback. Hence, while giving feedback, each one should adhere to

a certain protocol of decency, relevance, generalizability, and accuracy. Generalizability signifies that feedback should be predominantly based on the most frequent type of behaviour so that general conclusion could be drawn from such reported behaviour.

3. Involve managers and employees in developing appraisal criteria: To make the feedback system relevant to each employee, department, and hierarchy, the HR team must involve all the managers and employees to develop job- and individual-related data. This will allow accommodating and incorporating individual, departmental, and hierarchical peculiarities into the feedback-capturing instruments and processes.

4. Inform the employees about the whole process: Any intervention, initiated by the HR department, is often subject to collective resistance, individual insincerity, and unnecessary doubt. This could be, to a large extent, reduced with proper education and circulation of information, which will reduce initial phobia around the process as it is based on anonymity. Once anonymity is assured, this will enhance the likelihood of generating authentic feedback.

5. Pilot test: Each organization inherits a unique culture, process, and system of production of services. Hence, it is important to launch a pilot test with the newly developed 360-degree feedback system to examine the efficacy of the feedback process. This pilot test provides ample space to accommodate minor alterations to enhance the effectiveness of this feedback system.

6. Integration of the feedback data with individual growth plan and other organizational activities: The 360-degree feedback system should be integrated with the individual growth plan as this will make immense contribution to the development of individuals. Besides, feedback data could provide important guidance for developing relevant management- and leadership- development programmes.

7. Delinking with compensation and benefit management processes: The 360-degree feedback system should not be linked with the reward management scheme of the organization and should be used for individual development only. Linking it with reward management scheme will greatly erode the authenticity of the data and will potentially be clouded by organizational politics, social desirability, and manipulative administration.

8. Install flexibility: Any human design will inherit substantial amount of deficiencies; hence, there should be a provision for alteration of process, and also, the content may undergo substantial revisions for enhancing effectiveness. Organizational culture should be flexible for accommodating such alterations.

The 360-degree Feedback System and Its Content

This system is predominantly directed to provide feedback about an individual employee's performance, focusing on a few important issues.

1. Leadership style: This feedback system captures data pertaining to individual leadership style, which includes abilities of guiding subordinates, clarity of direction, instilling trust, and delegation style.

2. Stress management: Organizational workspace is constrained by resources and time. Hence, when each member accesses these resources for production of services, it inevitably creates substantial amount of stress and raises temperature in the workspace and automatically translates into stress for individual employees. This feedback system provides valuable information as to how this stress is managed by each role incumbent.

3. Consideration: Each leadership position in an organization is expected to invest considerable amount of time for the enhancement and development of others. However, daily organizational life is filled with deadlines and stress, and this takes away the space for developmental conversation among leaders, managers, and employees for individual growth. This feedback system could provide important information about the frequency and breadth of these practices.

4. Execution of job: Various stakeholders are located in advantageous positions to view how effectively each employee performs his or her job. Some stakeholders are even closely located to the service production process and can give interesting feedback about the service production process that each individual employee follows.

5. Proactive quality: Each job requires tremendous drive to initiate and follow up for final delivery of service. Proactive quality is indeed a great personal resource, which enables smooth execution of work. In the absence of this quality, a job cannot be executed well.

6. Development of subordinates: Nurturing talent and inspiring subordinates to achieve targets is one of the important functions for individuals in leadership positions. This generates a sense of care and bonding between leaders and subordinates, which works as a glue and reduces the intention of employee turnover. The absence of frequent changes in a group provides stability, which is necessary for performance.

7. Communication: Individuals working in leadership positions require communicating with other members. This multirater feedback system provides a unique opportunity to capture information pertaining to listening skills, information processing, and communication capabilities.

This enumeration is not necessarily exhaustive and should be considered as a suggestive example. Depending on the nature of the job, culture of the organization, and individual roles, this requires to be framed. In most cases, this is done in close cooperation with the role incumbent whose performance is required to be examined. One important observation could be made in this regard: the focus of this multirater feedback system is to gather information pertaining not only to employee performance but to all those personal qualities that are required to execute the performance.

FEEDBACK PARTNERS

The 360-degree feedback system is a multirater arrangement where various stakeholders associated with the consumption and production of services participate in the feedback generation system. Some stakeholders (i.e., peers, subordinates, and supervisors) witness the service production process, whereas customers experience the result of the service production process. Hence, each stakeholder is able to observe the employee from some vantage point and merit inclusion for the betterment of the service production process. Thus, the 360-degree feedback system becomes an assembly of viewpoints and interpretations of performance of employees from multiple vantage points. Investigation of differences of opinion provides valuable inputs to the employees for subsequent improvement in the service production process and for better business results. For example, the customer may be happy with the service outcomes but the concerned employee might not have created the quality of service that is expected by the organization.

Self-appraisal   Self-appraisal is an effective means of collection of data pertaining to performance. It also works as a base reference point to compare with feedbacks received from other sources and provides ample food for thought for each employee. The 360-degree feedback system includes self-appraisal in the feedback generation process, and this generates individual employee-level commitment, which works as a life-giving force for any system.

Disadvantages   Under the traditional appraisal system, each employee is subject to supervisory appraisal. However, the 360-degree feedback system considers self-interpretation of performance quality and process. Human behaviour is predominantly driven by self-interest, and because of this, each individual may generate exaggerated interpretation of his or her own performance. While evaluating with others' rating, the average self-appraisal rating, in most cases, scores higher than others' rating. Thus, leniency bias is a serious issue in self-appraisal process. Leniency bias occurs when the rater undeservedly allocates a higher score to self without valid supporting arguments.

Peer appraisal   Peer appraisal consists of reciprocal appraisal among the specified group members on certain dimensions of performance. This is based on the premise that employees who work closely with each other owing to the interdependent nature of tasks are closely located to observe the performance-generating processes and hence are more suitable to offer feedback. This is better than supervisors' evaluation, as a supervisor cannot observe the subordinate all the time, especially with the advent of flat organizational structure, where the span of management for each supervisor has increased substantially. This peer appraisal also potentially generates participative organizational culture, which is a prerequisite for a smooth service production process.

Disadvantages Each individual may adopt a less critical approach and may not raise all important issues. This collective play-safe behaviour will significantly contribute to the system failing. Each individual participating in peer appraisal process may intentionally engage in a popularity contest to achieve a higher score than others. Various ploys from the books on organizational politics could harm the organization more than the benefit the process can accrue. Each individual will compromise with the other in terms of performance standard and will be less aggressive in the pursuit of performance.

Subordinate appraisal It means that subordinates rate the performance of their immediate supervisor on several key performance criteria. Employees working under supervision are qualified to provide unique feedback as they are closely located in the service production process in relation to their supervisor. A customer can evaluate service quality, but may not and need not have knowledge about the back office operation where service has been produced, whereas subordinates are well informed about the service production process and its related constraints. From their vantage position where they can observe their supervisor's service production activities, they can observe the supervisor's leadership qualities, employee-responsive behaviour, clarity of direction, and quality of guidance. This also enhances a sense of employee participation and democratic organizational set-up. Thus, contribution of the subordinate to the improvement of the supervisor's performance is crucial and valuable.

Disadvantages Supervisor rating may curtail and erode a sense of managerial control over subordinates. Supervisors' restrained behaviour will generate a sense of powerlessness. Even when the situation demands, these supervisors will not engage in tough managerial practices, and mediocrity will take over the way the department functions. Employees may use this feedback for redressal of their personal problems with their supervisors and will not hesitate to put in their comments as a means of revenge.

MANAGING EMPLOYEE PERFORMANCE

Managing employees' performance requires deeper understanding about dynamic environmental and individual contexts where performance is being enacted. Two non-performers should not be equated with each other. Let us take a case where one is not able to perform as he or she has joined recently from a reputed hotel management institute. Although the individual is willing to perform, he or she does not possess the requisite skills to perform. The other non-performer may not be able to perform because of low motivation. This non-performer has been working for the company for the last 15 years, but believes that he or she has been unfairly treated and has not got the due that he or she deserves. Although he or she is not short of skill set, because of low motivation, he or she is being considered a non-performer.

In today's organizational context, the second type of non-performers is seen more. Recent Gallup surveys indicate that employee engagement is relatively low across the world. In other words, low employee engagement indicates that employees are predominantly physically present within the precinct of the organization; however, employees are not emotionally attached to the workplace. They do their job perfunctorily so as to not have complaints from customers. Their participation in organizational processes is deeply linked with the formal level of their job description. Employees do what their job description demands. Many of these employees maintain their jobs by performing a bare minimal level of work. In the service industry, as stated earlier, it is difficult to put every element of the job in the blueprint of the service design. Employees get ample opportunity to put additional values in the service composition collectively by adding smiles, providing additional explanation to the query of the customer, and so on. As employees require ample latitude to stretch beyond the call of duty to delight the customers, performance is required to be understood by the dynamic context where it is exposed to.

Theoretical Underpinning

An individual engages in various types of behaviour in order to maximize personal gains. Therefore, individuals who produce superior performance require reinforcement for repeat performance. Good behaviour reinforced by good experience will have more chances of repeat behaviour than otherwise. Using the argument advanced by Skinner (1938), behaviour is a function of stimulus.

Using a broader framework, we can classify all employees into four clusters (Fig. 5.4):

1. Excellent performers
2. Motivated learners
3. Demotivated performers
4. Deadwoods

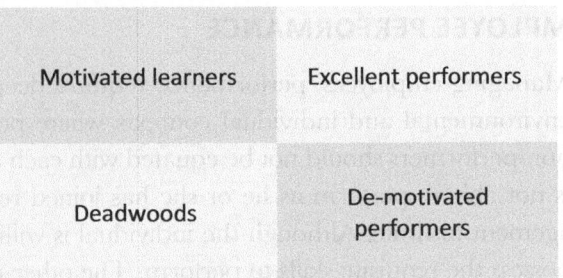

| Motivated learners | Excellent performers |
| Deadwoods | De-motivated performers |

Figure 5.4 Types of employees and managing performance

Excellent performers They have high motivation and ability to perform. These employees have the right combination of skills and knowledge required to perform and are vital for the organizational success. HR executives desire such employees and attempt to create a workforce consisting of such individuals and organize a wide range of HR initiatives to achieve this. To encourage their performance, the HR department should invest a good amount of resources for their developmental needs.

Motivated learners These employees are highly motivated; however, they do not have the requisite skills and knowledge to perform the job. Most of the new employees who join the hospitality industry after passing out of hotel management institutes fall under this profile. With their juvenile enthusiasm, they take every assignment positively and enthusiastically and are interested in learning. The HR department requires exercising the highest degree of care so that this enthusiasm could be maintained and the new employees get exposed to a good hospitality environment; adequate inputs are imparted so that they can graduate to becoming excellent performers. However, one of the most important dangers is the lack of tutelage and care that can generate unfair feeling, which could lead to them becoming demotivated performers.

Demotivated performers Demotivated performers are those employees who possess the requisite skills and knowledge but lack motivation. Behavioural science enlightens us that employees' performance is a function of knowledge, skills, and attitude (Fig. 5.5). Absence of any one of the elements may hamper the performance of the employees. In the case of demotivated performers, they do not have a positive outlook about the job. This may happen because of the unfair perception they hold about their company and their immediate world. In case the HR department fails to take proper and systematic care of the employees who have been working in the company for quite some time, the employees will become demotivated performers. It is important that the HR manager devises suitable processes and organizational and human infrastructure where the aspirations of the employees are accommodated with the progress of the company. Majority of the problems in our Indian hospitality industry are of this type. It is important that instead of blaming them for their non-performance, their concerns are addressed. Inevitably, they will become excellent performers. To increase the productivity of

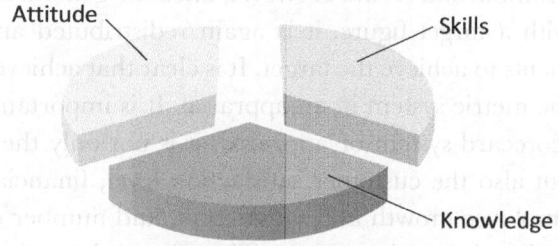

Figure 5.5 KSA Model

the hospitality industry, accommodating their aspiration is the only road to travel. Other strategic options available have proved to be costly.

Deadwoods   Deadwoods are those employees who possess low ability and motivation. They are believed to have reached a plateau of their capability. No easy conclusion can be made about employees being deadwood. The HR department must use all behavioural modification techniques to alter the status of these employees. An enlightened management does not make hasty conclusions about their ability and motivation. After providing all available supports to these individuals, if they fail to show a sign of improvement, managerial action could be initiated—this includes demotion, retirement, or firing.

EFFECTIVE PERFORMANCE APPRAISAL SYSTEM

Designing an effective performance appraisal system is one of the most important functions of the HR department. An effective performance appraisal system incorporates business strategies into measurable performance metric, which the employees are required to translate into service. For example, once the board of directors decides that the overall percentage of business growth over the next year is 25 per cent, it is the responsibility of the managing director to implement it during that period. With the advent of various regulatory bodies (e.g., Securities Exchange Board of India, SEBI), it is now customary that many reputed companies provide guidance to its shareholders about the growth they are going to achieve during the next few quarters. This guidance is usually given to restrain unnecessary fluctuation of the share price and to manage the expectations of the shareholders effectively. Thus, a formal announcement of 25 per cent growth over last year's performance is a commitment to its shareholders, which should be achieved without fail. Once the announcement is made, the HR department is required to reconfigure the performance infrastructure in such a way that it leads to achieving this objective. Thus, performance objectives are required to be cascaded down to each level of operation with adequate accountability. If the achievement target is 4000 crores in a year, then it should be distributed among the unit hotels. All hotels do not have equal potential to generate revenue. For example, hotels located in places such as Aurangabad do not have the same capacity to generate revenue as hotels located in Mumbai and Delhi. However, once the general manager of a unit hotel is assigned with a target figure, it is again redistributed among revenue-generating departments to achieve the target. It is clear that achievement of target becomes a part of the metric system in an appraisal. It is important to note that under the balanced scorecard system of appraisal, it is not only the financial target that is appraised but also the customer satisfaction level, financial implications of the operations, employee growth and satisfaction, and number of critical improvements made in various internal processes. Therefore, it is pertinent to know as to what constitutes an effective performance appraisal system.

Consistent The performance appraisal system should be consistently applied throughout the organization uniformly over a period of time. Each employee in the system is appraised using the same scale of measurement. Consistent application of the specific appraisal system will generate a sense of fairness, trust, and inspiration among employees.

Acceptable It is often seen that the performance appraisal process is not very credible in the eyes of employees. The performance appraisal system should be acceptable to the employees and should be construed as a fairness disbursement process, where the HR team acquires evidences for implementation of effective reward management. Therefore, before introducing a specific appraisal system, the HR executives need to dedicate substantial amount of resources and time to communicate and train employees about the way the appraisal system will work. For example, before introducing the balanced scorecard system of appraisal, employees need to be educated about the dynamics of the system, process, and time frame. Specific attempts should be made to convince employees that the multidimensional balanced scorecard system is fair, comprehensive, and employee friendly. In every system of human operation, there are sceptics who cannot be easily moved. The HR department needs to display special attention to them so that they graduate from a sceptic to a strong believer. Once an employee accepts a specific appraisal system, he or she will strive to achieve it.

Understandable The performance appraisal system should not be so complicated and ambiguous that the employees fail to understand its dynamics, process, and time frame. The HR manager should plan a special drive to educate employees about the performance appraisal system. At the time of induction, a newly recruited employee should be briefed about the performance appraisal process without fail. If employees are not convinced about its dynamics, process, and timing, they will provide the highest degree of resistance, and this will become complicated when the organizational workspace is dominated by multiple trade unions. In such a case, the HR manager should exercise the highest degree of caution before introducing any specific appraisal system, and the active trade union members should be convinced first before communicating it to the employees.

Manageable The performance appraisal system should be manageable. In most reputed hotel chains in India, it is integrated at the unit level and then subsequently at the corporate level. The overall architecture of the performance appraisal system should consist of simple processes with a clear outline and time frame for implementation. Once implemented, the HR manager should have access to critical information such as good performers and weak performers, as this information is crucial for compensation and benefit management (discussed in detail in Chapter 7).

Evidence driven The performance appraisal system should have a clear metric system for measurement and evaluation, and this system should have underlying valid and logical reasoning and should be able to discriminate between good and weak performers. A sound appraisal system also provides specific data support to review the exact weak zone of performance in an organizational context. This will provide useful assistance for initiating necessary actions regarding the corrective steps required to improve performance.

Ecological support   Organizational ecology should be able to support the performance appraisal system. Organizational ecology means various organizational artefacts that enable individual employees to perform, such as organizational culture and positive organizational and supervisory support systems. This is important because if organizational ecology is not congruent with performance-driven management system, installation of a robust performance appraisal system will collapse without producing any result. It signifies that the performance appraisal system, without supportive organizational culture and supervisory support, is bound to fail. Therefore, before installation of the performance appraisal system, the HR manager should install life-giving support for the successful its implementation.

Transparency   The performance appraisal system should embed all characteristics that provide the experience of transparency to the employees. This transparency can be achieved by clear articulation of objectives, provision of process map, evaluation criteria, and its linkage with the benefit management system. Minimal application of subjective interpretation of employee's level of performance will bring a sense of transparency, which is important for successful implementation and result-driven performance appraisal system.

Meaningful linkage   Performance appraisal should not by itself become the end result. It should be deeply integrated with recruitment, training, compensation, and benefit management so that it provides the rationale to the employees for sincere participation in the performance appraisal process. In other words, good performers who are identified by the performance appraisal process should be acknowledged by adequate compensation and provided adequate career growth whenever possible. This will work as a demonstrative display of reward, that is, performance linkage for other employees to emulate.

Solid feedback   The performance appraisal system often ends with superficial and token feedback. An effective performance system should be assessed by its result rather than the process itself. It has been reported that most supervisors refrain from disbursement of authentic feedback because of the fear of backlash. Predominantly, the performance appraisal process invites considerable stress among the appraisees and appraisers and is often hastened up to close the process at the earliest so that they can come out of these stressful moments—a kind of escapist ideology that is quite prevalent. There might be some exceptions; but predominantly, by providing some non-essential and superficial notation in the feedback form, a curtain is drawn over the performance appraisal process. In the absence of solid feedback, the whole process becomes a meaningless ritual of the HR department, rather than an instrument for distribution of fairness in the organizational context. This could be due to lack of time and self-confidence in the appraiser experiences, lack of faith in the system, and so on. The HR department should embed suitable elements in the performance appraisal process to record the theme of the feedback and examine its adequacy in relation to the performance score.

Confidentiality   Confidentiality is one of the important parts of the appraisal system, where exchange between the appraiser and the appraisee should be restrained within a veil of secrecy and privacy. Absence of confidentiality may cause serious harm to the performance appraisal process. Therefore, the HR team is required to embed adequate level of privacy around the process so that the performance appraisal process does not turn out to be merely a mode of prosecution but a medium of learning and growth.

Barney (1995) argued that a competitive edge over competition could be achieved by looking inside the organization, available at its disposal. One of these resources is human resource, which should be nurtured well by recognizing and rewarding good performers; however, provision for enhancement of average employees should also be embedded in the system. The HR department should be seen as effective, neutral, and transparent, and with the help of an effective performance appraisal system, it can achieve this easily.

SUMMARY

Performance appraisal system is an integral part of HR function. Performance appraisal process provides data for compensation management and training function. It helps identify excellent performers, deadwoods, motivated performers, and demotivated performers. Once this is known, specific policy is designed for the different types of performers. Thus, compensation management function depends heavily on the appraisal process and also provides data to the training department so that the weak spots in performance can be handled.

Performance appraisal process fails for various reasons: ill-designed appraisal process, political climate, poor knowledge about feedback system, guessed estimation by raters, and so on. It is important that all these shortcomings are eliminated to provide a robust performance appraisal framework.

Balanced scorecard is an appraisal system where the performance of an employee is evaluated using four criteria: finance, customer, employee, and internal process. Overdoing any one of the criteria may ruin the overall success. Thus, employees are required to exercise the highest degree of discretion to balance the four criteria to produce excellent services. Balanced scorecard is, in most cases, linked with compensation and benefit management function.

The 360-degree feedback system is a systematic process where employees' performance-related data is generated from multisources such as customers, colleagues, subordinates, and supervisors. Multiparty viewpoints attempt to provide feedback about an individual's performance, which is suitable for training and development. In most cases, this feedback is delinked with compensation and benefit management function.

Performance appraisal is a process by which employees' performance is assessed, whereas management of performance signifies how various types of performers could be managed so that performance level goes up in the near future. The various types of performers could be classified into four clusters: excellent performers, demotivated performers, deadwoods, and motivated learners.

KEY TERMS

Performance appraisal   Evaluating individual employee's performance against specific business targets.

Deadwoods   Individuals who are not motivated or do not have potential to perform.

Balanced score card   It is a performance appraisal framework, where performance is measured using four different types of performance targets, namely, customer-satisfaction-related targets, financial-performance-related targets, process-improvement-related targets, and employee-related targets.

Demotivated performers   Employees who have the capability to perform but are demotivated because of previous unjust treatments.

360-degree feedback system   It is a type of performance appraisal framework, where employee-related data is collected from a range of stakeholders, namely, subordinates, colleagues, self, supervisors, and customers.

Leniency error   It is error committed by the performance rater by loosely awarding higher marks to everybody.

Managing performance   HR department needs to devise a number of strategies to manage different types of employees for their respective efficient performance.

Goal setting theory   This theory highlights the importance of goal and its inherent contribution to motivate employees' performance.

Excellent performers   Employees who are highly motivated performers.

Motivated learners   Employees who are highly motivated to perform, but lack the skill to do so.

Johari window   It is a framework used to describe various dimensions of self. These various dimensions are open, blind, hidden, and unknown. 'Open' indicates that part of self which is known to self and others. 'Blind' indicates that part of the self which is not known to the self, but known to others. 'Hidden' indicates that part of the self which is privately known to individuals, but not available to others. 'Unknown' indicates that part of the self which is not known to the self as well as others.

EXERCISES

Concept Review Questions

1. Critically examine the role of performance appraisal process in Indian hospitality sector.
2. Elucidate performance appraisal process.
3. How is the 360-degree feedback system superior to other traditional appraisal methods?
4. To what extent do you believe that balanced scorecard architecture is suitable for measuring employees' performance?
5. Develop suitable framework to manage the performance of various types of employees.

Critical Thinking Questions

1. To what extent do you believe that the balanced scorecard captures all elements of performance? Is there any element missing that is not captured by the balanced scorecard framework?
2. How does the 360-degree feedback system generate authentic data pertaining to employees? What should be done to enhance the credibility of the data?
3. Employees' performance could not be managed by performance appraisal only. Critically comment various human infrastructure required for the production of services.

Assignments

1. Review the performance appraisal process you have encountered while undergoing on-the-job training and recommend suitable changes required to be incorporated to improve the system.
2. Review critical literature on performance appraisal systems to identify major hurdles as experienced by HR executives working in Indian hospitality sectors. Compare and contrast it with the global hospitality sector.

REFERENCES

Kaplan, R.S. and Norton, D.P., 'The balanced scorecard: measures that drive performance', *Harvard Business Review*, January–February 1992 p. 71–80.

Kaplan, R.S. and Norton, D.P., 'Putting the Balanced Scorecard to Work', *Harvard Business Review*, September– October 1993 p. 2–16.

Senge, P.M., *The Fifth Discipline*, Doubleday/Currency, New York, 1990.

Skinner, B.F., *The Behavior of Organisms: An Experimental Analysis*, Copley Publishing House, New York, 1938.

CASE COLLECTIVES

1. Two days after her appraisal, Sanya approaches the HR manager and complains that her performance appraisal score is inappropriate. She says that she has got low score in the department because she is a female employee. As she does not spend adequate time with other employees in her department in a non-working environment, it has affected her performance appraisal score. She states that most of the male employees in her department leave the hotel late, sometimes after 2 o' clock in the morning and then go to various places such as bars, where they spend quality time together. Being a lady, it is not possible for her to spend time like this and also, she is responsible for the well-being of her three-year-old daughter and elderly mother-in-law.

Discussion Question

As an HR manager, what would you do?

2. A trainee comes to meet the HR manager. He complains that his appraisal has been inaccurately done by his supervisor. He has worked for a minimum of 12 h in the kitchen most of the time and has never been absent from his workplace. Several positive customer feedbacks were available where he was successful in generating positive customer delight. He believes that he has been discriminated against just because he is a male trainee. He complains that all female trainees got excellent scores even though they remained absent on several occasions and never worked more than a few hours—mostly, they have only made some kind of report or presentation for the executive chef. Owing to this proximity to the executive chef, he believes that their scores are high. He complains that he worked in the hot kitchen and not in the air-conditioned office of the executive chef. In spite of all these, he failed to get good score from his supervisor. He says that his ranking will drastically go down if this appraisal score is given to the hotel management institute.

Discussion Question

As the HR manager, what would you do?

3. After taking over as the HR manager in a five-star hotel in Mumbai, you realize that the performance appraisal system is robust and a lot of paper work is done systematically throughout the year. When you invested a good amount of time to go through the paper work, you make one important observation. Although all employees are achieving their annual goals, the company is not performing well, and in the last two years, the company has made substantial loss. This year, the top management of the hotel is seeking fresh supply of money from the promoters for working capital.

Discussion Question

As the HR manager, what would you do?

6   Employee Motivation

INTRODUCTION

In Chapter 5, we learnt about the performance management systems. In this chapter, we will learn about employee motivation and ways of generating employee motivation. Employee motivation implies the level of energy, commitment, and passion deployed by employees to execute the job. Demotivated employees put relatively lower levels of energy and passion to the job, whereas motivated employees display high levels of commitment and energy to execute the job.

MOTIVATION

Historically, it is said that the term *motivation* has been derived from the Latin word for movement, *movere*. Therefore, motivation is a kind of drive full of 'direction, vigour, and persistence of action' as stated by Atkinson (1957) decades ago. In other words, it could be stated as a voluntary but sustained drive for achievement. Thus, motivation is in fact a kind of goal-oriented behaviour, which can be intrinsic (from within) or extrinsic (from outside) as shown in Fig. 6.1.

Intrinsic motivation signifies the drive for motivation in an individual that comes from within self, and the individual does not need to find any external reason to feel motivated. The inner core of the individual finds adequate drive to motivate oneself. On the other

LEARNING OBJECTIVES

After reading this chapter, you will be able to:
- understand employee motivation
- understand what generates employee motivation
- get to know ways of measuring employee motivation
- understand how to motivate employees

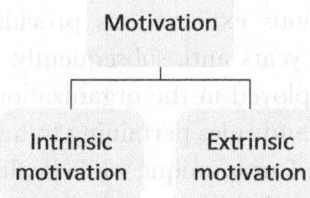

Figure 6.1   Types of motivation

hand, extrinsic motivation signifies that the source of drive is located outside, for example, good reward and recognition from supervisors.

Intrinsic motivation is more durable and requires less monitoring, whereas individuals who are driven by extrinsic motivation often require close monitoring. Research indicates that the introduction of extrinsic motivation has potential power to reduce the effect of intrinsic motivation. For example, children who are promised a reward on completion of a task spend less time playing and pay more time on completing the task, whereas children who are given unexpected rewards play for a longer time. Therefore, it is important that while introducing remuneration and compensation policy, the HR manager should be careful not to kill the joy one achieves out of completion of the job; rather it should be complementary to each other.

MOTIVATED EMPLOYEES—KEY TO GAINING COMPETITIVE EDGE

Motivated employees are an asset for any organization, especially so for the hospitality organization. A motivated employee provides better services to his or her customers and will be ready to go the extra mile to satisfy guests. They find creative solutions, almost exceeding the demand of the customers, thereby generating a delightful experience for the guest. Therefore, to have motivated employees in an organization is one of the most inimitable assets because this is not something that can be copied and implanted in another organization. This uniqueness makes it worthy to have motivated employees in a hospitality organization. It is easy to imitate a building; however, it is very difficult to replicate synergetic and harmonized productive human resource. The market is full of 'me too' products, and cheap imitation is available all around. Within weeks of launching a new product, the market is often overflooded with similar products with much lower rates. Therefore, it is difficult to convince the customers to purchase any specific product. In a similar situation, inimitability by itself is a great asset, and right configuration of human resources has indeed the potential to prevent this rampant imitation. The HR department makes considerable efforts to have motivated employees in the organization.

Therefore, it is important to know what motivates employees. A number of organizational psychologists endeavour to identify the critical factors, which potentially explain human motivation.

In this chapter, we examine various explanations provided by prominent organizational psychologists over the years and, subsequently, review the extent to which these learnings could be deployed in the organization. Human behaviour is diverse; to bring out a pattern and rules pertaining to human behaviour is indeed a very difficult task. Each one of us is unique while dealing with life issues, and even the same individual does not behave in a similar fashion at all times. Therefore, to bring out one simple rule about human behaviour is indeed a very difficult task.

EXAMPLES

1. SITO is a leading travel service provider in India that provides services to varieties of customer contacts for their diverse needs. Motivated employees in such travel services have indeed proved to be an asset for the company. Motivated employees will have genuine smiles, make efforts to listen to the needs of the customers, and will provide well-crafted travel services, which are suitable for the exact needs of the customers. Extra efforts that are exercised by the employees will be reflected in the customers' satisfaction and repurchase intention. Therefore, we can see that motivated employees are not only an asset, but they potentially generate provisions for future business.

2. HDCF Bank is a leading bank operating in India, which provides well-known banking services. Motivated employees endeavour to satisfy the customers. In one case, on the final reimbursement of bank loan, it is customary to issue a loan clearance certificate from the bank, along with returning original house property papers. One day, after issuance of the form, the customer discovered that the date printed on the certificate got smudged with the HDCF logo, which is an inadvertent error. A letter without proper date raises the question of authenticity of the document. When the customer contacted the bank officer, he immediately apologized to the customer and promised to send the certificate immediately. Several calls followed from the said office with enquiry about address, and on the very next day, the said certificate was delivered. The said bank officer enquired in the evening whether the customer received the letter. There is no doubt that the customer was highly satisfied with the bank and its employees.

VARIOUS MOTIVATION THEORIES

A number of theories have been advanced by organizational psychologists to explain employee motivation. Maslow attempted to explain human motivation using 'Need Hierarchy Theory' where individual motivation could be understood by the level of unfulfilled needs of individuals. Herzberg examined human motivation by highlighting the potential contribution of various organizational features such as quality of employee–supervisor relationship, recognition system, and good pay packet. However, as per his viewpoint, all these factors influence human motivation differently.

Maslow's Theory

Abraham Maslow's (1954) framework sets the historical background to motivational theories. It is one of the simplest representations of diverse human needs. Despite limitations, it presents various sources of human motivation. Maslow endeavoured to comprehend various types of needs, clustered them into five different categories, and organized them in some hierarchical segments: physiological needs, safety needs, belonging needs, esteem needs, and need for self-actualization. These needs are chained in hierarchical order. He argued that successful satisfaction of one level of needs leads to the next level. For instance, the primal human needs are food, water, and shelter. Once these needs are fulfilled, the second degree of need that arises is security. We engage in various activities to fulfil theis need, for example, by making a secure house, looking for a more permanent and secure job than contractual job, and so on. After achieving security, the next level is esteem need-fulfilling activities, which could be recognition from neighbour, any societal member, institution, and so on. Societal infrastructure has created various avenues to fulfil these needs, such as possession of a limited edition car and premier club membership. Once these needs are met, the individual graduates to the next level, that is, self-actualization, which is of a different order from the preceding needs. Drivers of the self-actualization state do not require any materialistic substance.

The essence of this theory is described here.

1. Human needs are diverse.
2. All needs can be viewed under comprehensive clusters: food and shelter, security, self-esteem, and self-actualization.
3. All needs are hierarchically organized.
4. On fulfilment of one kind of need, the individual graduates to the next level of satisfaction.

Critique   Although this theory is widely discussed and has advanced the understanding of human motivation, it has some weaknesses in its arguments. Needs are not necessarily hierarchical. It has been argued that human attention does not graduate only on completion of a lower need. Diverse needs can be simultaneously fulfilled; therefore, it does not necessarily adhere to the hierarchy, as prescribed by Maslow.

Herzberg's Two-factor Theory

Maslow's theory is focused on the individual, whereas Fredrick Irving Herzberg's (1959) theory of motivation is directed towards organizational infrastructure (relationship between supervisor and subordinates, good remuneration, working conditions, etc.). Herzberg reported two types of factors that are capable of driving employees' motivation: hygiene factors and motivating factors (Table 6.1). He identified certain factors such as good wages and working conditions whose presence in the organization does not generate satisfaction; however, their absence does lead

---

EXAMPLE

Ramnath works for a five-star hotel as a room boy. Presently, he is working on contractual basis and is eagerly waiting for the confirmation. As a confirmed job is relatively more secure, all his activities are centred around achievement of this goal. Using Maslow's hierarchy, he could be easily placed under 'seeking security'. Promise of a secure job will trigger high degree of motivation and engagement at the workplace. However, his supervisor has a bad reputation of managing employees and one day, he shouts at Ramnath in front of his colleagues. Although Ramnath tolerates the verbal abuse to avoid a confrontation, the supervisor takes advantage of his submissiveness and abuses him further. Ramnath loses control of his emotions and leaves the job. As per the theory, he is at the 'security need' strata, but his esteem need emerged as the most important need under this emotional experience. He has graduated to a higher level of need and responded as such.

Table 6.1 Motivating and hygiene factors

Motivating factors	Hygiene factors
Achievement	Company policy
Recognition	Supervision
Work itself	Relationship with boss
Responsibility	Work conditions
Advancement	Good salary
Growth	Relationship with peers
—	Security

to dissatisfaction. These factors are termed as hygiene factors. Similarly, there are some factors called motivating factors, which will generate satisfaction such as recognition, responsibility, and advancement; however, their absence will not generate dissatisfaction.

He developed new terminology to describe the state of satisfaction/dissatisfaction and argued that the opposite of dissatisfaction is not satisfaction, but 'no dissatisfaction'. Similarly, the opposite of satisfaction is not dissatisfaction, but 'no satisfaction' (Fig. 6.2).

Critique Arguments advanced by Herzberg appear to be true; however, this theory is not free from criticism. Majority of the critiques is centred on the methodology deployed by Herzberg in his research, and it is argued that it is the reason behind the unique outcome of the research. However, some of the research works (Matzler and Renzl 2007) found that the theory propounded by Herzberg appears to be true.

Adams' Equity Theory

Adams' equity theory provides another lens to advance our understanding about employee motivation. It indicates that each employee evaluates himself or herself against other employees of the organization in terms of workload, remuneration, supervisory treatment, and so on. In case this comparative evaluation provides negative results and indicates a lower return in comparison with the inputs, the employee concerned will be unhappy and demotivated. However, in case the employee finds positive results out of this comparison and sees that he or she is getting more than the input, he or she will be motivated.

Figure 6.2 Conceptual framework of Herzberg's theory

Thus,

Output/Input = Positive result $\rightarrow$ Employee will be motivated.

Output/Input = Negative result $\rightarrow$ Employee will not be motivated.

This theory provides important perspectives to advance our understanding as to how one individual arrives at a conclusion about the fairness in the organization. This theory gave birth to the theory of organizational justice. Unfair perception about the rules, procedures, and treatment from supervisors may grossly demotivate an individual. On the contrary, in case employees perceive that they are being fairly treated in the organization, they will be motivated.

B.F. Skinner's Reinforcement Theory

Skinner proposed a reinforcement theory that is based on manipulation of reward and punishment to achieve the desired level of performance. This theory endeavours to control human behaviour by controlling/manipulating punishment and reward. This theory assumes that human behaviour is controllable. Desirable behaviour could be reinforced by rewarding the performance, whereas undesirable behaviour could be reduced by imposing punishment. Reward becomes the language of desirability. Strengthening behaviour by reward is known as *positive reinforcement*, whereas weakening undesirable behaviour by punishment is known as *negative reinforcement*. The spirit of the theory is widely used in hospitality organizational context. The management provides increment to excellent performers to reinforce excellence in performance. Good increment will work as reinforcement for future performance. Thus, an HR professional uses reward and punishment to control employee behaviour.

Current status Employee motivation appears to be a critical issue for every organization. Therefore, every organization keeps a close watch on the employee motivation level. Various consultancy firms report that employee motivation is relatively down and is a critical challenge than ever before. It is very difficult to find employees who have not attempted for or applied for another job. In fact, in many cases, employees are working in the organization because they do not have better option elsewhere. Therefore, it is most likely to be reflected in the production and delivery of service.

MEASUREMENT OF EMPLOYEE MOTIVATION

The underlying logic and associated benefits that could be accrued from motivated workforce are clear from the earlier discussions. However, it is difficult to know whether employees are motivated. Each manager may have an inflated guess-estimation about the motivation level of their employees. However, with the advent of data-driven management practices, the HR manager deploys a number of measures to gauge the level of employee motivation. These are discussed in the following subsections.

Employee Satisfaction Survey

The HR department regularly conducts employee satisfaction surveys to estimate the level of job satisfaction among employees. This satisfaction score provides critical insights about the source of motivation/demotivation and helps pinpoint the source of motivation. Depending on the feedback received in the survey, the HR manager could undertake decisive actions to improve the employee satisfaction score. Interestingly, in a lot of performance-driven organizations, the employee satisfaction score is linked with the performance bonus of the HR manager, thereby making it their responsibility to work towards generating high employee satisfaction scores. This clearly indicates that the management understands that high level of employee motivation is crucial for the success of any organization, and by linking the bonus of the HR manager with the employee satisfaction score, it clearly communicates to the employees how seriously they consider the issue.

Turnover Rate

Turnover rate indicates the number of employees who leave an organization during a specific period. In case a good number of employees have left the organization during a specific period, it indicates that the employee motivation is not necessarily high—hence, they are opting out to join other organizations. Low turnover rate indicates that the organizational infrastructure is suitable for the employees.

Walk the Talk

Many HR executives undertake 'walk the talk' philosophy to get a first-hand feel of employee motivation. This indicates engaging employees near their workstations, in their natural workplace, or any other public place other than the HR manager's office. When the conversation unfolds in their natural setting with the HR person, it provides the employees informal opportunities to express their thoughts and provide feedback to the managers about the perceptions of the welfare initiatives undertaken by the HR department.

Incidence of Counterproductive Behaviour

In many organizations, it has been found that employees engage in various counterproductive behaviours such as stealing, fighting, breaking and damaging company's property. Regular cases such as these indicate that the motivational level of employees appears to be low and requires immediate attention and corrective action.

GOAL-SETTING THEORY

Setting goal increases the chance of getting success. Needless to say, clear articulation of the goal is very important, that is, 20 per cent growth in sales during next one quarter. Research indicates that by setting goals, an individual experiences a drive towards the goals to achieve. Employees focus their attention on goal-relevant activities, moving away from all the works, which does not contribute to the fulfilment of goals. Having a challenging target provides joy of achieving it—thus, goals work as energizers. Installing some superordinate goals in the work place such as 'to be a number one innovative company' unites employees for a mission and energizes the whole workspace. It generates a sense of belonging and a sense of purpose. Goal provides an external reference point for immediate comparison, thus providing immediate feedback on the level of performance. As a result, an employee becomes capable of taking immediate corrective actions required for the achievement of goals. Thus, the inherent capacity of setting attractive goals provides considerable impetus to guide employee's performance.

However, setting attractive goals may not necessarily produce excellent performance. Setting goals in an organization where employees do not display higher degree of commitment will not produce high level of performance. Setting goals among committed employees will definitely improve performance. Employees must believe that the goal set by the management is achievable within the time frame. However, if that goal is perceived as too high by the employees, they may not even try to achieve it. Thus, setting goal does not automatically translate into positive performance, unless it is orchestrated and nurtured well within the organization.

Creative Tension

Peter Senge (1990) attempted to explain the relationship between goal setting and performance. He argued that an individual needs to know two things in clear terms: (i) the goal that needs to be achieved and (ii) the current reality. He believed that acknowledgement of goal and realization of current reality will generate enough positive and creative tension. This process will automatically generate enough force for achievement of goals.

Management by Objectives

Management by objectives (MBO) is a structured approach to set goals in an organization. Peter Drucker (1954) popularized this concept in his book, *The Practice of Management*. Goals set by the top managements, after a thorough deliberation, subsequently have cascaded down across hierarchies. MBO provides a structured framework for developing organizational goals, devising a detailed roadmap for achievement of goals, allocating resources and responsibilities for achievement of goals, and correcting the actions in case of deviance from the grand gameplan. For example, suppose that the managing director of an Indian hospitality company fixes a sales target of ₹2750 crores for one year (Fig. 6.3). This target is planned to be achieved from three streams of business: travel business (250 crores), casino operations (1500 crores), and hotel operations (1000 crores). These targets again get distributed among its strategic business units (SBUs). Thus, irrespective of hierarchies, the employee shares some part of the grand objectives. This has been designed to generate enthusiasm, ownership of goal, linking employee functions with the grand game plan, and provide meaning to the employees.

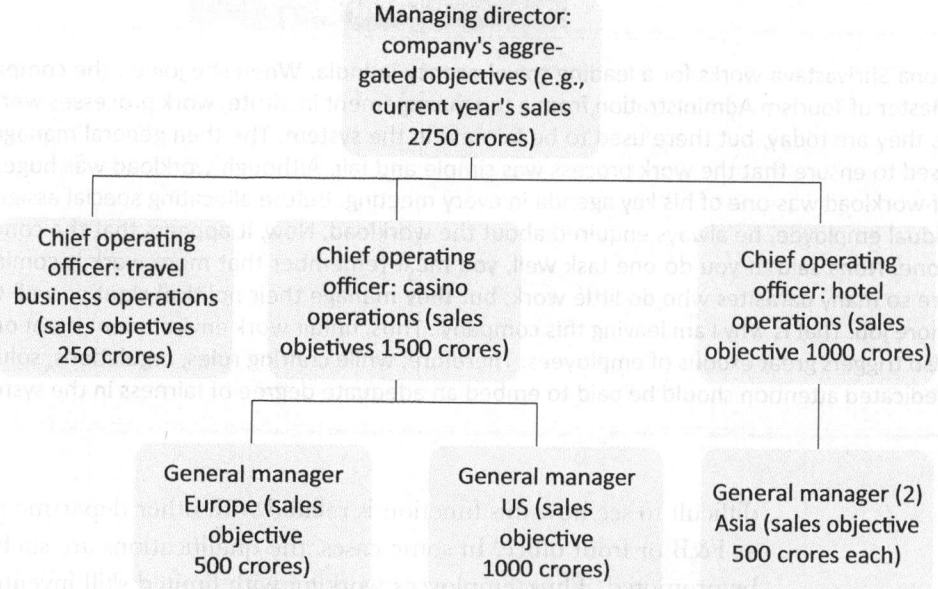

Figure 6.3 Management by objectives demonstrating cascading effect of goal setting

HOW TO MOTIVATE EMPLOYEES

To survive in today's chaotic business conditions, each organization needs to use its human resource effectively. Employees are guided and motivated to perform at their best. To ensure that employees perform effectively, an HR manager undertakes a number of initiatives.

Fair work process Work fairness perception is crucial for employee motivation. If employees perceive that their supervisor is biased towards certain individuals without sufficient reasons or merit, they will feel demotivated. They believe that the supervisory patronage could not be acquired by demonstrating good quality of work and thus, they will not be motivated to display positive behaviour towards their work. Most managers pay considerable attention to the development and maintenance of fair organizational infrastructure. Fair perception about the supervisor will provide sound logic to the employee to demonstrate the highest quality of work for supervisory patronage. Thus, in an unfair workspace, supervisory patronage is linked with other unscientific basis, whereas in a fair workspace, the supervisor is believed to be linked with good quality of work. It is important that the HR department maintains rules, policies, and procedures that are fair. This follows the recommendations provided by Adams' equity theory.

Job rotation Employees get bored with similar type of work. Sales agent in a sales counter may get bored with selling tickets over the years; a room boy in the housekeeping department may become so myopic in his perspectives that it will be

Nona Shrivastava works for a leading travel agency in India. When she joined the company after doing her Master of Tourism Administration from a top management institute, work processes were not as developed as they are today, but there used to be fairness in the system. The then general manager, Stuart Simpson, used to ensure that the work process was simple and fair. Although workload was huge, equal distribution of workload was one of his key agenda in every meeting. Before allocating special assignments to any individual employee, he always enquired about the workload. Now, it appears that the concept of workload is gone. Nona said 'If you do one task well, you must remember that more work is coming your way. There are so many parasites who do little work; but they manage their political clout so well that they never get more job. That is why I am leaving this company'. Thus, unfair work environment is not only demotivating, it also triggers great exodus of employees. Therefore, while crafting rules, regulations, solutions, and policies, dedicated attention should be paid to embed an adequate degree of fairness in the system.

difficult to see how this function is related with other departmental functions such as F&B or front office. In some cases, the qualifications are such that they cannot be promoted. Thus, employees working with limited skill inventory get stuck with low category of work, and it is difficult to motivate these employees. Most business institutions operating over the last few decades have inherited this problem. Job rotation could be a plausible way of motivating employees by rotating them among different types of jobs within/similar skill levels. In banks, employees continuously change their role between cashier, counter clerk, and so on. Job rotation brings in a variety of experience, uses different ways of handling a job, and thus gives enough freedom to each employee and helps him or her learn new skills. Monotony, which otherwise has been created over the years doing the same job, could be reduced by placing a job rotation programme for the employees. Such job rotation helps develop multiskilled workforce inventory, which could be utilized at the time of emergency. This recommendation adheres to the theory advanced by Herzberg.

For example, a hotel managed by a leading hotel chain in India was often confronted with labour shortage. Temporary deployment of contract workers reduced quality of service delivery, and as a result, customer complaints piled up. Contract workers were deployed from semi-skilled market, and they lacked in communication, service knowledge, and aesthetic attributes. It was important to stop deterioration in service delivery, so the general manager invited employees' contribution in this matter and promised to compensate by monetary measures. Twenty five employees responded to this invitation, and under this scheme, they were trained in various departmental activities across the hotel using job rotation. They were nicknamed RDF (rapid deployment force). They earned double wages for any additional work done, and they got high visibility and key employee status. Within two years, most of them were recommended for promotions in various hotels and most of them were selected for foreign postings, where earning in dollar terms always appears to be attractive among hospitality employees.

Job enrichment   Employees possess a number of skills; however, a fixed job provides limited opportunities to utilize all these skills that an employee possesses. Extending the thoughts outlined by Herzberg, job enrichment provides opportunity to utilize a wide variety of skills. Under this arrangement, employees are allowed to execute a wide variety of jobs or a complete sequence of tasks. For example, chefs in the kitchen traditionally remain limited at the kitchen. Under job enrichment plan, chefs are allowed to interact with the guests and gain wide variety of experience. Thus, a chef experiences a complete cycle of production of customer satisfaction.

Employee recognition programme   Employee recognition programmes are widely practised in service industry. Under such programmes, employees who display extraordinary service attitude and deliver exceptional services to customers are recognized publicly. Many organizations have dedicated display boards where they acknowledge the excellent service provided by employees. This public recognition is indeed a great encouragement for the employees, especially those working in the service delivery wing. This recommendation adheres to the theory advanced by Herzberg.

Joy at work   Happy employees will produce more spontaneous service to their customers. Joy at work signifies a wide range of activities, which are potentially designed for bringing happiness to the workplace. It involves public demonstration of drama, skit, dance, musical activities, and so on, for the consumption of employees and is an attempt to breed a sense of family. Employees in many good companies view themselves as an extended family. Cost benefit ratio is not considered while extending a helping hand to another family member, and in such an environment, the customer also becomes a part of the extended family. It is important to see that joy at work activities does not become a victim of bureaucratic procedures, which have the potential to kill the joy from the 'Joy at Work' programme. The designer of such a programme should be creative and should allow spontaneity to guide. Many a times, such programmes do not produce joy at all and have fallen

---

EXAMPLE

Taj Hotels, Resorts, and Palaces has launched a Special Thanks and Recognition System, which attempts to recognize the employees who have extended extraordinary services to guests. Employees could be recognized by fellow colleagues, supervisors, managers, or guests. Once a recommendation is received, it should be processed within 24 h. It is a web-based system that is integrated with other human resource information systems (HRISs). Employees also score points for recommendation and are graded as per the number of recommendations and number of points they have achieved, which makes them members of the prestigious COO's (Chief Operating Officer's) Club, Managing Director's Club, and so on. This is indeed an excellent attempt to bring in tireless efforts of hotel employees to the forefront of business achievement, and motivates employees to improve their service delivery.

victim of the design. This recommendation adheres to the theory advanced by Herzberg.

Good remuneration   Good remuneration works as a great motivator. It is an acknowledgement of good work demonstrated by the employee and encourages positive work attitude and excellence in service delivery. It has the potential to motivate; however, it should be exercised in conjunction with other initiatives mentioned earlier. HR executives undertake a number of initiatives to develop attractive remuneration packages as listed here.

Crafting it in tune with workforce requirement   The composition of workforce is undergoing a subtle change in India; it is predominantly the younger generation, which is the most productive workforce of our times. Life perspectives and expectations are not the same as it used to be, and the remuneration package should be in tune with their requirement. For example, the turnover rate among these young employees is very high, and they do not stay with a company for a long duration; hence, gratuity benefits, which are usually given on completion of five years of uninterrupted services, are not important to them, and they will prefer more real-time earning such as cash or other immediate benefits, which could be accrued during their limited relationship.

Design your own pay packet   Life requirement of each individual employee is unique and different from that of the other. Therefore, developing a comprehensive compensation and benefit policy is relatively difficult. Because of this, many organizations have introduced 'design your own pay packet'. During the job interview, only CTC (cost to company) is agreed on, and it is the employee who designs the salary structure within the limit of the CTC. Thus, the remuneration policy gets tuned to the requirement of the employees, which makes it realistic, contemporary, as if it is 'made for each other'. This recommendation adheres to the theory advanced by Skinner and Herzberg.

Income tax friendly manner   Some companies change the remuneration structure so that the tax burden on employees becomes relatively less. Under such a scheme, the designer of remuneration package takes the advantages of the various provisions of the Income Tax Act 1961 and its various amendments from time to time so as to have lower incidence of tax liability on individual employees.

Demonstrative linkage between performance and pay   HR managers look for new ways to link pay and performance. Traditional performance appraisal inherits weaknesses such as personal bias of the supervisor, subjective evaluation, and disagreement of what performance constitutes, and the scores achieved are hardly representative of the employee's performance. Therefore, it does not make sense to link it with performance. Balanced scorecard provides numeric indicators for the last year's performance. Attempts to link balanced scorecard score with performance appear to be on the rise. However, it requires further deliberation and subscription to the balanced scorecard philosophy.

Assurance of good supervision Employees do not often get the opportunity to meet top management personnel, but they meet their supervisor everyday. For these employees, the supervisor becomes the face and representative of the company. In most cases, employees do not leave the company. They leave their supervisors. It implies that the influence of a good supervisor is one of the critical factors for employee motivation. Assurance of good supervision potentially contributes a positive image about the company; similarly, the presence of a bad supervisor may ruin the reputation of the company. Thus, employees working at supervisory levels should be educated well so that their supervision does not ruin the reputation of the company, but they should work in tandem with the employee and ensure that the employee and supervisor collectively achieve the organizational goals, which would also ensure enhanced transparency in the practices. This recommendation adheres to the theory advanced by Herzberg.

Work–life balance In most cases, work stress level is very high among hotel employees, and they are connected with their workplace virtually throughout the day. Physical presence in the workplace for long hours has also gone up substantially, and this has snatched time, which can otherwise be used for personal life. With the advent of internet and mobile technology, the finer line between personal and work life has blurred, and employees are hardly able to spend quality and unperturbed time with their family members, as they constantly get, work-related calls on their mobiles and have to access mails on their internet-enabled mobiles or laptops. This is especially true for salespersons or those in reservations and causes substantial stress in the family. In addition, hotel employees have to work for long hours and might go for days without an off or might have to do odd shifts, which destroys the balance between work and life. This can potentially cause demotivation, and the HR department needs to create an adequate space so that each employee can spend time with his or her family and work optimally. This recommendation adheres to the theory advanced by Herzberg.

Employee training Employee training plays a crucial role in enhancing an employee's skill set and level of self-confidence. Inadequately trained employees experience difficulties while producing good-quality work. Bad quality of service to the customer makes the employee unhappy and demotivated. Thus, employee training contributes to enhance the confidence of the employees, which in turn motivates them. This recommendation adheres to the theory advanced by Herzberg.

Crafting an interesting job Job crafting should be done in such a way that the job itself becomes very interesting. For example, a job with adequate autonomy may generate satisfaction. Oldham and Hackman (1980) provided insight to make any job interesting. They argued that every job, no matter how small it is, should have the following characteristics:

- *Task significance* The task should be perceived by the employee as significant.
- *Task identity* The task should have a distinct identity.

- *Task variety*   It signifies whether the task involves a number of different types of work or repetitive task with monotonous experience.
- *Autonomy*   The job should provide adequate autonomy in decision making, designing, execution, and improvement.
- *Feedback*   The employee should receive timely feedback about the work.

These characteristics in any job potentially provide a range of experiences of meaningfulness of work and responsibilities for work outcomes. Research has indicated that a job composed with the help of the attributes mentioned earlier will potentially generate intrinsic motivation, and thereby positively affect job satisfaction. Each of these components provides job-specific satisfaction and makes it interesting, thereby causing positive experience. Therefore, companies initiate a wide range of programmes to make work interesting by launching job-enlargement and job-enrichment programmes, which motivate the employees to work harder. This recommendation adheres to the theory advanced by Herzberg.

Empowerment   Customers' demand is so prolific that it is difficult to predict. Although each organization makes considerable effort to design the blueprint of the service delivery system, the customer may make a demand that is beyond the standard design. To fulfil the demand of customers, each employee is given power and authority to deliver services. In many cases, employees may experience certain limitations of authority to execute the work and may believe that they are not empowered to handle the customer's request and need the necessary permission from higher authority to deliver a particular solution. In some organizations, employees are given abundant power to satisfy the guests. For example, it is said that in Ritz Carlton Hotel, each employee has been given a very high degree of empowerment and can even spend up to $3000 to satisfy the customer. This empowerment provides speed to the service delivery process, and also, employees experience satisfaction as they experience autonomy in execution of the work. This recommendation adheres to the theory advanced by Herzberg.

Welfare initiatives   Legal provisions mentioned in different labour legislations recommend bare minimum welfare provisions. Each hospitality organization has legal mandate to undertake a diverse range of welfare activities for their employees. However, most enlightened hospitality organizations have gone beyond the legal mandate of the Indian government and launched a wide variety of labour welfare schemes for the employees and their families. For example, most of these companies have schemes for children's education policy, medical and hospitalization policy, and so on. This recommendation adheres to the theory advanced by Herzberg.

Positive organizational support   Positive organizational support is a kind of perception held by individual employees pertaining to the value attributed by the organization. It is a kind of belief about the organization that individual employees hold. Some tentative thoughts, reflecting positive organizational support, could be as listed here:

1. My organization cares about my opinions.
2. My organization really cares about my well-being.
3. My organization strongly considers my goals and values.
4. Help is available from my organization when I have a problem.
5. My organization is willing to help me if I need a special favour.

When individual employees find that the contribution made to their organization is well appreciated, it generates a positive spirit and motivates them for more contribution towards the organization.

Stock option With the advent of knowledge economy, employee stock options policy (ESOP) has been launched to attract and retain talented employees in the organization. This scheme is essentially awarded to managerial and executive employees. There are certain SEBI (Securities and Exchange Board of India) guidelines regarding the administration of ESOP, which provide partial ownership to the company that the employees have built over the years. Besides regular salaries, stake in the growth of the company provides unlimited encouragement to be a part of what they contribute to build. Owning the future growth of the company works as great motivator for the employees. This recommendation adheres to the theory advanced by Skinner.

Offsite fun activities Employees regularly interact in the workplace, and their terms of interactions with each other always have work-related flavour. In many occasions, some interactions go bad and generate huge dissatisfaction. People develop a lot of unexpressed grudges, which may hold them from participating in work activities with full spirit, sour the relationship, and make the workplace toxic. This kind of environment is extremely dysfunctional and leaves a negative impact on the employees and eventually is harmful to the overall well-being of the company. In such a situation, employees mostly engage in routine activities and handle the job perfunctorily without any major concern for anything. Therefore, the HR department organizes employee interactions in offsite fun activities, which provides opportunity to employees to deal with each other on non-work-related issues. This recommendation adheres to the theory advanced by Herzberg.

Participative work processes Goal-setting theories suggest that fixation of goal should not be considered as the prerogative of managers and supervisors. Fixation of goals without involving the grass-root-level employees is bound to have malnourished solutions. In today's knowledge economy, grass-root employees have privilege knowledge of what is happening at the service delivery point, and supervisors and managers have access to comprehensive and summary perspective. Both these dimensions should be used to frame the solution and goal. Thus, when a goal is nourished with the collective wisdom of the group, the goal set by the employees will have higher challenge to achieve. Thus, collective goal setting could be highly inspiring and motivating. The goal set by collective efforts is owned by the group as well as the individual, and failure in such kind of collective environment does not remain an option.

This recommendation adheres to the theory advanced by Herzberg.

GROUP MOTIVATION

The scheme designed to motivate individuals may not motivate group effort. It is important to note that most of the service production is the ultimate expression of multiple members working in a synchronized manner. For example, while conversing with guests, the front-office assistant steward comes to know about their specific preference for a chocolate brand. He or she updates the customer databank regarding this preference and informs rooms division to put special chocolates in those guests' rooms, which is finally done. The guest will be delighted at such a gesture and comment positively. When most functions in the hospitality industry are centred on groups, there must be concurrent compensatory provisions for participation in group efforts.

Individuals should get dividend for participation in group performance, and there should be enough incentive to an individual for participation in group. The HR department should devise adequate measures to motivate individuals for group participation. For example, some part of the incentives could be linked with group achievement. A case in point could be sales target for the department and customer satisfaction score of the front-office department. Under the balanced scorecard scheme, a good number of metrics could be based on group target. Achievement of these group targets is usually linked with performance bonus. Thus, the right composition of individual- and group-based remuneration schemes is essential for smooth operation of functions.

BENCHMARKING

Benchmarking is a tool for identifying, comparing, and measuring best practices of industry leader and best practices from other industries. Is it possible to copy the best practices from most admired or successful organizations? Imitating organizational practices from successful companies is not new; academic literature provides rich data about the various practices among Fortune 500 companies. These visionary companies developed practices to integrate employees under meaningful pursuits. Newspaper, business, and academic journals report a huge number of good practices. Budgetary restrictions may not make this practice possible in every hotel, and even if it is followed, the hotel may not be as successful as Ritz Carlton hotels. The question is, 'what is to be done?'

Many hospitality organizations imitate current corporate practices; however, uprooting practices from one organization and fixing it for another organization, with completely different set of histories and unique culture, does not appear to be a great recommendation. It is important that before implementing any practice, highest degree of discretion is exercised. What is successful in one organization may not be successful in another, as each organization operates under specific dynamics, which could be social, political, and economic milestones of the company's history. Therefore, it is important to know what the other companies are doing; however, HR managers are encouraged to develop practices that are suitable for their own organization, as it will increase the likelihood of success.

Motivated employees have been described as the most inimitable resource, who definitely provide the hospitality organization an edge over competition. Imitating current successful practices of an admired and successful organization does not make another organization great, as each requires persistent and patient nurturing. Therefore, it is important that creative crafting of schemes for motivating employees should be the homework of each HR executive who should carve it out as per the history and unique culture of his or her organization.

SUMMARY

Employee motivation is very crucial for service excellence. Employee motivation is a crucial asset for any organization—lack of motivated staff in a hospitality organization will have the potential to destroy the hotel operation and its performance, whereas motivated staff will generate relatively higher degree of customer satisfaction. Therefore, most of the human resource managers in hospitality organizations allocate a significant amount of time to devise and implement strategies to motivate employees.

Without full-fledged support from the employees, no organization can achieve the success it aspires. Motivated and inspired employees are great assets because of the following reasons:

1. They are essential for fault-free delightful service delivery.
2. They cannot be easily imitated by other organizations; thus, potentially they provide a competitive edge over others.
3. Motivated employees fill up gaps, if any, in the organizational system proactively and do not let the customer know the deficiency in the system.
4. Employees go the extra mile to satisfy the guest, even if it is not within the mandate of the service design.

KEY TERMS

Equity This is a kind of perception that recommends rewarding employees as per their respective contributions to the organizational performance. Violation of this principle will bring unjust or inequitable experience for the employees.

Hygiene factors As per Herzberg, some of the factors, such as good salaries and working conditions, do not have the potency to motivate individuals; however, absence of these factors could potentially demotivate them. These factors are called hygiene factors.

Joy at work   Adding fun at the workplace potentially brings joy to the people.
Motivating factors   As per Herzberg, some of the factors, such as recognition and career advancement, have the potential power to improve employee motivation. These factors are called motivating factors.

EXERCISES

Concept Review Questions

1. Critically examine the framework developed by Maslow pertaining to hierarchy theories of employee motivation. To what extent do you agree with this theory? How could you use this theory?
2. It could be argued that Herzberg's two-factor theory provides excellent guidance to human resource professionals for making any workplace motivational. To what extent do you agree with the statement?
3. Devise several strategies to motivate employees in your workplace.

Critical Thinking Questions

1. Review various initiatives undertaken by HR managers to motivate employees of a five-star hotel/travel service agency, where you have undergone your industrial training. How far are these initiatives adequate for the current challenges faced by the employees?
2. Reflect about yourself as an employee/student. Find all the elements that potentially motivate you. Do all the theories adequately explain all the drivers that motivated you in your life so far?
3. Are crisis situations such as the Mumbai terror attacks or the Bali bombings exceptions to motivational theories?

Assignment

If you start a small restaurant in your hometown after passing out the hotel management examination, what different motivational techniques will you use to motivate your staff? Imagine a happy organization you will create there—how do you create happiness among your staff members?

REFERENCES

Atkinson, J.W., 'Motivational Determinants of Risk-taking Behavior', *Psychological Review*, Volume 64, 1957, p. 359–372.

Drucker, P., *The Practice of Management*, Harper Collins, New York, 1954.

Herzberg, F., *The Motivation to Work*, John Wiley & Sons, New York, 1959.

Matzler, K. and Renzl, B 'Assessing Asymmetric Effects in the Formation of Employee Satisfaction', *Tourism Management*, Volume 28, Issue 4, 2007, p.1093–1103.

Maslow, A., *Motivation and Personality*, Harper and Row, New York, 1954.

Senge, P.M., *The Fifth Discipline*, Doubleday/Currency, 1990.

Oldham, G.R. and Hackman, J.R., 'Work Design in the Organizational Context', *Research in Organizational Behaviour*, Volume 2, 1980 p. 247–278.

CASE STUDY I

VICTIM BY DESIGN

Florence has been working for a travel agency almost since the beginning of the company. She is skilled, hardworking, and sincere in her work. However, as she joined the company 20 years ago, right after school, she did not get time to study further. She feels that although she gets everyone's respect, college-educated, professionally qualified individuals are appointed her boss, giving her direction on what she should do. She has recently begun to feel left out. She feels that she should have been a little selfish and should have completed her graduation and postgraduation, rather than giving her full attention to her work. The company does not maintain any history; being a performance-driven organization, each day each individual needs to fulfil the need of the customer. Thus, she feels that she is a loser. She feels that she is the victim of her own design. She is feeling down. She is now 42 years old and does not have better opportunities outside. Hence, she cannot leave the job.

Discussion Questions

You are working as a human resource manager in this organization.
1. How would you motivate Florence?
2. Do you think that the career of Florence could have been managed better by the organization? Provide rationale.
3. Do you think Florence mismanaged her career? Provide adequate rationale for your answer.

CASE STUDY II

CHECKMATE

Raja works as a barman for the last 10 years. By the very nature of the job, he has extensive knowledge about wines, liquors, whiskey, and all other types of alcoholic beverages. He feels that the job is interesting because he likes the very nature of the job. Besides, he makes a lot of money out of tips he receives from the guests. However, recently, he has been a little worried. Many colleagues, who have worked with him and perhaps many of them who started their career together, have been promoted and transferred to other hotel properties. He thinks perhaps he is getting stuck with the job. He thinks that perhaps the very nature of his job is making him stagnant in one place. It is causing a little bit of uneasiness. Simon, the new food and beverage manager, has made some changes in the tips distribution system, where his seniority does not get any additional weightage; thus, his monthly earning has also gone down substantially.

Discussion Questions

You are working as the HR manager in the hotel; you are required to provide a suitable solution to this problem.

1. Do you think that Raja is getting stagnant in one place because of the very nature of his job? Provide rationale.
2. Do you think that Raja could be motivated in his existing position? Provide rationale.
3. Do you think that Raja deserves a promotion? Provide rationale.
4. How would you motivate Raja? Chalk out a detailed plan.

7 Compensation and Benefit Management

INTRODUCTION

In Chapter 6, we have discussed employee motivation. In this chapter, we discuss the key instrument of motivation—compensation and benefits. Compensation signifies all forms of payments made by an organization to its employees. It is called compensation because it is given for the work done by the employees. Compensation management is a critical function of the HR department. Wrong calculation and design of compensation package brings bad reputation in the labour market, and thus prevents access to good-quality employees. A badly designed compensation policy might lead to mass leaving of employees, leading to retention problem. On the contrary, a good compensation policy creates good reputation in the market; thus, the organization always finds adequate supply of good quality manpower. India witnessed economic stagnation for many decades, when Indian economic development was based on heavy industries that had been created by the government. To begin and operate private-run organizations, the Indian government instituted a strict License Raj system, which created limited opportunity for employment. This limited opportunity gave birth to labour union activism, leading to collective bargaining for compensation. During the last decade, substantial changes have been made. The Indian economic growth engine has achieved 8–9 per cent GDP growth, which has caused a radical change in the labour market. It has moved from a seller's market to a buyer's market. In this chapter, we examine issues around employee compensation in Indian hospitality industry, developed through an integrated view using human psychology, labour economics, and labour laws.

COMPONENTS OF A COMPENSATION POLICY

The various components of a compensation policy are discussed in the following subsections.

Basic pay This is a fixed amount to be paid at the end of the month to each employee. This amount is arrived at on mutual agreement at the time of recruitment and could be legally sanctioned (such as the minimum wages to be paid to entry-level staff). HR department pays special attention to the structure of the basic pay as it is significant in two ways:

1. This becomes a permanent cost figure, which cannot be changed during business downturn and is a commitment made to employees in terms of payment. Therefore, the HR team attempts to keep this component relatively less so that compensation paid to the employees could be changed in tune with the business cycle.

2. Most of the legal contributions (13 per cent of basic pay as provident fund subscription, 4.75 per cent of basic pay as employees' state insurance subscription, 15 days' basic pay as gratuity, 8.33 per cent to 20 per cent of basic as bonus, etc.) are made on the basis of basic pay. This entails huge cost burden to the companies. To have less cost incidence on payroll budget, the HR executives pay specific attention to this issue (Fig. 7.1).

Variable pay Variable pay is that part of the compensation policy which ensures payment as per the cost of living, performance of employees, and so on. This part of the compensation is not fixed and varies according to a number of criteria. Similarly, the amount of performance bonus paid by many hospitality organizations is pegged with last year's performance. This provides blanket coverage to contain the labour cost, especially in the years of recession or bad market conditions. Most of the enlightened companies give more emphasis on the payment of bonus to its executives. It is important to note that this performance bonus is over and above

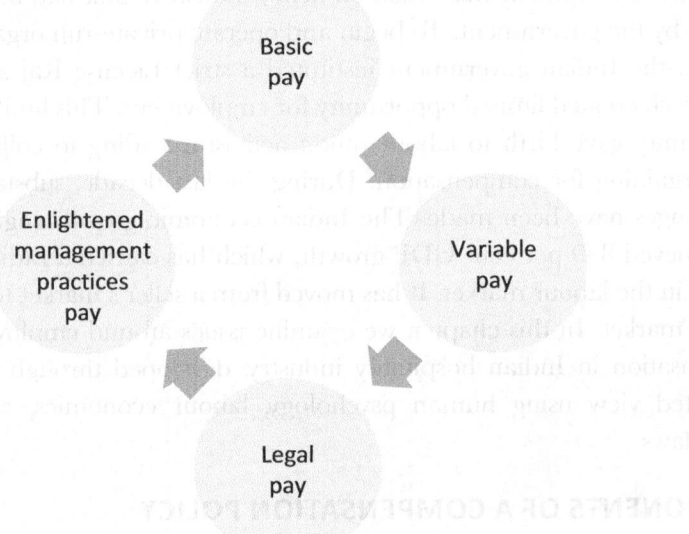

Figure 7.1 Components of compensation policy

the bonus granted under the Payment of Bonus Act, 1965. Variable pay aims at linking performance payment dynamics and brings accountability in the whole compensation policy (Fig. 7.1).

Legal benefits Indian labour legislations envisage a number of benefits for employees working in hospitality sectors, and no business institution can run its operation without adhering to the mandates given by the various labour legislations (Fig. 7.1). Some of them are briefly highlighted here.

The Minimum Wages Act This Act provides guidelines about the minimum wages to be paid to any employee for his or her work. No business institution should pay less than this mandatory wage rate, and violation of any clause or section of this Act attracts legal punishment, which includes fines and/or jail sentence.

The Equal Remuneration Act This Act mandates that no discrimination should be made between male and female employees working for any business institution.

The Payment of Wages Act This Act addresses two important issues pertaining to employee compensation:
1. The amount and type of deductions that could be made from the wages as penalty/punishment to employees.
2. Time of payment of wages: As per this Act, wages should be paid latest by the seventh or tenth day from the close of the previous month.

In industrial organizations employing less than 1000 persons, salary shall be paid before the end of the seventh day from the close of the previous month. In case the number of employees working for the organization is more than 1000, wages should be paid by the tenth day from the close of the previous month.

Employee Provident Fund and Miscellaneous Provisions Act This Act is a part of social security measures, which ensures that 12 per cent of basic pay is deducted and deposited with the provident fund commissioner, and an equal amount is paid by the employer. On retirement or termination of service, this amount is given back to the employee with interest.

Employees State Insurance Act Under this scheme, an employee gets a blanket coverage for five types of benefits (medical assistance, hospitalization, maternity benefit, etc.) against 1.5 per cent of wages as subscription. The employer needs to pay 4.75 per cent of wages against each employee (whose salary is less than ₹13,000 per month).

The Payment of Bonus Act Employees who have completed at least 30 days work in a year are eligible for bonus ranging from 8.33 per cent to 20 per cent of basic wages. This should be paid latest by 30 November the next year.

The Payment of Gratuity Act Employees are eligible for gratuity on completion of five years of services in an organization. Employees who have served the hospitality organization for five years or more are eligible for 15 days of basic wages for each completed year of service.

Enlightened management practices   Enlightened managements have introduced a number of employee benefits over and above the legal requirement. Some companies have introduced children education policy, medical policy, holiday policy, leave travel policy, and so on to encourage employees to stay with the company. These benefits help employees resolve issues arising out of their life stage. Taj Hotels, Resorts, and Palaces; SOTC; Thomas Cook; Oberoi Hotels; Lemon Tree; ITC; and so on—all have a number of employee-friendly policies to support employees.

OBJECTIVES OF A GOOD COMPENSATION SYSTEM

There are various objectives of a good compensation system. These are discussed in the following subsections.

Instrument for motivation   Compensation and benefits management is a key instrument to motivate employees in an organization. To reinforce good employee performance, organizations pay a good remuneration to excellent performers, whereas relatively less compensation is paid to average and below-average employees. Thus, compensation is the language and tool for effective management of employee motivation.

Equity in the organization   One of the basic objectives of compensation and benefit management is to maintain equitable salary and benefit structures, which is not only affordable for an organization to pay to its employees but also renders it attractive in the market so that they can attract good-quality manpower. Good compensation leads to happy employees who should be able to provide their best services to the customers. The world operates on the basis of these dynamics. Basic failure in adherence to equity principles could prove to be disastrous for any hospitality organization.

Discipline   Efficient compensation management also ensures industrial peace and harmony. Labour union participates with the management in negotiatiations over the wages and various benefits. The negotiated wage has been arrived at during a collective bargaining process between the management and the labour union, which ensured peaceful coexistence, especially during the last 60 years of industrial history of India. Deployment of wrong, inadequate, and inappropriate compensation policy will destroy industrial peace and harmony between the trade union and the management. Trade union members will not hesitate to undertake legal processes such as strike to redress the inequity in the compensation policy declared by the management. Therefore, a good compensation policy assures industrial peace and harmony and brings discipline into the system.

Language of desirability   Employees use remuneration as a yardstick for their performance. Receipt of good remuneration by the employees also indicates that the employee is important for the organization. Continuous acknowledgement by paying good remuneration to employees indicates how much importance an organization gives to the employee. Thus, remuneration becomes the language between employees and employers. In case employees perceive that the salary given in the present company is relatively less than the market price, then it could lead to mass resignations. On the contrary, in case an employee perceives the salary given by the company is higher than competition, this will motivate them to continue for a longer tenure in the organization.

Branded company   Good remuneration also helps build the brand in the labour market. Branded companies can easily access the labour market. They receive a lot of job applications from prospective employees. Therefore, good companies are always in a position to negotiate for lower wages. It also provides meaningful identity to the employees, which further enhances the chance of employability in the labour market.

DETERMINANTS OF AN EFFECTIVE COMPENSATION POLICY

There are various determinants of an effective compensation policy. These are discussed in the following subsections.

The labour market   The condition of the labour market plays a significant role in determining an appropriate compensation and benefit policy. High economic growth provides wider alternative employment opportunities to employees, whereas low economic growth reduces employment opportunity, and the compensation policy should be nimble enough to adjust itself in either of the market situations. Keeping these points in mind, the Indian hospitality industry has given more emphasis to variable pay.

Cost of living   Cost of living is one of the main determinants while deciding the salary structure. High cost of living could erode the real value of salary. Therefore, the hospitality organizations need to pay more to ensure that employees are able to maintain the same standard of living. Owing to the high cost of living in the United States, Canada, United Kingdom, and so on, a lot of top brands closed their respective production infrastructure there and moved to India, China, Brazil, and other emerging countries, the reason being that the lower cost of living in these countries works as an advantage as leading multinationals need to pay lower wages in emerging economies. Cost of living is not a fixed figure but a dynamic concept. The cost of items goes up because of inflation in the economy, which erodes the value of wages and salaries earned. Goods, products, and services become costlier because of inflation. You may not get the same quality and quantity of goods and services for ₹10,000 next month as you do this month, as the price for the items may increase (Table. 7.1). There is no legal regulation to link cost of living with wage structure for executives operating at managerial levels; however, the Indian government has enacted the Minimum Wages Act, which attempts to link

Table 7.1 Annual WPI inflation—new vis-à-vis old series

(per cent)

Items	Base year	Weight	Average 2005–06 to 2009–10	2010–2011*
WPI-all commodities	2004–2005	100.0	5.5	10.0
	1993–2004	100.0	5.4	10.6
1. Primary articles	2004–2005	20.1	9.2	19.3
	1993–1994	22.0	7.9	16.8
2. Fuel and power	2004–2005	14.9	5.9	13.5
	1993–1994	14.2	4.2	13.6
3. Manufactured products	2004–2005	65.0	4.1	5.6
	1993–1994	63.7	4.8	6.8
Memo items				
1. Food article and food products	2004–2005	24.3	8.1	14.2
	1993–1994	26.9	7.7	10.2
2. Non-food manufactured products	2004–2005	55.0	3.7	5.5
	1993–1994	52.2	4.2	7.2

*Relates to the period April–August.

Source: Mohanty, D. (2010).

the wages of marginal workers with the cost of living. Using various provisions of the Minimum Wages Act, the labour department revises dearness allowance twice a year, which is incorporated in the wage structure of the employees.

Labour unions   Labour unions exercised considerable amount of power to negotiate with the management for compensation and benefits. As discussed earlier, strong union leadership engages with the management under collective bargaining provisions. In terms of power dynamics, an individual employee is powerless while negotiating with the management to demand higher wages. Collective demands consist of a number of employees who garner strength to negotiate with the management for salary and wages. Over the last six decades, labour unions have significantly influenced the salary and wage growth of marginal employees, who otherwise do not get fair wages.

Economic condition of the country   Economic growth is deeply connected with the economic activities of the country. At the time of high economic growth, business institutions speed up the economic activities, and profitability goes up. To support economic growth, additional manpower is required, and recruitment function gears up to full swing. As each organization attempts to attract the best talent from the market, the salary range needs to be revised. On the contrary, during economic downturn, the speed of economic activities goes down, and most organizations make readjustments on a lower end of business operation and some reduce manpower count. Thus, the market has oversupply of manpower looking for job, and therefore, the remuneration package offered during business recession goes down substantially. In most cases, a depressed economy increases the labour supply, leading to lower average wage rate. Thus, economic growth is deeply connected with the remuneration package.

Legal provisions   In India, there are a number of legal provisions to extend social security benefits to employees, which are non-negotiable and should be fulfilled in order to operate in India (Table 7.2). For example, under the provisions of the Employees State Insurance (ESI) Act, all eligible employees should be members of the scheme and the employer should deposit an amount of 4.75 per cent of the wages of employees to the ESI authorities for onward disbursement, in case of any emergency. Similarly, each employee is eligible for provident fund contribution from employers. Table 7.2 highlights some legislations and their impact on the wages of employees.

There are some legal provisions that do not influence the salary amount directly but dictate terms for smooth wage and salary administration (Table 7.3). For example, the Equal Remuneration Act clearly articulates that the management should not make wage discrimination between male and female employees. Similarly, the Payment of Wages Act has framed rules and regulations about the administration

Table 7.2   Various labour legislations and their impact on employee compensation

Name of the legislations	Impact
The Employees State Insurance Act	4.75 per cent of the wages
The Employees Provident Fund and Miscellaneous Act	13.6 per cent of the wages (administrative charges included)
The Payment of Gratuity Act	15 days wages for every completed year of service
The Payment of Bonus Act	Minimum 8.33 per cent and maximum 20 per cent of wages

Table 7.3   Various labour legislations and their impact on wage administration

The Equal Remuneration Act	No discrimination between male and female employees
The Payment of Wages Act	Dictates terms of the date of wage distribution (seventh or tenth day after the close of the month)
	Dictates terms of various deductions that could be made from employee's wages
The Trade Union Act	Provides legal power to the union to negotiate for wage and benefit enhancements

of payment of wages, and this includes date of payment and various types of deductions, permitted under the provisions.

Ability to pay The compensation policy of a hospitality organization has a deeper linkage with what the organization can afford, that is, its ability to pay. For example, some hospitality organizations that were greatly affected by the economic downturn achieved stunted growth for a longer period. During that time, the economic bite on their profitability did not permit them to pay a higher salary to their employees. However, it is important to remember that hospitality organizations do not have the liberty to pay lower than the competitive organizations. It is very rare that some hospitality organizations find good quality of manpower in spite of paying lesser wages than the competition. In a hospitality organization, employee cost, food cost, and energy cost are the three most important pillars, which require skilful handling.

Nature of job Different types of jobs, done by different employees, bring or facilitate to bring monetary or non-monetary gains for the organizations they are working for. Thus, each job has its market price attached to it. Some of the skill sets are rare in the market place, while some are abundant in the market. Employees with rare skill sets attract high remuneration and vice versa. For example, even though receptionists and front-office associates do very important work in hospitality business, for these positions, the market receives huge supply every year through students who are passing out from the various hospitality management institutes. As this is an entry-level job, the salary negotiated for this job is relatively less than what a trained chef in the kitchen would negotiate for. Thus, acquisition of rare marketable skills is very important while getting educated in colleges.

Market information in pay Some hospitality organizations attempt to link the remuneration level with the market price attached to the specific job done by the individual employee. This reliance on market-based remuneration is outplayed by the brand value of different business organizations. For example, the HR executive is in a better position to negotiate lower wage/salary figures by arguing about the

---

EXAMPLE

Ghosh, the labour inspector, was conducting an inspection among small shops and found that none of the shop owners paid the minimum wages to their employees as per the Minimum Wages Act. They stated that they could not afford to pay the wages fixed by the labour department. Ghosh instructed them to pay the minimum wages and issued a notice. However, they continued to flout the provisions as their affordability did not permit them to pay such high wages to their employees. According to you, does their inability to pay override the legal provisions of the Minimum Wages Act? The answer is very clear—either they have to pay the minimum wages fixed under the legal provisions of the Minimum Wages Act or they should close their shop. Those who cannot afford to pay minimum wages do not have the right to operate—they have two options: either they should pay minimum wages, along with arrears, or should close their shops.

brand value of the company, which has a significant bearing on the career profile of employees; thus, it is not a bad thing to agree on salary figures a bit lower than the market rate. Some of the companies use market information in pay just as guidance; however, ultimately it has to be fine-tuned for specific candidates as per the experience, knowledge, and importance of the job. The HR department might experience difficulty in deciphering the market information regarding pay because most organizations put their employees under broadband of wages. Broadbanding gives the opportunity to put employees under some category of payment band as also it gives flexibility to fine-tune the exact amount of remuneration under a broad payment range. This kind of broadbanding practices essentially pose great problems to price employment positions. Broadbanding has created a huge range of possible remuneration, which could be fixed against a certain job. Broadbanding creates difficulties in providing guidance about job-based pricing. Thus, market survey pertaining to salary grade, along with the remuneration, is no longer useful. Therefore, market data should be used only to have broader guidance about the maximum and minimum remuneration that is paid against a certain job. The HR department needs to use a higher degree of discretion while using market information for fixing pay packets for employees.

PSYCHOLOGICAL THEORIES AND REMUNERATION

In Chapter 6, we have studied a number of psychological theories, which explained employee motivation. Let us now discuss how these theories are reflected in the current compensation and benefit management programmes of employees.

Maslow's need hierarchy theory   This theory postulated that all human needs are chained in hierarchy and once lower human needs are satisfied, an individual graduates to activities that satisfy higher needs. Compensation and benefit policies of most enlightened hospitality organizations adhere to these principles. Employees working in the lower hierarchy mostly have security needs, and a confirmed job in the company is considered by them to be more important. Executives working in managerial positions inherit esteem need, and benefits such as club membership and car with driver given to these employees will potentially fulfil this need.

Reinforcement theory   Various facets of the reinforcement theory, propounded by B.F. Skinner, are consistently used in the administration of compensation and benefit. To have repeated positive performance (exceeding sales target by 40 per cent, etc.), a few sales managers need to be rewarded. An individual failing to perform will not be given any increment. This kind of customer practice follows the basic theoretical and philosophical underpinning of reinforcement theory.

Herzberg two-factor theory   Good remuneration is considered to be a hygiene factor. As discussed in Chapter 6, hygiene factors indicate the presence of all those factors in an organization that do not have the potential to generate satisfaction; however, their absence generates dissatisfaction. Therefore, to motivate employees, utilization of compensation policy has its limitation and requires supplementary efforts, such as good supervisor–subordinate relationship and recognition for good performance.

EQUITY AND COMPENSATION MANAGEMENT

The HR manager, while designing the compensation policy, pays considerable amount of attention so that it adheres to the principles of equity. This is one of the critical factors that are given higher weightage by employees while comparing their contribution to the organization with the remuneration received. In case the employees perceive that their compensation policy violates the principles of equity, they will arrive at a conclusion that they are not fairly treated, which in turn will generate a high degree of employee dissatisfaction. This is not a good sign for any organization, and the HR team needs to actively manage equity perception among employees. Equity has different layers and forms, which include external equity, internal equity, employee equity, team equity.

External equity   Employees evaluate remuneration vis-à-vis the remuneration received by those who perform similar jobs in other firms. In case they discover that the market pays higher wages, the employees will feel that they are not being fairly treated by the organization. Dissatisfaction of employees will increase because of this feeling of receiving unfair treatment, which may find its expression in terms of sloppy service, high employee turnover, counterproductive behaviour, and so on.

Internal equity   Employees evaluate their remuneration vis-à-vis the remuneration of peers who are doing a similar type of work in the same organization. They expect that employees should be paid according to the relative value of their jobs within the organization. In case of breach of this perception, employees will feel that they are being unfairly treated, which will ultimately lead to employee dissatisfaction and other counterproductive behaviour within the organization.

Employee equity   Each employee inherits some degrees of uniqueness such as seniority, level of performance, and job experience. Employees expect that these unique qualities are given due weightage while fixing individual salaries. In case of violation, employees will feel discouraged to display specific skill sets at work for enhancement of customer experience. This will generate considerable service gap in the organization where the expectation of the customers will remain unmet. Sometimes, unique aspects such as seniority may not be marketable, as the new generation employees are efficient, fast, and dedicated. And the employee settles in the organization for lesser pay and works at the bare minimum level to preserve the job in the company and will not try to exceed customer expectations. Therefore, it is important that the unique qualities of employees are addressed through remuneration policy or other means.

Team equity   Hospitality organizations rely on team performance while providing services to its customers. It is akin to a relay race among individuals and groups. Therefore, the employee compensation policy should recognize team productivity as one of the determinants of the remuneration policy. Fairness in team-based performance indicates that successful teams should receive greater rewards than the less productive groups.

BUSINESS STRATEGY AND COMPENSATION

The business strategies of an organization also play a role while deciding the compensation and benefits of employees. Some of the strategies are discussed here.

Compensation Strategy during Recession

The hospitality industry flourishes when other industries do well in the market. Good business condition generates corporate travels, dealer meets, corporate launches, business gatherings, and so on. Hospitality industry fulfils the business need of corporate travellers. Banquet facility provides space for dealer meets, product launches, and business gatherings. The travel support services facilitate mass corporate travels. However, during recession, companies introduce measures such as huge travel cuts to restrain travel costs, postpone product launches, and refrain from business gatherings. Thus, hospitality organizations become tight-fisted, and the composition of the workforce requires fast changes in tune with the business situation. Some compensation strategies during recession include the following:

Salary structure   Most organizations discontinued salary hike and introduced performance-based bonus system. A salary hike is a permanent addition to the wage cost structure, which cannot be reduced at a later date. Performance bonus assures the achievement of performance targets against which bonus would be disbursed. Therefore, during recession, when most targets were not achieved, employees failed to get bonus. This meaningfully restrained the salary and wage cost structure for the organization.

Reduction of corporate travels   During recession, most companies restrained corporate travels, especially international travels. Several restrictions were imposed on travel of middle-level managers, such as prohibitions of first class air travel or requirement for permission from chief operating officer for domestic air travel. This helped reduce the organizational costs to a certain extent.

Reduction of employee costs   Some companies reduced employee cost by laying off employees, not hiring, and not replacing in case of voluntary turnover. This also resulted in substantial savings in labour costs.

Compensation Strategy during Business Boom

Compensation strategy during boom time requires careful interaction with the labour market. Economic boom creates a number of job opportunities in the labour market, which triggers a high turnover rate among employees. Besides, other segments of the service industry such as banking and retail poach talent from the hospitality sector. Although there are dedicated hotel management institutes producing hotel management graduates every year, there are very few dedicated programmes for the retail industry or banking until now. Therefore, as the employees from hospitality undergo training, interact with customers, and have the requisite skills and knowledge, employee poaching from the hospitality industry becomes a normal phenomenon. And it becomes difficult to recruit and retain good-quality staff or executives to run the business. As economic boom triggers huge employee turnover, recruitment becomes one of the prominent functions for the HR department during this time.

COMPENSATION AND DIVERSE PHILOSOPHICAL UNDERPINNINGS

Various aspects need to be kept in mind while deciding the compensation structure—the basis for pay, factors such as seniority or merit being the criteria to decide salaries to employees, and so on. Seniority as the criteria is the current practice being followed in government institutions. There are times when an individual may be a junior in terms of tenure of service but is a superior in terms of merit. Thus, the HR manager faces a critical dilemma while developing the compensation policy for the organization (Fig. 7.2). Here we examine various advantages and disadvantages of diverse philosophical underpinning and their impact on the employees, organization, and so on.

Seniority-based pay Seniority-based pay is usually followed in traditionally managed organizations. It is believed that a longer tenure will result in acquisition of new skills and better managerial control, which will result in career progression among individuals. In addition, they would have in-depth knowledge about the organization, processes, and systems. It also brings discipline in the implementation of compensation policy. This is widely followed in most of the government and traditionally managed hospitality organizations. However, this system is often punctured by problems associated with seniority-based payment system. Senior staff often transgress with accumulated unjust experiences suffered during the service tenure, which prevents them from using their best capabilities towards the execution of business objectives. They are mostly disappointed with the career progress, might be involved in political activities, have developed schemes for doing less for more gain, and may have developed a network of alliances for additional gains. Such possible dysfunctional behaviours do not need remunerative support from the organization. Seniority-based pay neglects the advantages of meritocracy and competency-based pay, which may work as demotivating factors for young employees and may trigger high employee turnover among new recruits. Therefore, this requires a balanced approach, especially when most organizations have become performance driven because of severe global competition.

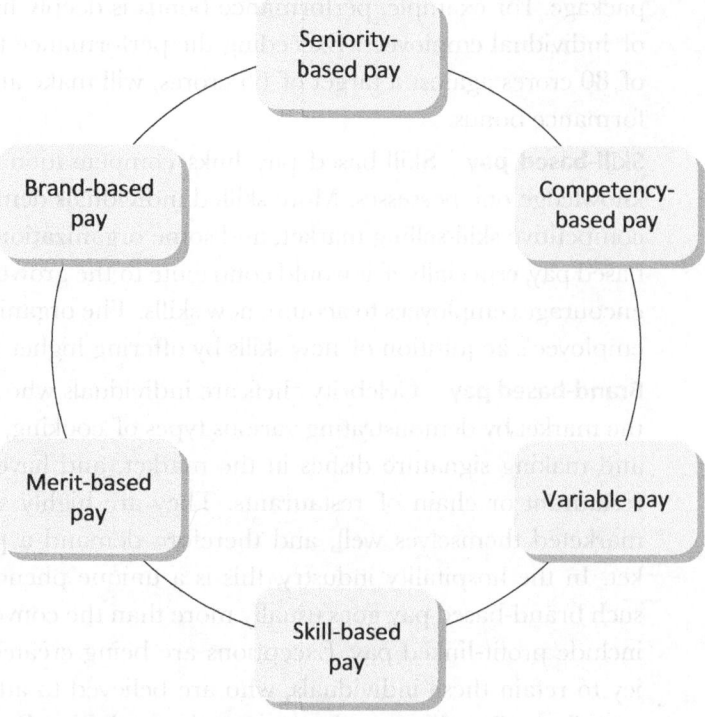

Figure 7.2 Various philosophical underpinnings that govern compensation policy

Competency-based pay In knowledge economy, competency plays a very important role in executing organizational performance. Each employee brings with him or her skills, knowledge, and experience at the time of joining the organization. While working in the organization, this base gets continuous nourishment, leading to a further development of competency. Competency provides the capacity for the organization to deliver solution to the customers. Although it does not necessarily provide guarantee that it will be deployed and translated into action, competency provides robust support. Competent individuals need to be encouraged to perform better for career growth as well as for organizational growth. Providing good remuneration to competent individuals will ensure that the highest degree of competency will be deployed while servicing customers. Thus, competency forms a base for remuneration.

Variable pay It is a part of the total remuneration schemes, which is linked with the performance of the business, group, individual, and so on. Hospitality business is highly cyclic and linked with the economic growth of the economy. More economic growth is reflected with the growth of industries and business institutions, which in turn increases the usage of hotels, restaurants, travel services, and so on by the consumers. Owing to this deeper level of linkage, HR managers from the hospitality industry install variable pay to a certain extent in the total remuneration package. For example, performance bonus is deeply linked with the performance of individual employees. Exceeding the performance target (achievement of sales of 80 crores against a target of 65 crores) will make an individual eligible for performance bonus.

Skill-based pay   Skill-based pay links compensation with the kind of skill and knowledge one possesses. More skilled individuals demand higher attention in the competitive skill-selling market, and some organizations are ready to provide skill-based pay, especially if it would contribute to the growth of the company. This also encourages employees to acquire new skills. The organization can acknowledge the employee's acquisition of new skills by offering higher pay.

Brand-based pay   Celebrity chefs are individuals who have gained a reputation in the market by demonstrating various types of cooking, presenting cookery advices, and making signature dishes in the market, and have become associated with a restaurant or chain of restaurants. They are highly skilled individuals and have marketed themselves well, and therefore demand a premium price in the market. In the hospitality industry, this is a unique phenomenon. Compensation for such brand-based pay goes usually more than the conventional pay range and may include profit-linked pay. Exceptions are being created in the compensation policy to retain these individuals, who are believed to attract food connoisseurs and contribute directly to revenue-generating activities. Restaurants managed by these celebrity chefs could demand higher prices from the guests as the economic and social profile of these visiting guests are not sensitive to the pricing, and what they are looking for is gourmet experience.

EXECUTIVE COMPENSATION IN INDIA

Most of the available literature on executive compensation is focused on CEO compensation. However, most of the studies have been conducted in the United States and European context, and relevant discourse on CEO compensation with reference to Indian context is relatively rare. Executive compensation has seen stunted growth owing to regulatory constraint for a long period as there was a specific direction in corporate laws that prohibited companies from pay compensation more than that of the President of India. However, the economic reforms introduced in the 1990s caused a transformational change in executive compensation. In globalized economy, uncertain business terrain forces hospitality organizations to recruit talented executives to ensure good shareholders' return (dividend) (Table 7.4). Some of the growth in executive compensation can be linked with the inflation that is prevailing in India.

Executive compensation depends on a number of factors, which include the following:

1. Chronological age of the executive

2. Pattern of shareholding
3. Public shareholding and CEO compensation

Chronological age of the executive CEO compensation is often found to be associated with the chronological age of the CEO. Chronological age signifies the actual age of an individual, that is, the number of years an individual has lived so far. A number of reasons could be cited to explain this phenomenon. Some authors (Ramaswamy et al. 2000) argued that the cultural bias in India could be one reason for such linkage. The role of accumulated wisdom is often equated with chronological age of individuals in India, and seniority is often respected in the Indian corporate power corridor. Besides, it could be argued that a long tenure with the companies provided opportunities to acquire various internal and external power bases. Internal power bases consist of a network of relationship among significant organizational members, whereas external power base signifies linkages with external stakeholders, which facilitates to execute the work in typical Indian socioeconomic context.

Pattern of shareholding The Indian hospitality industry is mostly owned and managed by family. This is not a unique phenomenon limited to this industry and

Table 7.4 Compensation received by top management personnel in 2009

Names	Designations and business entities	Annual compensation (in ₹ crores)
Kalanithi Maran	Managing director of Sun TV Network	37
Kaveri Kalanithi	Joint MD	37
Mukesh Ambani	Chief of Reliance Industries	15
Sajjan Jindal	Vice chairman, JSW Steels	10
Jeya Kumar	CEO, Patni Computers	12
Atul Sobti	CEO, Ranbaxy	8
Navin Aggarwal	Vice chairman, Sterlite Industries	7
Ajit Gulabchand	Chairman, HCC	6
Aditya Puri	Managing director, HDFC Bank	4
Seshagiri Rao	Joint MD and CFO, JSW Steels	3
Roopa Kudva	MD and CEO, Crisil	2
T.V. Mohandas Pai	Director, Infosys	3
Shikha Sharma	MD and CEO, Axis Bank	2
Chanda Kochhar	MD and CEO, ICICI Bank	2

Source: Various news reports: Compiled by the author.

can be extended to other reputed business houses too. Research indicates that family ownership and executive compensation are negatively related to each other. In simple terms, it signifies that family ownership is able to put a cap on executive compensation. As one of their family members is appointed as the CEO, the built-in relationship between the CEO and family ownership prevents exorbitant salary hike. It is argued that this remuneration constraint seen in family-owned businesses makes it the least attractive business institution to join, as reflected in a survey conducted by BT-Gallup (Piramal 1998).

Public shareholding and CEO compensation   Research indicates that public shareholding and CEO compensation have a negative relationship. It implies that public shareholders play an active role in restraining CEO compensation to be reasonable. Any significant cost management, entrusted to public shareholders, is believed to be managed well, which is reflected in the restrictive management of CEO compensation.

A research report published by internationally reputed hospitality consultants indicated that the median salaries of hospitality executives have seen a marginal decrease over the previous years (Table 7.5), which has been attributed to the recent economic downturn. This report highlights that resident managers have suffered the most because their salaries have gone down drastically. In some cases, resident managers were promoted as general managers and no replacement was made for that position (Interested readers can access some part of the report at

Table 7.5   Designation-wise annual median salary for the Indian hospitality industry

Position	Annual median salary (in Indian rupees)		Change over previous year (%)
	2007/2008	2009/2010	
General manager	2,118,000	2,042,000	−3.6
Resident manager	2,114,000	1,150,000	−45.6
Financial controller	1,487,000	1,311,000	−11.8
Director human resources	2,125,000	2,209,000	4.0
EAM/Director rooms division	1,815,000	1,938,000	6.8
Executive housekeeper	963,000	1,020,000	5.9
EAM/Director food & beverage	1,799,000	2,092,000	16.3
Executive chef	1,801,000	1,657,000	−8.0
Director sales & marketing	2,207,000	2,134,000	−3.3
Chief engineer	1,585,000	1,704,000	7.5

Source: Excerpt from the 2010 India Salary Report.

http://www.hvs.com/news/4615/hvs-executive-search-releases-the-2010-india-salary-report/).

As per the report, general managers have drawn 3.6 per cent less salaries in the year 2009–2010 in comparison with 2007–2008. Resident managers have drawn the maximum flak with a reduction in compensation amounting to 46 per cent. Financial controllers drew 11 per cent less in 2009–2010 than in 2007–2008. However, there has been a marginal increase (4 per cent) in the median salaries of HR directors. Surprisingly, executive chefs earned 8 per cent less than the previous years. Chief engineers drew 7.5 per cent more in the year 2009–2010. Thus, from the report, we can infer that the impact of downturn in business affects different professionals differently even if they work in the same industry.

EMPLOYEE STOCK OPTION PLAN

As we have discussed earlier, the hospitality industry is often marred by low salary and high turnover problem. This problem is not only limited to India but is a characteristic of this industry world over. High turnover of employees increases training and recruitment cost. Thus, retaining employees is a great challenge. Employee stock option plan (ESOP) is a stock option plan under which a company offers its shares to its designated employees, usually at a lower rate against the current market rate. If the business organization intending to offer ESOPs to its employees is not a public limited company (i.e., shares are not listed on any stock exchange), then the management fixes the price. ESOP is launched to offer the dividend of growth authored by employees and could potentially work as a great retaining tool. It could help the hospitality company put a cap on the movement of managerial staff by offering time-restricted shares of the company, wherein there are some time-related restrictions for the encashment of these shares. This share will grow with the contribution of the employees. ESOPs give a sense of ownership as stake in the company potentially generates a sense of belongingness, and also, it is an effective avenue to becoming millionaires within the shortest possible time. Dividend of growth is not restricted to its shareholders but also extends its reach to other stakeholders. Traditionally, employees are eligible for wages in return of their services. However, in the knowledge economy, employees are no longer passive wage earners, and the new role of knowledge workers is crafting their own part in the success story.

Owning an equity share means owning a share in the company business. Companies offer their shares to their employees because it is considered that having a stake in the company would increase loyalty and motivation substantially.

The eligibility criteria for participation in an ESOP depends on the policy of the company. Usually, all permanent employees will be eligible for ESOP, and in some companies, it is based on the grade and designation of employees. An employee who is a promoter or belongs to the promoter group shall not be eligible to participate in the ESOP. A director, who by himself or herself, through his or her relatives, or through anybody corporate, directly or indirectly holds more than 10 per cent of the outstanding equity shares of the company shall not be eligible to participate in the ESOP. Shareholders' approval is mandatory before launching the employee stock options scheme. Shareholders' approval could be achieved by passing a special resolution during the general body meeting with the shareholders. Usually, the shares issued to employees under ESOP inherit a lock-in period of one year from the date of issuance of the shares to the employee concerned. In case shares are issued to employees during public issues and the same price has been paid by the employees as public, the shares will not inherit any lock-in period. In some cases, ESOP is offered in a phased manner such as 30 per cent in the first year, 20 per cent in the next year, and then 10 per cent in subsequent years. Acquisition of shares is not taxed; however, profit made on sale of such shares is considered earning in that year and taxed accordingly.

EXECUTIVE BENEFIT MANAGEMENT

As a part of welfare measures, most reputed hospitality companies have a number of benefit schemes for its employees. These are discussed in the following subsections.

Executive accommodation scheme In hospitality organizations, executives are usually provided family accommodation as per the executive's grade and nature of the job. Usually these facilities are granted to departmental heads (e.g., executive chef, F&B manager, HR manager). However, most companies have flexible policies to extend these facilities to employees other than departmental heads, and for that special permission is sought from the HR director. Under this policy statement, maximum rental limit is fixed for different grades and current market rental practices.

Supplementary furnishing policy is also added in the policy, wherein, interest-free loans are provided for hard furnishing, and the maximum amount that can be utilized for furnishing is usually linked with the grade of the executives.

Medical benefit scheme Under this scheme, executives are eligible for reimbursement of medical expenses, which includes hospitalization and domiciliary expenses. Domiciliary expenses are those medical expenses that do not require hospitalization. All executives are eligible for these facilities, and the amount of medical allowance varies according to the grade of the executives. This facility extends to parents, spouse, and children, and usually, unclaimed hospitalization expenses are extended for the next two years. Under this scheme, executives over the age of 35 are eligible for special executive health check-up scheme. Executives are also allowed to spend an additional sum (varies according to grade) to undergo diagnostic health check-up, which is over and above the maximum amount fixed under domiciliary and hospitalization expenses.

Leave travel allowance   Usually, executives are given due financial assistance for personal and family travels once in a year. The maximum amount is linked to the basic salary of the executive. This is given to employees to facilitate their travelling during festival time or annual vacation with family.

Attire allowance   In the service industry, good presentation of self is important in the service production process. Non-executive employees usually get uniform during duty hours; however, executives are given allowance for the attire they need to wear during their office hours, and this attire allowance is also linked with the grade of the individual executives.

Children educational allowance   To extend financial support for the education of the executive's children, a fixed amount of financial assistance is given to the executives and is usually linked with the grade of the executives.

Maternity benefit   Female employees are entitled to maternity benefits at an average daily wage for a period of six weeks from the day before delivery to six weeks following that day, that is, three months leave for maternity.

Car entitlement   This facility is usually provided to the general manager or equivalent grade employees. The objective of this policy is to extend transport facilities to executives for their personal and official use. This policy usually has three components: type of car to be provided to the executives, petrol allowance, and driver's allowance. Executives working in a higher grade are given a more luxurious car than the lower grade. Similarly, the amount of petrol allowance and driver's allowance also varies according to the grade of the employees.

Dislocation or relocation allowance   Executives are eligible for dislocation/relocation allowance in case they are transferred across hotels/travel sales offices across the hotel chain. Under this scheme, executives are eligible for the following benefits: reimbursement for packing, unpacking, and transporting of personal household goods; insurance premium; travel entitlement; and so on. The maximum amount of this allowance is linked with the grade of the executives.

Performance bonus   Executives are eligible for performance bonus according to the performance score achieved by them through balanced scorecard mechanisms or other sophisticated frameworks. Usually, the bonus amount is linked with the performance score and the amount of basic salaries. Without giving salary hike, performance bonus works as a great proxy for economic boom or recession. Performance score is bound to be low during recession and goes up during economic boom. Thus, performance bonus works as a built-in self-balancing system that gets auto-adjusted to economic conditions. This facilitates flexible compensation according to the business achievement of the organization. In addition, this does not create permanent fixed expenses that are required to be borne by the companies, irrespective of the financial health of the company.

THE PRACTICE OF TIPPING

Hospitality industry inherits a unique practice where customers reward the employees for their good-quality service by paying over and above the bill amount. Frontline employees working in the F&B department, such as waiters, are the major beneficiaries of this practice. Employees working in the front office department of a hotel such as bell boys and drivers in a travel service company also earn tips that are much higher than their normal wages. Therefore, these positions are highly lucrative in the hospitality industry. Employees working in the housekeeping department or food production department (kitchen) are not as privileged, as they get less opportunity to interact on a one-on-one basis with guests. At present, in India, there are no dedicated legislations to govern employee tips, as is the case in the United States. It is common tradition in the hospitality industry that employees pool the money received through tips and share it among themselves as per the seniority and designation. Even if the compensation is relatively low in the hospitality industry, the practice of tipping helps staff level or marginal employees to supplement their earnings. This pooling of tips is managed on the basis of trust and blind faith. Although it is not mandatory that tips be shared among peers, tip sharing has taken a deep grounding in the Indian hospitality industry.

COMPENSATION POLICY AND ITS LIMITATIONS

Herzberg (1987) indicated that compensation is one of the hygiene factors for business organizations, and this highlights the limitation of the compensation policy with reference to employee motivation. Absence of a good compensation policy creates dissatisfaction, and the presence of a good compensation policy potentially removes dissatisfaction; however, it fails to motivate employees. Thus, a good compensation policy should be positioned as panacea for all motivation problems in the organization. The HR department needs to make supplementary efforts to build a good working environment and encourage positive relationships between supervisors and subordinates. Good employees should be recognized for performance; otherwise, lack of reinforcement will demotivate them. Thus, the HR team is required to pay specific attention to building a healthy and positive organizational infrastructure. Good compensation policy and healthy organizational infrastructure will potentially complement each other to generate motivation among staff employees and executives.

SUMMARY

Compensation in the hospitality industry is highly critical for its success in the market. It is noteworthy that the hospitality industry is characterized by a highly mobile workforce (resulting in high turnover), having relatively lower level of formal education, reliance on part time or contractual staff, and higher proportion of low-skilled job. Besides, this industry is also punctuated by structural and cyclical business demand. Usually, the hospitality industry follows various industry-specific yardsticks (e.g., room to number of employees ratio) to have overall control of cost arising out of wage and salary administration. Effective compensation policy needs to have a sense of internal and external equity. Internal equity signifies that the remuneration is linked with the nature and importance of the job performed by the employees. External equity signifies that the compensation policy is linked with the current market rate. Employees working at the staff level get compensation according to legal directives and current market rate for similar jobs, whereas employees working in executive grade are eligible for various benefits such as accommodation, performance bonus, and medical entitlement. Staff level employees are eligible for salaries with or without accommodation, dry-cleaning of uniform, duty time meal, and so on. Staff level wages also depend on agreement, arrived at during collective bargaining between the trade union and the management. These dynamic interactions provide voices to the staff level employees for a better deal.

KEY TERMS

Employees stock option plan (ESOP) It is a legal scheme where employees are allotted shares of the company at the market rate or subsidized rate.
Variable pay Employee remuneration amount depends on performance, business condition, inflation rate, and so on.
Equity Equity is the equitable principles with reference to compensation and other employee privileges.
Dislocation/relocation allowance This is a special allowance given to employees who are transferred from one business unit to another, which is located in a different region.
Medical benefit Benefits awarded to reimburse medical and other surgical procedures.
Skill-based pay Payment based on different layers of skills.
Seniority pay The basis of payment depends on the tenure of service within the company.

EXERCISES

Concept Review Questions

1. Critically examine the role of various determinants that influence compensation policy of a hospitality organization.
2. Review various legal provisions that govern employee compensation policy for hospitality organizations.
3. Discuss various benefits designed for executives to retain them in the industry.

Critical Thinking Questions

1. It could be argued that equity should be the cornerstone in employee compensation policy. To what extent do you agree with the statement? Give adequate rationale in support of your answer.

2. Some of the commentators and legal policy designers argue that top executive compensation has earned a colour of vulgarity for its excess. To what extent do you agree with the statement?

Assignments

1. Review the compensation policy of any reputed hotel chain, restaurant, or travel agency for which you have opportunity to access information. Report a good thing you found about their compensation policy. How can improvements be made in their compensation policy?
2. Collect Indian newspaper articles published during the last one year pertaining to employee compensation and report the new trends you see in employee compensation and benefit management.

REFERENCES

Mohanty, D., Perspective on Inflation in India, taken from the speech given at the Bankers' Club, Chennai, 28 September 2010.

Piramal, G., 'India's Business Families: The Inside Outside View', *Business Today*, January–February 1998.

Ramaswamy, K., Veliyath, R., and Gomes, L., 'A Study of the Determinants of CEO Compensation in India'. *Management International Review*. Volume 40 Issue 2, 2000 p. 167–191.

Herzberg, F.I., 'One More Time: How Do You Motivate Employees?', *Harvard Business Review*, Volume 65 Issue 5, September–October 1987 p. 109–112.

CASE STUDY

EMPLOYEE SATISFACTION SURVEY

Raj, director (HR) of one of the leading hospitality companies in India, got an annual employee survey report conducted by a leading HR consultancy agency. Last year, after joining the company, Raj launched a number of welfare schemes for the employees. However, it does not seem to produce any result. The feedback score, indicating employee satisfaction, has gone down drastically, and employees were not happy with the pay packet, benefit scheme, and bonus scheme. Raj observed an overall downfall of score in different aspects of the pay packet. One common perception that was prevailing among staff members was that the executives were paid very high salaries than the staff (non-executive employees), and the major complaints from executives were that they were not provided with trained staff to do the job. The executives of the company were also unhappy with the compensation packet. Some executives and staff members commented that there was no need for employee satisfaction survey as it did not help the employees in any way. In spite of launching a number of schemes for employees, using the input from last year's employee survey, there is a common perception that the survey is of no help to them. Raj is feeling helpless.

Discussion Questions

1. Should Raj continue with the annual employee satisfaction survey? Provide rationale for your line of arguments.
2. Why did the employee satisfaction score appear to be low? Recommend suitable strategies to overcome these problems.
3. Why did the executive satisfaction score appear to be low? Recommend suitable strategies to overcome these problems.
4. As a consultant, provide your recommendations to Raj on how he can boost his employees' morale.

8 Job Satisfaction

INTRODUCTION

To have a team of satisfied employees is one of the desirable outcomes/objectives of what every HR manager wants to achieve. Majority of managers expend a considerable amount of resources to improve the job satisfaction experience of the employees. They give this kind of importance to generate job satisfaction because it is considered to be the key for all types of employee behaviour in the organization. Satisfied employees put in extra efforts to satisfy customers and, generally, will not be always looking at opportunities to leave the organization. On the contrary, dissatisfied employees will not display positive employee behaviour, will do the job carelessly, and will attempt to evade work all the time. However, there is no final answer available of the factors that conclusively trigger job satisfaction. A number of reasons may be cited as the cause for employee satisfaction/dissatisfaction. Employees may be unhappy with the way the work is executed, the way the supervisor treats subordinates, the food provided in the staff cafeteria, the discriminatory treatment arising out of management policies, and so on. HR managers attempt to locate these sources of dissatisfaction and endeavour to improve the experience of the employees. We may wonder why employee satisfaction is important, especially in the hospitality industry. Job satisfaction is the prime driver for employee behaviour in the organizational workspace. Dissatisfaction will lead to different degrees of employee misbehaviours: low quality of customer interaction, not taking initiatives, breaking rules at random, causing harm to property and people, and even resignation. Termination of services of dissatisfied employees is not a lasting solution as new recruitment requires the HR department to spend more on training and other societal adjustment issues. Therefore, majority of the HR managers pay considerable attention to enhance employee satisfaction. Research indicates

LEARNING OBJECTIVES

After reading this chapter, you will be able to understand the following:
- the meaning of the term 'job satisfaction'
- the importance of job satisfaction among employees working in hospitality industry
- the determinants of job satisfaction
- the various measurement practices
- the effects of job satisfaction

that job satisfaction is the most frequently studied variable in organizational behaviour research (Spector 1997).

Definition   Job satisfaction is a kind of attitude that an individual employee holds about his or her job. It is, in fact, a kind of positive perception about the job. Thus, it is a kind of emotional state, which could be positive or negative. Vroom (1968) defined it as the positive orientation of an individual towards the work role. Job satisfaction could pertain to different facets of the job such as pay, relationship with supervisor, and autonomy.

THEORIES OF MOTIVATION

Maslow's Theory

As discussed in Chapter 6, Maslow endeavoured to comprehend various types of human needs and clustered them into five different hierarchical segments. These clusters are basic need, security need, social need, esteem need, and self-actualization need, and these are chained in hierarchical order (Fig. 8.1). Graduation from one level to another level is not automatic; it could be quite possible that one individual could get stuck in one level and fail to achieve the next state.

Essence of this theory

Human needs are diverse. All needs could be viewed under comprehensive clusters: food and shelter, security, social need, self-esteem, and self-actualization. All needs are hierarchically organized. On fulfilment of one kind of need, the individual graduates to the next level of satisfaction.

Critique   Although this theory is widely discussed and advanced to understand human motivation, it inherits considerable amount of weakness in its arguments:

1. Needs are not necessarily hierarchical. It is argued that human attention does not graduate only on completion of lower needs. Diverse needs are simultaneously fulfilled and do not necessarily adhere to the hierarchy as prescribed by Maslow. In today's media-dominated world, every day we are exposed to information pertaining to different life styles, different products, and so on. Although consumers cannot afford all the products advertised over the diverse range of media (television, newspapers, magazines, internet, bill board, etc.), it creates

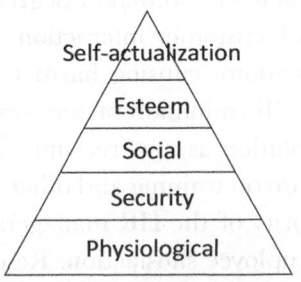

Figure 8.1   Maslow's theory

aspirational value in the mind of the consumers. It is quite possible that by just using the credit card one attempts to satisfy the diverse range of needs (security need, esteem need, social need, etc.) together. This makes Maslow's theory inoperable in organizational context.

2. Maslow's theory is consumption centric. It appears that the only gateway to self-actualization is through consumption. If the state of self-actualization is achieved through the gateway of consumption or achievement of security and esteem need, it will create a very sad picture for countries that do not have all these possibilities. In that case, Africa will never have self-actualized statesmen; but we have Nelson Mandela. Sanyasis (saints) of Indian origin have never walked through the stairs of consumption but have achieved nirvana. Therefore, the arguments advanced by Maslow appear to be truly representative of western consumption-focused world. It may not adequately explain all human pursuits.

Herzberg's Theory of Motivation

As discussed in Chapter 6, Herzberg identified hygiene factors, which even if present in the organization, do not generate satisfaction; however, their absence generates dissatisfaction, for example, good wages and working conditions. Similarly, there are motivating factors whose existence in the organization will generate satisfaction; however, their absence will not generate dissatisfaction. It signifies that one employee could be not dissatisfied with his job or workplace milieu; however, this does not automatically indicate employee satisfaction. As per the arguments advanced by Herzberg, 'no dissatisfaction' is 'not equivalent' to 'satisfaction'.

CORRELATES OF JOB SATISFACTION

Over a period, researchers attempted to find how job satisfaction is related to age, gender, personality, organizational justice, and so on. All these research works provide mixed results.

Age and job satisfaction   Research indicates that there is a positive relationship between age and job satisfaction. However, the true nature of relationship suffers from lack of clarity. Oshagbemi (2003) reported that age and job satisfaction are mutually related. One research indicates that employees over the age of 40 usually experience higher degree of job satisfaction than otherwise. Perhaps employees gain an enhanced capacity to cope and become emotionally stable as they grow old. Another study (Glenn et al. 1977) explained this relationship between age and job satisfaction that older employees fail to market themselves in the labour market owing to their limited education or non-marketable knowledge. Older employees are less educated. Lack of formal education prevents them from being able to acquire a new job at a new workplace. Hence, they feel fortunate to have a job in the present workplace, while the younger generation does not think so. Education and job satisfaction appear to share a negative relationship, that is, more educated employees will have higher employability in the market. They will be less likely to display a high degree of commitment to their existing organization and thus will have a natural tendency to have critical views on various treatments given to employees by the management. Employees working in organizations for long move fluently into lucrative segment of the jobs, create a comfort zone, and thus experience satisfaction. They also possess knowledge and skills to execute the job, and thus experience a sense of accomplishment. This leads to relatively higher job satisfaction to older employees than the younger employees. Luthans and Thomas (1989) reported that the relationship between age and job satisfaction is not linear. A linear relationship indicates that with increase in the age of employees, job satisfaction experience will also increase in a similar ratio. If this is true, then the oldest employee will be the happiest employee in the organization. In the real world, it may not be true. That is the reason the relationship between age and job satisfaction is not linear; it is curvilinear. A curvilinear relationship indicates that as the age progresses, job satisfaction goes up to a certain extent; however, subsequently, this relationship becomes negative as age creates adjustment problems due to changes in the usage of technology, process, and job depth.

Organizational culture and job satisfaction Organizational culture is the shared belief and values, collectively subscribed by majority of employees. It is a kind of thing one might have heard during his or her industrial exposure training in different business organizations such as 'we do it in this way' (refer to Chapter 9). Organizational culture could be traced in the following manner:

- Clan culture: This type of culture is characterized by biased orientation for teamwork, tradition, and loyalty, usually guided under the able leadership of one leader who works as a mentor.
- Adhocracy culture: This kind of culture emphasizes on creativity, flexibility, innovation, and entrepreneurship under a leader who is often a risk taker.
- Hierarchy culture: This kind of culture signifies adherence to rules, regulations, stability, and control under one strong leader who often wants to achieve control.
- Market culture: This kind of culture subscribes to competitiveness, goal orientation, competition, and market superiority, often orchestrated under a leader who is decisive and achievement oriented (Fig. 8.2).

Let us now discuss the relationship between various types of organizational culture and job satisfaction. A research (Lund 2003) indicated that clan and adhocracy will potentially generate job satisfaction in comparison to market and hierarchy cultures. This study provides further explanation as to why clan and adhocracy culture will generate a higher degree of job satisfaction than otherwise. This study indicated that although job satisfaction is generally high in clan and adhocracy type of organizational culture, job-related performance of the employees was not

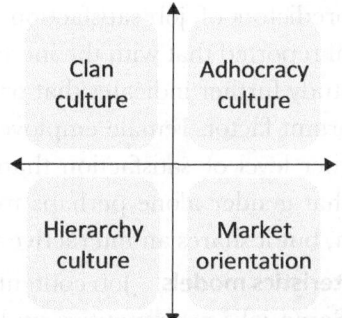

Figure 8.2 Various types of organizational culture

high in this type of culture. According to this study, job performance is reportedly observed highest in the market type of organizational culture, and subsequently in adhocracy, clan, and hierarchy. These arguments clearly indicate that job satisfaction and organizational cultures are intimately related with each other.

Gender There is no clear direction available to state that gender and job satisfaction are related with each other. Some studies indicate that men are more satisfied than women and some indicate the opposite. It is indeed very difficult to draw a line of conclusion on this because men and women use different evaluative criteria while assessing their job experience, and job satisfaction appears to play a significant role. For example, women place higher importance on social factors of a job, whereas men place higher value on the opportunity for self-expression in their workspace. So far as the important attributes are concerned, women look for opportunities to work with pleasant employees, whereas men give more importance to decision-making opportunities and leadership positions.

Length of service Length of service indicates the number of years spent in one workplace or organizational context. Some research indicates that job satisfaction and length of service are positively related with each other. It simply means that job satisfaction goes higher with the number of years spent in one organizational context. Some researchers argued that longer service provides a sense of protection against job loss and thus influences positively on job satisfaction. Oshagbemi (2003) said that job satisfaction among employees working in an organization for more than 10 years is relatively higher than among job-hopping individuals. He also indicated that job satisfaction gradually increased over time among employees working for one organization than among the job hoppers.

Organizational status Organizational status signifies one's relative position in the hierarchy of the organization. Research indicated that organizational status (level of work/designation) and job satisfaction are closely related with each other. One study (Near et al. 1978) examined the relative role of various job-related factors (pay, autonomy, etc.) for generation of employee satisfaction and reported that the strongest predictors of job satisfaction are organizational status or rank and age. Oshagbemi reported that with the increase in rank, job satisfaction goes up gradually. This study further indicates that organizational status or rank of an employee is an important factor. Female employees having higher organizational status displayed higher level of satisfaction than their male counterparts. Thus, it further indicates that gender alone perhaps may not be a significant contributor to job satisfaction, but it shares an interactive relationship with job satisfaction.

Job characteristics models Job content provides significant explanation to job satisfaction. Some jobs are repetitive and inherently uninteresting; others relatively provide space for self-expression and thus provide job satisfaction. Now a question arises: which are the factors that should be embedded in job content that will provide job satisfaction? One of the earliest answers came from the work of Oldham and Hackman (1976). They suggested that by designing interesting job content for subordinates, individual employees could be motivated. They further argued that there are five components that should be embedded in job content, which will provide meaning and thereby affect job satisfaction. These are discussed here.

- Task significance: Does an employee perceive his or her task as significant?
- Task identity: Does the task of an employee have a distinct identity?
- Task variety: Does the task of an employee provide diverse experience or is repetitive, providing monotonous experience?
- Autonomy: Does the job provide adequate autonomy in decision making, designing, execution, and improvement?
- Feedback: Does the employee receive timely feedback about the work?

These factors are related with each other. Oldham and Hackman argued that their relationship shares the following format:

$$\{(\text{Skill variety} + \text{Task identity} + \text{Task significance})/3\} \times \text{Autonomy} \times \text{Feedback} = \text{Motivating Potential Score (MPS)}$$

These characteristics, if successfully embedded in any job, potentially provide a range of experience of meaningfulness of work and responsibilities for work outcomes. Research indicated that a job composed of higher degree of autonomy and feedback provision will potentially generate intrinsic motivation and thereby positively affect job satisfaction. Each of these components provides job-specific satisfaction and makes it interesting, thereby causing positive experience. Therefore, most of the hospitality companies initiated a wide range of programmes to make

---

EXAMPLE

Employees working as contract employees may be the most unhappy individuals, and an employee's satisfaction may go up as he or she progresses over the years from being a contract or temporary employee to being regular employee and then in terms of designation and job content.

work interesting by launching job-enlargement and job-enrichment programmes. Job enlargement provides wide varieties of related works, whereas job enrichment provides enough depth in the work itself. For example, job enlargement for a room attendant in the housekeeping department would be to allow him or her to work on a wide variety of tasks (bed making, welcoming the guest by bringing luggage from the front desk to the respective rooms of the guests, etc.), whereas job enrichment involves diverse work under the room attendant's work portfolio. Job enrichment can improve employee performance and satisfaction by providing opportunities for adjustments required by individual employees and hence can provide a sense of personal growth. Cross-functional teams and job rotations are some of the widely practised frameworks, where employees could get diverse experience.

IMPORTANCE OF JOB SATISFACTION

Job satisfaction is considered to be the key to harness human energy and aspirations inside the organization. A lot of research has been done to find newer ways of explaining the role of job satisfaction in the workplace. It plays a significant role in improving employee commitment, performance, and generous work behaviour. It also plays a significant role in reducing work stress, employee turnover intention, and so on. Let us examine the role of each of these factors one by one.

Commitment   Commitment is defined as the relative strength of an individual employee's identification with the particular organization one is working for. It shows to what extent an individual employee identifies with the organization. Behavioural scientists have done a lot of research to examine the role of job satisfaction in employees' behaviour. For example, one research (Feinstein and Vondrasek, 2001) indicated that satisfied employees will display a higher degree of commitment towards their organization. In other words, hospitality employees who are satisfied in their workplace will display a higher degree of commitment towards their work.

Productivity and job satisfaction   Productivity and job satisfaction are positively related with each other. Although there are critical controversies regarding who influences whom, a positive relationship indicates that satisfied employees also will have higher productivity.

Job withdrawal behaviour and job satisfaction   Dissatisfied employees will withdraw from active participation in their work and will execute the work to a minimum level so as to maintain the job. This behaviour may be rampant especially when there is lack of opportunities in the market and a larger share of dissatisfied employees do not find opportunities to change their job but continue to remain in the workspace without enthusiastic participation at the workplace activities. This low level of engagement at the workplace may be harmful, as many services required by the guest require the employee to go beyond the blueprint of the service delivery system. Employees who are dissatisfied will show the rule book for not delivering the services to the customer, whereas satisfied employees will go beyond the blueprint of the service delivery system and deliver the services to the customer. Thus, it is very important that employees are satisfied so that the gap in the service delivery blueprint design could be filled by the enthusiastic employees and lacunae in the service delivery system are not known to the customer.

Job satisfaction across different cultures   Employees working under different cultural contexts appear to experience job satisfaction differently. Hofstede (2001) indicated that employees behave differently in different countries. Residents of one country share similar kind of history, politics, and societal changes; hence, it is not unusual to observe that citizens in one country collectively believe and share values. Hofstede (2001) attempted to explain why people from different countries behave differently while dealing with various life issues such as work, negotiation, and accepting supervisors/managers. They could be different by virtue of a number of issues such as power distance, ambiguity, and tolerance. For example, power distance signifies that the constellation of political power in an organization, as seen in Asian countries, could be different from western countries. High power distance is appropriate in oriental organizational context; however, this is not acceptable in any western organization. Thus, chair power driven world in oriental hospitality organizations is acceptable and rather finds its natural space in Asian countries; however, this will result in utter fiasco if practised in western business organizations.

With the advent of many foreign hotel chains in oriental countries, management principles and cultural yardstick of the western world should not be imported without major evaluations. In the Indian culture, individuals, irrespective of whether they are in their home or in office, are required to respect the elder members. The Indian society provides a number of gestures and expressions for display of respect. One hospitality organization in India, which has primary business connection with the western world, encourages employees to call each other by their first names. Employees working in these hotels practice contradictory cultural rituals in their personal lives where they need to express explicit gestures and rituals to respect senior members in the house and community. However, foreign hotel chains expect their employees to practise westernized cultural rituals in their organizational context. Managers need to be very careful before implementing any freshly imported rules, rituals, and fragments of tradition of western origin in oriental soil. Thus, employees bring a different set of expectations when they join the organization and potentially experience different levels of job satisfaction.

Job satisfaction and turnover intention   Research indicates that there is an inverse relationship between job satisfaction and employees' turnover intention. There is less likelihood that employees would consider leaving the organization if they are satisfied with it. In the years 2005–2007, India's economic progress (GDP growth) was around 8 per cent. It was found that even if employees were satisfied in an organization, they were leaving because of the abundant opportunities in the job market. Research also indicates that all those individuals who score high on money endorsement will leave the organization even if they are satisfied. Money endorsement signifies attributing higher weightage to money rather than other things in life. Therefore, those who attribute higher weightage to money for life satisfaction have shown the tendency to leave the organization even if they were satisfied with the existing organization. It indicates that at the time of recruitment, the HR manager should evaluate candidates or job applicants for their money endorsement orientation. In case a prospective candidate places higher importance on money over other things, it is most likely that the candidate will leave the organization if he or she finds another lucrative job offer from competition. Thus, HR managers should use higher degrees of discretion while recruiting these types of individuals.

Job satisfaction and organizational citizenship behaviour Organizational citizenship behaviour is a discretionary, voluntary, and non-remunerative employee behaviour that is beneficial to the organization. In other words, employees display certain positive behaviour for which they are not paid. This behaviour is not mentioned in their job description. Employees voluntarily engage in activities that are ultimately beneficial to the organization. This voluntary behaviour is desirable, but non-enforceable in an unmonitored service environment. This behaviour is not paid behaviour; however, employees engage in it voluntarily to benefit the organization, such as altruistic gestures to colleagues, putting extra smile on the face to have satisfied customers, finding information for the success of the organization, and staying late to do other's work. The HR managers are interested in generating a wide range of voluntary behaviour as it is not required to be supported by remunerative processes. Research indicates that satisfied employees are prone to engage in organizational citizenship behaviour. This indicates that job satisfaction and organizational voluntary behaviour are closely related.

MEASUREMENT OF JOB SATISFACTION

Measurement of job satisfaction is a challenge for HR managers. It is now gaining dominance as most of the enlightened organizations are migrating towards evidence-driven business context. It is a politically sensitive issue as many business organizations endeavour to increase job satisfaction by different sets of manipulative cultural environment to influence the score. For example, before administering job satisfaction surveys, employees are taken for picnic and on the very next day, satisfaction survey is conducted. This immediate exposure to the picnic environment provides a slight edge to the organization to generate a manipulative satisfaction score. This has been practised because many enlightened businesses endeavour to link performance bonus of the HR manager with subordinates'/employees' satisfaction score. The use of shortcut approach instead of orchestrating durable effort to generate employee satisfaction is hopelessly reprimandable.

Evidence-driven economy has increased the need to measure every attribute of a manager's work, and that has increased the need for measuring job satisfaction. A number of psychological instruments are available to measure job satisfaction, such as Minnesota Satisfaction Questionnaire (MSQ), Job Descriptive Index (JDI), and Porter Needs Satisfaction Questionnaire (PNSQ). Each of these psychological instruments is reliable and has been developed after a number of steps that are required to be followed before developing a scale.

Minnesota Satisfaction Questionnaire   This scale has been designed to determine employee satisfaction with reference to his or her work. This provides a detailed picture of the satisfaction of employees. It attempts to measure 10 facets of job satisfaction by using 100 measurement points. It is considered to be one of the most reliable and valid psychometric tools for measurement of job satisfaction (refer to Exhibit 8.1). This scale is relatively popular. This scale measures various facets of job experiences, such as compensation, moral values, security, advancement, working condition, company policies and practices, coworkers, and ability utilization. Although the scale is reliable, some facets measured by the scale have high correlation, that is, perhaps similar facets are being measured. These scales are available in two forms: long form and short form. The long form of the scale has 100 items, whereas the short form consists of 20 items. However, this scale inherits a number of difficulties such as lengthy questionnaire items. Employees filling up lengthy scale items may suffer from tiredness and may tick any one of them without paying particular attention to the scale question items.

Job Descriptive Index

This measures five facets of job satisfaction pertaining to pay, promotion, coworkers, supervisors, and the work itself. Researchers (such as Smith, Kendall, and Hulin 1969) argued that these five facets provide considerable understanding about how employees approach an organizational workspace. Although it is true that these five facets provide considerable understanding about various contributory factors for

Exhibit 8.1   Sample Representative Items from a Scale

	SD	D	NAND	A	SA
On my present job, this is how I feel about	1	2	3	4	5
My pay and the amount of work I do	1	2	3	4	5
The freedom to use my own judgement	1	2	3	4	5
The working condition	1	2	3	4	5
The feeling of accomplishment I get from the job	1	2	3	4	5

SD: strongly disagree; D: disagree; NAND: not agree nor disagree; A: agree; SA: strongly agree.

generation of job satisfaction, critics questioned this approach on the ground that there are more than five facets of job satisfaction. They believed that these five facets make employees' experience pertaining to job satisfaction. This scale is widely used and appears to be reliable.

HOW EMPLOYEES EXPRESS THEIR DISSATISFACTION

Employees express their discontent in various ways such as avoiding work, complaining about the work processes, stealing property, destroying property of the company, going for strike, and other democratic and undemocratic movements. The world witnessed the rise of the trade union movement; although its impact and visibility appeared to be on the wane, in India, five decades of post-independence era was often coloured by trade union activities. Trade union became the collective means of struggle against mighty, powerful, and politically connected business tycoons. Employee satisfaction used to be considered as the responsibility of the trade union. As India progressed towards a new developmental framework, the HR department was forced to take care of employee welfare owing to the highly competitive labour market; in addition, multiple job opportunities have reduced the role of the trade union in India. With the new performance-driven economy, employee satisfaction plays a very important role and is a top priority for HR managers. It is now well accepted that the benefits of a satisfied employee outweigh the cost of making him or her happy. The range of benefits could be traced in measurable and non-measurable terms. Satisfied employees work well, display higher degree of commitment towards the organization, and are regularly at work with minimal absenteeism. These can be measured. Praising the company in front of outsiders and making extra efforts to delight the customers are not necessarily measurable; however, they might be highly beneficial to the organization.

Employees' response can be categorized into two distinct precincts: constructive/destructive and activity/passivity. Constructive response implies that the action or response of the employee will not terminate the relationship but would improve it. Destructive response implies that the action or response of the employee will lead to the termination of the existing relationship with the organization. For example, exit is a destructive strategy as it intends to terminate future relationship with the organization. Active or passive behaviour indicates the degree of direct or indirect approach to resolve employee dissatisfaction issues at hand. For example, exit and voice are examples of active behaviour, whereas neglect and loyalty are examples of passive behaviour. Let us discuss the exit-voice-loyalty-neglect typology to dissatisfaction (Fig. 8.3) in detail.

Exit Unhappy employees choose to exit the organization. The exit decision of employees is one of the most widely followed mechanisms where disgruntled employees opt to exit from the existing organization. Such employees do not believe that they could do anything that could improve the present situation, and it

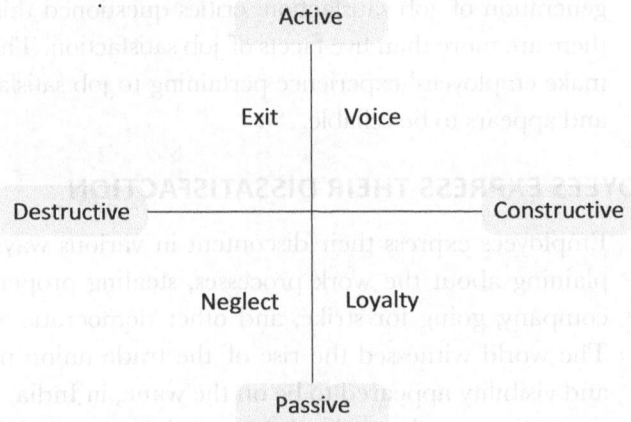

Figure 8.3 The exit-voice-loyalty-neglect typology to dissatisfaction. Adapted from Rusbult and Lowery (1985).

is believed that leaving the organization is the best solution available to the employees concerned.

Voice Unhappy employees raise concern and highlight various shortcomings, which are most often considered as complaints. Unless the organization develops adequate space for them, concern may be considered outrageous. This would most often be retaliated by punishing the employee.

Neglect An unhappy employee often neglects the job(s) allocated to him or her. In the service industry environment, where monitoring every human interaction is not possible, neglect shown by employees often remains untraced, but it has a negative impact on the external and internal customers.

Loyalty Loyal employees, even if they are unhappy over situations, remain in the organization. They might be suffering pain in silence waiting eagerly for good days ahead or waiting for improvement of relationships.

ADMINISTRATIVE AND MANAGERIAL IMPLICATIONS OF JOB SATISFACTION

It is often argued that the managers responsible for the well-being of employees should concentrate on employee satisfaction and attitude and attempt to influence their behaviour by launching a number of measures. Highly satisfied employees display low inclination to leave the job. By making the job interesting, showing human emotion to employee's craftsmanship, by paying attention to the exposed world where job is actually performed, job satisfaction is likely to go high. A satisfied employee naturally produces good quality of services for the customers, which significantly influences business positively.

Empowering employees Over a period, repetitive work experiences make one's job meaningless, dull, and boring. While awarding promotion is indeed an option for an employee, it is not possible all the time. Empowering the employee for executing a job provides a complete and broad range of job experience; a job potentially provides individual space and freedom—this, in turn, generates meaning in the job and eventually generates a higher degree of job satisfaction. Empowerment plays a significant role in generating employee satisfaction and thereby customer satisfaction.

Work–life balance With the advent of internet and mobile technologies, the difference between work and personal time is becoming blurred. Workspace is also becoming very demanding; fast delivery of service and a target-driven, performance-centric organization present unprecedented demands on individual employees. Office work has encroached private homes in many different forms: work-related phone calls, mails accessible on laptops, mobile phones, and so on; thus, the concept of private time is becoming extinct, which leads to a higher degree of stress in the family. This, in turn, causes employee dissatisfaction.

Training and development A number of reasons could be given to explain poor performance. Employee's inability to perform as per the standard of the organization could be due to lack of skill set that is required to perform the highly demanding job of the organization. This could in turn trigger job dissatisfaction, and therefore, arrangement for requisite training is crucial. In addition, the development of knowledge and skill sets is essential for the personal and professional growth of an individual, which leads to greater employee satisfaction.

Communication Management needs to communicate with all segments of employees pertaining to different issues such as business condition, competitor actions, company's strategy, employee benefits initiated to improve employee satisfaction, and pay and benefit structures. Communication with all segments of employees is a means of engagement. Organization provides a number of benefits to employees in different forms. In most cases, a high degree of secrecy is maintained around the compensation paid to employees. These states of affairs work as a breeding ground for rumours. Therefore, strong and well-articulated policies pertaining to employee benefits provide a level playing field to the employees. Personal relationship does not find a place while fixing employee benefits.

Responsive reward system A responsive reward system indicates that the system should be robust in relation to the employee's ability and the actual performance of the employee. It should also be in line with the changing times. Employees of different generations may have different sets of expectations, as each set of employees are located at different life stages. Therefore, reward system and its format should be in line with the expectation of the employees. This would lead to greater job satisfaction.

Joy at work Work should not be dull and boring. This can be achieved by allocating jobs as per the expectations and abilities of employees. The work should be meaningful to the incumbent, failing which, it will be done carelessly. In service industry, the responsive employee is the heart of the business and is capable of delivering high-quality services to the customer. To have responsive employees in hospitality organizations, the job itself should be embedded with provisions for task variety and autonomy. Thus, without much effort, organizations attempt to create fun-filled workspace. However, a number of enlightened management principles such as generous employee benefits and democratic work approaches could be followed to achieve real joy at work and to enhance satisfaction.

Employee feedback   Employee feedback signifies feedback from an employee's immediate supervisors, other senior staff, and colleagues. This enables them to steer the work in the right direction. Employee feedback should be timely and should be given in appropriate frequency. In many hospitality organizations, employee feedback is given on a yearly basis, during annual performance appraisal. Constructive employee feedback is very useful for enhancing one's work skills, thereby increasing their levels of satisfaction.

Understanding employees requirement   Each employee is different and brings different psychological orientations (e.g., extrovert: who has the tendency to enjoy engaging with the outside world; introvert: who has the tendency to enjoy engaging with self), located at different life stages (young/middle-aged/old employees), at different career graph (supervisor/employee/manager/director, etc.). Thus, it is natural that employees' expectations are likely to be different. Majority of the organizational rules, rituals, traditions, and policies are framed keeping the interest of the majority; thus, these broad-based frameworks fail to address individual needs. Therefore, some of the measures should be framed keeping in mind individual peculiarities to enhance satisfaction.

Fair and just organizational infrastructure   Research indicated that employees' perception of fairness and their perception pertaining to job satisfaction share a close relationship with each other. Thus, the HR department needs to maintain a fair and just organizational infrastructure, as any deficiency will lead to job dissatisfaction.

Human resource functions and employee satisfaction   Realizing the close link between job satisfaction and employee's engagement in hospitality organizations, many enlightened hospitality organizations have made explicit policy decisions to include job satisfaction score with performance bonus of the HR executives. At regular intervals (quarterly/half yearly), job satisfaction questionnaires are administered to gauge the feeling of the employees; the result of this survey is discussed among the heads of departments and their executives to improve upon the situation. A low score indicates possibilities of low performance bonus.

Thus, it is important for the HR manager to look for ways to enhance employee satisfaction, as dissatisfied employees would not only lower the performance bonus but also, in their interactions with customers, would not provide customer satisfaction and thereby, lower the company's revenues and repeat business opportunities.

SUMMARY

Incremental knowledge in organizational behaviour laid a lot of emphasis on job satisfaction. Job satisfaction has been explained as a central hub of explanation of positive employee behaviour. The benefit of a satisfied employee is so huge that it has become the focal effort of many HR managers. Thus, to be a successful professional in a hospitality business organization, understanding about job satisfaction is crucial. In fact, HR managers orchestrate a number of HR rituals (e.g., birthday celebration), activities (e.g., staff picnics), and processes (e.g., employee leave management) to improve upon job satisfaction of the employees. This chapter provides a brief sketch of the whole domain of job satisfaction discourse.

KEY TERMS

Job Descriptive Index (JDI) It is a psychometric scale used to measure job satisfaction.

Job characteristic model This model explains various features of job (task identity, task variety, task significance, feedback, and autonomy) that potentially generate meaning in the job, which in turn influences intrinsic motivation.

Job satisfaction This is the employee's attitude and perception about job and its immediate environment.

Minnesota Satisfaction Questionnaire (MSQ) It is a type of a widely used psychometric scale that measures job satisfaction.

Organizational citizenship behaviour It is a kind of voluntary behaviour, directed to benefit the individuals and organization for which no remuneration is paid.

Porter Need Satisfaction Questionnaire (PNSQ) It is a type of a widely used psychometric scale that measures job satisfaction.

Work–life balance It is a concern expressed by employees and organizational behavioural scientists that because of heavy work load and related work stress, employees are not able to draw a line of balance between work and life.

EXERCISES

Concept Review Questions

1. Identify various factors that potentially explain job satisfaction in the hospitality organizational context.
2. Elucidate various initiatives undertaken by the human resource professionals to enhance the level of job satisfaction among hospitality employees.

Critical Thinking Question

Critically examine the importance of job satisfaction, especially in the hospitality industry.

Assignments

1. Visit various web sites of various five-star hotels and travel support companies.

2. During your industrial training, what are the measures, instituted by the hotel concerned, found to be effective in generating employee satisfaction? Critique their welfare system.

REFERENCES

Feinstein, A.H. and Vondrasek, D., (2001). 'A Study of Relationships between Job Satisfaction and Organizational Commitment among Restaurant Employees'. *UNLV Journal of Hospitality, Tourism & Leisure Science: HTL Science, Article 2001-2*, 1-9, http://www.unlv.edu/Tourism.HTL2feinstein.html accessed on 24 October 2010.

Glenn, N.D., Taylor, P.A., and Weaver, C.D., 'Age and Job Satisfaction among Males and Females: A Multivariate, Multi survey Study'. *Journal of Applied Psychology*, Volume 62, p.189–193.

Hackman, J.R. and Oldham, G.R. 'Motivation through the Design of Work: Test of a Theory'. *Organizational Behavior and Human Performance*, Volume 16, 1976, 250–279.

Hofstede, G., *Culture's Consequences: Comparing Values, Behaviors, Institutions, and Organizations across Nations* (2nd ed.), Thousand Oaks, Sage Publications, 2001.

Lund, D., 'Organizational Culture and Job Satisfaction'. *The Journal of Business & Industrial Marketing*, Volume 18, Issue 2, 2003, p.219–237.

Luthans, F. and Thomas, L., 'The Relationship Between Age and Job Satisfaction: Curvilinear Results from an Empirical Study—A Research Note'. *Personnel Review*, Volume 18, Issue 1, 1989, p.23.

Near, J.P., Rice, R.W., and Hunt, R.G., 'Work and Extra Work Correlates of Life and Job Satisfaction'. *Academy of Management. Journal*. Volume 21, 1978, p.95–114.

Oshagbemi, T., 'Personal Correlates of Job Satisfaction: Empirical Evidence from UK Universities'. *Int. J. Soc. Econ.* Volume 30, Issue 12, 2003, p.1210–1231.

Rusbult, C.E. and Lowery, D., 'When Bureaucrats Get the Blues: Responses to Dissatisfaction among Federal Employees', *Journal of Applied Social Psychology*, Volume 15, 1985, p.80–103.

Smith, P.C., Kendall, L.M., and Hulin, C.L., *The Measurement of Satisfaction in Work and Retirement*. Chicago, Rand McNally, 1969.

Spector, P.E., *Job Satisfaction: Application, Assessment, Causes, and Consequences*, Sage, London, 1997.

Vroom, V. and MacCrimmon, K.R., 'Toward a Stochastic Model of Managerial Careers', *Administrative Science Quarterly*, Volume 13, Issue 1, June 1968, p.26–46.

CASE STUDY I

HEMANT'S DILEMMA

Hemant has joined a hospitality-related company very recently as an HR manager. His past exposures were from the manufacturing industry. In the corporate power corridor, it is often felt that employees are not happy, and it appears that employee dissatisfaction will find its expression in the form of strike or mass exodus (mass resignation) or some other means. There is no concrete evidence against this rumour; however, this story is gaining ground in the corporate HR office.

Hemant introduces a number of innovative ideas to increase the satisfaction of the employees such as five-day week, more manpower in every department, and increased remuneration. Hemant thinks of administering an employee survey to identify whether it is true that the employees are unhappy. However, one of the senior managers comes to his office one morning and expresses his displeasure on learning about this plan. He feels that instead of doing any good to employees, it will harm the relationship among managers; potentially a lot of dirt will be available in the public for general consumption.

Hemant does not understand why this senior manager is so sceptic and wonders whether he fears that his name might come into limelight and his subordinates might write against him. During lunch hour, one of his colleagues also tells him not to conduct such a survey. And that if he is so determined to conduct the survey, then this should be done after the annual day celebration, when the employees are entertained by managers, colourful staff party is organized, liquor is served, and family members of the employees are entertained. He feels that this would potentially be the right time to administer the survey.

Hemant is shocked as he believes in transparent dealing with employees. 'What is wrong in knowing where or what is wrong, rather than living in the dark to imagine about the darkness', Hemant wonders.

You are requested to provide Hemant suggestions for him to act. Provide suggestions that will help everybody.

1. Should he go ahead with his plan? What are the problems associated with his plan?
2. How could Hemant overcome the resistance from his colleagues?
3. Can his solution overcome the current problems faced by him? Provide rationale.

CASE STUDY II

RAM MURTHY'S CHALLENGES

Ram Murthy is the general manager of a hotel chain for the last seven years and is quite mature now to deal with the challenges associated with the business cycle. He has just read a report on his employees' satisfaction levels from a renowned HR consultancy agency. He finds that the employees are very unhappy owing to long working hours, less salary, and less time for their families. They also have complained against some managers about their unprofessional behaviour.

Discussion Question

Ram Murthy needs a consultant who will provide a workable solution to their problem. Suggest suitable strategies to overcome this problem.

CASE STUDY III

JOJO AND HIS BOSS

For the last several years, Jojo has been working for a reputed hotel chain. He has a great reputation among his colleagues. Jojo works very hard, guides other colleagues when they are in difficulty, and also some customers prefer his service over others. Some customers have recognized his services and have mentioned his quality service in customer feedback forms.

However, he has not been given promotion during these years. As some of his junior colleagues have already got promotions, he is feeling left out. He is being told by his manager that he is not getting promotion because he is not a hotel management graduate. His motivation is now at the lowest level.

Two years ago, he had joined a professional programme to earn an accredited degree from a privately run hotel management institute. However, his manager changed his schedule in such a way that he could not pursue this program in any way. He requested for a transfer to another hotel property, but his manager did not allow him to do so and resorted to a number of show-cause notices for small service problems, which happened in the hotel all the time. Other employees did not get any such reprimand for any display of deficiencies; but he is always picked for small mistakes. His supervisor made a report in writing against his name.

Discussion Questions

1. Jojo does not know what to do. You are required to suggest some way out to him.
2. As an HR manager, what actions would you recommend?

9 Organizational Culture

INTRODUCTION

What is organizational culture? Organizational culture refers to the personality of the organization. It is highly normative by nature and thus consists of the shared values, beliefs, signs (tangible) as well as assumptions that are shared among the members of the organization or as exhibited in their behaviours. So, the ambit of organizational culture is quite large and is normally perceived of through all our senses rather than being evident only to the eyes. The chapter discusses in detail the many facets of organizational culture, its characteristic features as well as the popular models in this domain.

Organizational culture provides diverse meaning to different research scholars. It could be described as 'observed behavioural regularities when people interact (language, customs and traditions, rituals), group norms, espoused values, formal philosophy, rules of the game, climate, embedded skills, habits of thinking/mental models/linguistic paradigms, shared meanings and "root" metaphors or integrating symbols' (Schein 1992). Organizational culture is the shared belief, attitude, and values that are nourished by the majority of the employees in an organization. These commonly held belief systems significantly determine the way of life in an organization. Organizational culture works as one of the most precious assets because it cannot be easily imitated and transplanted to other organizations, and doing the same organizational practices will not procreate another similar organization. Thus, organizational culture provides cushion for competitive advantage. This culture is embedded in the organizational architecture in the form of stories, rituals, ceremonies, history, dress, conversations, and symbols, which provides meaningful explanations to the people. It works as a fluid, which holds a group of people together for a certain purpose. Owing to these common threads, it provides guidance to the employees while doing their jobs as well as a similar interpretation uniting a group of people for a

LEARNING OBJECTIVES

After reading this chapter, you will be able to

- appreciate the basic understanding behind organizational culture constructs
- review various functions of organizational culture
- examine the role of organizational culture for delivering strategic competence
- utilize various theoretical models to advance understanding on organizational culture (cultural web model, OCTAPACE model, competing value framework models)
- describe how to diagnose basic tenets of organizational culture
- describe how organizations transmit cultural components among its employees
- examine the role of top leadership in creating and sustaining various tenets of organizational culture

common purpose. This interpretation works as a 'frame of reference' to deliver practical solutions.

OBSERVABLE ASPECT OF ORGANIZATIONAL CULTURE

Organizational culture exists in a subtle form and is often reflected in the collective behaviour of the employees, the story they share among each other, the way they do certain organizational operations, the way they celebrate their success, the way they deal with failure, and so on. For example, the vision statement of Oberoi Hotels (Exhibit 9.1) states, 'We see an organization where people are nurtured through permanent learning and skill improvement, and are respected, heard, and encouraged to do their best. Oberoi is recognized as a best practice for training and developing its people'. The management of Oberoi Hotels invests a lot of its financial resource to develop and nurture the talents. Learning orientation has been

---

Exhibit 9.1 Vision of Oberoi Hotels and Resorts

Vision

- We see an organization that aims at leadership in the hospitality industry by understanding its guests and designing and delivering products and services that enable it to exceed their expectations. We will always demonstrate care for our customers through anticipation of their needs, attention to detail, distinctive excellence, warmth, and concern.
- We see a lean responsive organization where decision making is encouraged at each level and which accepts change. It is committed and responsive to its guests and their stakeholders.
- We see a multi-skilled workforce that consists of team players who have pride of ownership, translating organizational vision into reality.
- We see an organization where people are nurtured through permanent learning and skill improvement, and are respected, heard, and encouraged to do their best. Oberoi is recognized as a best practice for training and developing its people.

- We see a multinational workforce that has been exposed to different cultures, problems, and situations and can use its experiences to enrich the local employees, whether in India or overseas.
- We see the world dotted with hotels of the Oberoi group in strategic commercial and resort locations.
- We see user-friendly technology enhancing value for our customers and helping our personnel by making information more accessible.
- We see an organization that is conscious of its role in the community, supporting social needs and ensuring employment from within the local community.
- We see an organization that is committed to the environment, using natural products and recycling items, thus ensuring proper use of the diminishing natural resources.

Source: Company Website.

embedded in the organizational culture of Oberoi Hotels. Let us examine some of these selective containers that capture organizational culture.

Stories Most of the organizations tell stories in the way they describe their past, their way of being. Some of these stories have linkages with the beginning of the business. The owner of the business often becomes the focal point of these stories. In Indian hotel industry, it is often seen that family ownership is predominantly a viable business option. Most of the stories chronicle the start of the hotel business by the entrepreneur; its growth under his/her leadership; and some heroic achievements that contributed to the building of the hotel chain. Some of these heroic stories determine the tone of the culture.

Rituals Most of the hotels use rituals to communicate and celebrate organizational culture. Most of the hotels have genuine practices that constitute their enduring tenets of the culture. While some of the rituals are centred on the way they celebrate success and address the pain of failure, most of these organizational cultures convey meaning to the participants and enforce its continuance by regularly practising the organization-specific rituals.

FUNCTIONS OF ORGANIZATIONAL CULTURE

Organizational culture serves a number of important functions. It unites employees of diverse backgrounds and aspirations under common goals, it gives identity to these people of diverse backgrounds, and it guides its employees on the appropriate pattern of behaviour acceptable within the organization as an unwritten rule book. Its functions are discussed here.

Integrating Employees join hospitality organizations from diverse educational, cultural, and economical backgrounds. Culture integrates the workforce under some purpose and provides identity. Organizational culture provides a sense of unique identity to these diverse groups of employees by integrating various facets of organizational life. Most of the hospitality organizations highlight various values they stand for while representing themselves as one single entity in the society. These value systems provide legitimacy and logic to unite employees at the grass root level, thus resulting in smooth operation of the function.

Describing Organizational culture helps describe itself in the language the members of the organization prefer. It gives a sense of belonging among employees and provides identity. This identity is used to differentiate it from other similar organizations and highlights formal and collective aspirations (refer Exhibits 9.2 and 9.3). In both the organizations, it is evident that the focus of the mission statements is on trying to describe what the organization stands for and the values shared among the management as well as the members of the organization.

Facilitating Culture creates informal language of conformity and provides colours to the web of rules and regulations to facilitate organizational activities. The

---

Exhibit 9.2   Mission Statements of Marriott and Oberoi

Marriott's Spirit to Serve, the foundation of our company culture, is simply the way we do business—everyday, everywhere—with our employees, our customers, and in the communities where we live and work.

We see an organization where people are nurtured through permanent learning and skill improvement, and are respected, heard, and encouraged to do their best. **Oberoi** is recognized as a best practice for training and developing its people.

Exhibit 9.3   Marriott Vision Statement

At Marriott, diversity is more than a goal—it's our business. From our global workforce to our customers, vendors, franchisees, and owners, our diverse differences give our company its strength and competitive edge. In the process, we've set the standard for the entire hospitality industry. Our global workforce mirrors the communities where we live and work every day. Our employees hail from dozens of nations, speak more than 50 languages, and work together as a team under the Marriott banner around the globe. Our diversity goes beyond backgrounds and nationalities—we pride ourselves on embracing the unique perspectives and talents of our employees. We know that our employees are our greatest asset, because it's through their dedication that we deliver exceptional customer service.

---

collective consensus removes dilemma from the system and works as unwritten guidelines for employee governance.

IS CULTURE A STRATEGIC RESOURCE OR SHADOW LIABILITY?

Culture is indeed a strategic resource, as it unites, integrates, and presents as one unified workforce. However, in some cases, organizational culture fails to fulfil its promise. For example, when organizational culture no longer fits the new business and market conditions, it becomes a shadow liability. Gordon Bethune took over the charge of Continental Airlines; he had the uphill task to save the company from immediate bankruptcy. In Continental Airlines, organizational culture was the bondage of its bureaucratic culture, created by the earlier predecessor. Gordon Bethune changed it all. He created a culture of performance and its due recognition. He declared freedom from a shadowy culture of bureaucracy by publicly burning the old service manual of 14,000 pages and heralded a new golden era for Continental Airlines.

It is a well-established viewpoint that each organization should have important and differentiable resources that will provide them with competitive advantage over others. Researchers have attempted to explain it in a number of ways. One of the leading thoughts on this area is called *resource-based view*, developed by Jay

Barney. As per this theory, each organization should have customer value, rareness, inimitability, and non-substitutability. The model is commonly referred to as the *VRIO framework* (Witcher and Chau 2010). Here the 'O' stands for 'organizable', referring to the ability to derive support from the other three.

Customer value will attract the customer to buy a specific product because it is a value purchase. Rareness will provide competitive edge because rare resources will provide certain advantages in terms of production cost, raw materials, location of business, and so on. For example, steel-making companies and mineral conglomerates are trying to acquire as many mines as possible worldwide so that they can play significant monopoly over the market. Inimitability enables companies to prevent imitation, which indeed is a great resource in today's me-too product market, the way the grey market in China produces every conceivable item in the world for which certain premium is there in the market. Thus, most of the companies use trademark and copyright legal provisions to protect their products from being copied. However, pirated copies of products create real problems for companies.

Organizational culture can be a great resource and has the potential to deliver competitive edge over others as it is very difficult to imitate. Therefore, if any organization is successful in developing productive architecture, it will deliver durable results over a period of time. These productive cultures may not be available to the competing companies even if they imitate everything. Unique combination of various cultural elements creates a metamorphosis, which is uniquely created and cannot be uprooted for further installation. Thus, human resource professionals should allocate adequate time to develop productive culture. Tata's leadership with trust, Epson's 'Built to Perform', A.T. Kearney's 'Ideas That Last', Accenture's 'High Performance. Delivered' are all compelling ideas that get materialized and embedded in the organizational culture.

Culture provides basic identity and guidance for future course of actions. It works as a binding force to a group of people, directed to achieve some meaningful objectives, and brings fluidity and speed in the working of the employees. It works as an unwritten rule book, adhered to by the employees without questioning the merit of it. It reduces the chance of misunderstanding and provides unifying lubricant to form a cohesive workforce. Culture is also a strategic resource, as it has the potential to attract good quality of workforce.

Stress is one of the factors that play a significant role in employee turnover. Productive working culture generates relatively less stress and agony among employees. In today's hypercompetitive environment, organizational performance is monitored by various stakeholders on a quarterly basis. Performance-driven organizational culture is capable of producing positive business results. Thus, organizational culture is a unique strategic resource.

On the contrary, organizational culture provides a stubborn way of dealing with its people, interaction, and service production. It is not an unmixed blessing for any organization. As productive organizational culture is capable of producing excellent business results, it is equally capable of causing damages to the business of the company. Organizational culture, unless managed well, may work against the company. Non-productive culture could write its own death sentence by engaging in non-functional behavioural pattern. For example, in Continental Airlines, before Gordon Bethune took over as CEO, a culture of bureaucracy held the company bondage, leading to ultimate financial disaster and bankruptcy. Moreover, organizational culture gives unique expression to its employees, which they hold very dearly. This presents an unbearable problem at the time of merger and acquisition. It presents a difficult challenge to disown their deeply held culture, which they believed to be true for a long period. In fact, some of the cultures require replenishment and alteration as the wheel of time moves on, as what is productive may not always remain productive over time. To alter certain parts of the culture is indeed a very difficult task. Therefore, culture requires careful nurturing.

Organizational culture could be a burden if it fails to contribute to business results. Over time, organizational leadership could take up certain behavioural cues, which provide negative contribution to the business results. For example, if an organizational leadership accepts highly aggressive behaviour as the norm of the organization, anybody failing to comply with will be severely punished. Aggressive behaviour then becomes the norm and increases and encourages risk-taking behaviour in the organization. Any business organization with too many risky adventures is prone to commit blunders and can bring down shareholders' wealth. Let's look at an example. Before Enron was engulfed into the quagmire of the scam, it actively selected and encouraged individual employees to take risk and make money for the company. Over time, too many risky adventures were no longer contributing to the top line and bottom line growth of the company. However, if reported, the shareholders would punish by selling the share in the market, which in turn would puncture the high share price of the company. This would have significantly affected the performance bonus of the top management. So, they created fictional companies to inflate the level of performance of the company. Thus, as can be seen from this example, if organizational culture is pegged around an unproductive web of interactions among employees, it could be a burden for stakeholders.

Organizational culture makes individuals follow certain commonly accepted behavioural norms. Adherence to these norms makes the organization 'stubborn' to ignore other positive behavioural norms, perhaps which, with the passing of time, makes sense to incorporate as new fibre in the existing culture. However, organizational members express a high degree of resistance to accepting new genre of norms, which may potentially generate a great degree of discomfort among employees. As in the case of Taj Hotels (Exhibit 9.4), the stubbornness on the part of the organizational culture has been done away with in order to accommodate a broader and much more diverse variety of people on board.

Exhibit 9.4   Taj Values

People diversity, integrity, and respect

Passion for excellence

Exceed expectations

Innovation

Sense of urgency and accountability

Social responsibility

Joy at work

People are our greatest asset and the key to our success.

We respect diversity of people, ideas, and cultures and honour the value of individuals in a team.

We believe in perfection to achieve excellence.

We continuously improve processes to surpass global benchmarks.

We succeed by exceeding expectations of all stakeholders and protecting the interest of our shareholders and playing by the rules.

We encourage innovation, embrace change, and support growth through knowledge and learning.

Source: Company Website.

Thus, strict adherence to existing cultural cues makes one organization less flexible to change. Flexibility is one of the qualities that provides longevity to organizations and maintains its relevance with reference to its market. Moreover, in today's competitive world, flexibility works as a great resource and helps quickly to get adjusted with the new norm of business. Peter and Waterman (1982) argued that flexibility provides durability to an organization. Stubborn adherence to its strong cultural cue makes an organization less open to change and takes away the spirit of flexibility. However, in a stable business environment, inflexible work approach may be suitable.

Alliance formation   Cultural uniqueness forces its member for conformity. Over time, this conformity gets embedded in the behaviour of employees. They accept ritualistic performance as an expression of the culture. Employees become accustomed to this behaviour as if it is their own and start feeling proud of being a part of it. Unquestionable acceptance of cultural cue by everybody generates peer pressure for conformity. Although this works as a facilitator for performance, it may work as a negative resource at the time of alliance formation. Alliance formation signifies that two companies unite under a common umbrella of objectives for strategic reasons. In today's hypercompetitive market, alliance formation is a necessity and an important requirement for long-term survival. However, relevant literature suggests that most of the alliances, although strategically and financially found to be prudent, experience difficulty to put people together under bigger canvas. Each culture works against another. Without strong, visionary, and inspirational leadership, alliance formation fails to deliver.

CULTURAL MODELS

Every human being has the liberty to behave in his/her own fashion, and it is true in the organizational context too. Each individual employee brings his or her own perspectives and ways of looking at the world. This creates possibilities of a diverse range of behaviour. Thus, to manage these diverse behaviour of a group of employees poses critical problem as to how to make sense out of it and channelize it productively for achievement of organizational aims and objectives without considerable friction. To avoid such difficulties, behavioural models can help us advance our understanding, which otherwise can become very difficult to observe. Certain behavioural patterns of human beings could be accurately described with the help of models that have been empirically verified for their relative robustness, accuracy, and replicability. Therefore, utilization of models provides straightforward answers to many difficult problems. Therefore, to advance our understanding on organizational culture, we use models that provide us reasonable clarity into the diverse colours of cultural nuances. The culture of Marriott is different from that of Taj Hotels, Resorts, and Palaces, as the operations of the former are managed by a very young bunch of employees, and Taj Hotels differs significantly in this regard. The culture of SOTC Travel Company is different from Cox and King's culture. Similarly, Kuoni Travels India's culture is different from that of other travel companies operating in India. Their HR policies clearly mention that the management expects certain clearly outlined behaviour in its employees, thereby differentiating their organizational culture from any others' (Kuoni 2012).

The question is why we find such differences. It is difficult to make any conclusive statement about any culture. It is all relative, and therefore, we invoke various theoretical models to understand organizational culture. Let us look at the various types of models.

Cultural Web

The first model we discuss here is cultural web. Culture is an indivisible part of any organization; however, it is difficult to articulate it in concrete forms and formats. Cultural web is one such framework that facilitates our understanding about any organizational culture. Cultural web framework consists of seven windows, which allows the viewer to see seven distinct dimensions of the same.

Stories   Stories are oral history, part of which is carried out by employees. Stories could be focused on the core belief system of the organization, collectively subscribed by the employees. Collective stories often remain in the minds of the employees and provide timely guidance to the employees. These stories could be positive or negative, success or failure, and achievement or disappointments. Stories could be centred on the heroic achievement of the employees and founders, which forms the base of the company. It could be about the organizational failures and how it failed in the past. However, conscious efforts are being made by human resource professionals to float and reinforce positive stories and encourage anybody who advances the merit and magnitude of the stories.

Symbols   It is the window that provides a privilege view of organizational culture. It signifies human behavioural cues expressed in the terminology, jargon, structure, logo, and so on they use to communicate what they are. Conscious efforts are being made by human resource professionals to highlight certain selective components of strategy in their articulation to state what the company is made of. For example, do all employees wear the same colour and type of uniforms? Different colours and types of uniform could indicate the status of employees, and different status in the organization is maintained.

Routines and rituals   These indicate the widely practised behavioural activities that are frequently enacted by the employees, for which they feel proud of. Elimination of these behavioural activities will potentially generate a high degree of dissonance and resistance. Which are the behavioural activities that are actively encouraged during training and new employee socialization phase? An answer to this question will provide a clear picture of durable human activities that are being practised without asking any questions. Some of the routines have been formed decades ago and are sincerely followed for years with or without much modification (Fig. 9.1).

Power structure   It is an important window that provides information about the power structure of the organization. This window of cultural web provides information about the distribution of power among its employees and how it is communicated among the workforce. Do they have an open door policy while finding solution for a nagging problem or do they follow hierarchy in ditto? Do they use a rectangular table or a circular table? A rectangular table signifies unequal power distribution, whereas a circular table indicates equal opportunity to every member. How does the leadership demonstrate what they claim to value? Does the power structure get reflected on the interactions among employees? Does it facilitate or truncate the workflow?

Control system   Control is one of the important functions, exercised more often by the management, to steer it to its objectives and plans. Thus, the organization may follow diverse types of control systems such as mechanistic control system and organic control system. Mechanistic control system is characterized by well laid down rules and regulations, flowing authority from top to bottom, and strict adherence to activity-based job descriptions, with overemphasis on salaries and wages, perquisites for execution of performance. Organic control system is characterized by minimum rules and regulations (invoked rarely), outcome-based job description,

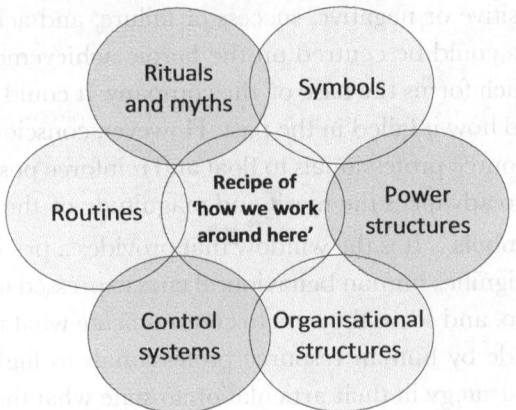

Figure 9.1   Cultural web

flexible authority structure, emphasis on creation of meaningful experience, and so on. Administration of control function builds the basic level and direction of interactions (Fig. 9.1). It provides colour to the core processes and composes unique combinations of elements for building unique culture.

Organizational structure   Organizational structure creates the level of interactions. Flat organizational structure provides width for human interaction and fluidity in the execution of work; it creates provisions for an informal level of communication and access to a vast amount of resources and facilitates innovations as it allows collaborating with experts located at any hierarchical level. This provides temper and speed of work, whereas a hierarchical structure limits human interaction, and emphasis is laid on adherence to governance protocol and provides formal interaction, which is often emphasized through written communication.

OCTAPACE Model

The OCTAPACE model was developed by T.V. Rao and Udai Pareek in order to facilitate the prerequisites of a culture conducive to harmony among the members of the organization (Singh 2008). The eight elements of the model can be seen as the essential determinants to the creation of an organizational climate that leads to successful human resource development within the organization (Fig. 9.2).

Openness   It signifies how spontaneously employees are to express their own feelings and thoughts without worrying about the consequences or fear. Openness indicates sharing personal viewpoints for public consumption. Fear of reprisal often prevents individuals from airing personal viewpoints. An organization enriched with openness often has the potential to know about the current experiences of the employees—this provides opportunity to address the cause of unhappiness, discontent, and so on. Openness could be characterized by allowing free flow of information across hierarchies, designations, and grades. HR executives allow openness to flourish by installing and fostering multiple frameworks such as open-door policy,

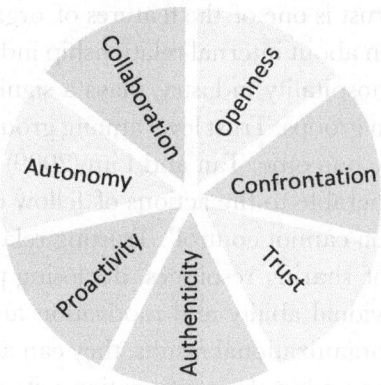

Figure 9.2 OCTAPACE model

unmoderated internal chat workspace, open mentoring facility across generations and designations, whistle-blower policy, data-driven performance management system with adequate feedback and improvement opportunities, and so on. Some hospitality organizations adhere to strict discipline and require to follow formal organizational structure while managing the workflow. In many traditionally run hospitality organizations, openness is not a widely practised phenomenon. Past traditions hold them back from using openness as a resource. A relatively higher degree of openness provides opportunity to find better solutions. A number of processes are required to deal with the openness. It requires space and framework to bring synergy and synthesis to deal with the data generated owing to the practice of openness. Many companies openly claim to practise openness as a fabric of their organization; however, how honestly they practise the virtue of openness is a serious question and is difficult to estimate. Thus, many companies give lip service to these resources and often follow reticence to deal with employees.

A number of characteristics could be indicative of openness practices:

- Do employees have freedom to air their view?
- Do employees know their performance score?
- Do employees get opportunity for performance feedback?
- Are the employees encouraged to share their pay packet details?

Confrontation It is one of the cultural characteristics that allows an organization to acknowledge the nature of the problem experienced by it and utilize its available resources to resolve it. It has been seen that some organizations do not want to know the truth of their organizational problem and always attempt to shy away from facing and acknowledging the true nature of the problem. Organizational members always play safe by denying the existence of the problem. Temporary relief provided by this denial, however, may appear as a bigger problem. Some organizations bring all the problems to the table and acknowledge them and use the collective wisdom of the group to solve them.

Trust   Trust is one of the features of organizational culture. It indicates a general disposition about internal relationship indicating their trustworthiness. Trust, especially in hospitality industry, plays a significant role, as most of the functions are enacted in groups. Trust level among group members could have a significant bearing on the outcome. Tan and Lim (2009) defined it as 'the willingness of a person to be vulnerable to the actions of fellow co-workers whose behaviour and actions that person cannot control'. Trusting relationship among co-workers increases the chances of sharing resources, disclosing privilege discovery of work processes. In case individual ability and motivation and knowledge of some employees fail to produce organizational results, they can access another resourceful person for help and advice within the organization without much hesitation. Interactions among co-workers potentially generate unspecified obligations, which may encourage more reciprocal exchanges. Co-workers, in this organizational context, will be less likely to invoke negative instruments such as social undermining to influence others to get the things done. Trusting relationship will not allow using anger and other negative emotions as an instrument for production of services. Under these reciprocal exchanges, symbiotic survival in the corporate world finds its meaning, provides fulfilling experiences, and unites workforce for greater causes. An individual using a common binding block of trust uses the positive side of human beings such as benevolence, integrity, and so on. An individual is believed to have or to be practising integrity when co-workers perceive that the individual adheres to a set of high ethical principles in dealing with individual and organizational responsibilities. Thus, the ability of an individual finds unrestrained expression in organizational pursuits, and working becomes an enjoyable experience. Trusting relationship among co-workers will ensure timely support, honour mutual commitments, and display more inclination to accept other individuals as they naturally are. Trust will create space for every individual according to the merit and ability of the individual. Trusting another individual has economic advantages, as it helps reduce paper work and support innovative practices. This leads to reduction in turnover intention and supports positive organizational behaviour. The workplace finds a healthy tone in dealing with collective aspirations.

Authenticity   The origin of work authenticity is believed to be linked with the Latin word *authenticus*. It signifies 'owing one's personal experiences, be they thoughts, emotions, needs, wants, preferences, or beliefs, and processes captured by the injunction to know oneself' (Harter 2005). The term *authentic* implies that one 'acts in accord with the true self, expressing oneself in ways that are consistent with inner thoughts and feelings' (Harter 2005). Some of the terms that reflect inauthenticity are 'hypocrite, charlatan, chameleon, imposter, phoney, fake, and fraud'. It could be said using the adjectival form of expressions such as 'elusive, evasive, phoney, artificial, manipulative, calculating, pretentious, crafty, conniving, duplicitous, deceitful, and dishonest'. Thus, becoming authentic implies getting in touch with the real self, without adding the colour of fake and inauthentic representation to the self. An authentic individual neither overestimates about self-worth nor attempts to present a glorified self to others. Inauthenticity could be achieved by 'fabricating, withholding, concealing, distorting, falsifying, pulling the wool over someone's eyes, posturing, charading, faking, and hiding behind a façade' (Harter 2005) Collective practice of inauthenticity may create multi-layer loops for suspicions and distrust, distort relationships, violate personal rights, and create space for speculations. This creates a dysfunctional workspace where employees show restricted participation and remain constrained within the scope of the job; it also discourages spontaneous and voluntary participations. Lack of authentic self also creates psychological tension for individuals while attempting to present false self to others knowing very well that the true self is in fact substantially different. An individual, living with glorified self, makes organizational function extremely difficult. For example, feedback, given during performance appraisal, will not be received well by the individual who subscribes to glorified self-estimation. Authentic organizational workspace encourages extension of positive support among co-workers and subordinates and enhances collective well-being, whereas lack of authenticity encourages scripted response and limited participation opportunity for individuals and creates an environment of suspicion. Employees show restricted participation because of fear of negative reaction and perception and thus want to play safe. Conversation among employees often gets distorted. Mistakes are often described as an outcome of co-workers' inability. The individual does not own up to the mistakes and often shifts the burden from self to others. Thus, authenticity is a great resource for any organization for smooth and productive functioning of the human system. Presence of authenticity in organizational dealings encourages employees to have a tolerant outlook towards mistakes committed by individuals. Thus, mistakes work as a stepping stone for future progression. Collective practice of authenticity builds and provides the base of the character of the workplace. Authentic ecology of the organization makes it habitable for humans.

Adams said it wonderfully,

In being loved, we become more open. In being open, we become more authentic. In being authentic, we become more loving and creative. Love, open awareness, and authentic existence are intimately inter-related. They co-arise interdependently and together comprise a coherent structure or well-being, allowing one to be most fully human and uniquely oneself.

Proactivity In most cases, proactivity has been described as a personal resource (individual quality). In the present context, proactivity is in fact an organizational resource, which requires different degrees of explanation. However, to have better synchronicity, proactivity is described as organizational and individual resources. Proactive behaviour is 'taking initiative in improving current circumstances or creating new ones; it involves challenging the status quo rather than passively adapting to present conditions' (Crant 2000). Individuals enriched with proactive tendencies usually do not only become the consumer of worldly resources but also alter the available worldly resources to bring changes for the betterment of lives around. Thus, it is about approach towards work. Proactive behaviour works on introduction of rules, regulations, methods, and procedures that are essentially a prime requirement to remain relevant in the ever-changing customers. Predominantly, proactive behaviour consists of personal initiatives and taking charge. Proactive behaviour is, thus, discretionary (volitional) behaviour that often engages in active search for improvement of work processes and invents newer ways of learning opportunity.

Autonomy Oldham and Hackman argued that autonomy embedded in the nature of the job provides intrinsic motivation to employees. Freedom to execute the job is the greatest reward for any capable employee. Autonomy increases higher degrees of involvement, enhances the speed of delivery of services, and reduces work-related stress. Autonomy indicates the practice of empowerment in an organization in its truest sense. Empowered employees find meaning in their work, provide grass-root-level solution deeply grounded in the pragmatic baseline, and give a sense of purpose. On the contrary, absence of autonomy reduces space for production of services required for varied demands of the customers. Absence of autonomy in organizational culture gives birth to a bureaucratic structure and brings inefficiency in the system, and eventually an inoperable human system.

At the individual level, it bestows a number of benefits. First, it gives a sense of self-determination. Self-determination indicates that they can choose the most appropriate action required to delight the customers. As the employees are located in the most proximate position with reference to the customers, employees with adequate autonomy could decide the most appropriate action. Besides, modern educated employees are not required to be micromanaged by supervisors. Second, perceived experience of autonomy provides meaning to the work as it has been designed by employees. As individual's voices and views find representation in the ultimate design, it generates high involvement. Thus, work becomes an appropriate avenue for self-expression. Work graduates from the mundane rituals to a highly evolved body of creativity. Third, autonomy in the workspace acknowledges individual talent, competence, and contribution. This enhances individual self-confidence and self-efficacy. Fourth, autonomy in the workspace allows individuals to believe that they are making distinctive contributions. Present day managers give a lot of lip service of giving autonomy to the grass-root-level employees; however, employees do not perceive it. In order to freely utilize resources, derived out of autonomy, individuals need to perceive or feel that they are empowered, have freedom, and are well rewarded for empowered behaviour.

Autonomy, embedded in the culture of the organization, makes employees innovative, fearless, and effective in their work. Employees working under highly assured autonomy could bring about transformational change in their workplace and assure mutual respect between subordinates and supervisors. Empowered employees find avenues to display their charismatic resources and abilities and deliver synergistic results.

Bureaucratic culture strongly impedes the autonomy of its employees. 'You need to take permissions from 10 people above your head to go for specific solutions. The biggest problem in our traditional old hotel is fear. Nobody takes a decision, and each managerial decision point becomes just a forwarding agent to the higher authority for decision. Fear of failure is so high that each decision point becomes redundant.' Tall hierarchy in the organizations often restrains autonomy in the system. Fear for decision in such a set-up never allows autonomy in the system. Nobody wants to undertake risk especially when there is a long tradition to follow top-down approach in decision making. Although some organizations claim to make changes in bureaucratic culture to assure autonomy to its employees, reward and other human resource management systems reward bureaucratic set-up. In the absence of relevant support from other human resource management functions, autonomy does not make sense to its employees. Thus, autonomy is a great resource and is difficult to achieve. Once the management acquires productive culture, it provides inimitable characteristic to the whole competition.

Collaboration   A collaborative workspace is highly desirable for any organization. Collaboration facilitates high-quality relationship to emerge in the organizational workspace. Collaboration indicates a few important and precious resources that exist in the organization. First, it indicates that emotion-carrying capacity in the organization is relatively high. Individuals display a diverse range of emotions. Negative emotion prevents collaboration, whereas psychological safety allows freedom to the employees to display a whole range of emotions. This potentially generates scope for a greater degree of communication among employees for collaboration rather than hiding it for later restrained behaviour. Second, organizational culture is enriched with tensility. Tensility indicates the capacity to bend and display flexibility while dealing with other individuals. Individuals need not be overtly cautious while dealing with each other. Third, organizational culture is enriched with connectivity with each other. Connectivity indicates a strong bond among employees and is open to ideas. High-quality relationships produce collaboration in the organization. Collaboration does not allow individual deficiency to affect the organization; rather, a collective approach makes individual efforts look larger than self. Work in the hospitality industry relies on collaboration across departments and team members. Break in collaboration will play havoc on the service-producing capability and destroy market reputation.

Experimentation   Experimentation is a precious genre of commonly held beliefs for proactive approach to organizational challenges. It signifies a range of collective beliefs that sustain constant attempt for improvization of collective actions undertaken by employees. It could mean self-starting, proactive, and a persistent effort to do things differently. Work in hospitality organizations is highly interdependent. Employees need to share perspectives and information to resolve issues that arise while delivering delightful service experience to the customers. Experimentation is encouraged by providing psychological safety to its employees. Psychological safety is 'a shared belief that the team is safe for interpersonal risk taking' (Edmondson 1999 p.354). Trying to do things differently invites the highest degree of risk of failure. Fear of failure among employees will hinder experimentation behaviour among employees if failure is reinforced by punishment. Individuals will not take risk. However, if failure is accommodated well in organizational life, it will provide psychological safety to its employees. For example, errors committed by individuals and teams are required to be acknowledged to redefine processes to make them error free. However, if error is constantly treated as stigma and it decides the career of employees, employees will not report it and continue to provide error-prone services to their customers. Increases in psychological safety perception will enhance error-reporting rate, and collective strength of the organization could be deployed to provide error-free services. Higher psychological safety perception will encourage employees to seek help from others. In this kind of environment, individuals, seeking help from others, will not be interpreted as a sign of incompetency. Seeking help provides recognition of each other's talent and provides space for each other. While seeking feedback from each other, a higher perception of psychological safety will provide an accurate picture regarding the original state of affairs and will not take refuge under sweet talk. Thus, experimentation in organizational culture is embedded by installation of psychological safety among employees. Experimentation increases the chance of challenging collective assumptions and takes the risk of doing it differently, efficiently, and effortlessly.

Competing Value Framework

University of Michigan faculty members developed competing value framework to develop understanding of organizational culture. This framework has been widely used as it was found to be robust and consistent. There are two axes producing four quadrants in the framework. The vertical axis indicates the range from flexibility to control, whereas the horizontal axis ranges from internal focus to an external focus. Thus, these ultimately create four quadrants: clan, adhocracy, market, and hierarchy (Fig. 9.3).

Clan Under this cultural orientation, individuals display a higher degree of intention to collaborate. Most of the managers and leaders operating in this type of culture display bias to facilitate the work process. Leaders are mostly mentors and build teams. The predominant value drivers are commitment and communication. The basic motto of this type of culture is to *do things together*.

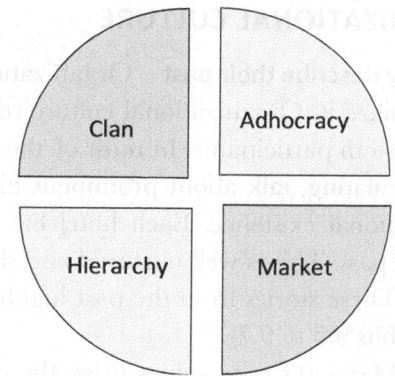

Figure 9.3 Salient dimensions of the competing value model

Adhocracy Adhocracy culture is overt bias towards creativity and innovative solutions. Leaders are seen as innovators, entrepreneurs, and visionaries. All the energy in the system is guided to build breakthrough in the process to deliver the most appropriate solution to the customer. The tendency in this culture is overchallenging the basic assumptions to *do things first over others*. Creative orientation makes this culture highly inspiring, and each individual contributes for the betterment of the world. The basic value drivers are innovative solutions and transformation of the world with agility. Experiencing constant change is the basic way of life in this kind of organization.

Market The competing values model emphasizes on decisive actions towards resolving organizational problems. Fast response to any organizational issues is the way of life here. Competitive spirit follows every bit of organizational life. The basic motto of this type of culture is to *do things first*. Leaders usually display distinctive orientation such as competition. They encourage competition as they believe that competition will bring the organizational system to perform at the most optimum level. The basic value drivers are market share, achievement of goal, and so on. Aggressively competing against each other is the way of life.

Hierarchy As the name implies, control culture is basically focused on enforcement of direct rules and regulations. Bringing stability in the system to produce business results is the basic aim in this type of culture. The basic motto of this type of culture is to *do things right*. Great emphasis on the foundation of measurement and enforcement of structure for improvement of efficiency is the tradition of this type of culture. The leaders are seen as coordinators, monitors, and organizers. Value drivers in this kind of organization are efficiency, timeliness, consistency, and uniformity.

DIAGNOSING ORGANIZATIONAL CULTURE

How they describe their past Organizational culture is invisible, and it is difficult to tangibilize it. Organizational culture resides in stories, histories, and memories of the system participants. In most of the organizations, stories of the past, which keep circulating, talk about prominent historical events that have prompted this organizational existence. Each hotel has stories to tell its guests and employees about its past. This is well nurtured and shared to reinforce a certain part of their culture. These stories from the past highlight the value of the entrepreneur. (Also see Exhibits 9.5 to 9.7)

> Marriott's core values drive the culture. Our culture influences the way we treat associates, customers, and the community, which impacts all our successes. In the words of J.W. Marriott, Jr, 'Culture is the life-thread and glue that links our past, present, and future'.

Exhibit 9.5 Marriott—Philosophy and Core Values

Our Global Diversity & Inclusion Philosophy

At Marriott, diversity is more than a goal—it's our business. From our global workforce to our customers, vendors, franchisees, and owners, our diverse differences give our company its strength and competitive edge. In the process, we've set the standard for the entire hospitality industry.

Our global workforce mirrors the communities where we live and work every day. Our employees hail from dozens of nations, speak more than 50 languages, and work together as a team under the Marriott banner around the globe.

And our diversity goes beyond backgrounds and nationalities—we pride ourselves on embracing the unique perspectives and talents of our employees. We know that our employees are our greatest asset because it's through their dedication that we deliver exceptional customer service.

Our Spirit to Serve

Marriott's Spirit to Serve, the foundation of our company culture, is simply the way we do business—everyday, everywhere—with our employees, our customers, and in the communities where we live and work.

Our Employees

Our Spirit to Serve is the unshakable conviction that our people are our most important asset. Our performance-reward system recognizes the important contributions of both our management and non-management employees. Our training and development programmes support our employees' goals of learning new skills, growing

Contd

Exhibit 9.5 *Contd*

their careers, and having rewarding experiences in whatever area of our business they choose.

Our Customers

Our Spirit to Serve is about our attention to detail and our pride in focusing on our guests. We know that our guests can count on our unique blend of quality, consistency, personalized service, and recognition almost anywhere in the world with whichever Marriott brand they choose.

Our Communities

Our Spirit to Serve is demonstrated every day through employee and company support of local, national, and global initiatives and programs. It's what we call doing business the Marriott way. It's an unmatched, deep commitment to giving back everywhere we can.

Source: Company Website.

Exhibit 9.6 Marriott's Core Values in Relation to Organizational Culture

- Marriott is committed to fair treatment of associates and to providing training and advancement opportunities to all.
- Marriott's reputation for superior customer service rises out of a long tradition that started with J. Willard Marriott's simple goal for Hot Shoppes to provide 'Good Food and Good Service at a Fair Price'.
  - 'Do Whatever it Takes to Take Care of the Customer'.
  - Pay extraordinary attention to detail.

- Take pride in their physical surroundings.
- Use their creativity to find new ways to meet the needs of customers.
- The company actively supports the community and encourages associate volunteerism through a variety of organizations.
- At Marriott, the perpetuation of a company's culture has a proven positive financial impact.

Source: http://www.marriott.com/corporateinfo/culture/coreCulture.mi last accessed on 11 March 2012.

How they differentiate with competition One of the members representing a leading hospitality company described themselves in relation to its competitor while making presentation during a campus interview: 'We do not make steel. We do not make salt. We are pure hotelier.' The aforementioned statement made by the executive is an attempt to differentiate his or her organization from the others operating in the industry. The point of differentiation in this case is incumbent on the exclusivity of their services to the extent of being restricted to hospitality services only and not broadening the gamut to other unrelated products and services, which many other conglomerates often do.

> We see an organization that aims at leadership in the hospitality industry by understanding its guests, and designing and delivering products and services, which enable it to exceed their expectations. We will always demonstrate care for our customers through anticipation of their needs, attention to detail, distinctive excellence, warmth, and concern.

– Oberoi Hotels

Exhibit 9.7   People Philosophy

HYATT INTERNATIONAL HOTELS & RESORTS

Who We Are

Hyatt International operates 91 hotels and resorts in 39 countries, with 32 new hotels under development.

In 1969, Hyatt International Hotels & Resorts opened its first hotel in Asia, the Hyatt Regency Hong Kong.

Today, Hyatt International Hotels & Resorts specializes in deluxe and luxury hotels with facilities and services for the discerning traveller. Hyatt has expanded its core brand, Hyatt Regency, to include Grand Hyatt, Park Hyatt, and Hyatt Resort properties worldwide.

With 32 new hotels under development, Hyatt International Hotels & Resorts is creating more than 20,000 exciting job opportunities in Europe, Africa, Middle East, Asia, Pacific, and Latin America within the next five years.

Our People Philosophy

It is our philosophy that it is the people of Hyatt International Hotels & Resorts who make the Hyatt experience an exceptional one. Guided by our Corporate Values, we strive to equip and empower our people to develop careers, not jobs, with Hyatt International Hotels & Resorts.

Innovation and an entrepreneurial spirit are the foundation for the way we conduct business. Our goal is to attract and retain a workforce that is motivated to provide a level of service, which is excellent, innovative, and customer-driven, and reflects the local cultures where we do business. We believe we can accomplish this by being a 'listening' company of well-informed, impassioned people.

Hyatt International Hotels & Resorts strives to provide a fair and ethical work environment for all its employees of all Hyatt International Hotels & Resorts worldwide. Our people are our principle asset, and it is their commitment to the Values of Hyatt International Hotels & Resorts that sets us apart from our competitors.

Source: http://www.hyatt.com/hyatt/careers/international/;jsessionid=42EFE2B559C3EA2FD2AD846683D19466.atg08-prd-atg1.

Pay attention to stories and anecdotes   In order to have an understanding about the fabric of culture, it is important to know the stories the organization uses to describe themselves. Each hospitality organization has its colourful past. This past timeline is used to energize human workforce.

With vision and imagination, Mr. Oberoi converted old and dilapidated palaces, historical monuments, and buildings into magnificent hotels such as The Oberoi Grand in Calcutta, the historic Mena House Oberoi in Cairo and The Windsor in Australia. It was, in fact, in the face of severe opposition that the State Government of Victoria awarded Mr. Oberoi the lease of The Windsor, a heritage building in Melbourne. He personally supervised the restoration of the hotel to its original grandeur and later acquired it. The Oberoi Cecil in Shimla, built in the early 20th century, reopened in April 1997 after extensive and meticulous renovation.

(From company website)

Read what the other says about the company In order to understand the true nature of organizational culture, it is important to listen to people who have the opportunity to access and the competency to speak. What people say about one organization originates from durable public perception and reflects some part of the truth.

'If we think of brands as stories about products, services, or people that buyers believe in, then the Tata brand has been through a series of narratives. In its early life, it offered a powerful counterpoint to the prevailing culture of traditional Indian business. It sought to show us that enlightened business was not a contradiction in terms of as it successfully reconciled diverse, often conflicting, interest (Desai 2010).

Read what the company says about itself Most of the companies follow a unique language to describe themselves. This language provides them identity, and they use it to achieve corporate objectives. Some of the languages are indicative of their organizational architecture and nature of dealing among their employees.

It is our philosophy that it is the people of Hyatt International Hotels & Resorts who make the Hyatt experience an exceptional one. Guided by our Corporate Values, we strive to equip and empower our people to develop careers, not jobs, with Hyatt International Hotels & Resorts.

Innovation and an entrepreneurial spirit are the foundation for the way we conduct business. Our goal is to attract and retain a workforce that is motivated to provide a level of service, which is excellent, innovative, and customer-driven, and reflects the local cultures where we do business. We believe we can accomplish this by being a 'listening' company of well-informed, impassioned people.

Hyatt International Hotels & Resorts strives to provide a fair and ethical work environment for all its employees of all Hyatt International Hotels & Resorts worldwide. Our people are our principle asset, and it is their commitment to the Values of Hyatt International Hotels & Resorts that sets us apart from our competitors.

Test how the company greets strangers The culture of a company could be reflected while dealing with strangers. Strangers have different occasions to interact with the organization such as conference call, meeting with the officer bearers of the company, and so on. In some cases, they are given time to talk over the issue, while sometimes they are kept waiting. This reflects a poor display of respect to others' time. Timely appointment signifies expression of respect and care. When they engage in conversation, the employee attempts to talk about the organizational life, provides socially desirable responses, and artificially inflates it with fake positive statements. It is wise to be careful before making speedy judgement about any work culture.

Talk to people and find how they describe way of life   Most of the employees develop a unique expression to describe their workplace. This brief description about the workplace reflects the essence of the culture the organization is able to instil in them.

> 'Here, nobody cares. You feel neglected. You need to survive on your strength. If you fall, do not expect people to rescue and save you. They will not hesitate to tread over you'.

> 'It is a great place to work: highly spontaneous, free from high emotion. Easy way to work is to be with the flow'.

Work culture is truly reflected in the Rule of Garage, as practised in Hewlett-Packard. It talks about the way of life in HP.

Observe how people spend their time   Spending time is reflected in organizational culture. Slow work culture talks about bureaucratic work process, whereas speedy decision highlights the urgency for achievement of results. Employees could be collaborative in dealing with solution—they will spend time to meet, plan, and seek assistance. Free gossip in the organization signifies existence of poor communication policy and non-functional allocation of workload. Wastage of time is the indication that a number of problems exist in the organization; one of them is definitely the leadership problem.

Look at the content of their discussions, especially at informal places   Employees are expected to display positive emotions in their workplace. In order to get positive performance appraisal, employees are trained to display a marketable range of emotions such as smile. In public places, employees speak as per the expectations of the enforcement authority, boss, or what the organization expects to hear. In some informal places such as staff cafeteria, staff washroom, and so on, it acquires some degree of privacy, where employees speak from their heart. They exchange notes with each other more frankly. Capturing some fragments of these conversations provides valuable clue about the work culture.

POSITIVE OR NEGATIVE CULTURE

The Rules of Garage as laid down by HP in Exhibit 9.8 have obvious effects on creating a positive culture that patronizes innovation and attempts at doing away with office politics or other aspects that impede organizational growth and sustenance.

It is difficult to differentiate between positive and negative culture as it is highly subjective and it is difficult to identify discernable traits of these cultures. Organizational culture should be accommodative towards new thoughts, feelings, views, and decisions, unlike the past. This requires adequate synthesis power in the organization, failing which it will become highly chaotic and unmanageable. Positive culture is progressive, inclusive, value based, performance orientated, institutional, and enduring (see Exhibit 9.9). Progressive signifies those tenets of the

---

Exhibit 9.8   Work Culture at HP

The Rules of Garage

'Believe you can change the world.

Work quickly, keep the tools unlocked, work whenever.

Know when to work alone and when to work together.

Share tools, ideas. Trust your colleagues.

No Politics. No bureaucracy. (These are ridiculous in a garage.)

The customer defines a job well done.

Radical ideas are not bad ideas.

Invent different ways of working.

Make a contribution every day. If it doesn't contribute, it doesn't leave the garage.

Believe that together we can do anything.

Invent'.

Exhibit 9.9   The Oberoi Group—People Philosophy

Key Principles

Organizational structure and manning   Organizational structures will be lean, with a minimum number of levels and with clear individual reporting and accountability.

Recruitment and selection   At every level of the organization, we will select people of the highest quality and with the highest potential to advance our business.

Performance appraisal   To inculcate a culture of personal growth and organizational excellence based on principles of performance-based results.

Learning and development   We will aim for world-class managerial and technical excellence using continuous learning and development to support the business and encourage growth from within.

Career development   We will provide careers, not merely jobs, to our people, through developing them in ways where organizational needs are matched with personal strengths and potential.

Succession planning   Our focus on development of people will reflect our international character and ensure that we have the right number of employees with the appropriate skills in the right place at the right time.

Contd

Exhibit 9.9 *Contd*

Training Transfers, national and international, will be based on organizational needs and career development requirements of the individual.

Compensation Our compensation philosophy will enable us to recruit and retain the best and the most highly motivated talent, and will encourage the highest level of performance amongst our employees through result-based reward and recognition, and be related to the Company's overall business performance.

Employee relations To create preserve and open harmonious environment in which employees at all levels will want to give off their very best in delivering world-class service at the highest level of productivity.

Retention Retention of talent is the key management responsibility as is separation of those whose performance is consistently below par or who breach the accepted ethical standards and rules of conduct.

culture that make the organization future ready. Inclusive culture signifies allowing and encouraging employees' participation in decision-making processes, and it does not eliminate anybody because of hierarchy, designation, and remuneration. It acknowledges the potential of the individual for organizational contribution. Performance-oriented culture signifies all those tenets of a culture that account for and are responsible for organizational performances. We need to exercise a cautious approach to understanding this aspect of the culture. Many cultures produce results, adequate for the time being. As the world is changing at a very rapid speed, organizational culture should be assured of future progressive performance too. The word 'institutional' signifies that organizational culture should have the potency to be embedded in the system, processes, and rituals.

CASE IN POINT

15 September 2010, 11.19 p.m. IST, Reuters
Goldman sued by women claiming gender bias

New York

Goldman Sachs Group Inc. was hit with a gender bias lawsuit by three women who said Wall Street's most profitable bank maintains an 'outdated corporate culture' that systematically deprives women of pay and promotions available to men. The plaintiffs are seeking class-action status on behalf of women who have worked as Goldman managing directors, vice presidents and associates in the last six years. It seeks punitive and other damages, and an end to gender bias at Goldman. The lawsuit, filed Wednesday in Manhattan federal court, contends that Goldman managers have unfettered discretion to assign accounts and responsibilities, and decide who gets administrative support and training. This has resulted in 'unchecked gender bias', the lawsuit said, that causes women to be underrepresented in management, at just 14 per cent of partners, 17 per cent of managing directors, and 29 per cent of vice presidents.

Contd

Case in Point *Contd*

The policies 'are part and parcel of an outdated corporate culture', the complaint said. 'Goldman Sachs has intentionally implemented these company-wide policies and practices in order to pay their male employees more money than their female counterparts, and to promote them more frequently'. Goldman denied the allegations. 'This suit is without merit', spokesman Lucas van Praag said in an email. 'People are critical to our business, and we make extraordinary efforts to recruit, develop, and retain outstanding women professionals'. The lawsuit was brought by Lisa Parisi, 48, a former managing director in asset management; Cristina Chen-Oster, 39, a former vice-president in convertible bonds; and Shanna Orlich, 30, a former associate in trading. 'Wall Street doesn't get it', said Kelly Dermody, a partner at Lieff Cabraser Heimann & Bernstein, LLP, representing the plaintiffs. 'Even as some (women) do crack the glass ceiling, Wall Street continues to pay them less, relegate them to jobs that have less upside potential, and exclude them from important clients and business opportunities', she added. Large banks and brokerages are regularly the target of US lawsuits alleging discrimination.

Improper Sexual Advance Alleged

Parisi alleged she was significantly underpaid compared with male colleagues, including a 60 per cent drop from 2005 to 2007, and had investments taken away from her despite her skill in stock picking. Chen-Oster alleged she was repeatedly shunted to lower-paying and lower-priority jobs, and had her accounts taken away after she returned from a maternity leave. She also said that after a dinner at a topless bar to celebrate a colleague's promotion, an event that all employees in her group were encouraged to attend, a male colleague attempted a sexual act with her. She also contended she was subjected to a sexually charged email by a male colleague that made fun of her Chinese heritage.

Orlich contended in the court papers that she was deprived of work and subjected to greater criticism than male workers. She said she once was kept from a golf outing because she was too 'junior' though several male colleagues just out of college attended. Chen-Oster resigned from Goldman after eight years in 2005, while Parisi and Orlich's jobs were terminated in 2008 after they had worked there since 2001 and 2006, respectively, the lawsuit said. Parisi lives in Georgia, and Chen-Oster and Orlich in New Jersey. They were not immediately available for comment.

The case is Chen-Oster et al. v Goldman Sachs & Co et al., US District Court, Southern District of New York, No. 10-06950.

Source: http://economictimes.indiatimes.com/news/international-business/goldman-sued-by-women-claiming-gender-bias/articleshow/6562270.cms accessed on 11 March 2012.

HOW ORGANIZATIONS TRANSMIT THEIR CULTURE

Through stories, myths, and heroes Organizations that have stood the test of time and have grown over the years generally owe their sustenance and growth to the heroics of certain key employees including the entrepreneurs themselves— something that is continually reinforced among the employees in order to impel others to outperform and thereby lead by example. This is normally done through the circulation of stories or myths or even heroes among the employees of the organization.

Through explicit language used during training and development As a new employee joins the organization, the learning and development department undertakes special efforts to talk about the culture of the organization. It is expected that the new employee should behave as per the collective aspiration of employees and the company. This process is called the *socialization process*. During this period, employees are given adequate input about the way of life inside the organization. Employees are receptive at the entry stage and learn quickly.

HOW LEADERS NURTURE, EMBED, AND COMMUNICATE CULTURE

Attention, measurement, and control Various components of culture are made visible by installing, maintaining, and reinforcing organizational processes. HR professionals make specific efforts to nurture these components in their overall organizational initiatives. Constant monitoring of these components is crucial for its survival as the organization undergoes constant change. These changes could be due to frequent change of employees, restructuring of organizational processes, and so on. Therefore, constant attention is being paid to nurture and reinforce the various components of culture.

Reaction to critical incidents and organizational crisis Organizational crisis gives opportunity and occasion to individual employees to play a key role in resolving it. On its successful completion, it produces heroes and provides stories, which will inspire employees over the years. Organizational life always provides opportunities to employees to rise above the ordinary and set exemplary behaviour. It is important that these stories are carried over the years for motivating employees.

Role modelling, teaching, and coaching Role modelling is systematically done with the help of informal buddy system or formal mentoring system. As a formal organizational system does not provide support to the individual, informal buddy system involves assigning co-workers and supervisors to the new employees for sharing, accessing, and seeking special help in case they require so. Formal mentoring system also provides suitable support to the new employees and indirectly enforces the various cultural rituals.

Formal set of values and philosophy Each organization stands for certain values that they hold dearly for organizational processes. They openly communicate it to all its stakeholders and set examples to reinforce it over time. Human resource professionals selectively float all those stories, taken from organizational lives, which reinforce all these values. This makes it possible for wider acceptance of those values among its employees and generates further support for adherence and adoption of those values.

Allocation of reward and status To reinforce cultural nuances among its stakeholders, especially among employees, organization makes specific efforts. It uses reward mechanism to reinforce value-based behaviour among its employees.

The Google Culture

Although Google has grown a lot since it opened in 1998, we still maintain a small company feel. At lunchtime, almost everyone eats in the office café, sitting at whatever table has an opening and enjoying conversations with Googlers from different teams. Our commitment to innovation depends on everyone being comfortable sharing ideas and opinions. Every employee is a hands-on contributor, and everyone wears several hats. Because we believe that each Googler is an equally important part of our success, no one hesitates to pose questions directly to Larry or Sergey in our weekly all-hands ('TGIF') meetings—or spike a volleyball across the net at a corporate officer.

We are aggressively inclusive in our hiring, and we favor ability over experience. We have offices around the world and dozens of languages are spoken by Google staffers, from Turkish to Telugu. The result is a team that reflects the global audience Google serves. When not at work, Googlers pursue interests from cross-country cycling to wine tasting, from flying to frisbee. 'As we continue to grow, we are always looking for those who share a commitment to creating search perfection and having a great time doing it'.

Source: http://www.google.com/corporate/culture.html accessed on 11 March 2012.

Reward is one of the widely used mechanisms and is considered to be an effective means of reinforcement. Thus, any employee who demonstrates a behaviour that reflects cultural nuances is reinforced by promotion, salary increments, and other types of remunerations.

Recruitment and selection   At the time of recruitment, HR professionals pay specific attention to recruit individuals who display or have the potential to display the characteristic of their corporate culture. Most of the HR professionals responsible for recruitment functions follow organization–person fit framework while selecting individuals for their organizations. Research indicates that an individual will seek a job and stay at it if there is a good amount of match between the applicant's self-concept and organizational culture. Similar tendency between organizational culture and individual personality orientation helps build harmonious relationship and potentially generates higher degree of satisfaction. Thus, similar value congruence between individual employees and organizational culture creates a 'fundamental and relatively enduring' relationship, which provides comfortable work experience. Organizational culture thus becomes a rare resource, which potentially attracts employees towards value-rich organization.

Physical space and building   Physical workspace and building structure speak about the organizational culture. Office workspace and its workflow management signify how top management imagined the work will be distributed and executed. For example, even though Google started its business quite some time ago, it is successful in giving college life experience in its workplace by doing things that are quite unheard of. Table 9.1 lists some of the best places to work for.

Table 9.1 Best places to work for (2010)

Rank	Companies
1	Google India Pvt. Ltd
2	**MakeMyTrip (India) Pvt. Ltd**
3	Intel Technology India Pvt. Ltd
4	**Marriott Hotels India Pvt. Ltd**
5	NetApp India Pvt. Ltd
6	American Express, India
7	NTPC Ltd
8	PayPal India Pvt. Ltd
9	Ajuba Solutions India Pvt. Ltd
10	SAS Institute (India) Pvt. Ltd
11	Crowne Plaza Today
12	Dow Corning India Pvt. Ltd
13	**Taj Hotels Resorts and Palaces**
14	Godrej Consumer Products Ltd
15	Whirlpool of India
16	InterGlobe Enterprises Ltd
17	iNautix Technologies India Pvt. Ltd
18	Hilti India Pvt. Ltd
19	Titan Industries Ltd
20	Intelenet Global Services
21	Qualcomm India Pvt. Ltd
22	Federal Express Corporation
23	Kotak Mahindra Bank Ltd
24	Jubilant Foodworks Ltd
25	Classic Stripes Ltd

The entries in bold represent the hospitality and travel and tourism business.

Corporate logo Corporate logo is a means of communication about corporate identity that is reflected in its logo design and colour. Along with providing trademark right, it provides visibility in public. Corporate logo provides symbolic

CASE IN POINT

Google Culture and Office Space

- Local expressions of each location, from a mural in Buenos Aires to ski gondolas in Zurich, showcasing each office's region and personality.
- Bicycles or scooters for efficient travel between meetings; dogs; lava lamps; massage chairs; large inflatable balls.
- Googlers sharing cubes, yurts, and huddle rooms, and very few solo offices.
- Laptops everywhere—standard issue for mobile coding, email on the go, and note-taking.
- Football, pool tables, volleyball courts, assorted video games, pianos, ping-pong tables, and gyms that offer yoga and dance classes.
- Grassroots employee groups for all interests, like meditation, film, wine tasting and salsa dancing.
- Healthy lunches and dinners for all staff at a variety of cafés.
- Break rooms packed with a variety of snacks and drinks to keep Googlers going.

Source: www.google.com/culture last accessed on 11 March 2012.

Figure 9.4   Logos of some leading hotels operating in India

meaning to its stakeholders, expresses the inner core value of the organization, and helps build the company's identity to its employees (Fig. 9.4).

MANAGING AND CHANGING CULTURE

Changing culture is a big challenge. The art of changing non-productive culture to productive culture in a hospitality organization is an important skill, which prospective hospitality professionals need to master.

Denial mode   Incorporating changes in the organization creates the highest degree of resistance among its employees. They fear from a wide range of issues such as fear of losing the job, work comfort, new rules and regulations, and so on. At the initial stage, the individual remains petrified into diverse types of fear, which in turn motivates them to believe that the change is not required. Therefore, it is important to note that the manager, responsible for orchestrating change in the organization, should acknowledge this human aspect and develop suitable emotive and non-emotive psychological initiatives to help employees overcome it.

New culture   The change manager must develop compelling reasons to articulate for its stakeholders. Whenever a change process is initiated, major questions are raised: Do we need change in our culture? Why can't we continue our old traditions? What is new in the new culture that will make employees' life better? These are a few questions required to be answered while orchestrating change in the organization.

Stories   The change manager must develop and identify suitable stories highlighting the essence of new values that are being incorporated in the system. A good number of people use stories to communicate that which is otherwise not possible to communicate. One emotive change session began with the following comment when the new chairman took over the company after dismissal of the previous chairman of the company for alleged ethical lapses:

> 'Stories are not new here. We do not bring new stories. We make our stories with our collective resources, which perhaps did not get noticed by the people. Stories are made from the daily lives of the housekeeper, room boy, or steward. We do not bring new stories. We tell stories that you have made. Our stories are about you. Stories do not speak about corporate structure and history. No illusion, no myth to sell here. We bring your stories. The stories which you wrote over the years. We sing with you. We are you'.

Need for change   The change manager must articulate the need for change. It should be stated from the perspective of the employees. What change offers to each of its employees should be relatively attractive and less risky to their career and remuneration. Educating employees on the necessity of the employees will increase early adoption of change among employees.

Spread the tenets of the new culture   It is difficult to orchestrate change in organizational culture. Many Indian hotel companies used to follow unique techniques to alter cultural change in the company. For example, every time this five-star hotel company bought, acquired, or took over the management control of another hotel, it sent a good number of employees from its parent hotels, especially the heads of all the departments. They used to deploy a few employees in each department. These employees used to set up their departments in a way that represented their parent company's culture. However, they used to do it slowly in every department. These employees were known as the Dirty Dozen. Their sole responsibility was to take over the new hotel property, install their parent company's culture, see it running successfully, and then leave it to a different set of people who will take it forward. Thus, employees deployed for mergers and acquisitions were not used for managing ordinary hotels. They were known as the Dirty Dozen in the history of the company.

Communicate new culture (informal and formal)   There are a number of ways new cultural tenets could be embedded in the existing culture leading it to a desirable state of new culture. Posters, presentation, speech, informal dinner, counselling staff members, walk the talk, and so on always helped install new culture.

Composition of the workforce   Composition of the workforce decides the tune of the organization. During mergers and acquisitions, newly acquired company experiences new power equation, and this in turn plays havoc on the existing employees. Uncertainty, fear of job loss, new power equations, and so on are the sources of great exodus among its key employees. Rank and file employees also follow the path shown by these key leaders' exit from the company. These create immense pressure on the organization. Employees from the acquiring company move in with their way of working style and change the composition of the workforce, which in turn gives birth to new culture.

Mergers and acquisitions   Literature review suggests that substantial proportion of the mergers and acquisitions cases fail to produce the desired results because of apparent mismatch between two organizational cultures. For example, Daimler-Chrysler merger failed because of durable difference in their respective engineering and corporate culture. They were considered to be equal partners. However, over the years, Daimler culture was given due importance, and that did not go well with the employees of Chrysler. It is important to note that Daimler Benz predominantly had German culture, whereas Chrysler had American work culture. When both attempted to refine administrative processes, it only created a mess, and it was difficult to indentify and hold the middle ground of goodness from both.

Therefore, even though financial, marketing, and strategic science suggests merger or acquisition between two companies, they may not be suitable from the behavioural science point of view. Most of the CEOs provide financial, marketing, and strategic logic for merger and acquisition. These types of explanations are usually widely accepted in the stock market and generate legitimacy for strategic actions such as merger and acquisition. However, these are not necessarily acceptable among employees, who are forced to accept organizational arrangement arising out of strategic action. This presents a blow to the overall survival of the strategic deal. To avoid this kind of problem arising out of cultural clash, most of the companies keep the newly acquired company as a separate entity for some considerable time. During this phase, HR professionals gradually incorporate changes in the company without creating much flutter or noise in the organizational system.

Axis-Enam Deal: Staff Integration Key to Merger's Success
18 November, 2010, 10.42 a.m. IST, Samidha Sharma, TNN

Mumbai

A merger or acquisition is branded a success in the corporate world only if the two organizations involved can integrate on the people front. Probably that is why the Axis Bank and Enam Securities management could not have enough of stressing on the point that they were a 'great strategic and cultural fit' while announcing the Rs 2,067 crore deal that brings the third largest private bank in India and a domestic boutique brokerage and investment banking firm together.

'We believe there are significant synergies, negligible overlaps, and a strong cultural fit between the two organizations', Axis Bank MD Shikha Sharma said while announcing the deal. Virtually the entire 450-strong Enam workforce will migrate to the new entity, but why did the Enam management choose Axis Bank over other suitors? The answer came from Vallabh Bhanshali, chairman, Enam Securities, who sought to stress on the human integration. 'The prospect of merging with an Indian bank with a corporate culture much like ours, along with having a value-oriented business driven by delivery and not marketing made Axis Bank a perfect fit for us', he said.

HR experts say that there can be other challenges to a merger of this kind where a smaller entity is acquired by a larger firm. 'A lot of people, especially in sectors such as investment banking, move from big companies to boutique firms to get a higher position. In such cases, the acquirer has to take special care to pay attention to such employees and address their needs', says Shiv Agrawal, CEO, ABC Consultants. Apart from issues on the people front, there can be client-related problems as well. 'There is apprehension among Enam clients as to whether they will be serviced as well by a bigger entity. The key here is communication,' Agrawal added.

K. Sudarshan, managing partner, EMA Partners, feels there are challenges ahead for both on the integration front. 'The biggest challenge for Axis Bank will be to transform individual relationships brought in by Enam and institutionalize them like a Goldman Sachs or a Deutsche Bank does. The idea is that people can move on but businesses should stay', he said.

Some HR experts believe there would be a definite upside for Enam employees. 'The advantages of being part of a large company is that you gain from its experience on every front and in the long term, the employees tend to benefit,' says Namr Kishore, head, organizational learning, Manpower India.

SUMMARY

Organizational culture is gaining currency among practitioners and researchers as its true potential emerges. Organizational culture is such a kind of collective belief and way of life practices that has the potential to bring in organizational effectiveness and provide durable strategic competency. Organizational culture is like a fabric that has the potency to unite the diverse workforce under some common thread of aspiration and motivate them to achieve it. Organizational culture is an important resource, capable of providing strategic advantage over the competition. Top leadership requires examining various tenets of organizational culture and its effectiveness and taking direct control to build the productive culture. They also need to play key role in sustaining and reinforcing the collective aspiration of the employees. At the same time, objective assessment is crucial to examine the merit of organizational culture and whether it is productive. Most of the organizations may enter into the loop of inefficiency by collectively practising approaches that are dysfunctional, unsustainable, and relatively unproductive. With the help of true leadership, organizational culture could be steered to all those values that are really reflected in organizational life.

KEY TERMS

Organizational culture   Organizational culture is shared belief, attitude, and values nourished by the majority of the employees in an organization.

Competing value framework   It is a framework, developed by University of Michigan faculty members, to explain our understanding of organizational culture.

Cultural web   It is a framework used to articulate the peculiarity of one organizational culture. It consists of seven dimensions, namely, symbols, power structures, control system, organizational structure, routines, ritual, and myth.

OCTAPACE   It is a framework used to explain organizational culture. It consists of openness, confrontation, trust, authenticity, proactivity, autonomy, collaboration, and experimentation.

EXERCISES

Concept Review Questions

1. Define organizational culture and describe various tenets of organizational culture construct.
2. Review various functions of organizational culture.
3. Examine the cultural web model and describe various elements of organizational culture using this model.
4. Describe how organizations transmit cultural components among its employees.

Critical Thinking Questions

1. Examine the role of top leadership for creation and sustenance of various tenets of organizational culture.
2. To what extent you believe that organizational culture could potentially deliver strategic advantage over competition? Provide relevant rationale for your answer.

Assignment

Using a cultural web model, carry out a cultural audit of your hotel management institute or the hotel where you have undergone training. How do you address the negative flavour of the culture and inject positivity into it?

REFERENCES

Desai, S., 'The Problem with Being Ratan Tata', *Economic Times*, dated 13 December 2010.

Edmondson A.C., 'Psychological Safety and Learning Behavior in Work Teams', *Administrative Science Quarterly*, Volume 44, 1999, 350–383.

Harter, S., 'Authenticity', *Handbook of Positive Psychology*, 2005, p.382–394.

Kuoni website, http://www.kuoniindia.com/career.asp accessed on 11 March 2012

Peters, Thomas J. and Waterman Jr, *In Search of Excellence: Lessons from America's Best Run Companies*, Warner Books, New York, 1982.

Schein, E. H., *Organizational Culture and Leadership* (2nd ed.), Jossey-Bass, San Francisco, 1992.

Singh, S. *Human Resource Development: HRD-IR Interface Approach*, Atlantic Publishers & Distributors, New Delhi, 2008.

Tan, H.H. and Lim, A.K.H., 'Trust in Co-workers and Trust in Organization', *Journal of Psychology: Interdisciplinary and Applied*, Volume 143, Issue 1, 2009, 45–66.

Witcher, B. and Chau, V., *Strategic Management: Principles and Practice*, South-Western Cengage Learning, Hampshire, 2010.

CASE STUDY

ORGANIZATION OF 'SIRS'

Shivkumar has worked for three years for an internationally reputed hotel chain. However, as he did not find adequate career growth in that hotel, he recently resigned and joined one of the Indian hotel chains. Although he got career growth, he is recently finding it difficult to cope up with the pressures, though not work pressure. He is experiencing great difficulty in talking to supervisors, colleagues, and managers and coping with the work culture in the new organization. In the previous organization, being an international hotel chain, everyone, from top boss to junior subordinates, was called by their first names. However, in the new organization everything is just the opposite. Here, the culture is a bit bureaucratic in nature where the boss needs to be addressed as 'sir'. He also experiences difficulty when his subordinates call him sir. It is indeed a great problem. Along with respectful exchange, what the new organization calls it, it brings forth new issues, restricts flow of information, and brings hesitation in the communication processes. He is thinking of speaking to the HR manager but can never gather the courage to do so, whereas in the previous organization, he could openly speak to him/her.

Discussion Question

Recommend suitable solution to Shivkumar and the HR manager of the new company.

10 Organizational Conflict and Collective Bargaining

INTRODUCTION

Conflict in an organization is inevitable, as employees from diverse psychological background and apparently different interest groups come together under one umbrella of organizational objectives. Conflicts could be centred on resource allocation (amount of money required to execute the work) or the advancement of self-interest in the organization (promotion, increment, etc). Organizational conflicts, in most cases, are not desirable and require an exhaustive mechanism embedded in the organization to resolve them. For an HR professional, it is one of the important responsibilities to ensure that organizational and industrial peace and harmony is maintained inside the organization. This enables the employees to concentrate on the work for which they are employed. Organizational conflict distracts employees from their assigned responsibilities; hence, it has the potential to reduce the productivity and organizational effectiveness.

WHAT IS ORGANIZATIONAL CONFLICT?

Conflict is an apparent contradictory pursuit of interests among employees with reference to their self or organizational role. For example, as an HR professional, it is important that adequate flexibility has been assured in the system so that minor manoeuvring is possible. A finance director, for example, uses a financial yardstick to restrain the manoeuvring. This will generate persistent problem inside the organization. Each one is perhaps right in asserting his or her point of view. However, it is important that the HR and finance directors find amicable solutions that are beneficial to the greater interest of the organization. Thus, organizational conflict is the pursuit of opposite directions with reference to resources, processes, and benefits.

ORGANIZATIONAL CONFLICT: IS IT DESIRABLE?

Organizational conflict is not desirable for any organization; however, it will emerge and is present in every organization. Although

LEARNING OBJECTIVES

After reading this chapter, you will learn about

- organizational conflict
- any harmful effects of organizational conflict on any hospitality organization
- various conflicts resolution techniques that potentially resolve organizational conflict
- various initiatives undertaken by human resource professionals to eliminate the effects of organizational conflict
- collective bargaining process in the hospitality organization

arguments are available to support the claim that organizational conflict, in some cases, provides positive results for the benefit of the organization, in the absence of efficient organizational routines and policies, in most of the cases, organizational conflict is destined to produce negative results for the organization.

Divisive Organizational conflict is divisive. It divides employees into various interest group clusters, and each one attempts to maximize his or her personal and organizational gain by politically manoeuvring various resources, people, and technology against each other. Theoretically, it is understood that employees join the organization to advance organizational goals and work together to achieve the mission and vision statement of the organization. However, organizational conflict divides employees and gives birth to political games, which is not good for any organization. Divisive employee groups will not extend support to each other; thus, owing to lack of teamwork, a lot of precious resources in the organization will be duplicated, leading to utter waste of energy and efforts. Thus, organizational conflict is dysfunctional in most cases.

Stressful Organizational conflict is stressful. Organizational conflict produces considerable amount of heat in the organizational system. Each participant in the conflict experiences stress for the same. Stressed employees will not be able to work at their full potential and their productivity will decrease. As a consequence, they will engage in various stress-relieving activities. This will bring in disorientation among employees. Thus, organizational conflict potentially reduces employees' full strength and takes them away from the objectives for which they were deployed. It is safe to state that organizational conflict is not desirable and should be avoided at all cost.

Communication Organizational communication is the bloodline for the success of any organization. Organizational conflict hinders communication among employees and departments, and each communication becomes a template for political and diplomatic dealing. Even a legitimate communication could become distorted during such times. Thus, distorted communication produces negative spirit and flavour in the organization.

Wastage Organizational conflict generates considerable amount of wastage. For example, owing to diverse political interest groups, in spite of having the knowledge to serve a specific customer, one group may prevent its member from communicating this information to the other group that is required to serve the customer now. In spite of having knowledge, capabilities, and resources, employees may withdraw themselves from participating in the system. This may generate duplicity of efforts, leading to considerable wastage.

Deferment of decision Owing to conflicting opinions and interests, organizations fail to achieve decisive action. This delay in decision making may cause considerable damage to the reputation and opportunity. In a hypercompetitive world, deferment of decision will always provide opportunity to competition to advance further. Thus, delay in decision is not a good sign for any organization.

Block listening   Owing to organizational conflict, block listening generates anger and affects smooth relationship. Because of anger in the system, it prevents employees from constraining within their own issues. This over-indulgence of self-interest prevents employees from listening to what other parties are saying. This blocks listening among conflicting parties; in the absence of healthy interaction, the conflicting parties are never able to achieve durable resolution of conflict.

Spoil the atmosphere   Organizational conflict has the potential to spoil the atmosphere. Organizational conflict, in the absence of effective resolution mechanism, can produce highly toxic atmosphere in hospitality organizations. This also provides adequate cushions for rumours.

Disrupt the work processes   Significant disruption is possible if conflicting parties are adamant in their demands. This prevents conflicting parties from participating in service-generating activities, and thus disrupts the work processes.

TYPES OF CONFLICT

Organizational conflicts could be of different types depending on the spread of the problem. While personal problem is centred on the individual, interpersonal conflict is focused between two individuals. Each problem is different and requires a unique approach to resolve it.

Personal conflict   Personal conflict is focused on the individual. In this case, an individual faces conflict with the self. Perhaps he or she is unable to decide what is required to be done in life. For example, the personal value system of one individual could be different from what one needs to display in his or her workplace, which may create a high degree of dissonance. An individual who fails to settle this internal tussle may suffer from pain, stress, and disorientation.

Interpersonal conflict   Interpersonal conflict originates between two individuals and requires careful handling to arrive at an amicable solution. An individual having two different value systems, interests, and academic background may look into a problem differently—this difference in perspective may generate conflicts among employees working in hospitality organizations.

Interdepartmental conflict   Interdepartmental conflict originates because of misunderstanding between departments in hotels. Strategic allocation of resources among different departments can cause departmental conflict and require diplomatic manoeuvre by the human resources professionals for an amicable solution and peaceful coexistence.

Interunit conflict   This type of conflict originates where each business unit (hotel) competes against another (another hotel under the same hospitality chain) for resources.

LABOUR LAWS AND ORGANIZATIONAL CONFLICT

Labour laws provide some guidelines and framework to resolve organizational conflict if it is centred on the conflict between employee and employer. Labour laws indicate the rights and responsibilities of employees and employers, and it is expected that each party adheres to its roles, as envisaged in the labour legislation.

Industrial Dispute Act 1947 This piece of legislation highlights the importance of management of relationship between employees and employers as well as their respective roles and responsibilities. This Act also provides the framework for restitution of rights, in case of violations. The Act designates various authorities (Labour Court, Conciliation Officer, Court of Enquiry) and their powers to resolve organizational conflicts.

Acts pertaining to compensation The Employees State Insurance Act 1948 (ESI Act) and the Workmen Compensation Act outline detailed guidelines to provide compensation to employees in case they meet with an accident.

Acts pertaining to salary and wages A number of legislations are there to provide guidelines pertaining to fixation and disbursement of salary and wages—for example, the Minimum Wages Act 1948, the Provident Fund and Miscellaneous Provisions Act 1956, the Payment of Wages Act 1936.

Acts pertaining to governance of relationship and other benefits The Factories Act 1948, the Shop and Establishment Act, the Payment of Gratuity Act 1972, the Payment of Bonus Act 1956, and so on provide detailed guidelines pertaining to management of relationship between employees and employers.

CONFLICT RESOLUTION

Although organizations invest considerable amount of resources to avoid organizational conflict, it appears in every organization without fail. Thus, although organizational conflict cannot be thoroughly eradicated, each organization requires robust organizational framework to address it to find amicable solutions. Conflict resolution means finding lines of solution acceptable to the conflicting parties. It is directed at achieving elimination or at least reduction of problem. Theoretically, to resolve any organizational conflict, five strategic options are available: avoiding, competing, accommodating, compromising, and collaborating. Let us examine each of the options in detail.

Avoidance Avoidance is one of the strategies deployed to handle organizational conflict. HR professionals devise exhaustive number of rules, regulations, and framework to avoid organizational problems from occurring. These strategies could be termed *preventive control system*. The organization attempts to prevent the occurrence of problems by devising systems and processes. Preventive mechanism is highly effective in resolving issues that are ordinary and frequently occurring.

Often, out of experience and organizational learning, the organization devises a blueprint of service design. If a problem occurs as per the blueprint of the service delivery, organizational rules and regulations are potentially capable of resolving it. However, if the problem is of extraordinary nature, avoidance strategies do not produce effective results.

Avoidance strategies include expression of ignorance about the problem and not reacting to the existence of the problem. This is effective in some cases—staying away from the typical problem makers of the organization and concentrating on more effective ways of dealing with other organizational issues. Not paying attention to the problem makers is not an effective way of dealing with organizational problems because these problem makers might have caused substantial loss of resources, time, and effort in the organization. As HR professionals, finding a way to deal with these problem makers is indeed a better strategy.

Accommodating This is one of the strategies frequently followed when one party is in a weaker position with reference to the opponent in the said conflict. Unequal position and relevant power force the weaker party to opt for appeasement and accommodate the demand of the stronger party. This solution is temporary and could be used to garner more power for subsequent revision of strategies. Weak position forces parties to opt for this solution. This is a win–loss game, where one party wins over the other. Thus, losing parties carry a lot of grudges and resentment. This affects their performance, and they may take revenge on issues where they are strong. Thus, the organization becomes a stage where display of power becomes more prominent rather than generation of excellent performance (Fig. 10.1).

Competing When both parties believe in their strength and superiority, each may opt for competing strategies for the resolution of conflict. This situation provides

EXAMPLES

1. Jane works as an assistant executive housekeeper for a hotel. She is efficient and concentrates on her work; however, there are a few people in the hotel who attempt to tarnish her image by spreading rumours about her personal life. She, rather than reacting to these rumours, focuses on her work and attempts to avoid these problem-creating politically strong individuals. She thinks that avoidance is the best strategy to deal with this situation as it is very difficult to prove the origin of the rumour as well as to deal with the rumour effectively.

2. Ram Gopal is a high school pass and has worked for the hotel for 25 years, almost from its beginning. He has seen a lot of trainees who learnt the work from him and subsequently became his boss. Although he is knowledgeable, he always opted for accommodating strategies to deal with the young boss. He does not have the requisite professional qualification (diploma/degree in hotel management) nor is he fluent in English, and it is difficult for him to find another job at this age. Thus, he is in a weak position. His young boss sometimes orders something that is not right; however, he always opts for appeasement of his boss to pass the day.

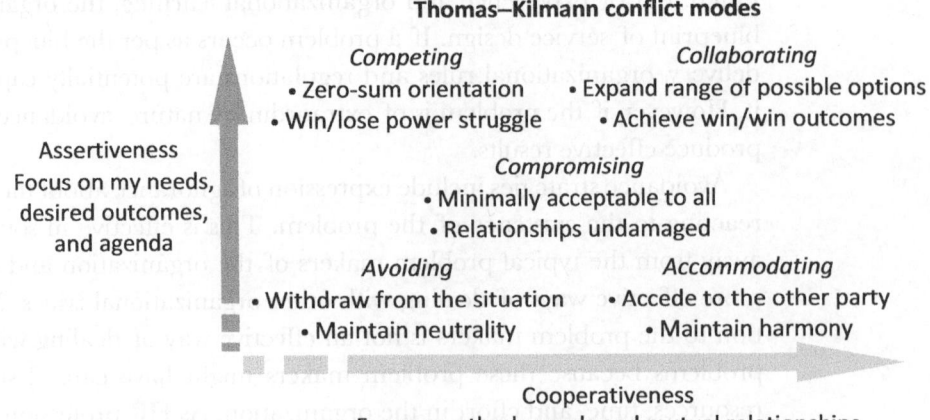

Figure 10.1 Conflict resolution framework

space for muscle flexing and power display behaviour to influence the stamina of the opposition party. Disregarding the interest of the other party, each party attempts to maximize gain. This win–loss framework produces a winning party and a losing party. The losing party may potentially take revenge by engaging in fight where they are relatively strong (Fig. 10.1).

EXAMPLE

The food and beverage department and the housekeeping department are at loggerheads over the minibar issue. Minibar is an extended facility provided to each of the resident guests. As a part of minibar facilities, each room is given a mini fridge containing a wide range of liquor, wines, whiskey, and so on. It is expected that each day guests write down their consumption details so that billing can be made by the front office. However, most of the time guests check out before the exact consumptions details can be procured. Front office employees usually rely on the guest's honesty. In most cases, the minibar facility is a loss-incurring function; hotels lose considerable amount of revenue as guest consumption has not been charged. Therefore, no department wants it under its umbrella. Although for sometime, in this particular hotel, the minibar facility has been considered to be under the housekeeping department, in most cases, it is managed by the food and beverage department. The general manager calls for revisit of the minibar management and asks for suitable recommendation to improve its monetary return. Each department wants the minibar facility to be managed by the other department. The food and beverage department believes that it is part of room business and mostly to be considered as extended room facility. The room boy already spends a considerable amount of time for servicing the room, why not add one simple task. Especially when additional manpower is extremely difficult to get sanctioned, this appears to be a durable solution. Housekeeping believes that serving beverages is ordinarily considered to be part of food and beverage function; besides, housekeeping staff may not be well conversant with the brand and procedure of maintenance. Both departments want to throw the responsibilities on others. Market analysis suggests that no significant trend could be traced about its current practice in the hospitality industry—in some hotels, it is managed by housekeeping and in some cases, it is managed by food and beverages department. In spite of several attempts to find a reasonable solution, the general manager fails to find a durable solution. Both departments endeavour to display muscle strength.

EXAMPLES

1. The management and the employees' union are at loggerheads. Employees' union seeks 50 per cent salary hike in their basic, whereas the management does not want to give more than 12 per cent. Both parties know that what they seek to achieve is not possible. Successive negotiations between the management and the employees' union yield a compromised formula. As a part of the compromised formula, the management hikes the salary up to 18 per cent of employees' basic salary, which is accepted by the employees' union. This has provided a win–win situation. Holding each party's position may have resulted in strike or lock out. Rather, the compromised formula has provided a reasonable solution with wider acceptance.

2. During economic downturn, employees can join hands with the management of the hospitality organizations to bring out wage-related settlement, acceptable to both parties. Employees need to have a job during economic slowdown, whereas the management of the hospitality organization needs to ensure economic survival of the business. These two needs could be fulfilled meaningfully through the adoption of collaborative approaches by the management and employees of the hospitality organizations.

Compromising   Compromising is an attempt to find an amicable solution by providing concession to each other. Compromising is like finding the middle path of the solution. Each party involved in the conflict provides concession to the other, as relevant concession provides a sense of win–win to each member. Potentially this could cause minimal damage to the relationship within the party and provide wider acceptance among members of the conflict (Fig. 10.1).

Collaborating   This is one of the best solutions where each party seeks to collaborate to find better solutions. Each party attempts to maximize the overall gain where both parties achieve maximum individual gain too. This approach is more desirable to bring out solution to the problems, as it generates less amount of stress among conflicting parties and provides wider acceptance. All other resolution-seeking behaviours generate negative energy in the form of anger, bad feeling, and sadness, whereas this solution provides a robust sense of inspiration among members. Conflicting parties do not carry any negative feeling with reference to the outcome of the resolution (Fig. 10.1).

VARIOUS MEASURES UNDERTAKEN TO MINIMIZE ORGANIZATIONAL CONFLICT

Organizations develop a number of formal frameworks designed to reduce the intensity of conflict. Organizational conflict, if not managed well, may appear to be a big problem for the survival of the organization.

Communication   Organizations invest considerable amount of money and effort to develop and maintain communication with the employees. Democratic exchange of information provides credibility and transparency. Each organization follows suitable principles to exchange information among members, which do not allow grudges to accumulate. Thus, organizational conflict is averted by sharing information.

Committee Each organization develops a number of committees or teams to look into a specific organizational question, for which it is not possible for any single individual to arrive at a solution. Collective contribution to a vexed problem provides wider acknowledgement of fairness and wider acceptance.

Mission and vision statement This provides wider goals to the conflicting parties on what is required to be done. Why are we here? What do we want to achieve? How do we achieve what we wanted to achieve? These broad questions provide solid guidance on what is required to be done. Narrow range of vision of conflicting parties finds wider reasons to exist and provides guidance on what is required to be done.

Commanding position In some cases, the directive from a significant individual in the organization provides a clear solution. Each member accepts the solution by the force of the chair power of the individual. Although this is not desirable, this is being used quite extensively throughout the organization.

Counselling Counselling is one of the important avenues to resolve individual conflicts. Individuals have unique psychological orientations—they may be introverts, extroverts—they may enjoy the relations, others may be conservative. These unique ways of self-expression may generate unique types of problems. Therefore, there is a great need to provide some special psychological assistance and guidance. They facilitate and guide individual employees to find their own solution.

Legal framework In some cases, it is legally mandatory to have some frameworks available on the shop floor to have a works committee resolve shop floor conflict. Needless to mention that as per the provision of the Industrial Dispute Act, an organization employing more than 100 workmen should have a works committee comprising equal number of representatives from employees and management to resolve shop floor problems. This effort is directed at resolving the root of the problem before it becomes bigger.

Fair organizational infrastructure Each organization aspires to design fair systems and processes in which employees get equal treatment. Each organization develops a number of policies to design fair processes, for example, salary advance policy, children education policy, leave encashment policy, and so on. Each of these policies attempts to clearly outline the eligibility criteria, the detail scheme, and how frequently it could be availed of. This provides fair opportunity to all.

COLLECTIVE BARGAINING AND NEGOTIATION

In India, organizational conflict is often marred by the conflict between capital and labour. In other words, organizational conflict is predominantly characterized by the conflict between the labour union and the management. Indian economy till the early 1990s was chained to the Licence Raj system where every business required permission from the government. Political patronage created limited opportunity for business, which in turn had created limited job opportunity. Thus, within the limited scope of money-making opportunity, labour unions fought with the management for various benefits. Indian labour laws envisaged the struggle and created avenues to resolve it with the help of collective bargaining and consequently lent strength to the labour union.

COLLECTIVE BARGAINING PROCESS

Each side of the bargaining process (labour union and management) usually follows a specific process to effectively participate in the bargaining. This collective bargaining is, in most cases, for good wages, benefits, and reinstatement of employees who have lost jobs because of some issues.

The management reviews the wage structure of the company and examines the scope for enhancement with reference to the directive of the board and business growth over the next few years. Then they compare their salary structure to the salary structure of other organizations.

Then, using this information and the directive of the management, HR professionals make a detailed argument for specific wage and benefit hike.

Similarly, labour unions also review their wages and call for meeting to prepare for demand charter. Then, to have a comparative benchmark, they send their representative to nearby factories to get the wage and benefit structure from the labour union of these factories. Further, in line with the expectations of the employees, a demand charter and wage structure are prepared. Subsequently, they present it to the management, but in most cases it is not accepted. These generate provisions for negotiation.

Several rounds of negotiations are undertaken. These generate a considerable stress inside the organization. Each party attempts to maximize gain by demonstrating the merit of their argument. While the labour union shows the wage structure of the competing companies, the management provides evidence that the wage structure is relatively better in their organization. The labour union argues for good salary in terms of the work load, process improvement initiative, economic hardship due to inflation, their contribution for the growth of the company, and so on. The management argues for limited business opportunity, frail market condition, fragile financial condition of the company, and so on. Each party negotiates using various strategies such as accommodating, competing, and collaborating.

Failing to achieve an amicable solution to their problem is often marred by lockout, strike, and industrial unrest. This has the potential to disrupt the production process. This is not desirable for any industry. Collective bargaining provides negotiated solution. Sincere adherence to these frameworks could potentially bring in industrial peace and harmony, which is crucial for the economic and social development of Indian labour. Otherwise, strike and lockout bring industrial unrest, loss of wages, loss of shareholders' wealth, and less taxes to the governments, leading to overall economic and social downfall. Therefore, HR managers need to maintain a collaborative and peaceful atmosphere for greater good.

SUMMARY

Organizational conflict is not desirable; however, it is present in every organization. HR professionals need to develop detailed measures to eliminate the effect of organizational conflict by developing fair programmes and policies. In spite of the procedures and policies, adequate space and time should be allotted to resolve any organizational conflict without fail by actively engaging conflicting parties to find amicable solution. These will bring in industrial peace and harmony in the Indian hospitality industry.

KEY TERMS

Accommodating It is one of the conflict resolution styles, where weak parties accept or accommodate the wish of the powerful parties.

Collaborating It is one of the most desirable and effective strategies where both parties attempt to collaborate to bring about more benefits by using each other's resources.

Collective bargaining It is the employees' effort to present their demand collectively before the management and negotiate as one united labour force for wages and benefits.

Competing It is one of the conflict resolution styles, where both parties believe that they are right and therefore compete with each other to win.

Compromising It is one of the strategies where both parties accommodate some of the wishes/interests of the other parties, and thereby attempt to arrive at some tentative or working solutions.

Organizational conflict Essentially, it signifies all kinds of conflicts that occur in organization among its stakeholders.

EXERCISES

Concept Review Questions

1. Examine the various problems associated with organizational conflict.
2. Identify various factors that potentially cause organizational conflict.
3. What are the various conflict resolution strategies that could be deployed to resolve organizational conflict?
4. Write a short note on collective bargaining and negotiation.

Critical Thinking Questions

1. Review one Hindi movie of your choice that effectively portrayed the Indian Labour Movement.
2. Could you identify various sources of organizational conflicts you have experienced during your industrial training in a hotel/travel agency?

Assignment

Reflect upon various conflicts you experience in your personal and professional life. Using Kilman's conflict resolution framework, do you think that you are vulnerable to opt for specific conflict resolution mode? Why? Is there a healthier or better way to address this conflict?

CASE STUDY

POWER WEB

Shyam Nath, the general manager of a hotel, has recently resigned from his job, and as a result, the new general manager Banerjee has been recruited. However, he will be joining after one and half months. In the meantime, the HR manager has been asked to maintain status quo and oversee the organizational discipline.

Banerjee has addressed employees on several occasions. However, uncertainty still prevails whether he is going to join or not. Rumour is that he may not be joining unless he gets the requisite salary hike, perks, and allowances. However, there is no such official confirmation available.

However, some of the senior staff have started meeting Banerjee in his hotel whenever he is in the city for some other work. They go there to brief him about the development and show their support for him. Besides, they send emails using various excuses and display their acute sense of responsibility.

Rumour is that all these senior staff want to develop a political relationship with the new general manager. Each senior staff is vying for space against the other. They demonstrate that they are very concerned about the well-being of the organization. Banerjee comes from a sales background and may not necessarily possess acute knowledge about organizational management. These individuals are said to have been ready to make gain out of the situation and spoil the image of other organizational members.

The HR manager is well informed about these activities. He ponders about what he needs to do.

Discussion Question

Provide suitable recommendations to the HR manager on what he needs to do.

11

Indian Labour Laws in the Hospitality Industry

INTRODUCTION

Indian labour laws govern and influence some of the human resource management practices in the hospitality organizations. For example, a number of welfare and regulatory frameworks have been devised to ensure the welfare and social security of the employees of these organizations. Indian labour laws provide broad frameworks to manage the relationship between the employees and the management of the hospitality organizations. We attempt to elucidate some selective issues in the labour legislations with the help of some examples.

CASE EXAMPLES

1. Kapadia has worked for the past 10 years in a leading travel agency in India. Recently, owing to ill health, she absented herself from work. She consulted doctors from the ESI (Employee State Insurance) hospital, and advancing age seems to be the reason for her ill health. Because of her frequent absence from the workplace, many clients were annoyed and they went to another travel agent. Her boss, Batliboi, under tremendous pressure to increase revenue, thought of firing Kapadia as she had not reported for work for the past 10 days. Can Batliboi fire Kapadia for her long absence?

2. Robert works for the F&B Department as steward. He always absented himself whenever the workload was heavy, for example, when arranging a party for 2000 people. Yesterday, when the hotel had heavy occupancy and a banquet for 2500 people was to be arranged on the lawns, he did not turn up. His manager wants to fire him immediately. Can he be fired for his absence?

These are a couple of snapshots from daily organizational life. Every day, managers responsible for human resource management undertake a number of decisions, some of them requiring sound behavioural science knowledge and others needing a robust legal base. Legally wrong decisions can jeopardize organizational discipline, attract considerable financial loss, and lower goodwill in the market, which in turn can make fresh hiring difficult. Therefore, decisions taken by the HR professionals should be congruent with current legal interpretations of law, currently applicable to employees. For example, employees utilizing medical assistance under the scheme of the ESI Act, 1948, cannot be fired under any circumstances. There is a dedicated clause in the said legislation that prohibits termination of service. Therefore, as stated in the first case, Kapadia's services cannot be terminated. The decision to fire Kapadia is not only ethically but also legally wrong. Hence, Kapadia cannot not be fired unless due legal provisions are adhered to.

Similarly, in the second case, Robert plays truant at his job and often takes the escapist route to solve his workload problem, which is indeed problematic for any organization. Employees who adopt such a practice create work overload for other employees. Such employees are undesirable and require severe punishment without fail. This matter needs to be strictly handled. However, although instant termination of services may seem correct from the behavioural science or practical point of view, it does not have legal sanction. The HR manager needs to adhere to a series of procedures before terminating the employees' services. Labour laws are based on the principles of fairness, equity, and natural justice. Without providing ample opportunity to Robert for an explanation for such behaviour, his services cannot be terminated.

Economists have argued that for the execution of any production process, four factors, in their relatively right proportions, should converge under one mission objective. These factors are land, labour, capital, and entrepreneurship. In a hedonistically constructed world, each resource provider will participate in the production processes with the sole objective of earning and fulfilling their self-interest. Thus, the land provider will get rent, the labourer will get wages, the capital provider will get interest, and the entrepreneur will get profit/loss. However, how much each one will get depends on the relative market and political power. Thus, a tussle among these participants is to be expected. History has witnessed a number of tussles, which sometimes have changed the face of the world. The most powerful incumbent in the production process is the entrepreneur. Under the command of the entrepreneur, land, labour, and capital converge in right proportions for completion of the production process. Thus, the entrepreneur will always endeavour to enhance his or her part of the share after settling the rightful claims of the other stakeholders, and the possibility of exploitation is radically possible. History has witnessed a number of bloodbaths, tussles, strikes, lockouts, and bankruptcy arising out of improper solutions of a stakeholder's conflict.

Industrial relations in India have often been marred by violence, exploitation, strikes, and lockouts. Various trade unions were formed to protect the interests of the labour force. A number of trade unions have often been affiliated to political parties. However, multiple unions in one organization often vied for a better foothold and failed to protect the interests of the common workers. It resulted in poverty, illness, and death among the workers. In the absence of alternative job opportunities in a closed economy, Indian workers were forced to spend their life in a strife-filled environment. In 1991, the Indian working scenario changed significantly with the opening up of the economy. India became the world's best back office service counter. The English-speaking workforce found new freedom, and were flooded with multiple job opportunities. New India is different from its recent past and requires to be seen in its own context.

The Indian government has framed multiple labour legislations to protect the interests of workers. Most of these labour legislations (Exhibit 11.1) are directed at achieving two objectives:

1. Dispute and administrative relative provisions, such as the Factories Act, Industrial Disputes Act, Industrial Standing Order Act, Contract Labour Regulation, and Abolition Act.

2. Regulatory framework for governance of employee remunerations, such as the Payment of Wages Act, 1936; Payment of Gratuity Act; Payment of Bonus Act; Equal Remuneration Act; Employees Provident Fund and Miscellaneous Provision Act; and Employees State Insurance Act.

Exhibit 11.1 Partial List of Labour Legislation

	Laws related to industrial relations
1	The Trade Unions Act, 1926
2	The Industrial Employment (Standing Orders) Act, 1946
3	The Industrial Disputes Act, 1947
	Laws related to wages
1	The Payment of Wages Act, 1936
2	The Minimum Wages Act, 1948
3	The Payment of Bonus Act, 1965
	Laws related to working hours, conditions of services
1	The Factories Act, 1948
2	The Contract Labour (Regulation and Abolition) Act, 1970
3	The Shops and Establishments Act
	Laws related to equality and empowerment of women
1	The Maternity Benefit Act, 1961
2	The Equal Remuneration Act, 1976
	Laws related to social security
1	The Workmen's Compensation Act, 1923
2	The Employees' State Insurance Act, 1948
3	The Employees' Provident Fund and Miscellaneous Provisions Act, 1952
4	The Payment of Gratuity Act, 1972

LABOUR LEGISLATIONS IMPACTING HOSPITALITY

We examine a few pieces of legislation that have a significant bearing on the hospitality industry, more broadly the service sector employees.

Payment of Gratuity Act, 1972

This Act applies to

1. every factory, mine, oilfield, plantation, port, and railway company
2. every shop or establishment, registered under the Shops and Establishment Act in a state, in which 10 or more persons are employed or were employed on any days of the preceding 12 months
3. such other establishment, or class of employment where 10 or more employees are employed or were employed on any day of the preceding 12 months, as the central government may by notification specify in this behalf

Does It Apply to the Hospitality Industry?

From the definition stated earlier, it clearly indicates that travel agents, hotels, restaurants, car providers, and so on should come under this legislation. While examining the criteria for application of the Payment of Gratuity Act, the number of employees indeed provides the crucial test for inclusion or exclusion. Deployment of 10 or more employees in any establishment attracts the application of the Payment of Gratuity Act. Any attempt to reduce the number of employees to lower than 10 to avoid the application of the Act to an establishment has been eliminated. Therefore, the law provided a dedicated subclause to indicate that once the provision of the Payment of Gratuity Act applies to one organization, it will continue to prevail even if the number of employees goes down below 10.

Does this Act apply to industrial trainees or apprentices who are working in any five-star hotels? The conclusive answer is 'no'. This Act does not apply to apprentices or industrial trainees. It also does not apply to persons who hold civil posts under the central government or a state government and are governed by any other Act or by any rule providing for payment of gratuity.

Gratuity applicability   Gratuity becomes due only on the occasion of termination of employment, provided that the employee concerned has completed service not less than five years. This gratuity is payable on termination of services due to superannuation, retirement, resignation, death, or disablement on account of accident or disease. One important factor that should be considered is that this Act does not make any distinction between regular employees and those on contract or on daily or monthly wage basis. Any employee, whatever the form of employment, is eligible for gratuity on termination of service (termination due to resignation, retirement, disablement, or death).

Rate of Gratuity

The rate of gratuity is calculated as described here.

1. The rate of gratuity for regular employees is 15 days' wages based on the rate of wages last drawn by the employee for every completed year of service or part thereof in excess of six months.
2. The rate of gratuity for employees who are provided with wages on a monthly basis is 15 days' wages for every completed year of service or part thereof in excess of six months. However, the rate of wages will be calculated on the basis of the last drawn monthly rate of wages divided by 26 and multiplying the quotient by 15.
3. An employee drawing wages on a piece-rate is also eligible for gratuity for each completed year of service. For convenience of calculation, total wages will be the average of the last three drawn by the employee before termination of employment.
4. In case of seasonal employees, the employee will get seven days' wages for each season.

Prescribed time limit for claiming of gratuity This Act prescribes a time limit for an employee or his or her legal heir presenting a claim of gratuity. It is the responsibility of the employer to settle the claim for gratuity at the time of making the final payment; in case the employer fails to fulfil this legal responsibility, then the claim must be made by the employee concerned or his or her legal heir within a period of one year. However, the honourable court can condone the delay and entertain the claim after the expiry of this time limit.

Mode of payment Gratuity can be paid either by cash, cheque, or bank draft to the eligible employee or the nominee or the legal heir as the case may be.

Obligations of the employer This Act imposes a responsibility on the employer for dissemination of information of the Act by presenting an abstract of the Act in the language of the majority of the staff members at the staff entrance and also designating an individual officer who will be responsible for disbursement of payment.

Penal liabilities This Act prescribes strict penal punishment for employers who fail to comply with the provisions of the rules and regulations of the Payment of Gratuity Act:

1. In case of a false statement or a false representation made to avoid any payment being made to employees, the Act prescribes a punishment with imprisonment for a maximum period of six months or with a fine, which could be extended to ₹10,000.
2. In case an employer contravenes any provisions of this Act, the punishment is imprisonment for a minimum period of three months, extendable to one year or with a fine between ₹10,000 and ₹20,000.

3. In case the employer fails to pay the gratuity under this Act, the employer shall be punished with imprisonment for a period between six months and two years.

Workmen Compensation Act, 1923

This piece of labour legislation was enacted during the British rule. The objective was to provide assistance to employees who were injured in accidents arising out of and in the course of employment. This provides adequate social security to the employee who is exposed to risk of injury while at work. Although the provisions of the Act provide limited social security support, it should be remembered that this piece of legal template was the maiden attempt to extend support to the employee injured in accidents arising out of and in the course of employment. This Act applies to the employees in certain situations, especially when the hospitality organization is not covered under the Employees State Insurance Act. During the construction phase of a hospitality project, The Workmen Compensation Act, 1923, provides some relief to the employees who are injured while at work.

This Act applies to the whole of India, except Jammu and Kashmir.

When Can Claims be Entertained under This Act?

In case of injury/death caused to an employee 'out of and in the course of employment', the employee or his or her dependents will have the legal right to claim compensation from the employer. This clearly outlines one simple principle that the injury should have a connection or relation to the actual fact of injury. If an employee was loitering around in a dangerous production process area without the mandate from the management, and the employee suffered an injury, it will be difficult to accommodate the said injury under the definition of 'arising out of and in the course of employment'. When the injury to the employee causes disablement for not less than three days, the employee concerned could present a claim under various provisions of the Act.

This Act also provides guidance on what constitutes a dependent. Dependent means relatives who rely on the worker at least to some extent for their daily needs at the time of the accident. This accident does not conjure up all heirs of the workman as dependents, but only those who to some extent rely on him. Therefore, kinship plus dependency for daily survival are the sole criteria for identification of a dependent. The dependency should be at the time of the accident and the subsequent development of relationship between a widow and other individual will not debar the person from claiming the benefits under the Act. Therefore, the immediate aftermath of the accident should be the status that should be utilized to entertain the claim and not the subsequent development of a relationship or remarriage.

Workmen Compensation Commissioner

The state government appoints an officer, designated as Workmen Compensation Commissioner, to look after the interest of the employees. The government enforces it by a requisite notification in the official gazette. All cases are required to be channelized through the Workmen Compensation Commissioner.

Eligibility   This refers to an employee working for the employer irrespective of the status of the employment. This indicates that any employee, whether on regular or contract or fixed term or daily wages basis, deployed for production of services, will be eligible for benefits. This poses considerable financial risks for the management.

Procedures for making a claim   The Act provides guidance as to how to claim financial benefits envisaged in the Act.

1. Anybody who wishes to claim financial benefits under the various provisions of the Act requires to send a notice to the commissioner, instituted under the Workmen Compensation Act, 1923. This notice must contain the name and address of the person injured, with details pertaining to the cause of injury, date, and time of the accident.
2. This notice should be addressed to the employer, who is responsible for settlement of claims, under the provisions of the Workmen Compensation Act, 1923. It is a legal requirement under this Act that the employer should designate an officer to be responsible for the settlement of the claim.

Occupational disease   When employees work for specified industries for at least six months, he or she can claim for contraction of occupational disease. Usually, in the case of employees working for specified industries, certain diseases are considered as occupational disease and are thus claimable.

Disablement   Disablement signifies partial or total loss of capacity to work or to move. Two types of disablement have been recognized under this Act: partial and total disablement.

Partial disablement   This indicates any type of disablement that decreases the earning capacity of a workman because of accidental exposures. It could be temporary or permanent.

Total disablement   This means such types of disablement that incapacitates an employee or denies him or her opportunities of gaining meaningful access to employment because of the injury. In other words, the injury prevents him or her from doing similar kind of work he or she was doing before the accident.

Liabilities   The Workmen Compensation Act imposes liabilities on the employer to settle the claim made by the legally eligible claimant. The notice for claim substantially provides details pertaining to the injury suffered by the claimant. This could have reference to the schedule of the Act that highlights and defines various types of injuries. However, in case the injury cannot be clubbed meaningfully under the descriptions of any schedule, then the claimant needs to provide adequate evidence of incapacity. In case after presenting a legally sound claim the employer fails to settle the case within a specified time, the employer will be liable to pay 6 per cent interest on the payable amount. However, in case the employer, without any valid reason, delays the reimbursement of claims, then a penalty up to a maximum of 50 per cent can be imposed on the employer.

The employer cannot be liable for compensation

1. in case the injury does not cause total or partial disablement for more than three days
2. in case the injury, which did not cause death, is, in fact, due to the workman
   (a) being under the influence of drinks or drugs at the time of accident
   (b) being wilfully disobedient to the expressed order of the management, which is usually directed to ensure the safety of the employees
   (c) wilfully removing safety gears, designed and embedded in the machine to secure the safety of the employees

Payment process The payment is usually made to the Workmen Compensation Commissioner for onward disbursement to the claimant. In case the employer disagrees to pay the claimed amount, the employer requires depositing only the amount, provisionally accepted by the employer.

Amount of compensation The Act provides detailed guidelines as to how the compensation amount can be derived. The amount of compensation is calculated on the basis of (a) the last drawn monthly wages of the workman, (b) the nature of injury, and (c) the relevant factor, as specified in Schedule IV of the Act.

Trade Union Act, 1926

A trade union is an association of employees predominantly formed to look after the interests of the workers while facing the mighty employer.

As per Section 2(H) of the Trade Union Act, a trade union means any combination, whether temporary or permanent, formed primarily for the purpose of

1. regulating the relations between employer and workmen or between workmen *inter se* or between employers *inter se*
2. imposing restrictive conditions on the conduct of any trade or business and includes any federation of two or more trade unions

The trade union movement has a long history in India. Most trade unions have a political affiliation and often engage with employers for better terms of employment.

The Trade Union Act provides a unique range of safety coverage to its members. A trade union formed according to the provisions of the Trade Union Act, 1926, accrues a good number of benefits:

1. With the registration of a trade union as per the provisions of the Act, the trade union acquires the identity of a legal personality.
2. The provisions of the Act clearly articulate the registration process and organization structure of the trade union.
3. This Act also provides immunities to its registered trade union members.
4. Outsiders are allowed to join and lead the union.
5. A trade union acquires the legal right to participate in political activities.

6. Members are allowed to go on a peaceful strike.
7. Trade unions are allowed to be a negotiating party for collective bargaining. The collective agreement between the trade union and the employer acquires legal sanction with the explicit provision of Section 18(1) of the Industrial Disputes Act.

Minimum Number of Members Required for the Registration of a Trade Union

Seven or more members wilfully joining together may form a trade union by adhering to the rules and regulations of the Act. This minimum requirement of seven members is a prerequisite for the registration of a trade union. The registration of members can be done by a registrar, notified by the state government through the requisite notification in the state gazette. At the time of the registration process, withdrawal of one or a few members does not affect the registration process; however, this withdrawal of members should not be more than half of the total number. In that case, the registration process will be interrupted by this majority withdrawal.

Process of Registration

A minimum of seven members wilfully forward the application for registration to the registrar in order to get the union registered along with the following set of documents:

1. The rules of the trade union
2. The name and head office address of the trade union
3. The title, names, age, addresses, and the occupations of the office bearers of the trade union office bearer
4. Accounts statement showing the assets and liabilities, if the trade union is already more than one year old

The registrar does not have judicial power; he or she just utilizes the administrative power while examining the merit of the trade union application.

The rules of the trade union must have the following details:

1. The name of the union
2. The major objectives of the trade union intended to be formed
3. Clear articulation as to how subscription received should be spent
4. All details regarding membership and provision for inspection of books of record pertaining to numbers of members, wilfully subscribe the trade union
5. Process of admission of new members
6. Amount and process of collection of subscription from the member of the trade union
7. Clear articulations of regulatory frameworks for disbursement of benefits to its members at different crisis moments
8. Process for incorporating changes in the rules and regulations of the union
9. Process of induction and removal of executive office bearers

10. Management of treasury function for management of subscription and process of inspection of the books of record
11. The process for dissolving the trade union

Cancellation of registration   The registrar, appointed under the Trade Union Act, 1926, is empowered to cancel the registration of the trade union on satisfactory fulfilment of the following conditions:

1. if the trade union, on its own, applies for cancellation
2. if the registrar is satisfied that
   (a) the certificate has been obtained by fraud or mistake
   (b) the trade union has ceased to exist
   (c) wilful violation of any provision of the Trade Union Act, 1926, after obtaining the certificate
   (d) framed and continued rules are, in fact, inconsistent with the provisions of the Trade Union Act, 1926

However, before cancelling the registration of any trade union, the registrar needs to give notice two months prior to the cancellation. This notice will provide opportunity to present arguments against the impending cancellation order. This show cause notice is in line with natural justice and fairness. In case the trade union does not agree with the decision of the registrar, then the only legal relief lies in approaching the local high court or district court, where the trade union was registered. All the notices should be served at the head office of the trade union.

Fund utilization   Trade unions are allowed to collect subscription from its members. Thus, it requires clear guidelines where these funds could be utilized. There are two funds that can be maintained under the Trade Union Act. These funds are called the *general fund* and *political fund*.

General fund   The Trade Union Act clearly outlines as to how general fund money can be utilized:

1. the payment of salaries, allowances, and official expenses to office bearers of the trade union
2. the payment of expenses for the administration of the trade union audit of the books of records
3. legal expenses for cases involving the trade union or its members with their employers
4. the conduct of trade disputes on behalf of the trade union or any members thereof
5. the compensation of members for loss arising out of trade disputes
6. allowances to members or their dependents on account of a member's death, old age, sickness, accident, or unemployment
7. liability under the policy of assurance of the lives of members or under policies insuring members against sickness, accident, or unemployment

8. the provisions of educational, social, and religious benefits for members
9. the publication of a journal, discussing questions affecting employers and workmen as such
10. on programmes intended to benefit workmen in general; this amount should not be more than one-fourth the gross income collected during that year and of the balance at the credit of those funds at the commencement of that year

Political fund   A separately levied fund could be formed with a view of promoting the political interests of its members. Contribution to this fund is voluntary and cannot be imposed on the members. The fund organised under this Act could be utilized to

1. meet the expenses incurred by a candidate for election to any legislative body
2. meet the expenses for holding meetings and for distributing literature in support of the election of a candidate
3. meet the expenses of maintaining a member of a legislative assembly
4. finance the expenses for the selection of a candidate for a legislative body

The disqualification of an office bearer   Section 21A highlights various reasons for the disqualification of a trade union office bearer:

1. The member has not attained the age of 18.
2. Any member convicted by a court in India for an offence of moral turpitude and sentenced to imprisonment. On expiry of the five-year time ban from the release date, the member can again be the office bearer of the trade union.

Immunity   The office bearer of the trade union engages in various agitations, processions, protests, and so on. Hence, the Trade Union Act has provided several immunities to its members for furtherance of the interests of the workers.

1. Criminal conspiracy: Office bearers of a registered trade union can be punished under Subsection (2) of Section 120-B of the IPC with reference to an agreement among members if it is conceived and implemented for the purpose of furthering the interest of the trade union. However, this agreement among its members should not be an agreement to commit an offence; in that case, the immunity granted under the umbrella of the Trade Union Act, 1926, cannot be applied.
2. Any legal proceeding in any civil court in respect of tortuous Act cannot be entertained against any registered trade union. This immunity is available when the action in question has been done in accordance with the furtherance of the interest of the employees and with the explicit instructions given by the executive of the trade union.
3. Civil liabilities: No suit or other legal proceeding can be entertained in the court against any office bearer when it has been done in furtherance of the trade dispute. Immunity is considered to be crucial as the enforcement of labour rights requires inducement to mass labour to undertake mass action against the

employer, which under other pieces of legislation active in India construe as crime and invite civil liabilities.

This immunity provides an adequate safety net around the trade union office bearer for engaging in activities for protection of its employee's interest against the mighty employers. This safety net is crucial and provides assurance of not inviting legal proceedings while done in furtherance of the trade dispute.

Outsider or insider   The Trade Union Act, 1926, provides clear guidelines pertaining to the outsider and insider ratio with reference to office bearers. In India, multiplicity of trade unions is one of the major problems. It could be attributed as the main cause for poor performance in protecting the right of the employees. Some of the prominent trade unions are INTUC, AITUC, and HMS.

Indian National Trade Union Congress (INTUC)   It is a strong presence in West Bengal, Assam, Gujarat, and Maharashtra. This union has affiliation to the Congress party.

Hind Mazdoor Sabha (HMS)   It is another powerful trade union, predominantly limited in its spread in comparison with other trade unions.

All India Trade Union Congress (AITUC)   It is one of the oldest trade union federations in India and one of the five largest. It is governed by a body headed by the General Secretary of the Communist Party of India.

Industrial Dispute and Collective Bargaining

Industrial disputes can arise from a number of issues such as retrenchment of employees, unfair terms of employment contract, additional job responsibilities, percentage of bonus and salary hike, rivalry among trade unions, and perceived negative attitude of management towards labour.

A mechanism to bring out an agreed solution to the above-mentioned issue is often arrived at with the help of the collective bargaining process. Collective bargaining means a process of negotiation between the management and the trade union/representative of employees to arrive at an agreed solution that will remain active for a specified period. Collective bargaining may be about wage-related issues, additional and supplementary benefit issues, work-related issues, etc. Collective bargaining requires an elaborate protocol comprising collection and analysis of data. The negotiation process allows each party (employer and trade union/ employee) to present its expectations—exchange of view points from both parties allows them to arrive at an acceptable solution, acceptable at both ends. Once the terms of agreement are decided, the trade union goes back to its employees and puts the matter up for vote. Once endorsement from the employees is achieved with the help of voting, the trade union representative is authorized to sign the agreement on behalf of the employees. Thus, the terms of the agreement remain valid for a certain period.

Industrial Dispute Act, 1947

This Act applies to all states in India. Its objective is to provide a regulatory and administrative framework to resolve industrial disputes that may arise during the course of its operation. It provides various regulatory processes and administrative architectures to resolve industrial disputes. In other words, this Act provides the institutional mechanism with its elaborate procedures to settle industrial disputes. It applies to all employees engaged in commercial organization. However, it does not apply to persons in managerial and administrative positions in the air force, army, navy, police, prisons, and civil services of the government.

Industry

An industry means any business, trade, or undertaking engaged in manufacturing processes. In one of the famous court cases, Bangalore Water Supply and Sewerage Board vs A. Rajappa, AIR 1978, the Supreme Court devised the triple test formula to ascertain the existence of the spirit of industry.

The triple test formula is

1. systematic activity
2. organized by cooperation between employer and employee
3. for the production/distribution of goods and services calculated to satisfy human wants and wishes.

This formula has enlarged the scope of the definition of industry, and thus clubs, educational institutions, hotels, travel agencies, travel and transport companies, charitable institutions, cooperatives, research institutions, banks, and insurance-service-providing companies are all arguably within the ambit of industry. The triple test formula provided more clearance on the applicability of the Act.

Industrial dispute It means any dispute or difference between employers and workmen or between employers and employers or between workmen and workmen that is connected with employment or non-employment or terms of employment or with condition of labour of any person.

Dispute Resolution Architecture

To resolve industrial conflicts, the Industrial Disputes Act has provided various authorities. These authorities are

1. Works committee
2. Conciliation officer
3. Board of conciliation
4. Court of inquiry
5. Labour courts
6. Industrial tribunals
7. National tribunals

Works committee A works committee is required to be formed where the number of workers in an establishment is more than 100. The objective of the committee is to provide a mechanism to resolve conflicts that may arise at the shop floor. An equal number of members from the management and workmen usually constitute the works committee. They are entrusted with the responsibility of arriving at solutions amicably. Problems at the shop floor level inherit various peculiarities. Shop-floor-level employees are located in the most proximate position—hence, their familiarity with the intricate nature of the shop-floor-level issues will provide an additional advantage to the works committee members to resolve the conflict.

Conciliation officer In case the works committee fails to resolve a dispute, it is referred to the conciliation officer. The officer investigates and attempts to arrive at an amicable solution. However, in case the officer fails to deliver a solution, it is referred to the Board of Conciliation.

Board of conciliation The board of conciliation endeavours to resolve the dispute by enquiring and negotiating between the parties involved. In case the board fails to resolve the issue, it is referred to a court of inquiry.

Court of inquiry The important responsibility of the court of inquiry is to collect data and to investigate the matter and refer it to the labour court. Information gathering and reporting is the important function of the court of inquiry.

Labour court The labour court executes the following functions:
1. the legality of the employer's order issued under a standing order
2. application and interpretation of a standing order
3. discharge, dismissal, reinstatement of and grant of relief to any workman
4. withdrawal of any concession or privilege that was being paid/given to any workman as a customary payment or privilege
5. legality or illegality of a strike or lockout

The decision of the labour court, industrial tribunal, and the national tribunal is binding on all parties. On expiry of 30 days, it is published in the official gazette. However, it cannot be extended for more than three years.

It is often reported that excessive state intervention in industrial disputes makes the whole system cumbersome and vulnerable for political manoeuvring. The Industrial Disputes Act provides enormous power to the government to decide the timing of intervention, whether through conciliation or an adjudication process.

Arbitration Parties to the dispute may refer the case to an arbitrator who is acceptable to both parties. When the case is referred to a number of arbitrators, they must ensure that an umpire is appointed. In case the opinion of the arbitrators over the dispute is found to be divided, the decision of the umpire will be final and binding and the said order will be published in the official gazette.

Relief available under various provisions of the Industrial Disputes Act The labour court, industrial tribunal, or national tribunal may direct the management to reinstate an employee if it is found that the dismissal cannot be legally justified. If an employer fails to accept the order of these legislative authorities and seeks legal remedy from higher courts, then the employer is required to pay full wages during the pendency period, provided the employee concerned is not employed anywhere.

Employees Provident Fund and Miscellaneous Provision Act, 1951

This Act is designed with the intention of providing social security to employees for the retirement years. According to the scheme of the Act, 12 per cent of wages/salary (basic and dearness allowance) is deducted from every eligible employee, and an equivalent sum is contributed by the management and deposited with the Employees Provident Fund authority. On retirement or cessation of services, the employee can withdraw the amount.

An employee, as defined in Section 2(f) of the Act, means any person who is employed for wages in any kind of work, manual or otherwise, in or in connection with the work of an establishment and who gets wages directly or indirectly from the employer and includes any person employed by or through a contract in or in connection with the work of the establishment.

It signifies that employees, whether working as casual, part time, or on daily wage or contractual basis, are eligible for provident fund benefits. Employees also get interest on the accumulated fund that is deposited with the Employee Provident Fund authority. When an employee leaves one organization for another, the employee can simply transfer the fund from one account to the new account by filling up specified forms. Under this Act, the employee can nominate family members, who stand to benefit from the fund in case the employee concerned dies before arriving at the retirement age. Each member gets an annual books of record for the contribution made.

Employees State Insurance Act, 1948

Before enactment of the Employees State Insurance Act, 1948, the Workmen Compensation Act, 1923, was in operation. However, the range of benefits prescribed under the Act was rather limited and only available on occurrence of injury or death. It was felt that more comprehensive arrangements were required to assist low-paid employees when they fall sick. To fulfil this objective, the Employees State Insurance Act was enacted.

Who are eligible? The wage limit is the central criteria to provide coverage under this Act. From time to time, this wage limit criteria is changed, and at present it is ₹13,000 per month. Any employee whose wage (basic + dearness allowance+ house rent allowance) is not more than ₹13,000 is eligible to access the benefits provided under the various provisions of the Act.

Rate of contribution Eligible employees are required to contribute equivalent to 1.75 per cent of wages (basic + dearness allowance + house rent allowance) every month. The employer is also required to make a contribution of 4.75 per cent of the wages (basic + dearness allowance + house rent allowance) every month. Within 20 days of the month end, this contribution is required to be deposited with the Employees State Insurance authorities.

Range of benefits Eligible employees can avail of the following benefits: (a) sickness benefit, (b) maternity benefit, (c) dependent benefit, and (d) medical benefit. Any eligible employee availing of benefits, while in service, cannot be terminated or punished. The Employees State Insurance Legislations clearly articulate that

No employer shall dismiss, discharge, or reduce or otherwise punish an employee during the period the employee is in receipt of sickness benefit or maternity benefit, nor shall he or she, except as provided under the regulations, dismiss, discharge or reduce or otherwise punish an employee during the period he or she is in receipt of disablement benefit for temporary disablement or is under medical treatment for sickness or is absent from work as a result of illness duly certified in accordance with the regulations to arise out of the pregnancy or confinement rendering the employee unfit for work (Section 73).

At one time, only one type of benefit could be availed of. Two benefits could not be combined; for example, sickness benefit and maternity benefit or sickness benefit and disablement benefit for temporary disablement, or maternity benefit and disablement benefit could not be availed of together. When an insured employee is entitled to more than one type of benefits, he or she shall be entitled to choose which benefit the employee shall receive.

Medical benefit An insured person, within the meaning of the Employees State Insurance Act, can avail of medical benefit for the family members whose medical conditions warrant medical treatment.

Disablement benefit (a) An insured person who sustains a temporary disablement for not less than three days excluding the day of accident, shall be entitled to disablement benefits. (b) An insured employee who sustains permanent disablement, whether total or partial, shall be entitled to disablement benefits.

Dependent's benefit If an insured employee dies as a result of an injury sustained out of and in the course of employment, dependent benefits are to be paid to his dependents.

Maternity benefit An insured woman shall be qualified to claim maternity benefits for a confinement occurring or expected to occur in a benefit period if the contributions in respect of her were payable for not less than 80 days in the immediately preceding two consecutive contribution periods. A contribution period consists of a half year time span, April–September and October–March.

Payment of Bonus Act, 1965

The Payment of Bonus Act, 1965, envisaged an additional remunerative mechanism where workers can claim some shares out of the profit made by the organization. The provisions of the Act regularize the worker's participation in profit sharing to some extent.

Rate of bonus   The minimum amount of bonus sanctioned under the Payment of Bonus Act, 1965, is 8.33 per cent of the wages (basic and dearness allowance), and the maximum amount is about 20 per cent of the wages.

Time limit   The bonus for a year should be paid within nine months of the close of the financial books of record. If the accounts books of record are closed on 31 March 2010, then the bonus must be paid before 1 December 2010.

Eligible employees   Any employee who has worked at least 30 days in a year is eligible for bonus on a pro-rata basis.

Shops and Establishment Act

This Act aims to provide legal coverage in terms of wages, weekly holidays, earned leave, working hours, and spread over of working hours. It indeed attempts to provide legal remedies for millions of employees working in various organizations such as shops, restaurants, and hotels. Different states enacted this Act at different points of time. Therefore, it is known differently in different states:

- The Bombay Shops and Establishment Act, 1948
- The Punjab Shops and Commercial Establishment Act, 1948
- The Kerala Shops and Commercial Establishment Act, 1960

Objective of the Act   The objective of the Act is to provide statutory obligation to employers and rights to employees. This Act applies to shops, commercial establishments, residential hotels, restaurants, eating houses, theatres, and other places of public amusement or entertainment.

Scope of the Act   It is a state legislation that implies that each state has the liberty to frame its own rules for the Act. The state of Maharashtra has framed the Bombay Shops and Establishments Act, 1948. Therefore, it is important that Human Resource professionals need to be familiar with the nuances of this Act, as applicable to the state. This Act applies to all persons employed in an establishment with or without wages, except the members of the employer's family.

Main provisions   The main provisions of the Act are listed here.

- Compulsory registration of shop/establishment within 30 days of commencement of work: Each establishment, referred to in the Act, requires registering with the labour department and should obtain necessary licences.
- Communication of closure of the establishment within 15 days of the closing of the establishment: It is important to note that specific communication

should be made to the labour department regarding the closure of the shop within 15 days of its closure.

- Working hours per day and week: It gives detailed guidelines regarding working hours and weekly offs. It also provides the following:
  ○ Guidelines for spread-over, rest interval, opening and closing hours, closed days, national and religious holidays, and overtime work
  ○ Rules for employment of children, young persons, and women
  ○ Rules for annual leave, maternity leave, sickness, casual leave, and so on. The Shop and Establishment Act provides due guidelines about annual leave, casual leave, and other type of leave.
- Rules for employment and termination of service: The Act gives rules and regulations for employment and termination of services.

Critique This Act regulates the management of shops and establishments with reference to deployment of labour. It provides some bare minimum support to employees working in various shops and establishments. However, awareness of regulatory remedies available in case of violations of any provision of the Act is mostly not known to the employees. Implementation of the Act provides a unique challenge as the shops and establishments are located in diverse business locations.

CONTRACT WORKERS AND LABOUR LAWS

It is a worldwide phenomenon now to utilize contingent manpower in the production process. 'Another important trend in the global labour market is the continued increase in the contingent workforce—the workers whose jobs are dependent or contingent upon present work demand' (Vance and Paik 2006 p.73). Against this worldwide wave, India cannot stay isolated. Deployment of contract workers in India is on the rise, as seen in the global arena. The prime drivers for deployment of the contingent workforce in the Indian service sector could be explained by 'intensified competition, fuelled by globalization, deregulation and rapid technological change' (Byoung-Hoon and Frenkel 2004 p.508), cost containment and incorporation of embedding flexibility at the time of faster changing landscape (Kalleberg 2001). Indian industry is not free from these global influences as it has developed a deeper level of connections with the outside world. Many internationally reputed companies are operating in India. Similarly, a large number of Indian companies are acquiring foreign competitors and establishing footprints across the globe. Looking beyond the License-Raj-protected Swadeshi system, Indian entrepreneurial aspirations match that of any internationally reputed company. Many of these companies are now managed by foreign CEOs. Compulsion to survive in a competitive world is a reality and a driving force governing organizational architecture. Hence, incorporating a contingent workforce is becoming a regular routine and will gradually play a significant role in the coming decades. Many researchers have termed this underlying changes in the composition of the labour force as a 'new deal' (Herriot and Pemberton 1995), a protean career (Hall and Moss 1998), a boundaryless career (DeFillippi and Arthur 1994), and alternative form of employment (Gallagher et al. 2001).

Growth in Numbers of Contract Workers

No accurate data is available pertaining to the prevalence of contract workers in the Indian service sector. Some tentative data is available for scrutiny, which provides a few snapshots about the overall deployment of contract workers in Indian industries. In one estimate, contract workers constitute 19, 20.68, and 22.38 per cent of the total Indian workforce in the financial year of 2003–2004, 2004–2005, 2005–2006 (Table 11.1).

This is one of the latest estimations available from the repositories of the Indian government. In another news report, 'No accurate data exists on how many such workers are employed by the Indian industry and government departments, but the labour ministry estimates that they make up nearly 28% of India's 459 million-strong workforce' (Livemint 2009).

Reason for Deployment of Contract Workers

Polivka and Nardone (1989) defined contingent works as 'any job in which an individual does not have an explicit or implicit contract for long term employment

Table 11.1 Comparative labour statistics

Sl. No.	Parameters	Years			% increase in 2005–06 over 2004–05
		2003–04	2004–05	2005–06	
1.	Absenteeism rate (%)	10.01	8.96	8.10	−9.60
2.	Labour turnover rates (%)				
	1. Accession	16.79	18.45	18.25	−1.09
	2. Separation	18.11	16.94	22.37	32.06
3.	Employment				
	1. All employees (No.)	7870081	8453624	9081024	7.43
	2. All workers (%)	77.34	78.06	78.31	0.32
	3. Contract workers (%)	19.00	20.68	22.38	8.22
4.	Wages/salaries per man-day worked (Rs)				
	1. All employees	233.71	239.91	255.94	6.69
	2. All workers	165.55	168.58	174.73	3.65
	3. Contract workers	100.96	109.71	116.40	6.10
5.	Labour cost per man-day worked on employees (Rs)	305.89	307.76	323.64	5.16

Source: Indian Labour Bureau, Annual Report, 2008–2009, Chapter 17, downloaded from labour.nic.in/annrep/annrep0809/Chapter-17.pdf accessed 15 November 2009.

and one in which the minimum hours can vary in a non-systematic manner'. Thus, contingent workers are different by virtue of the type of relationship they share (relational vs transactional; high involvement vs low involvement) with the hospitality organization; it indeed has reason to believe to have distinct impact on performance (such as work commitment). Deployment of contract workers is clearly seen in the Indian hospitality industry too. Most of the hospitality companies deploy considerable number of employees on contractual basis. One of the main reasons to deploy a contingent workforce is to achieve cost efficiency with low long-term financial liability. This also helps hospitality organizations to overcome problems arising out of the cyclic nature of the business, especially business downturn.

According to one of the research reports (October 2009), in Asian countries, predominantly contract workers are deployed to handle the peak load during seasonal points. Other important reasons for temporary utilization of contingent workforces sometimes is to cover employees who may be on leave, sourcing talent quickly that requires specialized training, and so on (Figure 11.1).

Contract Labour (Regulation and Abolitions) Act, 1971

In India, the Contract Labour (Regulation and Abolitions) Act, 1971, governs the relationship between employer and contract workers. This piece of legislation provides a few rudimentary safeguards for contract employees working in the Indian hospitality industry.

Asia Pacific

Complete work during peak seasonal periods	(17%)
Source talent quickly that requires specialized training	(5%)
Cover for employees who may be on leave	(4%)
Screen/test drive candidates for permanent positions	(3%)
Provide longer term workforce flexibility	(3%)
Work with limits imposed by HQ during hiring freeze, etc	(3%)
Outsource tasks not part of core business	(1%)
Let and expense become a direct cost	(1%)
Other	(15%)
Do not use contingent labour	(48%)

Source: www.manpower.com/researchcentre titled Rules of Engagement: Harnessing the Potential of the Contingent Workforce, accessed 17 November 2009.

Figure 11.1 Asia Pacific trends—Reasons for deployment of contract workers

This Act has provisions regarding registration and revocation process licences of contractors, a sector where contract labour could be deployed, basic guidelines regarding health and welfare such as canteens, rest rooms, drinking water, first aid facilities, liabilities of the principal employer, penalty, and procedures. These provide an elementary safety net around the contract workers.

Recent reports suggest that a few cases of prosecution have been made under this legislation; however, implementation of the legislative provisions is merely nominal and face saving in nature. Figure 11.2 highlights various prosecutions made under this Act.

In 2007–2008, the number of licenses issued to contractors was 9587, as compared to 9280 and 7313 in 2006–2007 and 2005–2006, respectively. However, implementation of the Act is not so impressive. The number of irregularities detected by the inspectors of the Contract Labour (Regulation and Abolition) Act was 6843 in 2007–2008 as compared to 5365 in 2006–2007 (Figure 11.2). The number of cases of prosecution has gone up to 3675 in the financial year 2007–2008 against 2648 and 2991 in the financial years 2006–2007 and 2005–2006, respectively.

The Contract Labour (Regulation & Abolition) Act, 1971, requires a serious revisit and alteration to accommodate the growing need of the young employees. About 22 per cent of the workforce is working as contract workers and it is increasing by more than 8 per cent in a year. This requires serious reexamination to incorporate changes to accommodate various safety and welfare requirements. Some research papers (Saini 2010) severely criticized the state government for failing to enforce the bare minimum provisions of the Act.

Minimum Wages Act, 1948

The Minimum Wages Act deals with minimum amount of wages that are required to be paid for deployment of employees in any establishment. The labour department declares the minimum rate of wages, on a half-yearly basis. Adherence to this notification is expected from each notified establishment. Hotels, restaurants, travel agents, transportation businesses, and so on, are governed by the terms and regulations of this Act.

The question then arises: if one establishment is in a dire financial condition—can it pay wages less than the minimum wages? The simple answer to the question is an absolute 'no'. In fact, no deviation can be made from the prescribed rate of wages, as announced by the state government. The poor financial condition of an establishment cannot be used as an argument for deviation from the prescribed rate. It is believed that any establishment, which cannot afford to pay minimum wages, should not be in the business, first of all.

This Act signifies that each employee working at the lowest level of an organization should not get lower wages than the prescribed rate of wages as declared by the state government, under the provisions of the Minimum Wages Act, 1948.

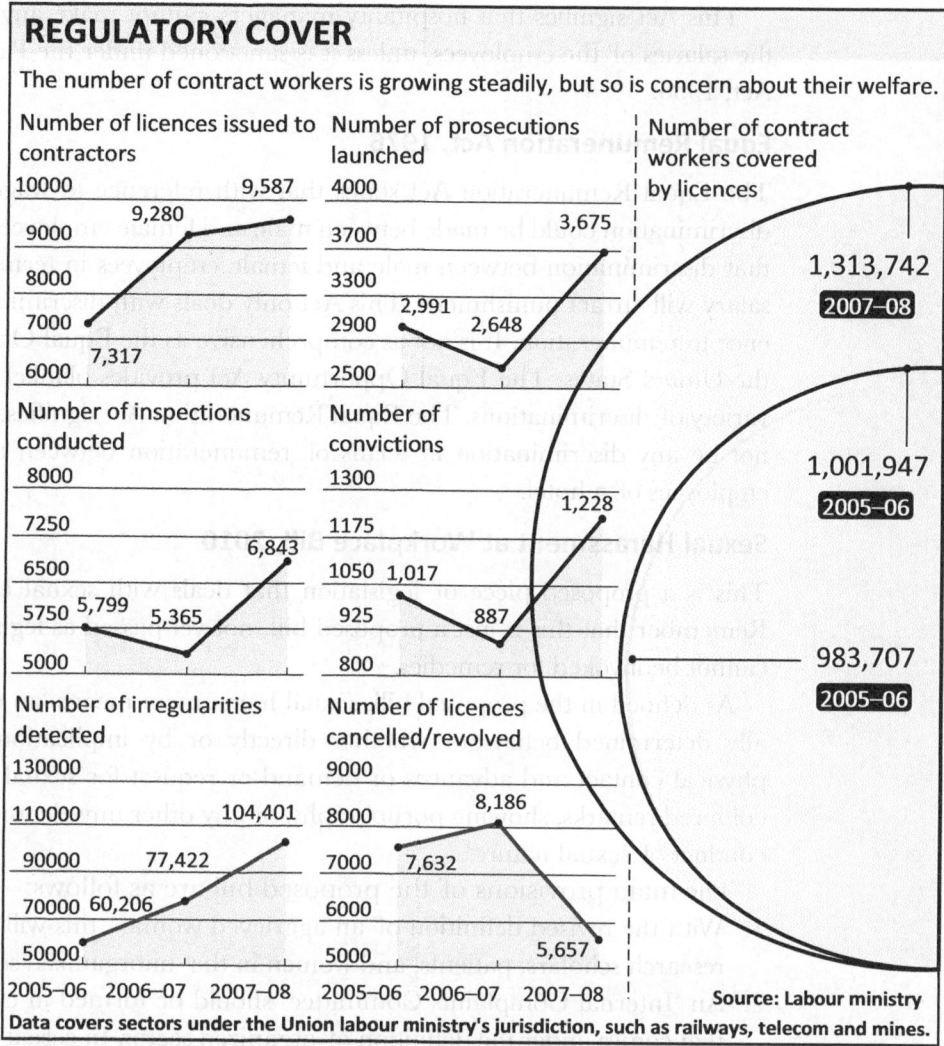

REGULATORY COVER

The number of contract workers is growing steadily, but so is concern about their welfare.

Source: Labour ministry

Data covers sectors under the Union labour ministry's jurisdiction, such as railways, telecom and mines.

Source: http://www.livemint.com/2009/08/03214654/No-end-in-sight-to-contract-la.html accessed 15 November 2009.

Figure 11.2 Contract labour—Regulatory implementation

Payment of Wages Act, 1936

The objective of this Act is to ensure the following:

1. Timely payment: The wages should be paid within the seventh day of the month or the tenth day of the month, depending on the number of employees deployed by the organization.

2. Prevention of unauthorized deduction: This Act states a number of regulations regarding various types of deductions that can be entertained as a deduction from the wages. No other type of deduction can be made from the wages.

This Act signifies that hospitality managers cannot make any deduction from the salaries of the employees, unless it is sanctioned under the Payment of Wages Act, 1936.

Equal Remuneration Act, 1976

The Equal Remuneration Act states that with reference to wages and salary no discrimination could be made between male and female employees. This Act states that discrimination between male and female employees in terms of payment of salary will attract punishment. This Act only deals with discrimination with reference to remuneration. It is not as comprehensive as the Equal Opportunity Act of the United States. The Equal Opportunity Act provides blanket coverage from a variety of discriminations. The Equal Remuneration Act signifies that there should not be any discrimination in terms of remuneration between male and female employees of a hotel.

Sexual Harassment at Workplace Bill, 2010

This is a proposed piece of legislation that deals with sexual harassment cases. Remember that this is just a proposed bill, not yet passed as legislation. Hence, it cannot be invoked for remedies.

As defined in the proposed bill, sexual harassment means 'an unwelcome sexually determined behaviour whether directly or by implication which includes physical contact and advances or demand or request for sexual favours, sexually coloured remarks, showing pornography, or any other unwelcome physical, verbal conduct of sexual nature'.

The main provisions of the proposed bill are as follows:

1. With the revised definition of an aggrieved woman, this will include students, research scholars, patients, and women in the 'unorganized sector' also.

2. An 'Internal Complaints Committee' should be formed in every organization that comes under the definition of organized sector. In case it fails to form such a committee, there is a provision of penalty, which includes deregistration of the institutions or a fine of ₹50,000 for a first-time offence. The employer will be liable to twice the punishment imposed earlier, for the second offence.

3. The district officer will be authorized to enforce that all organized sectors should have formed such committees.

4. The bill envisages that the committee should have a minimum of 2 and a maximum of 10 members and the presiding officer should be a woman. While one of the members will be from the institution, necessarily a woman, one more should be from an NGO. The penalty will be the decision of the committee.

5. The organized sector, as defined under this bill is 'any department, organisation, undertaking and establishment or branch which is established, owned or

controlled, financed by funds provided directly or indirectly by the appropriate government or local authority or a corporation or a cooperative society'. Any private sector organization, institution, unit, or service provider carrying on commercial, professional or industrial activities has been defined as a workplace. 'This includes an established private sector, institution, nursing homes, all industries, agencies involved in financial activity and having more than 10 employees'.

6. For the unorganized sector, the district collector will be responsible. The unorganized sector has been defined as a workplace owned by an individual or a group having less than 10 employees. This proposed law envisages for a mandatory district-level local complaint committee to investigate sexual harassment complaints, especially registered by women working in the unorganized sector such as domestic help and labourers.

Critique One of the prominent critiques is that the Sexual Harassment at Workplace Bill, 2010, is not 'gender neutral'. It means that men and women, both working in the organization, are equally vulnerable to sexual harassment. Therefore, there should be enough provisions in the Act that prevents misuse. Many critics argue that this bill could be misused to a great length.

LABOUR LAW—IS IT TIME FOR HEALTHY DIALOGUES?

It has been reported that in 2008, 4.5 lakh workers were affected because of strikes and lockouts; this number has gone down to only 90,000. It is difficult to agree that it is an indication of employee satisfaction. In one of the half-yearly estimates of the Ministry of Labour, the Indian government suggests that 2010 has seen only 41 strikes and 15 lockouts. This is a radically low figure against that of the two previous years. For example, 109 strikes and 148 lockouts were reported in 2008, whereas 2009 witnessed about 62 strikes and 172 lockouts. Employment opportunities available in the Indian economy perhaps caused this slowdown. However, labour protection finds a complete new meaning in new India. A new type of employee interest is required to be protected. Therefore, it is important to have open debates about the relevance of many age-old labour provisions, which are not able to deliver protection and security to new-age employees. Debate makes an informed society. An informed society can deliver better protection. Prime Minister Manmohan Singh advocated for some changes in the labour laws as some of the provisions are hurting the growth of employment in the country.

Labour laws provide a structural framework for employees and employers for the management of their relative relationships. In economic terms, employers are always located in association with a powerful social structure. Hence, the authors of the labour laws often devised exhaustive provisions with a view of promoting safety and security of powerless employees. Labour laws are quite generous in awarding right to form associates and free speech; this is also in line with the spirit reflected in the Constitution of India.

Labour laws also provide a safeguard to employees for restraining a powerful employer from using autocratic power, available in the societal structure because of their affluence. Labour laws provide assurance of financial safety by preventing an employer from abruptly closing a business organization. A number of safety procedures have been installed in the various provisions of the Industrial Disputes Act. Termination of service cannot be executed without following the rule of law. This has made termination of service relatively difficult.

Employees were not only taken care of when in service but labour law also envisaged the difficulties of unemployed individuals. In the absence of any other social security measures, the authors of the labour laws took an advanced bold step by installing provisions such as gratuity and provident fund. These supports provided ample relief to Indian workers. Therefore, it is indeed true that without the support of the labour laws, Indian workers could not have achieved a lifestyle or survived the onslaughts of the powerful employers.

However, most of these labour laws were composed when India was coming out of the persistent saga of under-development, unemployment, and other associated diseases of closed economies. The labour force was not educated in relation to today's age. Have the ground realities changed so much that labour laws have become an edict of the past, failing to fulfil the aspiration of the younger generation? (See Exhibit 11.2.) For example, the younger generation no longer joins companies

---

Exhibit 11.2   Changes in the Labour Legislation

23 November 2010, 11.27 a.m. IST, PTI

Labour laws hurting employment growth need to be revisited: PM

New Delhi: Acknowledging that some labour laws have not yielded the desired results, Prime Minister Manmohan Singh today said there is a need to revisit some of them which have hurt the growth of employment.

'We have enacted several progressive labour laws since independence and some even before that. But it appears that not all these laws have had the intended good effects that we would like to see on the ground', he said inaugurating the 43rd session of Indian Labour Conference. Singh said there is a need to consider the possible role of some of the labour laws in 'contributing to rigidities in the labour market which hurt the growth of employment'.

'Is it possible that our best intentions for labour are not actually met by laws that sound progressive on paper but end up hurting the very workers they are meant to protect', he said in his address to the delegates who included representatives from trade union, employees and employers. The Prime Minister also said the government was making serious efforts to moderate the inflation rate. 'We have difficulties but we shall overcome', he said referring to the prices of essential commodities.

Noting that the government was keen on not only making growth faster but also more inclusive, he said, 'There have been many successes in our initiatives for social and economic inclusion. But we need to do much more'.

Source: http://www4.economictimes.indiatimes.com/news/news-by-industry/jobs/labour-laws-hurting-employment-growth-need-to-be-revisited-pm/articleshow/6974298.cms accessed on 21 March 2012.

for life; bigger challenges and opportunities always attract its attention and it leaves companies for whoever offers such challenges. Thus, young employees are not staying with one company for a long time. The Payment of Gratuity Act states that in order to become eligible for gratuity benefit, an employee requires working with one business organization for at least five years without a break. New-age employees frequently change their workplace; this makes the selective provisions of the Payment of Gratuity Act almost redundant. The closure of any business organization requires specific permission from the appropriate government, as notified by the state government. Although economic sense does not allow continuing the production process, legal reason keeps it going. This allows sick companies to continue to be sick for a longer duration with the finance of the tax payers' money, which otherwise can be utilized for development. The Industrial Disputes Act has dedicated provisions for organizations deploying more than 100 employees not to declare closure of the business without the requisite permission of the government. This poses a critical problem where flow of money into any country in the form of diverse range of investments follows commercial consideration, labour market flexibility, and industrial peace. Research indicates that relative entry and exit of business into any country becomes easier with the introduction of flexible labour laws, and real benefit will go to the employee with more termination benefit. The employer also will save considerable money by moving the production centre where efficiency and return of capital are relatively high.

The provisions stated in the Contract Labour Regulation and Abolition Act, 1971, require considerable changes. With the considerable increase in the number of contract employees, the provisions of the Contract Labour Regulations and Abolition Act require a thorough revisit. There is an urgent need to recommend additional benefits to the contract employees. At present, the Contract Labour (Regulations and Abolition) Act provides barely rudimentary benefits such as a hygienic workplace where the contract labour is employed. Thus, there is an urgent need to incorporate changes in the scheme of labour laws, in sync with the grassroot reality of new India. It requires strong political will and unbending courage, which is almost extinct in the present political system.

Maintenance of a huge number of registers, under various labour legislations, is indeed a very cumbersome process. (See Exhibit 11.3.) Various labour laws have been enacted at different points of time; therefore, each piece of legislation has its own formats, registers, and so on. It becomes difficult to comply with multiple labour laws, especially for small and medium enterprises. In order to increase the rate of compliance of multiple labour laws, there is an urgent need to make it simple. At this point of time, having multiple registers and books of records is not serving anybody, at least the employees. It is of utmost importance that some kind

Exhibit 11.3 Outsourcing Legal Support

19 August 2010, 12.14 p.m. IST, PTI

Business booms for labour laws outsourcing units Chennai: The pan-India expansion of telecom, insurance, banking and financial services companies and the near extinction of the tribe of personnel managers have resulted in booming business for labour laws compliance outsourcing units. 'It is an opportunity that has arisen out of an Indian tragedy—the tragedy of having to deal with multitude of labour laws by human resources (HR) managers of companies with pan-India presence', Manish Sabharwal, chairman of TeamLease Services, told IANS. Earlier, the personnel managers were entrusted with the task of labour law compliance, said Bharath Krishna Sankar, chairman and managing director of Aparajitha Corporate Services (P) Ltd.

'With HR managers grappling with tasks like employee retention, remuneration and other measures to increase productivity and employee satisfaction they find routine legal compliance activities as non-core functions and can be outsourced', Sankar told IANS. He said with competition increasing, companies are forced to have a pan-India presence. But the problem is complying with various local laws, either by appointing a dedicated person or getting it outsourced to domain experts. Aparajitha is the largest stand-alone labour law compliance services outfit with a pan-India presence and boasts of the who's who of Indian corporate world on its client's list. Spread out in nearly 20 locations, the Rs130-crore revenue company has around 400 employees deployed in this space.

Sankar said a non-manufacturing establishment with pan-India branch offices have to comply with more than 15 labour laws. Failure to comply with labour laws will result in one of company's director's landing in jail. Further, most of the labour laws are antiquated and the dictum ignorantia legis non exusat (ignorance of the law is no excuse) is the sword that dangles dangerously over businesses. 'Outsourcing is definitely a cheaper option for corporates. We can complete the task at nearly 60 percent of the cost that a company would incur on its own', N. Hariharan, head of Compliance Services at TalentPro India, told IANS. Meanwhile, the field, dominated largely by unorganized regional players, is now attracting staffing solutions companies like TeamLease. 'We will be formally launching our regulatory compliance services in two months' time. What we have been doing for our staff is being extended as a service to others. A cost centre has now turned into a revenue generator', Sabharwal said.

Staffing solutions companies like Team-Lease and TalentPro are trying to leverage their existing corporate relationship for this line of activity. On the other hand, Aparajitha, which started as a regulatory compliance services company, is offering staffing solutions to its clients, said Sankar. All the players agree that scaling up the operations by expanding to newer cities is a big challenge and at times acts as an entry barrier for others. 'Tying up with consultants or other smaller players to service a client is a big no as it involves sharing of critical data', P.S. Srikumar, vice president (Sales and Marketing), TalentPro, told IANS. 'With competition increasing in the traditional regulatory compliance services space, we are now looking at the growing mining, energy and hospitality sectors for our services', said K.Nagaraj, joint managing director of Aparajitha. According to Sankar, the company is also studying markets like Sri Lanka and Bangladesh whose labour laws are similar to Indian legislation.

Source: http://www4.economictimes.indiatimes.com/news/news-by-industry/services/consultancy-/-audit/business-booms-for-labour-laws-outsourcing-units/articleshow/6335987.cms accessed 2 January 2010.

of coherent efforts are undertaken to make labour rules 'implementable'. With the development of information technology, data managements under various labour legislations require urgent re-evaluation. Submission of annual returns under various laws requires to be made simpler than the present multiple submissions. This system should be done away with for easy and higher degree of compliance. It is only a matter of imagination as to how all these returns, submitted by various organizations, are maintained at the labour office. Thus, by bringing in simplicity, the government and the labour department will be highly benefitted indeed.

Inspection of organizations should be evidence based and some form of accountability is required to be installed in the process. Under various labour legislations, it has been envisaged that inspectors will enforce various provisions of the labour legislation. By bringing in transparency in the relationship between government, employees, and employers, it will potentially promote the true objectives of the labour legislations, that is, labour welfare.

The Indian Labour Court, envisaged under the Industrial Disputes Act, does not have sharp teeth to implement its ruling. Thus, stakeholders of labour laws, employees, and employers, equally perceive it as inferior to civil courts. Whenever labour laws are going to be revised, it is an important issue that requires fine-tuning. Therefore, it is highly recommended that the Indian labour court should get equal stature with any civil court and should get enough teeth to implement its ruling.

SUMMARY

Indian labour legislation is at the crossroads. It has attempted to give voice to the weaker sections of the workforce over the past 70 years. However, India is no longer an isolated nation—it is deeply connected with the world. India's progress is unprecedented in its history, achieving economic growth of about 8 per cent or more while other developed nations languished in the vicious cycle of marginal or no growth. With this renewed condition of world competition, India badly requires a progressive and inclusive labour policy in tune with the requirement of the present workforce. It is not an option; it is a strategic need for India. It is required to fuel the growth and cascade the benefit of growth to all sections of society. India should have labour laws that facilitate these objectives. Therefore, simplification, inclusivity, and speed are the three terms crucial for the new progressive labour legislation. Simplification will bring about simplicity, whereas inclusivity will make a broader arrangement for a more inclusive approach, such as pragmatic labour welfare for unorganized sector employees. Speed is a non-negotiable element in the new labour legislation, which will provide deterministic decision by various judiciary and executive authorities, fixed in the labour legislations. The dynamic force of these three elements will indeed facilitate India's progress. Labour laws provide inconclusive guidelines about deployment of contract labour in the hospitality industry. Critical evidence suggests that there are violations of fragments of laws, which exist today to govern contract labour in the hospitality industry. Industry needs clear guidelines and enforcement without compromise.

KEY TERMS

Salary or wages   All remuneration (other than the remuneration in respect of overtime work) capable of being expressed in terms of money, which would, if the terms of employment, express or implied, were fulfilled, be payable to an employee in respect of his or her employment or of work done in such employment and includes dearness allowance.

Sexual harassment   It means an unwelcome sexually determined behaviour whether directly or by implication, which includes physical contact and advances or demand or request for sexual favours, sexually coloured remarks, showing pornography, or any other unwelcome physical, verbal conduct of sexual nature.

Works committee   Works committee is formed with equal number of members from management representatives and employee representatives in any industrial establishment employing 100 or more number of employees to address shop floor level of conflicts and issues.

EXERCISES

Concept Review Questions

1. Examine various provisions of the Payment of Gratuity Act and the Payment of Bonus Act, 1965. Recommend changes to be incorporated in the various provisions of these acts.
2. What are the various regulatory frameworks applicable to any hospitality organization for management of compensation and remuneration?

Critical Thinking Questions

1. Critically examine various provisions of the Employees State Insurance Act, 1948 with reference to various benefits sanctioned for insured employees.
2. Critically examine the regulatory frameworks, applicable to any hospitality organization, with a view to administering discipline among employees.
3. Critically examine various changes that are required to be incorporated for making a wide variety of labour laws in tune with the present state of labour affairs.

Assignments

1. Record various problems employees expressed during your industrial exposure training in five-star hotels, travel agencies, and restaurants and to what extent these list of problems could be solved by legal and regulatory supports.

2. Consider yourself as the general manager of a hospitality business organization. Design a scheme for resolving various problems faced by employees working in the hospitality industry.

REFERENCES

Byoung-Hoon, L. and Frenkel, S.J., 'Divided Workers: Social Relations between Contract and Regular Workers in a Korean Auto Company', *Work, Employment and Society*, Volume 18, Issue 3, 2004 p.507–530.

DeFillippi, R.J. and Arthur, M.B., 'The Boundaryless Career: A Competency-Based Perspective', *Journal of Organizational Behavior*, Volume 15, 1994, 307–324.

Gallagher, D.G., Gilley, M.K., Nelson,D., Connelly, C. ., and Michie,S., *Work–home conflict and distress: The role of volition in temporary employment arrangements.* Presented at The 7th European Conference on Organizational Psychology and Health Care, October 11–13, 2001, Stockholm, Sweden.

Hall, D.T., and Moss, J.E., 'The New Protean Career Contract: Helping Organizations and Employees Adapt'. *Organizational Dynamics*, Volume 26, Issue 3, 1998, 22–37.

Herriot, P. and Pemberton, C., 'A New Deal for Middle Managers', *People Management*, Volume 15, June 1995, p.32–34.

Kalleberg, A.L., 'Organizing Flexibility: The Flexible Firm in a New Century,' *British Journal of Industrial Relations*, Volume 39, 2001, 479–504.

Livemint, http://www.livemint.com/2009/08/03214654/No-end-in-sight-to-contract-la.html accessed 15 November 2009

Polivka, A.E., and Nardone, T., 'The Definition of Contingent Work,' *Monthly Labor Review*, Volume 112, 1989, 9–16.

Saini, D., 'The Contract Labour Act 1970: Issues and Concerns', *Indian Journal of Industrial Relations*, Volume 46, Issue 1, 2010, p.32–44.

Vance, C. and Paik, Y. *Managing a Global Workforce: Challenges and Opportunities in International Human Resource Management.* M.E. Sharpe, New York, 2006.

CASE COLLECTIVES

1. You are selected as a management trainee with a consolidated salary of ₹12,000/-. However, your friend Sitaram has been selected as an operation trainee with a lower salary package, ₹7500/-. Do you think, Employees State Insurance Act, Employees Provident Fund Act, Minimum Wages Act, Payment of Gratuity Act, and Payment of Bonus Act will apply to you and your friend? Provide your rationale in line with your answer.

2. Twenty contract workers are working as drivers in your travel agency. They draw a salary of ₹8000/-. Do you think Employees State Insurance Act, Employees Provident Fund Act, Minimum Wages Act, Payment of Gratuity Act, and Payment of Bonus Act will apply to these contract workers? Provide your rationale in line with your answer.

3. Banerjee is not well for the last three months; he works in the F&B department. His continuous absence causes typical problems in the department. The F&B manager is angry and tells the HR manager to terminate his services immediately and replace him with another employee. Banerjee has availed medical and hospital facilities from a hospital, notified under Employee State Insurance Corporation. You are working as the HR manager. Will you fire Banerjee from his job? Justify.

4. Chatterjee had started his business 20 years ago. It grew quite well in the initial years. However, cheap Chinese products spoiled the fate of this great company. He has employed about 180 employees. Now he wants to close his business as it is no longer profitable. He feels that selling the land where the factory is located will bring better value. You are working as a consultant to him. You need to update him about the various procedures, required to be followed before the closure of the business unit. Enumerate the procedures he is required to follow.

12 Disciplinary Action

INTRODUCTION

12 Disciplinary Action

INTRODUCTION

Legal dispensation is one of the effective ways to deal with employee misconduct. HR personnel should adopt a balanced approach about employee misconduct. Each employee joins an organization in order to become a successful individual. The individual refrains from engaging in misconduct and other negatively identified behaviours. So, individual misconduct is the reaction of abusive organizational infrastructures (oppressive rules and regulations, abusive supervisors, etc.). Thus, employee misconduct should be seen in the light of contribution from deformed organizational infrastructure.

However, it is equally true that employee misconduct should not be dismissed without proper scrutiny and punitive actions. Absence of due deliberation on employee misconduct will generate serious difficulties in the maintenance of discipline in the organization. Owing to demonstration effect, other employees will also imitate and engage in various misconducts. Therefore, punishment becomes one of the legitimate instruments and one of the effective administrative tools for organizational discipline. Punishment will prevent mass imitation inside the organization, leading to organizational discipline (Fig. 12.1).

Employees predominantly engage in positive behaviour as it is desirable for maintenance of discipline. A number of reward systems operate in the organizations for reinforcement of this continuous display of positive organizational behaviour. Similarly, negative behaviour from the employees is certainly not desirable, and hence, the human resource manager attempts to maintain strict control over discipline so as to maintain organizational peace and harmony. Providing organizational support in the form of reward to reinforce positive behaviour is called *positive reinforcement*, whereas not remunerating individuals who display negative behaviour is called *negative reinforcement*. Some of the negative behaviours demonstrated by individuals require explicit dealing by human resource professionals. The

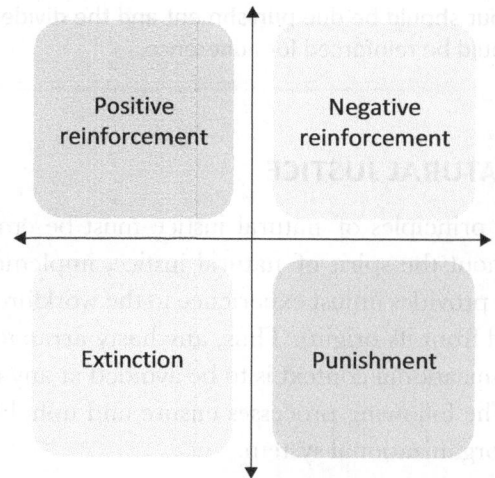

Figure 12.1 Typology: Multiple approaches for different employees

severity and magnitude of negative behaviour such as theft is relatively problematic for the hospitality industry. HR professionals administer different degrees of punishment to deal with delinquent employees. Suitable rewards are most effective if they immediately follow the desired response. Similarly, negative behaviour is not desirable and hence should be curbed from the beginning by providing negative experience. This negative association between undesirable employee performances with punitive action will help the management of the hotel to reinforce good performance. The management often attempts to associate pain along with the occurrence of negative behaviour, such as theft, with a belief that negative experience will prevent a repeat of similar incidents. It is of utmost importance for any management that they successfully manage employee behaviour for organizational performance. Behaviour not reinforced by the management with adequate positive/negative reinforcement will become extinct over a period of time. Discontinuation of negative behaviour displayed by the employees automatically is responded to with withdrawal of punishment—this is called *extinction*.

EXAMPLES

Situation A: The sales manager achieved a sales target of ₹5 crores against a target of ₹3.5 crores. This is desirable, and good performance is required to be acknowledged by providing good remuneration and package. This positive appreciation will be considered as a positive reinforcement for a repeat performance in the next year. This positive reinforcement will ensure recurrence of good performance with increased vigour.

Situation B: Report of theft in the F&B department by the steward. This is not desirable in any organizational context. Hence, not awarding a salary hike as was given to other performers will work as an effective intervention to manage employee's performance. Management of consequence of employee's activities provides useful guidance on what is expected, what is remunerated, and what is not desirable. The cost of undesirable behaviour should be due punishment and the dividend for diligent, hard-working, and law-abiding employees should be reinforced for adherence.

PRINCIPLES OF NATURAL JUSTICE

The principles of natural justice must be embedded in the disciplinary process. Without the spirit of natural justice, implementation of disciplinary process not only provides unjust experience to the workforce but is also illegal and void ab initio (void from its origin). Thus, any hasty arrangement to administer discipline in an organizational context is to be avoided at any cost.

The following processes ensure and uphold the principles of natural justice in the organizational system.

Prior notice of the hearing Natural justice assures that the person allegedly charged for any offence should be given adequate time and information regarding the allegations. This provides opportunity to the allegedly delinquent individual to prepare the required defence. This signifies that the notice served to an employee, who purportedly committed a crime, should include the time and location of the hearing.

The opportunity to be heard The employee, who has allegedly been charged with misconduct, should have the right to attend the hearing and present adequate defence.

The conduct of hearing The conduct of hearing should follow fair processes where the employee concerned should be able to consider, challenge, or contradict any evidence presented against him or her. The objective of this process is not to assign any preconceived notion on the employee concerned but to derive a conclusion, indepently without any preconceived notion or prejudice.

The right to legal representation The employee charged with misconduct should have the right to represent his or her case, either by himself or herself or through any other legally qualified person.

The decision and the reasons for it The final verdict should have reference to the detailed logical base for awarding any sanction, injunction, and penalty to the employee concerned. The ladder of logic deployed by the decision maker to arrive at the final punishment, if any, should be informed to the employee concerned. This will enable the employee concerned to examine whether the decision is based on the principles of equity and fairness.

Decision maker free from pecuniary and proprietary interest The decision maker should be free from pecuniary and proprietary interest so far as the case in question is concerned. It is believed that relationship, whether pecuniary or any other proprietary, with the case, or the parties involved, could potentially cause bias for outcome.

Equity The whole disciplinary process, including its outcome, should adhere to equity principles. Equity principles indicate that punishment should not be more than the magnitude of the crime. During disciplinary process, equity principles indicate allocation of adequate time for defence, honestly evaluating the merit of the arguments provided by the employee concerned, and so on. This principle powerfully advances the arguments that disciplinary process itself should not end up as a punishment or become a platform to harass the employee concerned.

Due process The concerned employee should be assumed innocent till the time the charges are proved with the help of a transparent, equitable, fair disciplinary process. Conclusion could only be derived after evaluating all the relevant facts and figures. The decision maker should not allow himself or herself to be influenced by common sense or by what others have already made up their minds. Due process principles ensure basic decision context for arriving at a fair and equitable decision.

POSITIVE DISCIPLINE—COUNSELLING

HR managers from hospitality organizations practising enlightened management philosophy may not necessarily apply legal provisions as enumerated. In most cases, the HR personnel are well equipped with behavioural knowledge and skills. Hence, they provide counselling services to the individual who exhibited employee misconduct. Counselling should not be equated with a session of advice. Counselling session is directed to provide adequate information about alternative life options available to the delinquent employees.

FACTORS TO CONSIDER WHEN DISCIPLINING

Magnitude of the problem Disciplinary action should be commensurate with the nature of the problem. Coming late for one day may not invite termination of services; drinking during duty hours, at the same time, attracts a severe degree of punishment. Therefore, disciplinary action should correspond with the magnitude of the problem. To understand what should constitute a grievous crime or minor crime, the Model Standing Order Regulations should be referred, which classifies the wide range of misconducts into two: grievous and minor. This clarifies an important issue that disciplinary action does not depend on the discretion of the management; rather, it is governed by legal frameworks.

Disciplinary action is not equivalent to punishment Disciplinary action does not automatically correspond to punishment. Disciplinary action is undertaken as a disbursement of justice in the organizational context. Justice should adhere to the principles of fairness and natural justice. This should be administered with due care. Disciplinary action is administered as a part of prevention of repeat enactment of similar crime in future by the same employee or any other employee of the hotel.

Duration, frequency, and nature of the problem   If employee misconduct occurs frequently in any organizational context, it forms part of a pattern. Then, the response should be more organization specific than specific to the concerned employee who is causing it. For example, if only the employees from a specific department are taking part in counterproductive behaviour, then specific investigation might reveal that the counterproductive behaviour is the reaction to a supervisor who is abusive to his or her subordinates. Then, addressing employee misconduct does not include the delinquent employees only; to have durable solution, it must include treating the concerned supervisor, who is involved in abusive supervision.

Justifying/extenuating factors   Misconduct should not be seen in isolation and should be seen in a cause-and-effect format. Investigation should be made to understand the circumstances where actual crime has been committed, although the seriousness of the crime does not get eroded when the management attempts to comprehend and develop a big picture of the issues. This information could be derived from a number of sources: (a) deviant employee's explanations, (b) reporting of similar kind of incidents earlier, (c) examination of workspace where the misconduct happened, and so on.

Organizational precedents   Organizational precedent provides crucial guidance about the organizational responses given against similar nature of crime. Major deviation from past precedents will attract the charge of discrimination, which can prove to be legally costly. Thus, the management should devote considerable amount of effort to link and comprehend the occurrence of crime in the light of past actions. Organizational precedents simplify the decision-making process. In case of no previous precedents, current misconduct should be evaluated critically, as this will become a precedent for future reference of misconduct.

Agreement with legal framework   Disciplinary action is mostly governed by a number of labour legislations. Therefore, the gravity of the misconduct should be seen in the light of legal provisions. In case the type of misconduct does not feature in the list as per the Model Standing Order Act, then the veil should be removed from the incident to extract the major ingredient of the incident, and this will provide adequate reasons to find its corresponding similarity with major or minor misconduct. Adherence to legal framework is a compulsion, and it is essential to abide by the legal provisions while addressing employee misconduct in an organization.

Support from the organizational system   Disciplinary process will be impotent unless it is congruent with other organizational policies. Disciplinary process is the last resort to bring change; primarily, other enlightened approaches such as installation and maintenance of fair organizational processes, reasonably good remuneration, employee recognition system, and so on should be used to tame employees so as to guide them into positive organizational practices. The organizational system should have enough provisions for disbursement of dividend to anybody who is subscribing, practising, and reinforcing positive organizational forces.

DISCIPLINARY GUIDELINES

The HR manager should follow certain basic principles while administering disciplinary process. Some of the principles are as follows.

Punitive vs corrective   Disciplinary action should not be seen in the light of punitive measures. Thus, disciplinary procedures should be based on corrective measures rather than punitive. Administration of justice should be the ultimate goal while dealing with organizational misconduct.

Progressive disciplinary process   Disciplinary process should be progressive. Starting with lower intensity punishment, the HR manager may have the liberty to increase the intensity of the punishment. This brings back the responsibility to the deviant employee for attracting various degrees of punishment (Fig. 12.2).

Adherence to hot-stove rule   'Hot-stove' rule is a metaphor and is often applied with reference to disciplinary process. A hot stove does not make distinctions; it equally influences anybody who violates the basic principles of precaution while dealing with a hot stove. Hot-stove rules are as follows.

Immediate response   Hot stove provides immediate response to the individual who violates the basic safety precaution.

Consistency   Hot stove provides feedback consistently irrespective of the background of the violator.

Ample warning   Hot stove provides ample warning for the violators not to break the rules; in spite of ample warning, if anybody violates the basic modality of dealing with hot stove, it does not hesitate to respond to the violators.

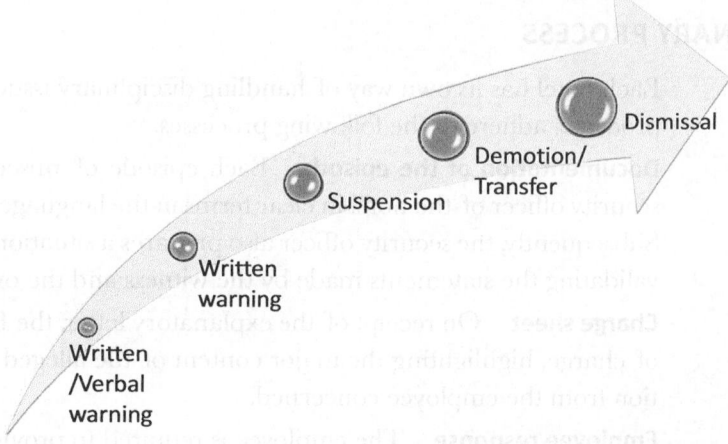

Figure 12.2   Progressive nature of disciplinary process

Impersonal Impersonal signifies that it treats each violator with equal intensity without any preconceived bias or discrimination. Whether the violator is the managing director of the company or a steward of the hotel, it will be equally generous to burn anybody who approaches it disrespectfully.

BRINGING MORE TRANSPARENCY INTO THE PROCESS

Transparency in a disciplinary process is essential and indispensable. When the organization fails to incorporate transparency, employees will lose trust from the justice framework of the organization. Employees will take the law in their hands and will attempt to deliver the justice they believe their hotel administration should have done. This will break down the discipline in the hotel. Therefore, for greater interest, the hotel administration needs to incorporate a sound justice framework with transparent processes.

Equity Disciplinary action should be based on the principles of equity. Equity signifies an equivalent disciplinary action/punishment commensurate with the nature of the crime. The hotel administration should not administer punishment disproportionate to the nature of the crime. Crimes similar in nature should attract equal punishment irrespective of any other subjective ground, which will potentially indicate personal bias and prejudice. Equity principles provide legitimacy to the whole disciplinary process.

Promptness Promptness is one of the characteristics of the disciplinary process. Timely disbursement of justice is one of the prime characteristics of disciplinary processes in any hospitality organization. Lapsing of considerable amount of time nullifies the meaning and importance of the disciplinary process. Lengthy disciplinary process brings unnecessary stress and suspicion on the whole justice delivery process, and thus potentially, the employee may lose faith in the efficacy of the process.

DISCIPLINARY PROCESS

Each hotel has its own way of handling disciplinary issues. However, most of these processes adhere to the following processes.

Documentation of the episode Each episode of misconduct is recorded by the security officer of the hotel in clear terms in the language of the witness and victim. Subsequently, the security officer also prepares a situation report, summarizing and validating the statements made by the witness and the on-duty security guard.

Charge sheet On receipt of the explanatory letter, the HR manager issues a letter of charge, highlighting the major content of the alleged episode, and seeks validation from the employee concerned.

Employee response The employee is required to provide adequate answer to the question raised in the charge sheet.

Show cause notice On receipt of the report, the HR department issues a letter to the employee concerned, titled 'Show Cause Notice'. The main objective of the letter is to provide an opportunity to the employee concerned to explain the delinquent act within a specific deadline. This letter clearly indicates the exact description of the problem reported to the HR department (Exhibit 12.1).

Explanation of Delinquent Act The employee concerned is required to state the episode in clear terms, with a line of acceptance or denial. This letter should examine the merit of the charge made in the show cause notice and provide adequate clarification, if required, to arrive at a more fair conclusion. The tone of this letter is one of the critical factors that are often referred to while decision on appropriateness of the punishment is pondered upon. This explanation is designed to give another opportunity to the employee concerned to defend.

Exhibit 12.1   Example of Show Cause Notice

To
Mr. Arvind Sharma,
Ticket No.25349
2/15, Second Floor
Rashi Apartments
Sion, Mumbai
Maharashtra – 400 022

It is reported to the undersigned against you that on 25 March 2010 at 4.30 p.m. when you were leaving the hotel after your shift, certain articles belonging to the company were recovered from your possession by the hotel's security guards while taking a search at the security gate. The following items were recovered from your possession:

1. Shampoo bottle (50 g)   5 nos
2. Sugar sachet (50 g)   10 nos
3. Scotch whisky (60 ml)   7 nos (mini bar)

The act stated above if proven to have been committed by you would amount to theft of the company's property. This act is a serious misconduct and attracts severe disciplinary action, including dismissal of your service from the company.

You are hereby called upon to show causes within 48 h of the receipt of this letter as to why disciplinary action should not be initiated.

Should you fail to provide your explanation within the stipulated period, as mentioned above, it will be presumed that you have no explanation to offer and an appropriate action will be taken without further reference to you.

Meena Gupta
Human Resource Manager

Enquiry   Domestic inquiry is initiated with a notice of enquiry highlighting the name of the enquiry officer, date, time, and venue of this enquiry. This enquiry adheres to the principles of natural justice and is the final chance given to the employee concerned to defend or rebut the charges. This enquiry requires documents of all the evidences and responses given by the witness, victim, and the concerned employee, who allegedly committed misconduct.

Punishment   Once misconduct is proved beyond doubt, punishment is awarded to the employee concerned. This punishment should adhere to the Industrial Standing Order Regulation (as modified). While awarding punishment, a lot of other factors, such as employee's past record, implication of the decision on the discipline of the organization, and veracity of the crime are given due consideration.

Employee's response   On receipt of the punishment order, in case the employee concerned feels that the punishment is not proper or right in relation to the misconduct, he can make an appeal within a specified time limit. This appeal must explain as to why the punishment order is not appropriate in relation to the misconduct committed.

The HR manager can examine the ground for the appeal. In case it is found that the punishment needs to be relooked at in the light of the arguments provided in the letter of appeal, a less stringent punishment could be awarded; however, if after due consideration, punishment is found to be equivalent of the crime committed, then the HR manager can inform by issuance of final order.

ESSENTIAL FEATURES OF A CHARGE SHEET

Various pieces of labour legislations do not provide any specific guidelines as to how a charge sheet is required to be framed, nor does it provide any specific forms in its rules. Therefore, charge sheet in India is mostly developed with various inputs extracted from various judgements, given by various courts. However, while drafting a charge sheet, a number of principles, derived from various judgements delivered by Honourable Courts, are required to be adhered to. Some of these principles are discussed as follows.

The objective of issuance of a charge sheet is to inform the accused about the reported act of misconduct committed in violation of the terms of employment contract. Accuracy in terms of the time, place, and the nature of the crime will enable the accused employee to defend himself or herself. Therefore, it is important that each charge sheet issued by the empowered authority of the hotel administration should provide precise description of the misconduct so that the accused employee can provide adequate defence against the charges.

Charge sheet   A charge sheet is an allegation of misconduct arising out of misbehaviour, indiscipline, lack of interest, revengeful intentions, and so on. It is a statement of allegations outlining various breaches against the terms of contract, the Standing Order Regulations, and so on.

Initiation of the disciplinary process In the absence of any dedicated guidelines on what constitutes a charge sheet, a few steps are required to be followed. However, this question arises: how do we know that misconduct has occurred in the organizational system? The Standing Orders usually provide exemplary guidelines on what constitutes employee misconduct. If a new genre of employee conduct resembles the description of 'employee misconduct', as articulated in the Industrial Standing Order, it gives occasion for issuance of charge sheet. The charge sheet should not be in contravention of any legal provisions. It should adhere to the principles of natural justice.

Content of a charge sheet There is no specific guideline available on what constitutes a desirable form of charge sheet. Careful consideration should be given to the various legal proceedings and judgments awarded by the courts. Therefore, a charge sheet should be construed as a medium to communicate with the employee concerned with clear articulation of various allegations. It should be precise, clear, and unambiguous. No abbreviation is to be used while drafting a charge sheet against any employee. The use of abbreviations such as 'etc.' or 'any other provisions/documents' with an intention to broaden the horizon of the scope of the crime should be refrained from. The charge sheet provides precise description of the crime by providing time, venue, and how it differs from the legal force in operations by highlighting various reference points. For example, in case of theft, a clear description of the time of occurrence, the venue where it happened, the ownership of the items involved in the alleged theft cases, the process of discovery of theft, and the witness present at the time of occurrence of theft or during the discovery process should be provided. The word 'about' with reference to time provides enough latitude to the interpretation of the crime and hence should be included whenever time of the crime is mentioned. The exact time might not have been recorded while reporting by various people involved. Hence, the word 'about' with reference to time provides ample scope for inclusion of crime committed by employee. It is not necessary to mention about the gravity of punishment, legally imagined against a specific type of crime; however, highlighting the punishment against a specific misconduct will leave the concerned employee caught off guarded. However, relevant clauses highlighting the punishment reserved for a specific employee misconduct are common. Hence, the linguistic expression should be well managed so as not to communicate the punishment before advancing defence by the employee concerned.

Issuing authority This is an important question: who can issue a charge sheet? Executive chef, in charge and final authority over food production process in the kitchen, cannot issue a charge sheet to the commis (chef) working in the kitchen department, unless specific provisions have been made in the modified Industrial Standing Order Regulations. In other words, a charge sheet can be issued only by the authority that has the power of recruitment. This is an important issue, which should be followed while issuing a charge sheet. Refer to Exhibits 12.2 and 12.3 for examples of suspension order and discharge letter.

Exhibit 12.2   Suspension Order—Sample

Date: 6 March 2012

To
Mr S.K. Mishra
50, Sadar Bazar
Ahmedabad – 380 003

This is in continuation of the charge sheet dated 4 March 2010, issued to you by the undersigned and your explanation dated 5 March 2010, received in response thereto.

After giving due consideration to all the facts and circumstances, with reference to the above case, it has been found that you are guilty of serious misconduct, liable to be dismissed from the service. However, in view of your sincere and unqualified admission of the charge made in the charge sheet along with an unconditional apology with a firm assurance that in future you will not repeat any type of misconduct, the management of the hotel has taken a lenient view of the case and hereby imposes a suspension for a period of five days with immediate effect, instead of dismissing you from the job. This suspension should not be construed as an indicator of gravity of the misconduct. The management of the hotel has taken a considerate view only for this case. In future, should you act in any way prejudicial to the interest or discipline of the hotel, no leniency will be shown to you.

For Indian SAT Hotels

Raj Kumar
Human Resource Manager

Exhibit 12.3   Sample Copy of Discharge Letter

Date: 12 January 2012

To
Mr Raja Kumar
50, Sadar Bazar
Ahmedabad – 380 003

You were charge sheeted on 15 March 2010 for the misconducts of riotous and disorderly behaviour. Since the explanation submitted

Contd

Exhibit 12.3 *Contd*

by you is grossly inadequate, evasive, and unsatisfactory, an enquiry was conducted adhering to the principles of fairness, justice, and natural justice against the charges labelled against you. During this enquiry, you were given due opportunity to defend and present required facts before them. The enquiry process was fair and objectively examined the merit of the case during the last one month.

In line with the findings of the enquiry officer, we have come to the conclusion that the charges labelled against you have been fully proved beyond doubt.

You are, therefore, hereby informed that you are discharged from the services of the company with immediate effect. You are required to collect your dues on any working day during the working hours from the Accounts Department.

For Indian SAT Hotels

Hemant Gupta
Human Resource Manager

SUMMARY

Indiscipline among hospitality employees is undesirable, and hence, the management of any hotel should be concerned. The hotel administration must launch preventive as well as corrective control mechanisms. Time to time, the hotel administration needs to revisit and re-evaluate the effectiveness of all these mechanisms. Suitable changes are required to be incorporated to strengthen the discipline framework of the organization.

KEY TERMS

Counterproductive behaviour It is a revengeful behaviour, secretly or openly exercised by the employee who believes to have suffered because of wrongful decision, policy, and behaviour of the management.

Disciplinary action It is the managerial action to address employee misconducts.

Industrial Standing Order Act, 1946 It provides general rule of governance directed to maintain organizational discipline. It is a rule book required to be adhered to by the employee and the management.

The principles of natural justice The principles of natural justice ensure that justice is assured to every individual without any bias or prejudice.

Equity It is the fairness in the dealings received by the employees in any hospitality organization.

EXERCISES

Concept Review Questions

1. Discuss various legal provisions that are required to be adhered to while administering disciplinary action in a hospitality organization.
2. Critically review various dimensions of counterproductive behaviour and the extent to which legal provisions are adequate in relation to the magnitude of the problem.
3. Recommend suitable strategies required to be embedded in organizational architecture to prevent counterproductive behaviour in an organizational context.

Critical Thinking Questions

1. To what extent do you believe that the legal frameworks available for delinquent employees are adequate? Do various legal provisions adequately address the true nature of the problem?
2. While devising suitable disciplinary action, can it go beyond the legal injunctions as envisaged in the Indian labour legislations? Will you recommend any change? Provide adequate rationale for your answer.

Assignments

1. Review various justice administration processes followed in various societal contexts in the world. (For example, in Maori justice system in New Zealand or in wisdom culture, the role of forgiveness and justice is very different. Is it possible?)
2. Draft a show cause notice addressed to a steward who has broken 200 plates out of a rage against the supervisor.

CASE STUDY I

THE PLIGHT OF RANA KUMAR

(The following case study is totally fictional and developed for academic learning purpose. Any similarity of event is a mere coincidence and drawing further conclusions should be refrained from.)

It was indeed hot evening news. Rana Kumar, the store helper, was caught red-handed while stealing branded rice and dal packets from the hotel. It was an elaborate plan. His brother was the general manager's driver and therefore had a number of privileges. These included that his car would not be checked by the security guard while leaving the hotel and also, employees will not ask any question about his movements. All these helped them devise a suitable strategy to steal. There was an occasion when Rana Kumar was alone in the store. Other employees had gone to attend other departments for accounts reconciliation or other related works. That time, he called his brother and gave some of these grocery items—rice and dal packets. His brother kept them in the general manager's car.

No history was available about past incidents similar to this where they have done it before. They ran out of luck as the security guard on duty was a keen observer. While keeping these grocery items into the car, the driver was looking all around in a suspicious way, which generated interest in the security guard responsible for managing the car park. He inquired about the sources of the grocery items. The driver told boldly that he had taken them from the store for the general manager (GM). The security guard reported it to the security officer who promptly reviewed the case and verified the case with the GM. The general manger called the driver immediately who said that it was given to him by the store people for the GM. By that point of time, the store officer had already been called, and it had been verified that no call was made from the GM for these grocery items. Then, further investigation brought out the truth and their game plan.

They were given a show cause notice, which indicated immediate suspension pending investigation and reply within 24 h of the receipt of the notice. Both of them asked for forgiveness citing family responsibility, financial burden, and age. Both of them had been working for this company for the last nine years. They highlighted that during their tenure of service this was an isolated incident. They also highlighted that other members also steal from the company. They also wrote that they could give details as to how other employees were stealing money from the company. Starting from the F&B department, purchase department, and the front-office department, they claimed that in every department, employees were involved in some kind of theft.

As they had only stolen small grocery items, they sought pardon. They said that the salaries they received were not adequate to manage their family, and that they were not able to feed their school-going kids properly. In addition, one of their kids was not able to go to school for the last one week because the school administration had asked for school fees. They were in deep financial trouble. If they lost a job in the current scenario at the age of 45, it would be difficult to find a similar job. They also said that over the years, they had been working with almost no salary hike, whereas all other employees working as executives were increasingly getting higher salary. Their salary was stuck at the minimum wages level, fixed under the Minimum Wages Act. That made their life miserable and difficult to sustain when the annual inflation was very high. They just wanted to sustain during this phase of their life.

Suggest suitable strategy to handle this case.

CASE STUDY II

THE CURIOUS CASE OF THE 'KING OF GOOD TIMES'

On Monday morning, you, the HR manager, come to your office a little early to organize your papers before a morning meeting. However, as soon as you come in, the executive chef of the hotel, Chef Mukherjee calls you up. You get a bit surprised to receive a call from him so early in the morning. He is almost howling:

Mukherjee: Raja is a real....... (abusive term frequently used in kitchen)—real headache. I do not want him in my kitchen. Fire him now. He should not enter my kitchen.

HR manager: What happened?

Mukherjee: He ... does not come for shift whenever we have heavy workload. Yesterday we had party for 2000 pax; he was not there. Today he has come, and I have stopped him at the security gate. He should not enter the hotel. With this amount of workload, I cannot entertain him. I do not need employees of good times. What are you going to do with this king of good times?

HR manager: Did you speak to him? I mean, why he did not come yesterday?

Mukherjee: Is there any shortage of excuses in the world? What are we going to do with the excuses? We need to do our job.

HR manager: Ok, I will issue a notice to him.

Mukherjee: Do whatever you like to do; ensure that he does not enter my kitchen. I am not going to take him in the kitchen. Fire him now. Just fire him.

Conversation ends abruptly.

Discussion Questions

1. How would you handle the delinquent employee as highlighted in the case?
2. Should the HR manager fire the employee? What are the legal implications?
3. Should Raja, the allegedly delinquent employee, be given any opportunity to defend himself?
4. Suggest a suitable strategy to the HR manager for dealing with the king of good times.

ANNEXURE A

RELEVANT PROVISIONS FROM THE INDUSTRIAL STANDING ORDER CENTRAL RULES, 1946

Termination of Employment

1. For terminating employment of a permanent workmen, notice in writing shall be given either by the employer or the workmen - one month's notice in the case of monthly-rated workmen and two weeks' notice in the case of other workmen: one month's or two week's pay, as the case may be, may be paid in lieu of notice.

2. No temporary workman, whether monthly-rated, weekly-rated or piece-rated and no probationer or *badli*, shall be entitled to any notice or pay in lieu thereof if his services are terminated, but the services of a temporary workman shall not be terminated as a punishment unless he has been given an opportunity of explaining the charges of misconduct alleged against him in the manner prescribed in The Industrial Standing Order Central Rules, 1946.

3. Where the employment of any workmen is terminated, the wages earned by him and other dues, if any, shall be paid before the expiry of the second working day from the day on which his employment is terminated.

ANNEXURE B

RELEVANT PROVISIONS FROM THE INDUSTRIAL STANDING ORDER CENTRAL RULES, 1946 WITH REFERENCE TO DOMESTIC ENQUIRY

Disciplinary Action for Misconduct

1. A workman may be fined up to two per cent of his wages in a month for the following acts and omissions, namely:

   Note: Specify the acts and omissions which the employer may notify with the previous approval of the......................Government or of the prescribed authority in pursuance of section 8 of the Payment of Wages Act, 1936.

2. A workman may be suspended for a period not exceeding four days at a time, or dismissed without notice or any compensation in lieu of notice, if he is found to be guilty of misconduct.

4. (a) Where a disciplinary proceeding against a workman is contemplated or is pending or where criminal proceedings against him in respect of any offence are under investigation or trial and the employer is satisfied that it is necessary or desirable to place the workman under suspension, he

may, by order in writing suspend him with effect from such date as may be specified in the order. A statement setting out in detail the reasons for such suspension shall be supplied to the workman within a week from the date of suspension.

(b) A workman who is placed under suspension under Cl. (a) shall, during the period of such suspension, be paid a subsistence allowance at the following rates, namely:

(i) Where the enquiry contemplated or pending is departmental, the subsistence allowance shall, for the first ninety days from the date of suspension, be equal to one-half of the basic wages, dearness allowance and other compensatory allowances to which the workmen would have been entitled if he were on leave with wages. If the departmental enquiry gets prolonged and the workman continues to be under suspension for a period exceeding ninety days, the subsistence allowance shall for such period be equal to three-fourths of such basic wages, dearness allowance and other compensatory allowances:

Provided that where such enquiry is prolonged beyond a period of ninety days for reasons directly attributable to the workman, the subsistence allowance shall, for the period exceeding ninety days, be reduced to one-fourth of such basic wages, dearness allowance and other compensatory allowances.

(ii) Where the enquiry is by an outside agency or, as the case may be, where criminal proceedings against workman are under investigation or trial, the subsistence allowance shall, for the first one hundred and eighty days from the date of suspension, be equal to one half of his basic wages, dearness allowance and other compensatory allowances to which the workman would have been entitled to if he was on leave. If such enquiry or criminal proceedings gets prolonged and the workman continues to be under suspension for a period exceeding one hundred and eighty days, the subsistence allowance shall for such period be equal to three-fourths of such wages:

Provided that where such enquiry or criminal proceeding is prolonged beyond a period of one hundred and eighty days for reasons directly attributable to the workman, the subsistence allowance shall, for the period exceeding one hundred and eighty days, be reduced to one-fourth of such wages.

15[(b-a) In the enquiry, the workman shall be entitled to appear in person or to be represented by an office-bearer of a trade union of which he is a member.

(b-b) The proceedings of the enquiry shall be recorded in Hindi or in English, the language of the State where the industrial establishment is located, whichever is preferred by the workman.

(b-c) The proceedings of the inquiry shall be completed within a period of three months:

Provided that the period of three months may, for reasons to be recorded in writing, be extended by such further period as may be deemed necessary by the inquiry officer.]

(c) If on the conclusion of the enquiry or, as the case may be, of the criminal proceedings, the workman has been found guilty of the charges framed against him and it is considered, after giving the workman concerned a reasonable opportunity of making representation on the penalty proposed, that an order of dismissal or suspension or fine or stoppage of annual increment or reduction in rank would meet the ends of justice, the employer shall pass an order accordingly:

Provided that when an order of dismissal is passed under this clause, the workman shall be deemed to have been absent from duty during the period of suspension and shall not be entitled to any remuneration for such period, and the subsistence allowance already paid to him shall not be recovered:

Provided further that where the period between the date on which the workman was suspended from duty pending the inquiry or investigation or trial and the date on which an order or suspension was passed under this clause exceeds four days, the workman shall be deemed to have been suspended only for four days or for such shorter period as is specified in the said order of suspension and for the remaining period he shall be entitled to the same wages as he would have received if he had not been placed under suspension, after deducting the subsistence allowance paid to him for such period:

Provided also that where an order imposing fine or stoppage of annual increment or reduction in rank is passed under this clause, the workman shall be deemed to have been on duty during the period of suspension and shall be entitled to the same wages as he would have received if he had not been placed under suspension, after deducting the subsistence allowance paid to him for such period:

Provided also that in the case of a workman to whom the provisions of clause (2) of Article 311 of the Constitution apply, the provisions of that article shall be complied with.

(d) If on the conclusion of the inquiry, or as the case may be, or the criminal proceedings, the workman has been found to be not guilty of any of the charges framed against him, he shall be deemed to have been on duty during the period of suspension and shall be entitled to the same wages as he would have received if he had not been placed under suspension after deducting the subsistence allowance paid to him for such period.

(e) The payment of subsistence allowance under this standing order shall be subject to the workman concerned not taking up any employment during the period of suspension.

5. In awarding punishment under this standing order, the 17[authority imposing the punishment] shall take into account any gravity of the misconduct, the previous record, if any, of the workman and any other extenuating or aggravating circumstances, that may exist. A copy of the order passed by the 17[authority imposing the punishment] shall be supplied to the workman concerned.

6. (a) A workman aggrieved by an order imposing punishment may within twenty-one days from the date of receipt of the order, appeal to the appellate authority.

(b) The employer shall, for the purposes of Cl. (a) specify the appellate authority.

(c) The appellate authority, after giving an opportunity to the workman of being heard shall pass order as he thinks proper on the appeal within fifteen days of its receipt and communicate the same to the workman in writing.

13 Human Resource Information System

INTRODUCTION

Human resource information system (HRIS) is a concept that integrates various HR functions for better synergy, efficiency, and accountability. The HR functions, as discussed through the book, are manpower planning, recruitment and selection, training, performance appraisal, compensation and benefit management, disciplinary actions, exit management, human competency management, and so on. Although these functions are scattered and performed at different points of time, they are interrelated, and data generated under one function is required as raw data under another function. To support the diverse nature of HR functions, technology provides ample opportunities for implementation. SAP, PeopleSoft, and Oracle provide necessary support to implement this. The advantages of HRIS are as follows:

LEARNING OBJECTIVES

After reading this chapter, you will be able to understand
- human resource information system (HRIS)
- modules of HRIS
- various benefits that can accrue from installation of HRIS in an organization

- HRIS helps transform HR practices from a mere administrative function to a strategic function.
- It automates clerical and administrative tasks, allows a panoramic picture about diverse HR functions, brings in efficiency in overall HR administration, and facilitates pinpointing of corrective actions.
- It explores industry best practices to enable strategic actions.
- It creates an organization-wide HR database to support diverse business processes, maintain past records and performance-related data, produce real-time report about the progress on critical HR functions, and thereby facilitate prompt and informed decision making.
- It creates job applicant profiles; manages contingent workers, helps hire employees, or track and manipulate applicants' data, in line with business requirements.
- It accommodates a range of worldwide and local regulatory compliances and produces relevant reports—classifying and

monitoring business data by region or country—or helps drill down to individual data from macro analysis.

- It creates the database for the management for basic compensation practices and extends scalability and capabilities into more complex pay programs to include cash and non-cash items, variable compensation plans; multiple components of pay, and so on.

- It allows installation and modification of diverse HR-relevant metrics, which can be used to compare and evaluate HR functionalities across individual roles, functions, and industries. It also provides diverse reporting templates that give the capability to produce and drill the data down to individual, group, business unit, strategic business unit (SBU), and so on.

- It allows HR professionals to manage employee-related data and reproduce it whenever required and whatever format it is required in. It brings transparency and democracy in the HR management system as it forces the management to put up seniority rules and promotion criteria under one roof to make the system operational (Table 13.1).

- It also records all employee-benefit-related data to track, manage, and facilitate an employee welfare support system. This provides clarity in the system and helps improvise the system whenever required (Table 13.1).

- It also manages and enhances workforce talent by identifying skills and competencies, supporting their adult learning process, and helps the employees' career growth. In a way, it helps to highlight, identify, and then use that data to manage careers, fill vacant or key positions, and develop the best performers (Table 13.1).

Table 13.1 Significant benefits Peoplesoft Enterprise HCM offers

Leverage	Capabilities offered	Benefits offered
Global core human capital management (HCM)	Consolidate onto a single web-based system	Cut costs, increase user adoption, and gain insight
	Compete globally while complying locally	Reduce risk/improve data integrity
	Build a core foundation of HR data and processes that will expand to accommodate your growth	Lower total cost of ownership
		Grow easily into new regions and markets
		Increase HR operational efficiency and productivity

Contd

Table 13.1 *Contd*

Workforce management	Implement flexible role-based user interfaces for time reporting	Ensure accuracy; monitor productivity, in-time reporting, and labour demand planning
	Integrate with third-party time capture devices	Enable integration to collect time and labour data from multiple sources/solutions
	Monitor actual time worked to plan and manage schedule changes	Ensure adherence to schedules to mitigate understaffing/lost productivity
	Apply a global, flexible rule-based solution for calculating absence accruals, eligibility, and gross pay	Ability to adhere to all legislative, union, corporate labour laws, and calculation of gross pay
Workforce service delivery	Deploy HR data and transactions to all members of the enterprise	Cut HR administrative costs
	Enable managers and employees self-service to reduce administrative costs	Increase employee satisfaction
	Improve employee satisfaction with a shared services model	Boost productivity
		Achieve best practices
		Streamline business processes
		Streamline problem resolution
		Reduce or eliminate process barriers
Integrated talent management	Analyse and model your workforce skill pool to accurately plan for your future workforce and leadership	Ensure success and longevity
	Attract and retain ideal employees to fit your workforce plan	Maintain competitive edge
	Optimize employee contribution by delivering the right learning, in the most effective format, for the lowest price	Cut costs
	Align employee contribution with organizational needs with appropriate rewards, performance plans, and career plans	Increase employee productivity and engagement

Contd

Table 13.1 *Contd*

		Reward the right people
		Improve succession and leadership development

Source: http://www.oracle.com/us/products/applications/peoplesoft-enterprise/hcm/052833.html.

Source: http://help.sap.com/saphelp_45b/helpdata/en/bb/db05144a3011d189490000e8323c4f/frameset.htm, accessed on 20 February 2012.

MODULES OF HUMAN RESOURCE INFORMATION SYSTEM

HR function has a number of modules and integrates them using different software. Each software configuration is different and provides a unique solution to its users. HRIS architecture is predominantly constituted by a number of individual but interrelated modules (also see Exhibit 13.1) such as the following:

1. Time office management
2. Payroll management
3. Compensation and benefits administration
4. HR information/record management
5. Recruiting/selection management
6. Training/learning and development management
7. Performance appraisal data management
8. Employee self-service system

Exhibit 13.1 Oracle PeopleSoft HR Management System

Global Core HCM
Benefits administration
Payroll interface
Payroll interface for ADP Connection
Payroll for North America
Pension administration
Global payroll
Human resources
Stock administration
Country extensions
Workforce Management
Absence management

Contd

Exhibit 13.1 *Contd*

Resource management
Time and labour
Travel and expense management
Workforce scheduling
Activity-based management
Workforce Service Delivery
Directory interface
eBenefits
ePay
eProfile
eProfile Manager Desktop
Fusion Middleware
HelpDesk for Human Resources
Workforce Communications
Integrated Talent Management
eCompensation
eDevelopment
ePerformance
Succession planning
Incentive compensation
Learning management
Services procurement
Tutor
User productivity kit (UPK)
Recruiting solutions
HR Analytics
Oracle HR analytics

Source: http://www.oracle.com/us/products/applications/peoplesoft-enterprise/hcm/053827.html last accessed on 28 February 2012.

Time office management In the hospitality business, it is important to manage the movement of employees inside the premises. Electronic time office management system provides the in-time and out-time of the employees. This is crucial for payroll and disciplinary functions. The data generated through this time office function is used to prepare the salary for the month after accommodating leave records. In many companies, the time office function has been replaced by the flexible time system where employees need to complete the work whether sitting in their residence or inside the company premises. With the advent of high-speed Internet connection, cloud computing has made it easy to implement this kind of system; however, in the hospitality industry, employees are required to be present inside the premises to produce the service. Hence, the time office function is one of the inevitable requirements of the hospitality industry.

Data collected by the time office management module is linked with the capacity management module, security module, payroll module, and the costing module (Fig. 13.1). The data collection process varies from a simple electronic identity card to a biometric card reading system. However, owing to the problem of proxy swiping of cards and costing, payroll- and security-related problem, the electronic card appears difficult to manage (Exhibit 13.2). Hence, a lot of companies are moving towards a biometric-based data collection process.

Payroll management Payroll management system is a part of HRIS that allows to process compensation- and benefit-related data swiftly. This is integrated with a number of modules and depends on a number of issues. For example, it is linked to the time office management system for attendance and leave records, with the

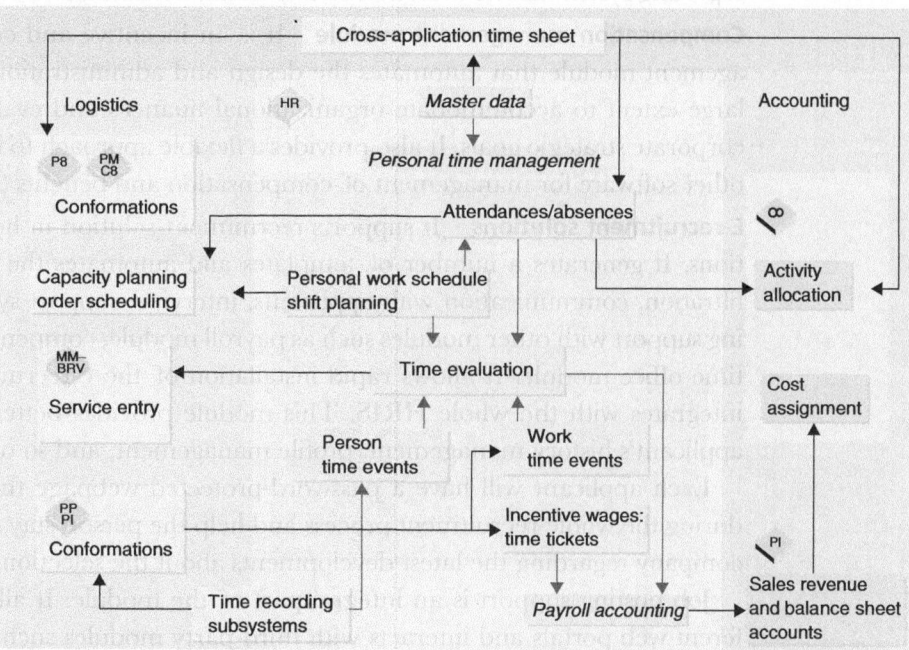

Source: http://help.sap.com/saphelp_45b/helpdata/en/8a/9868bc46c411d189470000e829fbbd/frameset.htm last accessed on 28 February 2012.

Figure 13.1 Showing SAP personnel time management module map

Exhibit 13.2 Features of SAP Personnel Time Management Component

Defines requirements and employee shifts
Complies with legal, pay scale, and contractual working time provisions
Records time data manually supported by the system
Processes data from time recording devices or employee self-service applications
Evaluates time data and provides bonus and overtime wage types for R/3 Payroll Accounting or a third-party payroll system
Administrates time accounts (e.g., flextime balances, leave entitlements, annual working time accounts)
Records and administrates data for piecework wage or bonus payment
Generates time tickets automatically based on postings from Plant Data Collection

Source: http://help.sap.com/saphelp_45b/helpdata/en/8a/9868bc46c411d189470000e829fbbd/frameset.htm.

performance management module for incentive and related benefits, with the financial management module for banking and costing purpose, and so on. This module provides a number of reporting modules for costing and legal compliance. It also allows cost forecasting and budgeting (Exhibit 13.3 and Fig. 13.2). The elaborate reporting system allows detection of any fraud, deviance, and so on, with ease.

Compensation management module It is an incentive and compensation management module that automates the design and administration. It is flexible to a large extent to accommodate organizational nuances and evaluate it against the corporate strategic goals. It also provides a flexible approach to integrate data from other software for management of compensation and benefits (Exhibit 13.4).

E-recruitment solutions It supports recruitment solution in hospitality organizations. It generates a number of templates and automates the process of resumé filtration, communication with applicants, interview support system, and processing support with other modules such as payroll module, compensation module, and time office module. It allows rapid installation of the e-recruitment module and integrates with the whole HRIS. This module provides better search capability, applicant's history management, profile management, and so on.

Each applicant will have a password-protected webpage that can be accessed during the whole recruitment process and help the person stay connected with the company regarding the latest developments about the selection decisions.

Job posting support is an integral part of the module. It allows posting in different web portals and interacts with third-party modules such as monster.com or naukri.com. It deals with the posting of job advertisements and helps generate interest among candidates to apply for the post. It also helps integrate with other internal processes such as job requisition formality.

Exhibit 13.3 Oracle Payroll—Benefits

Flexible Eligibility Rules
Defines comprehensive eligibility rules that link user-defined criteria
Defines standard rules for automatically assigning and changing employee compensation and benefits
Minimizes workforce inquiries by providing near real-time remuneration data and history
Simplifies Management of Processing Rules
Utilizes simple, configurable formulas
Controls unique processing rules and calculations using FastFormula
Uses conditional logic for more complex cases
Streamlines administrative processes
Reduces set-up costs and processing time and errors
Manages Global Payroll Activities
Manages global compensation with one application
Implements Oracle Payroll's core payroll engine by adding local extensions to attain the legislative functionality and country reporting requirements
Controls organization-wide workforce payroll and compensation data
Configures and manages personalized compensation policies and programs with one global payroll engine
Processing Efficiencies
Monitors payroll processes end to end
Reconciles errors while maintaining current calculations
Processes payrolls of multiple groups of employees simultaneously
Reduces administrative costs with online paperless payslips
Monitors Performance and Security
Utilizes standard and personalized reports to view and analyse payroll data
Provides configurable security for unique access
Maintains audit logs of changes

Source: http://www.oracle.com/us/products/applications/ebusiness/hrm/053360.html

Screening The e-recruitment module generates a substantial number of job applications; therefore, it is highly important to screen the applications. Using a number of criteria, the module facilitates screening of applications. Criteria selection and modification can be done with ease, which helps facilitate screening.

Training Plan Budget Model

Budget Model Id: 12
Training Plan Id: [12   ]🔍

Run

As of Date:	01/01/2010	Finalization Date:	
Start Date:	01/01/2000	End Date:	01/01/2010
Business Unit:		Learning Environment:	North America
Company:		Establishment:	

[Run]

Budget Model   Find First 1 of 1 Last

Name:	Human Resources	Budgeted Amount:	10000.00	Currency Code:	USD
Ratio (%):	17.00	Total Activity Cost:	1700.00	Currency Code:	USD

Budget Items   Customize | Find | 🖼 | ⊞ First 1-16 of 16 Last

Item Type	Long Description	Base Cost	Training Demand	What If Demand	Current Cost	Budgeted Cost	Currency Code
Activity	IBS RES CONFLICT ILT 01 - Resolving Conflict	100.00	2	2	200.00	200.00	USD
Activity	EXT COMM ETIQUETTE WBT 01 - Communication Etiquette	100.00	2	2	200.00	200.00	USD
Activity	EXT EMAIL MARKET WBT 01 - Email as a Marketing Tool	100.00	1	1	100.00	100.00	USD
Activity	EXT SHARED VISION WBT 01 - Communicating a Shared Vision	100.00	1	1	100.00	100.00	
Activity	EXT WORK IMPROVE WBT 01 - Continuous Workplace Improveme	100.00	1	1	100.00	100.00	USD
Program	BasMgmt01 - Basics of Management	500.00	2	2	1000.00	1000.00	USD

[Recalculate]

Total Cost: 1700.00
Total Budgeted Cost: 1700.00

Source: http://www.oracle.com/us/products/applications/peoplesoft-enterprise/...... visited on 29 March 2012.

Figure 13.2   Learning management module sample workbench

Exhibit 13.4   Features and Benefits of Oracle Incentive Compensation

Increases Productivity

Keeps sales representatives motivated with on-time and reliable payments and direct access to compensation plans, calculations, and transactions

Aligns Your Workforce

Increases sales line of sight to corporate strategy to increase sales success rates

Gains Flexibility

Provides complete coverage for any compensation plan design; plans can be quickly created, modelled, and rolled out to meet changing business needs

Financial Control

Manages administrative costs and gains visibility into your variable payouts; supports corporate governance initiatives

Source: http://www.oracle.com/us/products/applications/ebusiness/sales/051341.html.

It also helps process the applications through a diverse range of processes and can easily help generate an employee-wise, job-wise report that empowers the HR professionals to decide the next course of action. It also generates a filtered applicant pool, which can be utilized at a later date if not required at the present time horizon. These applicant lists can be managed effectively for further processing. For that, they should be linked with the contact management system. Most software provide support in this regard. All e-mail communication can now be clubbed against each candidate, and this can be used for further processing.

Some software also provide data management capability to process internal recruitment. If employees are working and opting for new recruitment processes, these data can be managed. Contract workers already working for the organization can apply for better job opportunities, and past data pertaining to the contract workers can be used during the recruitment processes.

Employee self-service human resource information system module   Under the traditional system, dealing with employee-related data used to be the prerogative of staff members working in the HR department. The role of the employee was limited to the submission of data to the HR department. However, it has been seen that a number of problems prevented the HR department from updating this HRIS. Thus, the very basic objective of supporting the HR department while making informed decisions failed at the very beginning because of the lack of support from the HR staff members. With the advent of smart and wide use of technology, the self-service module has made HRIS a ground of dual participation of employee and HR staff members. Under this module, the employee is empowered to incorporate, enter, and alter data pertaining to the self. For important developments such as acquisition of new educational qualification, address change, and filing leave application, HRIS has become the key process of the employee management scheme where the employee is not a dormant spectator but an equal partner. A number of options are available for inclusion of the self-service module with HRIS. The Oracle self-service HR information module allows its easy implementation (Exhibit 13.5).

Learning and development module for human resource management system   This module helps consolidate all learning activities under one umbrella. This system facilitates standard of learning, monitors progress of the learners, links this learning while assigning the work, updates competency details of the employee, and seamlessly connects with other modules of HRIS.

It can also organize test and examination modules and provide geographical proximity by uploading the system through a web portal. Learners have access to the module they need to learn about and monitor their progress (Fig. 13.3). It also provides an opportunity to maintain a catalogue of programmes and other details.

It also gives the capability to announce the programme through its dedicated contact management system. Thus, learning becomes democratic and does not

Exhibit 13.5 Benefits of Oracle Self-service HR

Works from a single source of truth
Increases accuracy and timeliness by providing both managers and employees a single point of entry to all HR information and processes. Delivers workforce intelligence to those who need it—managers, HR professionals, and executives. Uses embedded online advice to reduce errors.
Drives employee self-service
Enables employees to manage everything from profiles—including skills, resumés, contact details, and bank data to learning, benefits, payroll, and more, through self-service portals. Increases worker productivity. Authorizes employees to maintain their own information, including personal profiles, benefits, expenses, and more, in their own language.
Empowers managers
Enables managers to perform transfers, re-grading, employees training enrolment, terminations, skills searches, and more. Manages the recruiting process.
Supports career development
Provides employee access to targeted training and job opportunities. Enables managers to graphically search for suitably skilled individuals or groups and then match them to work or learning opportunities. Enrols employees in benefits and training courses.
Speeds up processes with workflow
Routes information of any type according to user-defined business rules. Delivers reports, status messages, and approval requests to approvers in sequence via workflow. Streamlines processes, removes bottlenecks, and reduces administrative costs. Integrates approvals with workflow. Identifies employee- and manager-specific functionality. Supports large numbers of transactions, including legislative processes.

Source: http://www.oracle.com/us/products/applications/ebusiness/hrm/053681.html.

prevent individual employees who do not have access to corporate resources otherwise. The benefits of such a system are listed in Exhibit 13.6.

Employee exit management   The employee exit management module is a part of the HRIS system. Employee exit management involves a professional way of dealing with employee resignation or termination and captures information that can be useful for the organisation. Mostly an HR professional takes the final exit interview before an employee leaves an organization. This data provides interesting clues about the functioning of the organization. As the employee is set to leave, he or she relatively experiences little political compulsion to make feel good/look good statements about the company. This data, if collected properly, can support the employee management system and contribute to the improvement of the human workspace ecology. This module helps capture the exit interview data and plough back with the mainstream HR management module for necessary actions. Without the HR management system, it is difficult to manage this data and account for it.

My Learning

You can view five of your most current activities and programs or select the All My Learning link to view all of your activities and programs. You can search for learning using a keyword search or access the Advanced Search or Browse Catalog by selecting the corresponding link. To view your scheduled activities, select the View Calendar link. Submit a learning request by selecting the Request New Learning link.

Search Learning Catalog

Select Search Category: **Activities** | Catalog Items | Programs | All

Search the Catalog: [   ] [Search Activities]

Advanced Search   Browse Catalog   Request New Learning

My Learning Activities   Customize | 1-5 of 5

Title	Type		Status	Date	Action	Launch
Time Management	External Vendor Self Paced		In-Progress	11/13/2002	Drop	Launch
Building Customer Loyalty	External Vendor Scheduled Lrn		Enrolled	11/13/2002	Drop	
Communication Etiquette	External Vendor Self Paced		Enrolled	08/24/2009	Drop	Launch
PeopleTools-1	Web-based Training		Enrolled	08/24/2009	Drop	Launch
Network Design and Administration (Part 1)	Blended Learning		Completed	08/25/2009		Launch

All My Learning   View Calendar

My Certification Status   Customize | 1 of 1

Program Name		Status	Status Date	Recertify
Network Engineer Level 01 Certification		Complete	2009-08-25	Recertify

My Learning Objectives   Customize | 1 of 1

Title	Proficiency	Status	Target Completion	Assigned By	Learning	
Relationship Building		In-Progress		Luis Martinez	Building Customer Loyalty	

Source: http://www.oracle.com/us/products/applications/peoplesoft-enterprise/...... visited on 29 March 2012.

Figure 13.3   Learning and development module sample workbench

HRIS forces the system to recognize the value of the data and put responsibility and accountability for the data recorded. This is an important contribution.

E-SERVICE AND HUMAN RESOURCE INFORMATION SYSTEM

HRIS facilitates improvement of the efficiency level of the HR department. The traditional approach to manage an employee was predominantly paper based. To avail of every kind of facilities envisaged under HR policy employee participation, usage of the pen and paper method is indeed cumbersome, untidy, and vulnerable to mistakes. The pen-and-paper-based method of disbursement of employee benefits brings inefficiency and gives rise to lack of transparency

Exhibit 13.6 Benefits of Oracle Learning Management Module

Develops Your Workforce
Leverages a common, reusable framework for describing learning objectives, defines competencies attained by the learner, automatically updates competency profiles, and creates learning paths and certifications to guide and manage workforce learning and development
Ties Training to Organizational Goals
Measures the effectiveness of training initiatives
Reduces Costs through Online Learning Delivery
Gains a content player that delivers any web-accessible content; deploys content to a global learning community; and collaborates via forums, chats, and web conferencing
Simplifies Administration through a Unified Catalogue
Creates a single catalogue for all online, offline, synchronous, and asynchronous learning; supports blended learning; and enables administrators to see the entities they create and directly edit their properties.
Increases Efficiency by Managing Learning Content
Assembles and delivers learning content rapidly, enables the reuse and assembly of learning content that makes use of mixed media and multiple learning modalities, and delivers the optimal blend of classroom and online training
Extends Solution Value by Providing Learning to Customers and Partners
Provides self-service access to learning for customers and partners, retains one-stop administration, and automates catalogue distribution and enrolment
Simplifies Administration by Efficiently Scheduling and Managing Resources
Places the right resources and equipment in the right locations, defines learning event needs only once, ensures that instructors possess the necessary competencies and experience, consolidates training initiatives on a scalable, cost-effective LMS.

Source: http://www.oracle.com/us/products/applications/ebusiness/hrm/053815.html accessed 28 February 2012.

and accountability. E-service is possible under the new HR information architecture, where employee benefits can be accessed, utilized, and requested for using the software-based system. HR information architecture comprises a number of modules such as recruitment module and learning management module. Under this system, each employee will find every possible benefit scheme under one umbrella and service requests can be triggered by a simple e-application. Respective authorities are required to respond to the request within a certain time limit. As all these data are executed through the system, every particular such as data and time of application and decision of the head of the department can be viewed clearly. This makes the system transparent, fair, and convenient to the users, employees, and employers, and consequently makes the HR department more efficient and dedicate more time on other developmental issues rather than managing leave applications and other such matters.

SUMMARY

During the life cycle of an employee in any organization, huge quantities of data are generated. These data could be biological, professional qualification data, performance-related data, achievement data, and so on. These employee activities are useless unless ploughed back into the system for further utilization. This utilization is enhanced, facilitated, and improved by organization HRIS. It forces HR professionals to articulate HR metrics to make systems operational and thus provides objectivity in the system and takes away prejudice and bias from the system. It saves a huge amount of time for preparation of report writing and allows HR professionals a lot of time to engage with employees, for which they are recruited.

KEY TERMS

HRIS   It is a software-based system to manage and utilize employee-related information for organizational requirements.

Learning management   It is a set of validated *modules* designed for *managing, utilizing,* and optimizing enterprise-wide *learning* and information.

Payroll management   It is a wages/salary management system that streamlines employee payment management functions and improves accuracy by eliminating time-consuming and error-prone manual systems.

EXERCISES

Concept Review Questions

1. Discuss the various important modules of an HRIS.
2. Discuss the various benefits that can accrue from the payroll module of HRIS.
3. Discuss the various benefits that can accrue from the learning and development module of HRIS.

Critical Thinking Questions

1. Critically examine the various benefits of installing HRIS.
2. Examine the role of HRIS in disbursing transparency and democracy in employee management.

Assignment

Do you think that your experience as an industrial trainee could have been enhanced by managing your personal and professional information well? Chart out your experience.

Did you get your industrial training certificate at the right time? Do you think your induction in the hotel was smooth? Is there any provision for improvement?

CASE STUDY I

NO TAKER

Srinath is the HR manager managing one of the leading travel companies of India. It has about 1000 employees working in offices located across 20 states in India. With this geographical separation, HRIS should work as the blood stream of the HR management; however, it is rarely used by the HR department staff. Employees display less interest in updating their personal details in the system. A number of e-mails to each individual employee do not generate good participation.

Last month, during one of the board meetings, the finance director questioned the very necessity of such kind of HRIS, which does not serve any purpose and is not useful to anybody, whether it is the employee, HR department, or the management.

He was inquiring about the discontinuance of such a system. Srinath asked for more time before such a decision could be taken. He is looking for ideas that will increase employee participation. HR staff members are also not highly encouraged to feed the data in HRIS. Their concerns also need to be addressed.

Discussion Questions
1. You are a consultant who needs to advice Srinath. Suggest ways to enhance participation among employees all across.
2. How can employees be encouraged to update their individual records?
3. How can HRIS be made an effective tool?

CASE STUDY II

SYSTEM MIGRATION

Jay Mukerjee is the HR director of one of the leading hospitality management companies. As per the new corporate policy, the company is migrating to an enterprise resource management system; hence, the HR management also needs to migrate to the enterprise management system. He is facing a number of problems. However, he fears that the HR department is not ready for this migration. He thinks that the department operates with bare minimum policy and rules. However, in order to have a successful HRIS, a number of HR policies need to be articulated. With these articulations, the department can develop a number of metrics for the operation of the system. However, it is difficult to have all the policies within the next 2 months because it is required to be negotiated with the employees before implementation.

Discussion Questions

1. You are a consultant who needs to advice Mukerjee. Suggest ways to enhance participation among employees all across.
2. Suggest critical steps HR managers need to undertake to make it a successful migration to a new ERP (enterprise resource planning) platform?
3. Why is development of an HR policy a prime requirement for successful and effective HRIS?

14 International Human Resource Management

INTRODUCTION

International human resource management is gaining in importance among HR professionals. Most hospitality organizations operate in multicultural contexts across the globe. Some of the Indian hospitality multinationals are acquiring hotel properties in foreign countries. Indian travel chains are spreading their network across nations. Managing employees in a multicultural context is indeed challenging. Each country has its own economic, social, political, and technological peculiarities. This presents a competing demand on the management as to what extent the current human resource policy should align with the local contexts. A successfully operational standardized human resource policy is often constrained by differing national business systems, cultural norms, educational systems, labour laws, and local HR practices. Accommodating a vast degree of diversity of prevailing practices in different countries under one HR policy is difficult and requires delicate dealings. To manage multicultural employees, a 'new managerial mentality' is required. In this chapter, we examine the various issues related to international HR management.

NEED FOR INTERNATIONAL HUMAN RESOURCE MANAGEMENT

Most successful business organizations do not rely on domestic customers for their survival because it is too risky to rely on one market for business growth. Globalization brought about scale and efficiency. Therefore, it is important to advance our knowledge in this area.

Scale and scope of economics The scale and scope of economic activities are no longer restricted within the geographic boundary or political boundaries of a nation. The term 'scale' of economic activities signifies that relatively larger organizations earn significant benefits that otherwise are not available in the case of small organizations. Some of these benefits could be cheaper bank loans, higher

bargaining power, and so on. Likewise, the term *scope* of economic activities signifies having a large bouquet of offerings rather than one type of hospitality product. For example, having different types of hotel properties, which could be appropriately classified as five-star luxury, five-star, four-star, and budget hotels, provides wider latitudes and higher synergetic values. The increased level of interdependence among nations and bigger scale of operations across nations to serve diverse global customers has made it necessary to look into the HR practice beyond the boundary of a domestic framework of activities.

Shorter product life cycles   Each product has a distinct life cycle similar to any other living being. The increased level of changes in technology and customers' tastes and preferences have reduced the life cycle of the product. Imitation of products by some companies, especially from China, further dented the survival of new products. Restaurant concepts (different cuisines, fast food) require constant changes in design and delivery of composition of product and service to remain relevant in the market. This is an important development.

Technology   Technology made it possible to have a global presence for delivery of products. All companies have their own websites and also rely on market intermediaries such as Galileo International, Amadeus, Sabre, and Worldspan. These are the four global distribution systems currently operating as the backbone to the Internet travel distribution channel. Thus, business opportunity is unprecedented. This global reach and interaction with global customers has increased the need for competent employees. Inexpensive, rapid, and extensive global communication facilitates virtual interaction between the company and the customers.

Growing linkage with the world through trade, foreign competition   The world is getting integrated for trade and foreign competition. This unifying force is powerful and almost unstoppable. The inevitable dense relationship among nations will require more understanding about the global workforce. International HR management facilitates advancing our understanding about the workforce on a global scale.

Improving education   Education standards, especially in Asian countries, are improving. This has made the supply of labour inexpensive, which helps multinationals start manufacturing, and service centre hubs in all those countries make them highly competitive.

Growth of Indian hospitality industry   After a stagnating growth in India over the past 100 years, many Indian hospitality organizations are looking abroad for growth. Reputed international hotel chains are allowed to make 100 per cent foreign direct investment in the Indian hospitality sector; therefore, a number of international hotel chains such as Hyatt, Carlson, Hilton, and Marriott made inroads into the Indian hospitality sector. This has increased the level of competition. Some of the reputed Indian hospitality companies are looking outside, especially in the Southeast Asian market for their next phase of growth.

Thus, when a lot of Indian hospitality organizations are growing abroad, it is important to advance our knowledge in this field.

CHARACTERISTICS OF INDIAN MULTINATIONALS

Indian multinationals, after achieving a stunted growth over the past 80 years, are now looking to acquire and manage new businesses in Southeast Asia, Europe, and the United States. Multinationals from emerging economies are being called by different names, such as multinationals from developing countries (Monkiewicz 1986), dragon multinationals (Mathews 2006), emerging multinationals, and third world multinationals. Multinationals from the emerging economies have a significantly different history, compulsion, challenges, affiliations, timing, and reputation. Most of these multinationals operated in a closed economy for a long period and have now endeavoured to internationalize their business because of new markets, technology, and domestic pressure. Airtel, the Indian telecommunication giant, looked to markets in Africa and Bangladesh when domestic pressure was relatively high. Similarly, Tata Steel also went ahead with acquisitions and bought Corus. Taj Hotels, Resorts and Palaces also bought a number of hotels in the United States and Australia and is reportedly making efforts to enter the Southeast and Middle East markets soon.

Late comer Most of these MNCs are late comers in the business canvas and have inherited several disadvantages. Therefore, it has been observed that they play catch-up games and endeavour to have accelerated growth, which potentially allows them to be equated with other competition. Accelerated growth should be understood by the magnitude of the action. For example, Tata Steel started its business by 1910, during the British rule. However, threatened by Mittal's attempt to start its steel base in India, Tata Steel aspired to be a big player in the competitive landscape. Thus, history demanded bigger action. Their acquisition of Corus Steel made them the fifth largest steel producing company in the world, quite a substantial jump from the twenty-third rank.

Competition against another Indian player Indian companies have been seen fighting against each other in the international market. For example, in 2011, Essar Energy Holdings and Jindal Steel acquired Zisco, Zimbabwe's state-owned steel maker with an annual capacity of 1 million tons. Similarly, in 2010, JSW Steel and GMR Group competed against each other to acquire CIC Energy, a Canadian energy company. Tata Steel and SAIL fought for coal blocks in Indonesia, and in early 2011, they joined hands to form a Tata Steel SAIL joint venture to access coal blocks in Indonesia. Similar types of expansion needs, control over natural resources and technology, and global scale of operations are some of the reasons that play a significant role in such competition.

Accelerated growth Indian multinationals rely on the international operations for their growth and revenue. Reliance on wider and diverse markets gives a wider base of operations, and thus total risks get redistributed across the market. Failure in one market is compensated for by success in another. For example, the recent recession affected business growth in the US market; hence, multinationals emphasized that the European and Asian markets should compensate for the lost opportunity in the US market.

Acquisition   Usually, acquisition is defined as acquiring managerial, strategic, and ownership rights of one small business organization by a big business organization. This has been violated with the acquisition of Corus by the smaller and less known Tata Steel. Acquisition and greenfield projects are the most successful ways of market entry, observed among Indian multinationals. Taj Hotels made a number of national and international acquisitions.

Liabilities of foreignness   Most of these Indian multinational companies operate in diverse social, economic, and political environments and inherit the burden and liabilities of foreignness (implies a number of disadvantages that Indian multinational companies inherit because of their foreign roots while accessing diverse stakeholders, that is, customers, employees, governments, etc.). Customers experience discomfort about the foreign brand compared to well-known native brands (high learning cost). These Indian multinationals are deprived of home turf advantages and some of the Asian brands especially have made inroads into the US and European markets. Literature recorded the experience of these brands in all those countries and highlighted the associated difficulties experienced by these brands in comparison to the local brand. Lack of local roots, a perceived lack of host country legitimacy, and origin from emerging economies create an inferior market sense among the sophisticated customers of Europe and the United States, and thus liabilities of foreignness becomes an additional issue to resolve while accessing foreign markets.

ROLE OF NATIONAL CULTURE

Most classic books on F&B style recommend a specific sequential style of serving food when the incoming guests are of different age groups. These books suggest that it is customary to serve food first to children, senior members, female guests, and subsequently to gentleman. Although most of the nations accept these traditions, in the Middle East, it is absolutely not acceptable. Employees, while operating in a local context, do not necessarily have significant bearings; however, while operating in foreign countries, cultural competency is a critical factor. National culture provides a way of life, which is accepted by the majority of the nationals. It is pervasive and touches every aspect of life. Denial of such a powerful influence while doing business does not appear to be a prudent strategy.

Culture is a kind of abstract and common belief, collectively subscribed to by the majority of people in a country. It is a kind of cognitive structure (belief and values) or 'collective programming of mind' that gives substance and meaning to people residing within the specific boundary of a country. This works as unstated practices, often reflected in festivals, life style, eating habits, and a whole set of practices representing a way of life. Several authors have attempted to appreciate the cultural differences and developed rules to understand them. Among these are Hofstede's theory of cultural dimension, where he defined national culture as a set of collective beliefs and values that are durable and represent a way of life for a nation. As this set of beliefs is country specific, it can only be understood by comparing against each other. He undertook comprehensive research to develop rules to understand individual working across nations (Fig. 14.1).

Uncertainty avoidance   It is said that the true character of an individual is known while facing adverse/uncertain/ambiguous situations. This, in fact, forms the true basis for differentiating nationals. People across countries can be differentiated on the basis of uncertainty avoidance. It signifies that while nationals in some countries can tolerate a higher degree of uncertainty than others, those from certain countries require formal rules and regulations to bring about predictability in the way of life; some others prefer flexibility and relative ambiguity. This influences the risk-taking behaviour of a country. Therefore, nationals from a low uncertainty tolerant country reduce the risk perception by development of formal rules and regulations, whereas nationals from a high uncertainty avoidance country will rely on informal communication and like to work having less rules and regulations (Table 14.1).

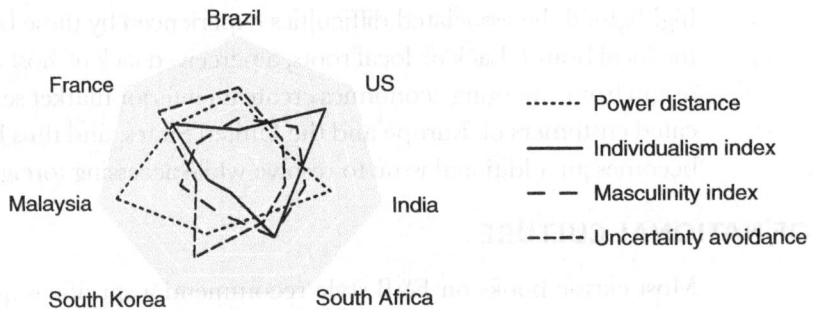

Figure 14.1 Cross-cultural comparison

Table 14.1 Contrasting high and low uncertainty avoidance

Low uncertainty avoidance	High uncertainty avoidance
Easy going, relatively low stress	Higher degree of stress, anxiety
Aggression and emotions not expected to be shown	Display of aggression and related emotion permitted
Competitive approach to life considered to be fair	Competition and conflict reduce predictability, so undesirable
Need for few rules and regulations	Need for rules and regulations
Willingness to take risks	Predominantly risk aversive behaviour seen

EXAMPLE

Jamesford, a German, took over a five-star property in India. He was quite appalled by the condition of the hotel. Although the hotel enjoyed a major chunk of the market share and had a huge loyal customer base, it lacked formal standardization of process. Each department had its unwritten code of conduct governing the business and customer satisfaction was relatively high. Jamesford wanted to develop rules and regulations. The F&B and HR managers raised objections against this initiative. They particularly did not like to chain employees with rules. However, Jamesford was adamant. He believed that standardization of processes would improve the efficiency and performance of the hotel. The HR manager, not wanting to shock the employees, counselled Jamesford to go slow with his ambition. This difference in their respective management styles could be attributed to their national origin. Jamesford comes from a country having a low uncertainty tolerance, whereas Indian managers are quite comfortable within an informal cultural web.

Power distance   The power distance perception is a distinguishing factor across nations. In some cultures, it is a socially accepted fact that power is located in the hands of a few significant others. In some others, power is more democratically distributed or aspires to be perceived in that way. Power distance perception has a significant bearing on the way an individual deals with workplace relationship. Therefore, managers working in high power distance cultures can fluently give instructions to employees located at a lower hierarchy. Taking instructions from a higher authority is considered to be natural (Table 14.2).

Table 14.2   Hofstede's cultural dimensions for international business

Power distance							
Country		**Country**		**Country**		**Country**	
Malaysia	104	Singapore	74	Portugal	63	Jamaica	45
Guatemala	95	Brazil	69	Uruguay	61	United States	40
Panama	95	France	68	Greece	60	Canada	39
Philippines	94	Hong Kong	68	South Korea	60	The Netherlands	38
Mexico	81	Columbia	67	Iran	58	Australia	36
Venezuela	81	El Salvador	66	Taiwan	58	Costa Rica	35
Arab countries	80	Turkey	66	Spain	57	Germany	35
Ecuador	78	Belgium	65	Pakistan	55	Great Britain	35
Indonesia	78	East Africa	64	Japan	54	Switzerland	34
India	77	Peru	64	Italy	50	Finland	33
West Africa	77	Thailand	64	Argentina	49	Norway	31
Yugoslavia	76	Chile	63	South Africa	49	Sweden	31

Contd

Table 14.2 *Contd*

Individualism							
Country		**Country**		**Country**		**Country**	
United States	91	Norway	69	Jamaica	39	Hong Kong	25
Australia	90	Switzerland	68	Brazil	38	Chile	23
Great Britain	89	Germany	67	Arab countries	38	West Africa	20
Canada	80	South Africa	65	Turkey	37	Singapore	20
The Netherlands	80	Finland	63	Uruguay	36	Thailand	20
New Zealand	79	Austria	55	Greece	35	El Salvador	19
Italy	76	Israel	54	Philippines	32	South Korea	18
Belgium	75	Spain	51	Mexico	30	Taiwan	17
Denmark	74	India	48	East Africa	27	Peru	16
Sweden	71	Japan	46	Yugoslavia	27	Costa Rica	15
France	71	Argentina	46	Portugal	27	Pakistan	14
Ireland	70	Iran	41	Malaysia	26	Indonesia	14

Thus, in a high power distance culture, communication becomes rather more restricted, and business is done with strict central control. This may prevent innovation and increase monotony and average solutions to the problems faced by the organization. In a high power culture, expatriate managers need to pay serious attention to this power dynamics and should refrain from the practice of extreme democracy and participative management principles. On the other hand, in a low power distance culture, it is expected to have lateral communication, to give less importance to authority and rules, and encourage free interaction among employees to bring about efficiency, encourage innovation, and bring forth the best solutions making the most use of available resources. All participants in the free flow of information get an opportunity to demonstrate collective solutions to the problems faced by the organization (Table 14.3). Therefore, it can be possible that

Table 14.3 Contrasting collectivism and individualism

Collectivism	Individualism
Harmony is the objective, to be maintained in group dealings	Personality dominates
Opinion does not have automatic rights to free flow	Private opinions are respected
Obligations to collective structures such as family, society, and groups	Individual-centric approach, obsessed with self
Indirect communication works	Direct communication works

Table 14.4 Contrasting low and high power distance

Low power distance	High power distance
Inequality is undesirable, hence minimized	Inequality ensures order and space for everybody
Higher authorities in organization is expected to be accessible	Higher authorities should not be accessible
Organizational democracy where equal rights for everybody is expected	Powerful roles are expected to have privileges

an organization operating in a relatively high power distance context operates at a less optimum level (Table 14.4).

Masculinity versus femininity   Masculine culture is characterized by a higher attribution of values to an achievement-oriented society, where accomplishment and recognition of social accomplishment are respected. Materialistic achievement, financial reward, and prestige are predominant in this culture. People are not risk aversive in this kind of society, but rather demonstrate entrepreneurship and undertake risks. Society renders respect to the achiever. Working in a masculine culture requires individuals to be assertive, encourages them to be dominant as a way of executing work, and appreciates success (Table 14.5).

Feminine culture is characterized by higher attribution of values to quality of life rather than achievement in society. It discourages the pursuits of overambitious

Table 14.5 Ranking of countries by masculine culture

Masculinity Index							
Country		Country		Country		Country	
Japan	95	South Africa	63	Malaysia	50	Spain	42
Austria	79	Ecuador	63	Pakistan	50	Peru	42
Venezuela	73	United States	62	Brazil	49	East Africa	41
Italy	70	Australia	61	Singapore	48	El Salvador	40
Switzerland	70	New Zealand	58	Israel	47	South Korea	39
Mexico	69	Greece	57	Indonesia	46	Uruguay	38
Ireland	68	Hong Kong	57	West Africa	46	Guatemala	37
Jamaica	68	Argentina	56	Turkey	45	Thailand	34
Great Britain	66	India	56	Taiwan	45	Portugal	31
Germany	66	Belgium	54	Panama	44	Chile	28
Philippines	64	Arab countries	53	Iran	43	Finland	26
Columbia	64	Canada	52	France	43	Yugoslavia	21

Contd

Table 14.5 *Contd*

Uncertainty avoidance							
Country		**Country**		**Country**		**Country**	
Greece	112	Costa Rica	86	Austria	70	Australia	51
Portugal	104	Panama	86	Taiwan	69	Norway	50
Guatemala	101	Argentina	86	Arab. countries	68	South Africa	49
Uruguay	100	Turkey	85	Ecuador	67	New Zealand	49
Belgium	94	South Korea	85	Germany	65	Indonesia	48
El Salvador	94	Mexico	82	Thailand	64	Canada	48
Japan	92	Israel	81	Iran	59	United States	46
Yugoslavia	88	Columbia	80	Finland	59	Philippines	44
Peru	87	Venezuela	76	Switzerland	58	India	40
France	86	Brazil	76	West Africa	54	Malaysia	36
Chile	86	Italy	75	The Netherlands	53	Great Britain	35
Spain	86	Pakistan	70	East Africa	52	Ireland	35

projects. In this culture, life is governed by non-monetized drivers such as quality of life, human generosity, and concern for others. A feminine society is less competitive than masculine culture as it gives due consideration to others. Working in a feminine culture encourages individuals to be more concerned about the long-term effect of their actions; therefore, environmental sustainability, durability of the solution, and generosity to the less privileged are paid due attention.

It is important to note that individuals are expected to display their national culture. This generalization is required to be taken with much care. However, an exception to the above generalization of culture is possible and evidently visible. Individuals may not adhere to the cultural orientation described above as they are exposed to diverse education and open to diverse cultural contexts (by travel, virtual interaction, MTV). Hence, two individuals from one cultural domain may possibly behave differently. It is suggested that the highest degree of discretion is required to be used while using the above cultural frameworks.

RECRUITMENT PRACTICE IN THE GLOBAL MARKET

The recruitment practice for global companies, stretching across nations, is diverse in nature. In general, three types of recruitment practices have been noticed: ethnocentric, polycentric, and geocentric (Fig. 14.2). Each of these strategies has its pros and cons. Let us examine each one separately.

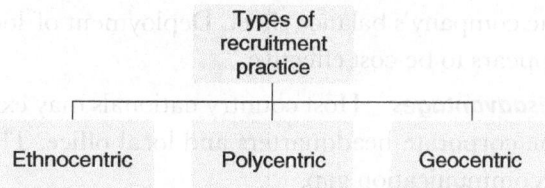

Figure 14.2 Types of recruitment practices

Ethnocentric approach   It signifies that all important and senior management positions are filled by parent company nationals. Ethnocentric strategies are followed when there is relatively less trust on the competency of the domestically available employees. Under this policy, all key decisions are taken by the corporate headquarters. In this kind of system, a higher degree of control is made possible as a result of the structural arrangements.

Advantages   This strategy should be followed when employees available in the host country appear to be less qualified in fulfilling their corporate aspirations. This strategy is usually considered to be an interim measure and is believed to hand over responsibilities of the company gradually to the local employees. However, this process is extremely slow in some companies. This is usually done to maintain corporate standards and culture across companies. Demonstrative behaviour of the senior managers helps enforce cultural and operational fluency in the system and works as a role model.

Disadvantages   Each country is unique and complex in its dynamic expression. Competent managers are those who are deeply connected with the local market and possess important market intelligence. The ethnocentric approach provides a lower level of importance to the knowledge of the local market. Therefore, newly appointed managers of foreign origin need to pay special attention to acquire the local cultural competency to survive in a host country. Failure to appreciate the cultural differences assures ultimate failure. Recruitment of foreign nationals in senior positions creates a sense of frustration among the host country nationals. This potentially leads to lower productivity and high employee turnover.

Polycentric approach   Under this kind of approach, host country nationals manage subsidiaries and report to the corporate office. All senior positions are occupied by the local seasoned managers.

Advantages   Under this system, local professionals are at the helm and they can take prompt managerial decisions; the system does not have the problem of cultural myopia as in the case of expatriate managers and hence no dedicated time is required to acclimatize. This also provides considerable cost saving, especially as top foreign expatriate managers demand salaries in foreign currency and as per the lifestyle of the countries of origin. This presents a considerable cost burden on the company's balance sheet. Deployment of local managers in the operation thus appears to be cost effective.

Disadvantages   Host country nationals may experience cultural distance between the corporate headquarters and local office. The cultural differentials may create a communication gap.

Geocentric approach   The geocentric approach goes beyond the narrow cultural and linguistic competency and seeks to recruit the most competent people for the job available in the company. Thus, the prime criterion for recruitment is competency of the individual, irrespective of nationality.

Advantages   This provides the best chance to the company to grow with the help of the best possible constellation of human workforce. As organization dynamics are based on competency, the unifying force among employees is not limited to the narrow range of nationality. This inspires employees to acquire new skills for remaining relevant in the ever depreciating world. This culture openly supports global competency and organizational excellence.

Disadvantages   Immigration rules and regulations restrict recruitment of foreign nationals in some sectors. There might be a cap on the compensation to be paid to the foreign nationals, which creates problems in finding and recruiting individuals who will fit the legal as well as competence frameworks. The cost associated with the recruitment and training is very high. In some cases, even if the person is recruited because of competency, it does not guarantee the success in the current company. Very high differentiation between locally recruited employees and international recruitment can be the cause of high dissatisfaction.

GLOBAL MANPOWER PLANNING

Hospitality organizations in India realized that they need to reinvent themselves to be meaningful in the globalized world. A lot of foreign hotel chains have started business. Therefore, a few of the Indian organizations are looking to the European and Southeast Asian markets for future growth. To support this extraordinary development, HR professionals need to have a robust global manpower planning process that will ensure deployment of the right kind of people at the right time in the right numbers. Indian hospitality companies have relied on domestic employees for too long for its daily operations. These companies had always refrained from going to the international market, as they were happy with their organic growth. However, each passing day heralds a new change in the Indian corporate houses. Gradually, they are gaining confidence to grow their business inorganically, especially in international markets by acquisitions and mergers. Indian Hotels (Taj Group) is acquiring foreign hotels in Australia, the United States, and the Middle East regions. Most of the hospitality companies make enough investment to develop leader-managers, capable of working in foreign lands. Therefore, there are important questions to address:

- How to manage international hotel properties?
- Do they need to transfer managers to all these newly acquired properties?
- Should somebody from the local market be selected, who is familiar with the local laws?

Parent country nationals (PCNs)   PCNs are nationals whose citizenship and residency match the nationality of the parent company. Deployment of PCNs in a newly acquired hospitality business appears to be advantageous for the following reasons:

- PCNs will be more comfortable to deal with the headquarters because of proximity and familiarity with the national and organizational culture. Linguistic similarity and cultural proximity facilitate and bring about ease of communication.
- PCNs will have a higher level of network at the corporate headquarters. High-density network is an important social capital that provides a wider level of choice to bring out the best level of solution.

However, deployment of PCNs in foreign countries presents the unique problem of social adjustment. Although PCNs finds it easier to deal with the corporate headquarters, they find it difficult to adjust in the working environment of the host countries. High adaptability, fast learning, and a high awakening state of being are helpful qualities that PCNs should have for success in a host country.

Host country nationals (HCNs)   HCNs are the citizens or residents of the host country. They are well informed about the local culture and the legal and economic framework, and are fluent in doing business in the host country environment. Individuals having exposure in international environments are majorly given preference while selecting HCNs. Lack of familiarity in the corporate headquarters may limit the HCNs for utilization of best resources available within the company. Language and cultural distance between HCNs and international headquarters pose a critical problem. So as to avoid this kind of problem, most HCNs get adequate exposure at the corporate headquarters to acquire knowledge pertaining to organizational culture, rituals, and protocols.

Third country nationals (TCNs)   TCNs are those nationals who are legally related with the host country or corporate headquarters. On the basis of the competency and experience of TCNs, they are recruited in the host country. The policy required to be followed pertaining to the deployment of manpower depends on the views of the majority shareholders/owners. Pressure to generate shareholders' value every quarter has increased the chances of recruiting competent employees in responsible positions, as competency is the best guarantee for excellent performance. Another important dimension of recruitment of personnel is the maintenance of power and political balance in the organization. Cruise ships usually accommodate employees from diverse cultures and nations. Overdominance of any one culture and nation may create potential political problems, and maintaining peaceful industrial relations becomes difficult especially at the time of a labour crisis.

TRAINING AND DEVELOPMENT IN INTERNATIONAL HR MANAGEMENT

Working in a global platform requires a number of critical competencies that facilitate organizational performance. Some of these competencies are business, role, and organization specific. Another aspect of these competencies is that all these competencies are not readily available in the labour market. Therefore, it is important to nurture and develop all these competencies in the long run. However, a number of Indian hospitality organizations failed to address this concern. They never had enough workforce strength that could be readily deployed in international business operations, resulting in a stunted corporate growth. They took shelter under the Licence Raj policies of the Indian government, which made them domestic players.

With expansion into the international market, Indian hospitality organizations were forced to pay attention to talent acquisition and development. Because of the lack of in-house talent capable of handling international organizations, a number of Indian hospitality organizations have recruited individuals of foreign origin, having international market and operational knowledge. They have been given responsibility for global strategic market actions.

To be successful in the international work environment, employees need to have certain competencies. Some of these competencies are discussed here.

Historical or past connections It is advantageous to have past connections and experience with the host country. It provides a unique competency to the individual who has connections or some kind of connection with the host country. Many of the top executives have a multicultural upbringing. Constant exposure in diverse cultural contexts provides solid competency to tolerate a high degree of dissonance and engage in the international organizational workspace.

Language skills It is an important competency that is given due weightage at the time of selecting an individual for an international assignment. Language proficiency brings clarity in communication and builds a relationship with the host countries. Relying on an interpreter to do business is problematic, and the meaning often gets diluted during translation. Therefore, doing business in the language and style of the host country brings about fluency in dealings.

Managing uncertainty Operating in an international environment inherits a number of risks, such as political, economic, and social. Each one of them alone or in interaction with others potentially creates a huge amount of uncertainty. To deal with this, an individual not only needs to know how to deal with the situation in the host country but also requires a control on the nerves. For example, you are working as a general manager of a five-star hotel in China for the past one year. You receive a notice from the local authorities that your hotel is violating certain environmental laws applicable in the hotel industry. They have threatened to close down your hotel within the next 15 days. It is important to know how this kind of problem is solved in China. It could be a sincere effort from the Chinese authorities to enforce the environmental laws or it could be an invitation to negotiate for an exchange of bribe. Thus, managing in an international workspace requires skill sets to manage uncertainty.

Cross-cultural awareness Cross-cultural awareness is crucial for survival in an international environment. For example, employees of different nationalities assume their way of life is normal in certain ways. However, when they interact with each other, it is important that they should be careful that their way of life is not misinterpreted by the host country employees.

Cross-cultural adjustment Cross-cultural adjustment is one of the important competencies. Once individuals are exposed to the nuances of a national culture, it poses considerable pressure on the expatriates to unlearn some of the assumptions and ways of lifestyle and adopt the new one. This is a painful process and requires psychological, social, and economic adjustments. Americans are accustomed to traffic discipline, whereas in some of the Asian countries such discipline is somewhat compromised and, therefore, delay to report in office is seen as quite inevitable. Using the US yardstick to understand local employees may be seen to be rude, and local employees may respond to that through uncooperative and unhelpful behaviour when expatriates count on them to get the job done. Therefore, expatriates need to be flexible and adaptable to the tune of the new culture.

Global business acumen Working in a global business arena requires multi-country global business knowledge. Previous exposure and performance in an international market and an international educational degree often provide convincing credentials for global business acumen.

Emotional intelligence Emotional intelligence is the kind of ability that allows an individual to respond to others emotionally. This competency includes the ability to be aware of, read, and manage self and others' emotions effectively. Working in an international business poses problems of alien culture and customs. Using the native emotional framework to interpret the emotions of local people could be quite troublesome. A successful expatriate needs to borrow a new cultural lens to understand the web of emotions prevailing inside the organization and to invest substantial energy to deal with local employees effectively.

Managing a cross-cultural workforce Sensitivity and self-adjustment to the foreign culture is a unique competency; however, working and managing diverse workforces with mixed nationalities is relatively difficult. Therefore, previous knowledge and work exposure in a multicultural work environment is crucial. For example, managing the multicultural workspace in cruise ships is indeed a difficult task. Most cruise ships provide a multicultural workforce to work together to offer the visitors a memorable experience.

Flexible work approach   The native yardstick learned, acquired, and sharpened in a domestic work environment cannot be used to deal with other employees in the international workspace. An expatriate needs to display a higher degree of flexibility in approach while dealing with other nationals working as colleagues, subordinates, and bosses. The stubborn usage of own culture to deal with foreign nationals without adopting any flexibility in outlook is a sure sign formula for failure. Many foreign nationals, after coming to India, learn to accept nuances and effectively use jargon and rituals to deal with employees.

Legal knowledge   Legal knowledge in the foreign country requires some amount of understanding, especially all those rules and regulations that have a significant bearing on the way of life. In some countries, carrying and transporting alcohol while travelling is restricted. HR professionals usually develop a country brief and ritual sessions before departing for international assignments.

Change management competency   Orchestrating change in a familiar organizational and national culture in itself is a difficult challenge. To achieve successful organizational change in an international business is extremely difficult because of cultural, social, economic, and legal consequences. Change, of any kind, is essential to survive in today's hypercompetitive world. Everything is changing from customer taste, technological platform, and mode of delivery to workforce compositions (new generation taking over the position of the old), competitor's strategy, and so on. In order to survive in the hypercompetitive business environment, individuals need to be competent in change management.

Self-management   Self-management is crucial for any individual. Individuals confront the outside world to meaningfully derive solutions to survive and prosper. It is an interesting dimension to review if an individual is successful in resolving life-related issues. The way each individual negotiates with life issues is an art and a reflection of the self. For example, the recently divorced may indicate problems in family relationship. Whether this problem spills over in the working of individuals, especially in an international business environment, is a matter of speculation. Self-management is a critical indicator for success in life. Individuals confronting too many life issues are most likely to get distracted and may fail to allocate a high degree of attention to work and work-related problems.

Ethical work competency   Representing well-known brands or domestic companies in the international market requires delicate dealings. Research indicates that internationally reputed brands are expected to have a formal organizational approach to deal with business ethics and hence will be less vulnerable to unethical behaviour in dealings with government, political parties, employees, and customers. In most of the cases, to build an internationally reputed brand, considerable investment has been made over the years. Therefore, it is important that ethical competency is an important issue while working for such internationally reputed brands. The unethical behaviour of any individual employee representing an internationally reputed brand can cause tremendous damage to the prestige of the company. Various stakeholders react differently to the unethical behaviour of the organization.

International negotiation skills   Depending on the hierarchy, expatriates on an international assignment require negotiation skills. If the expatriate is deployed for a higher executive position, it requires a high degree of negotiation skills for dealing with suppliers, customers, and employees. The expatriate should also have knowledge of cultural nuances, with particular reference to negotiation. For example, in a European and US business environment, time-bound discussion is usually encouraged to achieve a specific result; however, in some Middle East countries, especially Saudi Arabia, time-bound discussion is considered to be an insult and not being sincere to the deal. In Saudi Arabia, it is believed that it takes time for durable business results.

It is difficult to have a skilled employee ready for international business pursuits. Therefore, most business organizations, operating on a global scale or aspiring to operate on a global scale, require good investment to have abundant manpower support. HR professionals need to develop a well-planned pipeline structure to have suitable manpower supply to fuel business growth.

TYPES OF TRAINING FOR EXPATRIATES

Some skill sets can be acquired while working for organizations, some developed by cultural events, some acquired while attending training, and so on. Therefore, HR professionals make the structure that potentially develops these skills.

Making local workspace multicultural   Whenever the local law permits and the opportunity arises, HR professionals should attempt to induct a few employees from foreign nations where future business developmental activities will be undertaken during next few years/months. This will increase the competency among local employees to deal with employees from diverse cultural backgrounds. This cross-cultural learning will take place in the safe and secure setting of their familiar work environment, which will reduce the stress and increase the chances of learning.

Short-term educational programmes   Executives should be encouraged to attend educational programmes that empower their business skill in an international business area. A number of universities impart short-term educational programmes. These programmes emphasize the executives' performance in the international field; therefore, the syllabus provides more attention to cultural sensitivity and management, legal complexity, negotiation skills for global positions, and so on.

Short-term assignment   Before assigning employees for foreign postings, they should be encouraged to execute short-term business assignments. Short term signifies exposure to an international workspace from three to six months. This assignment works as a training ground for future executives and also provides first-hand feedback about employees who have a high likelihood to survive and achieve business results.

Training before departure Employees selected for international assignments need to be given suitable training. Such training should focus on language, legal framework, cultural nuances, and workplace history. In some cases, the spouse should be included in this training to the extent that it appears to be accretive and valuable for them. HR professionals are required to develop robust training syllabi and material that make relevant contributions to enhance the employees' confidence for success. Training content should be changed in tune with the times, requirement, and hierarchy of the expatriates. The employees should be briefed about the way most expatriates experience the new work environment. Individuals who have worked in those international environments could work as mentors to provide assistance if required. Many companies host in-house dialogues among employees using various e-platforms (Microsoft's Sharepoints facilitates this)—perhaps this e-platform conversation among experienced employees and novice expatriates could work as a support mentor for immediate and emergency assistance. Informed expatriates are better equipped to deal with the business situation. Several research reports indicate that in most hospitality organizations, minuscule or no training before departure poses considerable problems for expatriates.

Training during an international assignment The HR management system should provide constant support framework and training support to expatriates and their family members in the host country. This will increase the likelihood of success.

Training during repatriation This is one of the most critical and neglected issues observed in the Indian hospitality industry. Repatriation management is almost non-existent and not expatriate friendly. The Indian hospitality industry has witnessed the highest number of employee turnover after coming back to the native land. They were not given due status and asked to report to juniors who might have reached higher corporate positions during the years. These aspects often create adjustment problems in the organization.

Cultural events Hospitality organizations, especially hotels, organize food festivals to promote their restaurants. In these events, only a part of F&B and the Food Production Department become familiar with the events, food, cultural nuances, and so on. HR professionals could organize supplementary quiz, cultural video (cafeteria TV), and so on to raise the overall awareness about food and cultural nuances. This will increase the level of cultural awareness of a specific country or region among the lower level staff members. In case special chefs from other nations are invited during such festivals, they should be encouraged to make formal presentations about their culture. Local staff could highlight, report, and record the technical and behavioural learning from them.

Expatriate management   The selection criteria for a foreign assignment depend on a number of factors. In the hospitality industry, the highest priority is given to previous foreign experiences, technical competence, past performance, tolerance for ambiguity, life stage, cross-cultural expertise, adaptability, family support and composition, and so on. It is often seen that an international academic qualification is a qualifying criterion for selection for an international assignment. Individuals with previous international experience provide a higher degree of assurance for survival in the foreign land. Many of the employees consider an international posting as an achievement, at least in the Indian hospitality industry. Therefore, past performance is often used as a criterion for selecting individuals for an international posting. Working in an international work space is typical, often constrained by cultural nuances. Individuals who performed well in the domestic environment are most likely to achieve success than individuals who failed to do so. Past success is remunerated by providing international and prestigious postings. Cross-cultural competence is crucial for achieving an international posting. The huge literature on cross-cultural competence supports the claim that each country has a tendency to behave in a specific manner. It is important to have a high degree of competence to get adjusted in the foreign culture. Family support is extremely crucial. Individuals having resistance from family will have difficulties in adjusting in the foreign culture. In some Indian families, family members use a high degree of resistance to foreign postings. Similarly, there are some segments of employees who prefer an international assignment in the early stage of their career; for example, skilled and semi-skilled personnel prefer an international posting in the Middle East for money; however, after marriage, the same individual attempts to avoid an international assignment.

FIVE-STAGE PROCESS OF INTERNATIONAL ADJUSTMENT

Each international assignment poses a critical challenge to the employee, which should be negotiated, adapted, and adopted to lessen the discomfort. This adjustment could be physical, social, and emotional. Physical adjustment signifies adhering to a new set of rules and regulations, quite different from that in the country of origin. This could be in terms of driving on a different side of the road and a different set of rules. New sets of social rules in the host country may affect family life. This new set of rules may create a disruption in the routine and the way of life. This creates considerable stress.

Literature reviews suggest that individuals posted on international assignments undergo five distinct processes:

1. Initial euphoria and excitement
2. Culture shock
3. Adjustment and acceptance

4. Gradual performance improvement
5. International mastery

Initial euphoria   After getting an international assignment, an individual experiences an initial euphoria for the new role. In the organization, especially in the Indian context, an international assignment is prestigious and works as a sign of achievement. Employees consider it as a sign of acknowledgement for all the work done for the organization. This also opens up a vista of opportunity for further career growth. All these factors generate excitement and euphoria.

Culture shock   After experiencing initial euphoria, the individual starts experiencing a new set of rules, regulations, and routines that potentially brings disruption in the way of life. Continuous interaction with unfamiliar rules and behavioural cues increases the degree of stress as it demands a huge adjustment. This increases irritability and frustration. To adjust to the work and social environment, the individual needs to invest huge psychological energy. Failing to allocate substantial energy in reducing dissonance from multiple interactions, the individual may withdraw from social and workplace interactions. This in turn creates alienation in the workplace. Family adjustment (spouse getting familiar with the local markets and new levels of interaction, children's issues pertaining to adjustment in the school, society, playground, etc.) also poses additional stress and collectively causes a number of physical symptoms such as fatigue, lack of interest, and depression. This stage is extremely crucial for future survival of the individual employee. In some cases, the individual employee fails to adjust in the new environment and leaves for the home country within a few months, leaving the assignment incomplete. Research indicates that expatriates need to adjust to the new rules and regulations and fix reasonable and practical objectives. Initial euphoria usually colours the expectation from the assignment. The induction process for the new assignment could reduce the dissonance. Local HR professionals could extend support to acclimatize to the new environment. It is important that during the induction process the expatriate gets feedback about the current social norms, support for children's education (such as admission to good schools, transportation, connecting with social frameworks), and so on. This works as a great help.

Adjustment and acceptance   In case the expatriate invests energy to adjust to the new social and work milieu and accepts it as an additional challenge, he or she arrests the downfall in performance. However, a number of adjustments are required to be undertaken by the expatriate. Learning the new language, jargon, social rules, the pattern of employee behaviour, and so on, are the additional workload that the expatriate needs to accomplish for initial survival. A lot of organizational and social practices could be undesirable or different from the recent past practices that the expatriate has been comfortable with. The expatriate needs to accept it even if he or she holds other opinions on it. This adjustment could be social. Social norms, in some societies, allow children to behave in a manner that may not be acceptable to the expatriate. The initial euphoria painted a rosy picture about the accomplishment. The expatriate needs to adjust and accept the new reality and attempt to adjust in tune with the demand. This is a critical phase. Continuous efforts are required to be successful during this phase. Each day, a small level of adjustment should be celebrated and used as progress towards success for the successful completion of the international assignment. A comprehensive support system for the expatriate manager is required. Thus, the nature of support may be different as the expatriate attempts to adjust with the new environment. Initial support including arrangement of accommodation for the expatriate family, familiarization with the local market, school, social rules and regulations, and so on help the family to settle in the new social environment; however, the expatriate requires ongoing support to be successful in the new organizational workspace.

Performance improvement With successful assimilation into the local culture, the expatriate has fewer issues to get adjusted to in the new environment. This allows him or her to allocate attention to productive purposes, which in turn improves performance. With deeper knowledge of social behaviour cues and workplace nuances, the expatriate becomes confident and increases self-efficacy. Accidental interaction with new social norms does not generate shock because with the passing of time, the expatriate develops successful ways to deal with stress. This directly contributes to improve his or her performance.

International mastery Over time, the expatriate becomes successful in dealing with the cultural and workplace nuances and enhances effectiveness. He or she learns to accept the new way of being in the international workplace, acquires competence to work in the international workplace, and becomes fluent in dealing with the workplace challenges (Fig. 14.3).

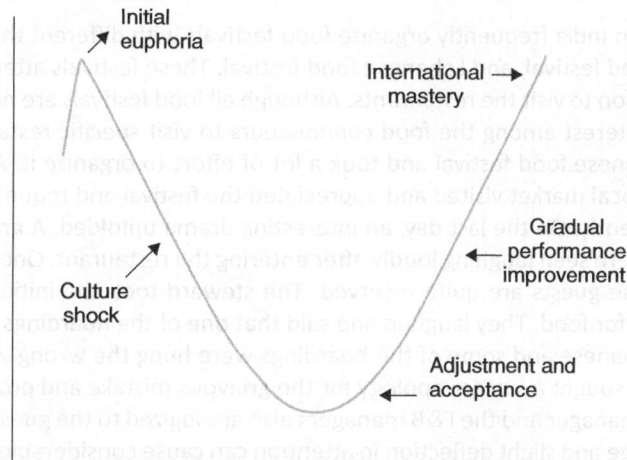

Figure 14.3 Expatriate adjustment life cycle

There are a number of processes that HR professionals could devise to help expatriates get adjusted in the international workspace. Some of these are realistic relocation preview, mentoring and coaching, short-duration exposure in the international workspace before allocating an international assignment, and so on. Realistic relocation preview signifies that the expatriate should get a realistic preview about the nature of the assignment and the associated challenges. This preview of the challenge will moderate the degree of initial euphoria and help set realistic objectives. A number of training programmes could be organized to provide cultural tutorials that will enlighten the expatriate about the cultural nuances in the new international assignment.

COMPONENT OF PERFORMANCE IN THE GLOBAL CONTEXT

Communication is considered to be one of the significant competencies in international business.

In another incident, a restaurant organized a Mexican food festival because the song Macarena was popular in those days. Everybody liked it. The general manager took the opportunity and invited two Mexican chefs with the help of the Mexican Embassy. It was one of the most successful food festivals in the history of the hotel. These two chefs used to have a lot of fun with the employees working in the restaurant and also used to dance with the guests. Local guests used to participate in the process with a high degree of amusement. It was obvious that the cash counter also danced to the tune of Macarena. Although linguistically these chefs failed to communicate, they compensated for it with music and dance and obviously with the delicious Mexican food.

EXAMPLE

Five-star hotels in India frequently organize food festivals with different themes, such as Mexican food festival, Chinese food festival, and Lebanese food festival. These festivals attempt to give the existing and new customers a reason to visit the restaurants. Although all food festivals are not successful in terms of earning, they generate interest among the food connoisseurs to visit specific restaurants. A five-star hotel in India organized a Japanese food festival and took a lot of effort to organize it. A good number of food connoisseurs from the local market visited and appreciated the festival and requested that such festivals be organized more frequently. On the last day, an interesting drama unfolded. A group of Japanese guests came in; however, they were seen laughing loudly after entering the restaurant. One of the stewards found it unusual because Japanese guests are quite reserved. The steward took the initiative and inquired about it while taking the order for food. They laughed and said that one of the hoardings written in Japanese was in fact a dirty word in Japanese and some of the hoardings were hung the wrong way, that is, upside down. Laughing, the steward sought a sincere apology for the grievous mistake and promised to take immediate action. The restaurant manager and the F&B managers also apologized to the guests when they finished their meal. Lack of knowledge and slight deflection in attention can cause considerable damage to the reputation of the hotel, which perhaps takes a long time to build.

Communicative language consists of verbal and non-verbal cues. A verbal cue is in the language; however, when a specific language is spoken, it carries a number of non-verbal cues, such as body language, combination of words, tone and diction of the language, and the status of the individual. Therefore, it is crucial to have good communication skills.

Frequency of performance appraisal   Usually twice in a year, a performance appraisal is conducted. However, in tune with the rules and regulations of the financial markets the world over, it is becoming customary to report a company's performance quarter by quarter. The share price of the companies fluctuates heavily in tune with the quarterly business performance. Therefore, it is being increasingly felt that employees' performance also requires to be appraised on a quarterly basis. It is important to remember that such measurement and appraisal are not free from deficiencies. Linking employees' performance (especially top leadership performance) with the quarterly performance will trigger adventurous strategic actions, which can potentially increase the chance of gaining market acceptance and inflates share prices—this might not be good for long-term organizational performance. The top leadership could easily engage in a short-sighted approach, which increases the chance of their performance-linked bonus; however, this may not be suitable for long-term business health. Therefore, performance appraisals should give adequate attention to the long-term as well as short-term targets. Some of the performance weightage should be accretive to shareholder's value over the period of three to four years. Performance captured over the years will provide the real worth of the employees' performance. This will truly reflect the performance of the employees, especially the top management level.

COMPENSATION MANAGEMENT IN THE GLOBAL CONTEXT

Compensation in managing employees on a global scale is a very complex issue. It requires an integrated approach where compensation across nations needs to follow distinct approaches. Some of these distinct approaches are linking performance with pay. With the increased accountability for performance and reporting to its shareholders, quarter by quarter with advanced guidelines for business action, pay for performance is considered the preferred choice. Pay for performance philosophy is reflected in the compensation policy in different forms: performance bonus, employee stock options scheme, profit sharing, and so on. Some companies use a balanced score card as a base for allocating performance bonus. Depending on the culture of the organization, HR professionals develop different variations and bases for implementation of the performance for pay philosophy. Some companies use the average stock price as a guiding star for determining the performance-related pay of the executives. For example, Table 14.6 highlights the compensation package for top global chief executives, published by Forbes Magazine.

Table 14.6 Remuneration package for top global chief executive officers

Rank	Name	Company	Pay (in million dollars)	Five-year pay ($million)	Shares owned (in million dollars)	Age	Efficiency
1	H. Lawrence Culp Jr	Danaher	141.36	188.52	49.3	47	90
2	Lawrence J. Ellison	Oracle	130.23	1028.31	29,896.20	65	82
3	Aubrey K. McClendon	Chesapeake Energy	114.30	293.35	25.7	49	163
4	Ray R Irani	Occidental Petroleum	103.07	782.48	622.3	75	89
5	David C. Novak	Yum Brands	76.49	207.63	9.2	57	78
6	John C. Martin	Gilead Sciences	60.40	184.37	73.1	58	38
7	Sol J. Barer	Celgene	59.32	108.943	39.4	63	NA
8	Keith A. Hutton	XTO Energy	54.78	NA	153.1	51	NA
9	Richard C. Adkerson	Freeport Copper	48.76	177.48	47.6	63	NA
10	Jen-Hsun Huang	Nvidia	31.40	137.25	356.5	47	31
11	Ivan G. Seidenberg	Verizon Communications	30.93	101.53	57.1	63	184
12	Louis C. Camilleri	Philip Morris International	30.08	NA	91.8	55	NA
13	Ralph Lauren	Polo Ralph Lauren	30.05	126.61	3690.30	70	82
14	Howard D. Schultz	Starbucks	29.21	129.773	482.3	56	NA
15	Robert W. Selander	MasterCard	28.97	97.45	10.3	58	NA
16	Laurence D. Fink	BlackRock	28.21	105.62	278.2	57	20
17	J. Wayne Leonard	Entergy	27.32	89.43	21.1	59	98
18	Leslie Moonves	CBS	26.48	123.56	17	61	NA
19	Hugh Grant	Monsanto	26.08	157.17	29.5	52	40
20	Gregg L. Engles	Dean Foods	25.52	116.38	40.7	52	181
21	Samuel J. Palmisano	IBM	25.20	118.78	76.8	58	166
22	John H. Hammergren	McKesson	25.18	149.59	32.7	51	79
23	David B. Snow Jr	Medco Health	25.05	67.49	19.3	55	14
24	William H. Swanson	Raytheon	24.88	97.77	52.7	61	141
25	James C. Mullen	Biogen Idec	24.78	61.84	11.6	51	NA

Source: http://www.forbes.com/lists/2010/12/boss-10_CEO-Compensation_Rank.html.

Compensation payment frameworks   International compensation signifies provisions for monetary and non-monetary rewards, as valued by employees for an international work engagement. Compensation is devised in such a way as to attract and retain good quality employees for successful international operations.

Headquarters-based compensation framework   Under this system, expatriates are paid as per the salary structure of the headquarters' compensation structure. One unified structure is followed for compensation irrespective of the country the expatriate is exposed to. This is beneficial if the prevailing headquarters' compensation policy is relatively higher than the life style expense of the host country. This kind of policy is relatively costly and difficult to implement. The compensation will not have linkage with the host country operation. When most of the business entities are graduating to be a performance-driven organization, this kind of compensation cannot be sustained as it disowns performance-linked compensation. Individuals will be interested to work only in those nations where the relative cost of life style expenses is less and will not go for a high-cost country.

Revised home country compensation framework   Under this system, home-country-based compensation is given with revised factors after considering the host country life style cost factors. It is called *balance sheet approach,* where any loss of compensation arising out of an international posting is compensated for by introducing incentives that address and compensate any such loss.

CLOSING THOUGHTS

In this book, we have examined a whole range of issues starting from manpower planning to deployment and management of personnel in the international context. Although a generalized discourse has been presented in the book, a number of delicate issues could not be explored owing to the limited mandate of a textbook. The book outlined general processes that are required to be adhered to while managing workforce in the hospitality organizational context. It is needless to mention that each hospitality organization has its own glorious history and unique culture. HR practices are intimately related with the history of the organization and the unique culture it inherits. Hence, each organization attributes greater importance to some of the selective values and the whole human organizational practices revolves around it. Hence, a receptive mind will be able to see this inner web of culture and how human resource functions enable employees to perform.

SUMMARY

Global competition is changing its colour at a lightning speed. Most of the industries, including the hospitality industry, are undergoing unprecedented changes. The Indian hospitality industry enjoyed protection from international competition during the past 100 years. However, India is opening up its market and internationally reputed brands are making inroads into the domestic market. To survive in this hypercompetitive market, some of the reputed hotel brands are making attempts to spread their business in the international market. Thus, HR professionals require a well-coordinated approach to develop trained manpower suitable for taking up international assignments. This chapter provides a very brief review of the various practices required to manage and nurture a workforce suitable for the international market.

KEY TERMS

Expatriate   An expatriate is an employee working in a country other than the country of birth.

Hofstede model   Geert Hofstede developed a framework to explain how national cultures are relatively different from each other.

Host country nationals (HCNs)   Host country nationals are the citizens or residents of the host country. They are well informed about the local culture and the legal and economic framework of the host country and fluent in doing business in a host country environment.

Third country nationals (TCNs)   Third country nationals are those nationals who are legally related with the host country or corporate headquarters.

Parent country nationals (PCNs)   Parent country nationals are those nationals whose citizenship and residency match the nationality of the parent company.

Cultural ambiguity   It is the ambiguity experienced by the individual while exposed to an unfamiliar national culture.

Uncertainty tolerance   It explores the degree of tolerance with reference to uncertainty.

EXERCISES

Concept Review Questions

1. Critically examine the various competencies required for international postings.
2. Recommend suitable strategies to develop skilled manpower for international posting, especially for the Indian hospitality sector.
3. How useful is the 360-degree feedback system to an expatriate? Present critical review in support of your arguments.
4. Critically review the cultural adjustment process predominantly experienced by expatriates during their international assignment.
5. It is said that a balanced scorecard should be used to appraise the performance of expatriates. To what extent do you agree with the statement? Provide your rationale in favour of your arguments.

Critical Thinking Question

Are you professionally ready for an international posting? What additional training could have made you more professionally competent?

Assignments

1. Assume that you have been selected by your company for an international posting. The HR manager has given you an option to select the country of your choice:
   (a) South Korea
   (b) Russia
   (c) Brazil
   (d) Malaysia
   (e) South Africa
   Which country would you like to choose and why?
2. During your industrial exposure training, record the experience of expatriates who had international experience. Prepare a comprehensive report with your reflective note from their experience.

CASE STUDY

EXPAT REPATRIATION

Kuldeep works for a reputed hotel chain. After several efforts, he was selected for one of the Middle East hotel properties as an assistant sales manager. He considered it to be a great achievement and organized a big party before departure for the said foreign assignment. During this international posting, he used to send photographs to his friends/former colleagues through e-mail, which communicated his happiness. However, after two years, he requested the corporate office to allow him to move back to India. After considerable efforts, he was asked to come back; however, there was no word about his new posting in India. After coming back to India, he contacted the corporate office again. However, there was no direct or immediate answer. He was asked to wait. After several months, he was asked to report to the sales manager of their Bangalore branch of the hotel. He observed that no change had been made in his scale, grade, and position. He observed that he lost seniority, pay hike, and all other benefits that other colleagues had got as they were posted in India. He was very unhappy with this development. When asked about his compensation packet, a direct answer was not available from the corporate office. It appeared to him that his service during the international posting had been ignored, and he needed to start from scratch. He resigned from the job and joined the competition at a higher compensation. He activated all his old contacts again in the city. He diverted a number of good customers to the new company. He was considered to be the best sales manager of the year in the new company. Over time, he was promoted as national sales manager. The old company changed two general managers from their Bangalore hotels; however, it did not improve the business condition of the Bangalore hotel.

Discussion Questions

1. Identify the major problem in the case.
2. Recommend suitable solutions for the Bangalore hotels.
3. Did Kuldeep take the right decision to leave the Bangalore hotel?

Appendix A:
Counterproductive Behaviour

Counterproductive behaviour includes all those behaviours wilfully undertaken by employees with an intention to harm people and the organization. Thus, counterproductive behaviour comprises theft, sabotage, workplace violence, workplace aggression, incivility, revenge, and so on. Conceptualization of counterproductive behaviour at the very beginning was disparate, disconnected, and focused on a variety of employee misbehaviour such as lateness, absenteeism, and sabotage. Gruys and Sackett (2003) identified various dimensions of counterproductive work behaviour: (a) theft, (b) destruction of property, (c) misuse of information, (d) misuse of time and resources, (e) unsafe behaviour, (f) poor attendance, (g) poor quality work, (h) alcohol use, (i) drug use, (j) inappropriate verbal action, and (k) inappropriate physical actions.

Robinson and Bennett (1995) attempted to present the first comprehensive and integrative view, suitably accommodating a wide range of disparate negative behaviour. This model is robust and comprehensive: robust because a number of independent studies successfully validated this typology and comprehensive because it successfully accommodates a wide range of negative employee behaviour. Robinson and Bennett (1995) proposed a two-dimensional model, measuring severity and target. Severity dimension indicates a continuum with a range from minor to severe. Target dimension indicates the recipient of harmful behaviour, ranging from individual to organizational. Thus, the cross section of these two dimensions delivers apparently four quadrants, and each one has been named after the themes production deviance, property deviance, political deviance, and personal aggression (Fig. A.1)

Production deviance   It is a range of counterproductive behaviour that is directed towards the organization. The severity of impact of such behaviour is relatively less. Production deviance behaviour includes presentation of a fragile excuse for not reporting for job/non-performance of job, wilfully extending break time, and so on. It is the organization that is at the receiving end of this type of counterproductive behaviour.

Political deviance   It is a range of counterproductive behaviour that is directed towards individuals within the organization. The severity of impact of such behaviour is also relatively less. Political deviance behaviour includes spreading unsubstantiated rumours and blaming others for their own mistakes. An individual employee or a group of employees becomes a victim of such behaviour.

Property deviance   It is a range of counterproductive behaviour that is directed towards the organization. The severity of impact of such behaviour on the organization is relatively high. Some examples of property deviance behaviour are stealing and sabotaging properties, availing

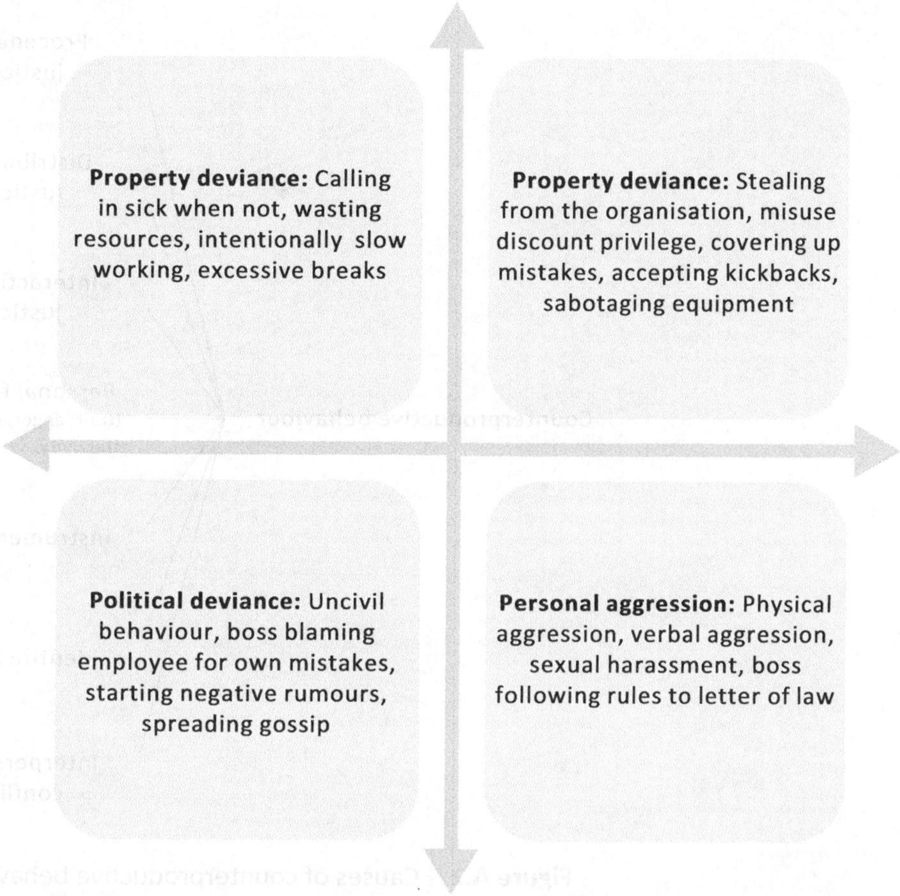

Property deviance: Calling in sick when not, wasting resources, intentionally slow working, excessive breaks

Property deviance: Stealing from the organisation, misuse discount privilege, covering up mistakes, accepting kickbacks, sabotaging equipment

Political deviance: Uncivil behaviour, boss blaming employee for own mistakes, starting negative rumours, spreading gossip

Personal aggression: Physical aggression, verbal aggression, sexual harassment, boss following rules to letter of law

Figure A.1   Typology of deviant work behaviour (Robinson and Bennett 1995)

facilities inappropriately, accepting bribe, and so on. This is a serious problem for the organization.

Personal aggression   It is a range of counterproductive behaviour that is directed towards other employees of the organization. The severity of impact of such behaviour is relatively very high. An example of personal aggression behaviour includes sexual harassment. Such behaviour where legal jurisprudence is relatively developed attracts severe financial penalty.

CAUSES OF COUNTERPRODUCTIVE BEHAVIOUR

There could be a number of reasons for counterproductive behaviour among employees. However, it is difficult to summarize all the factors responsible for such behaviour. Some of the factors are discussed here (Fig. A.2)

Interpersonal conflict   Overpowering nature of employee conflict often generates a sense of powerlessness. In some cases, a sense of perceived incompatibilities

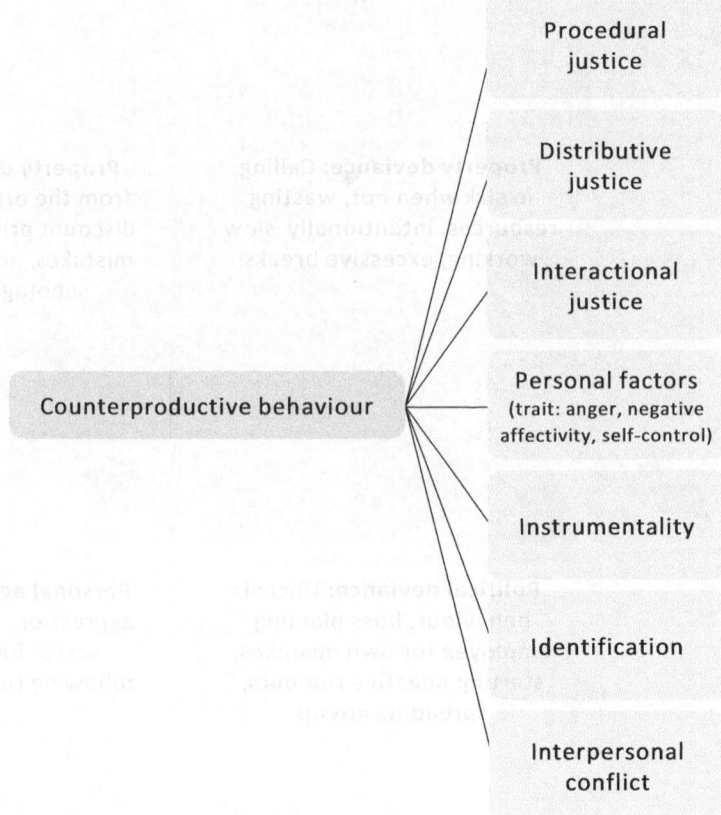

Figure A.2   Causes of counterproductive behaviour

among employees potentially generates workplace incivility. Employees reciprocate workplace incivility with a higher degree of aggressiveness. This increases the chance of mistreatment and social norms of workplace civility. Thus, interpersonal conflict is a reason for counterproductive behaviour as a part of redressal efforts, engineered by the affected employees.

Procedural justice   It is a kind of perceived unfairness pertaining to the procedure followed by the management for arriving at a specific outcome. Distribution of organizational resources has a strong bearing on the performance outcome of the employees. Each organization has processes and procedures to allocate resources. Unfair distribution of organizational resources, leading to a specific outcome, bears significant importance. Thus, counterproductive behaviour could be targeted towards the individuals who have designed and executed unjust procedure or benefited from the unjust procedures.

Job status   An individual employee with minimal job stake will be vulnerable to counterproductive behaviour. For example, a temporary employee receives discriminatory treatment from the organization in terms of salary, facilities, treatment from supervisors, and so on. Temporary workers tolerate this human exploitation as they have limited options for an alternate job. They comply with the rules and regulations till the time they are under intense scrutiny. However, some of these temporary employees may have lesser threshold of toleration, and subsequently, may engage in a range of counterproductive behaviour.

Individual characteristic Each employee manages his or her psychic energy in a certain preferred way, which turns out to be the driving force of the personality of the individual. Thus, when confronted with worldly problems, each individual attempts to solve the problem using these preferred means, which predominates and guides the individual to resolve life issues. Eventually, this durable psychic energy forms the person's individuality. When an individual prioritizes certain psychic energy over others, it potentially triggers a wide range of behaviour. For example, a narcissistic personality or an employee with higher trait anger will be more vulnerable to engaging in counterproductive behaviour.

Abusive supervision As defined by Tepper (2000), it is considered as a perception of the subordinates pertaining to a supervisor, who is claimed to be practising and displaying verbal and non-verbal hostility in a sustained manner towards subordinates. Examples of abusive supervision include public and private ridicule, rude behaviour of supervisor, and taking credit for a subordinate's work. Counterproductive behaviour is the reaction to the abusive behaviour exhibited by the supervisor.

Job dissatisfaction Job dissatisfaction is also one of the critical factors, especially when the job is menial in nature. Boring, dirty, and low-paid job performers are mostly confronted with on-job problems, and their family life is also constrained by financial, health, and other problems. For them, life is harsh, boring, and cruel. Little degree of application of discretion is available to them in the organizational context—they always experience the harsh and rude side of life. These employees are more vulnerable to engaging in counterproductive employee behaviour.

SITUATIONAL CONSTRAINTS

Perceived low risk of detection Perceived low risk of detection plays a critical role in the counterproductive behaviour of employees. Uncertainty of receipt of punishment for a crime provides encouragement for committing crimes. Committing crime without detection increases the chance of counterproductive behaviour. The incidence of theft cases is likely to be high where perception of low detection risk exists.

Influence of deviant group A deviant work group almost creates peer pressure to engage in collective or individual crime. Group norms existing among deviant work group play a critical role and enhance the likelihood of crime.

Political power distribution in organization   Workplace deviance is often a product of organizational power distribution. Power distribution installs legitimate authority at different hierarchies—a unique proportion of usage of reward, sanction, and punishment—organizational actors communicate about the desirables. Higher concentration of power to a few without democratic arrangements prepares the ground for autocratic oppression and denial of collective wisdom. The ordinary employee often experiences denial and alienation in the system. Individuals prefer different degrees of autonomy and self-control, as this gives them belief that they can control their own destinies. Concentration of power in only a few designations takes away this privilege belief and could possibly undermine or threaten one's identity in the organization as a strong and independent individual. Research indicates that this threat to individual identity activates defensive self-presentation and is more likely to provoke revengeful behaviour. This unequivocal submission to the altar of selected power gods generates frustration, anger, and revenge. Counterproductive behaviour is the natural result of this kind of system. Counterproductive behaviour is revenge, directed to demonstrate that they deserve better respectful treatment than their current situation.

Instrumentality   Instrumentality is often considered an important and indispensable ingredient for human motivation. Instrumentality means a belief that efforts/actions will likely achieve relevant goals. Research indicates that most students join public rallies when relevant instrumentality for the achievement of objective is relatively strong. Most of the academically serious students engage in serious studies because they believe that their effort will bring in the desired results.

A few authors deployed this concept in explanation of counterproductive behaviour. Instrumentality plays a catalytic role in the culmination of the ultimate expression of counterproductive behaviour. Having suffered under the abusive system of the organization, the aggrieved employee intentionally engages in deviant behaviour as a protest against the system. In case of unfair action by abusive supervisor or unfair organizational infrastructure, the aggrieved employee undertakes deviant action, when supported by positive instrumentality. This means that when the aggrieved employee, in his or her own assessment, believes that deviant action will redress the magnitude of the distress, the likelihood of practice of counterproductive behaviour increased substantially.

Identification   Identification with the victim, group, and organization often works as one of the critical factors in human behaviour. When corresponding identification with target for counterproductive behaviour is relatively low, there is a high likelihood that the aggrieved employee will engage in deviant action. Even if the deviant employee is not directly affected by the abusive supervision, however, strong solidarity and identification with the victim may trigger deviant behaviour.

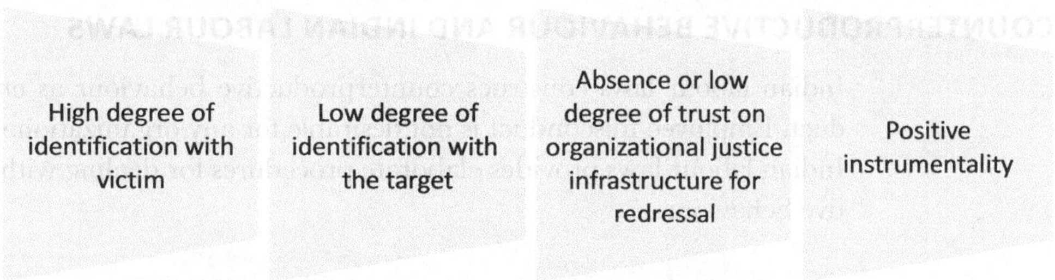

High degree of identification with victim	Low degree of identification with the target	Absence or low degree of trust on organizational justice infrastructure for redressal	Positive instrumentality

Figure A.3 Counterproductive behaviour model

Thus, strong identification with any victimized individual, whether it is a friend, colleague, team mate, supervisor, or individual employee, will potentially lead to deviant behaviour (Fig. A.3).

IMPLICATIONS OF COUNTERPRODUCTIVE BEHAVIOUR

Counterproductive behaviour is undesirable for any organizational context as it causes tremendous harm to the individuals who are exposed to it directly or indirectly. It is equally harmful for the organization as it facilitates squandering of precious organizational resources and causes economic loss.

Financial Employees are exposed to and are responsible for costly and precious products of the hotel and customers. Therefore, stealing and sabotaging pose considerable financial constraints on hotels. This problem becomes more complicated and costly, when the customer is at the receiving end of counterproductive behaviour. It not only causes financial loss but also causes considerable damage to the reputation of the hotel. Therefore, employee counterproductive behaviour is not desirable. It is not uncommon to see disgruntled employees throwing imported and costly vegetables into the dustbin. When counterproductive behaviour is exhibited in the presence of third party (for example, suppliers), the company ends up paying higher prices for the products the hotel purchases. As decision making is entrusted with the senior management team of the hotel, serious vigilance and strong organizational infrastructure should be provided.

Personal Counterproductive behaviour generates considerable stress in the organizational system. When employees engage in counterproductive behaviour, they have lost faith in the current justice system operating in the organizational context. As a last resort, employees take law in their hand to take revenge against the oppressive organizational infrastructure. A lot of productive time goes waste when employees engage in counterproductive behaviour. In addition, the relationship among employees goes sour. Internal conflict produces a lot of negative energy in the system, such as vanishing spirit of team work, demotivation, toxic work relationship, and employee turnover. In extreme cases, it leads to workplace violence.

COUNTERPRODUCTIVE BEHAVIOUR AND INDIAN LABOUR LAWS

Indian labour laws construes counterproductive behaviour as employee misconduct. Employee misconduct is not desirable for any organizational context; hence, Indian labour laws provides elaborate procedures for dealing with counterproductive behaviour.

REFERENCES

Gruys, M.L. and Sackett, P.R., 'The Dimensionality of Counterproductive Work Behavior', *International Journal of Selection and Assessment*, Volume 11, Issue 1, 2003, 30–42.

Robinson, S.L. and Bennett, R.J., 'A Typology of Deviant Workplace Behaviors: A Multidimensional Scaling Study', *Academy of Management Journal*, Volume 38, 1995, 555–752.

Tepper, B.J., 'Consequences of Abusive Supervision', *Academy of Management Journal*, Volume 43, 2000, 178–190.

Appendix B: Abusive Supervision

As defined by Tepper (2000), abusive supervision is considered as a perception of the subordinates pertaining to a supervisor, who is claimed to be practising and displaying verbal and non-verbal hostility in a sustained manner towards the subordinates. Examples of abusive supervision include public and private ridicule, rude behaviour of supervisor, and taking credit for a subordinate's work.

Generalized hierarchical abuse   It signifies the perception of mistreatment by superior. The mistreatment might have originated from any higher position directed towards subordinates. This mistreatment includes physical, non-physical, and sexual harassment (Fig. B.1).

Petty tyranny   Ashforth (1994) conceptualized a unique supervisory behaviour, which involves exorbitant, vindictive, and whimsical display of power to oppress subordinates. Petty tyranny is constituted by six dimensions: arbitrariness and self-aggrandizement, belittling subordinates, lack of consideration, a forceful style of conflict resolution, discouraging initiatives, and non-contingent punishment. Tepper argued that petty tyranny is a broader concept than abusive supervision. Petty tyranny does not indicate downward hostility towards subordinates. For example, petty tyrants are mostly unapproachable and unfriendly, which makes group environment unpleasant, but does not necessarily reflect hostility and focal negative intention as is predominant in abusive supervision.

Figure B.1   Abusive supervision and related concepts

One of the critical aspects of pretty tyrannical supervision involves discouraging initiatives. Discouraging initiatives signifies adherence to the routine ways of responding to organizational outcomes, and not allowing creative minds to operate in resolving organizational problems—this potentially creates depressing situations and a sense of repression.

Workplace victimization   Aquino and his colleagues (2000, 2002) conceptualized workplace victimization. Their research reported interesting dimensions that set it apart from abusive supervision. Borrowing the lenses from sociology and criminology, they reported that victimization is not always directed downward, that is, supervisor to subordinates. The range of victimization may originate from laterally located employees (co-workers) and may even be directed upward (at the supervisor). Hostility reaches the level of physical manifestation. Thus, abusive supervision is markedly different.

Workplace bullying   It is a sustained receipt of negative actions from one or several persons when the recipient is relatively in a weak situation failing to defend appropriately. Bullying does not necessarily originate from superior authority; it might be from collegial communities.

Supervisor undermining   It involves a wide range of behaviour, directed to prevent the formation of positive self-concept, work-related success, and maintenance of reputation by the individual employee. This undermining precludes physical hostility. The employee joins the organization for a range of benefits, which includes good remuneration, sense of success, achievement, and identity. Supervisor undermining deprives the recipient employee of pride in the job and hinders the processes to harm the reputation of employees. Supervisor undermining is one of the successful means of silencing lively employees into shattered individuals at the workplace. Supervisor undermining is a silent killer in the workplace. Although there are variations in describing supervisory abuse, the discussion presented above directs attention at the fact that abusive supervision is evidently present in the organizational context. Abusive supervision is not desirable as it brings toxicity in the workplace and enhances stress and the potential to reach violence. Hence, organizational infrastructure should provide adequate regulatory and normative provisions to curtail and restrain the power of abusive supervision.

ANTECEDENTS OF ABUSIVE SUPERVISION

Some research work that examined various antecedents of abusive supervision is available for academic scrutiny. Antecedents refer to the cause of something, or to the potential agent that causes something. The following are some antecedents that are responsible for abusive supervision.

Underlying Theories Explaining Aggressive Behaviour of the Supervisor

Drive theory of aggression   Drive theory suggests that external factors such as frustration trigger the harm intention, which will be expressed in some form of aggressive behaviour. Adequate empirical support to this theory is not readily available; however, it works as a popular belief and has wider acceptance (Fig. B.2).

Social learning perspective   This theory suggests that aggression is a learned behaviour often incorporated into behaviour from social environment. This could be due to the direct or indirect exposure to hostile environment. Past experience often helps determine how to find a target, ways to harm, and so on. The extent to which the past learning will be deployed in the current scenario depends on the current reward and current support to that practice.

For example, in some hotels, employees in the kitchen department often use slang and other obscene language with each other. Most of them have lost their sensitivity about the slang; new employees/industrial trainees face considerable difficulty in surviving in this environment. Many of the employees recount joyfully that they have been exposed to this 'culture of expression' quite from the beginning of their career; now, they practise it with subordinates as an 'expression of care'. New trainees often undergo great difficulty in adjusting with this environment. Some trainees will even bring it to the notice of the human resource manager. However, experienced human resource professionals are accustomed to listening to such problems. Kitchen staff learn directly; human resource professionals learn indirectly. Constant exposure to this culture makees them experienced and sensitive towards this culture. Aggression in hotels' kitchen is often linked with the treatments received earlier by their supervisor.

Social Explanation of Aggression

Frustration   Frustrating experience often leads to aggressive behaviour; however, it is not necessary that frustration always be accompanied by aggression. However, whenever frustration originates or is viewed as illegitimate or unjustified, the likelihood of frustration translating into aggressive behaviour becomes high.

Provocation   An aggressive approach is highly likely to be reciprocated in the same order or more, unless some other constraints operate there. Disdain and condescension operate as a predictor of aggressive behaviour.

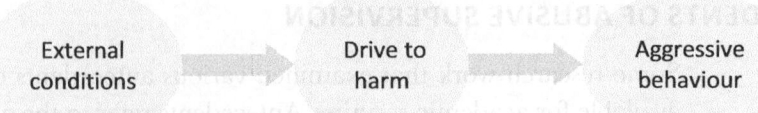

External conditions ⟶ Drive to harm ⟶ Aggressive behaviour

Figure B.2   Frustration–aggression hypothesis

Excitation transfer theory   This theory suggests that receipt of negative behaviour in one situation can dwell on and find its way in to subsequent events in a magnified manner. Subsequent events should not necessarily be related with the previous event—it could be completely unrelated. An individual may not be aware of the long intensity experience of residuals of negative events; however, negative behaviour may likely reappear in completely new and unrelated events.

Sustained exposure to media violence   Various experimental research studies indicated that sustained exposure to media depicting violent events increases the likelihood of engagement in aggressive behaviour and aggressive expectation; the individual tends to be biased towards violent adventure, leading to aggressive behaviour (Fig. B.3).

Violent pornography   Research indicates that because of exposure to violent pornography, men will likely exhibit increased aggressiveness against women. With the advent of the internet, access to such material has become easier, leading to increased exposure to lurid portrayal of violent and erotic behaviour. This generates rumination and tends to bias towards aggressive expression in behaviour.

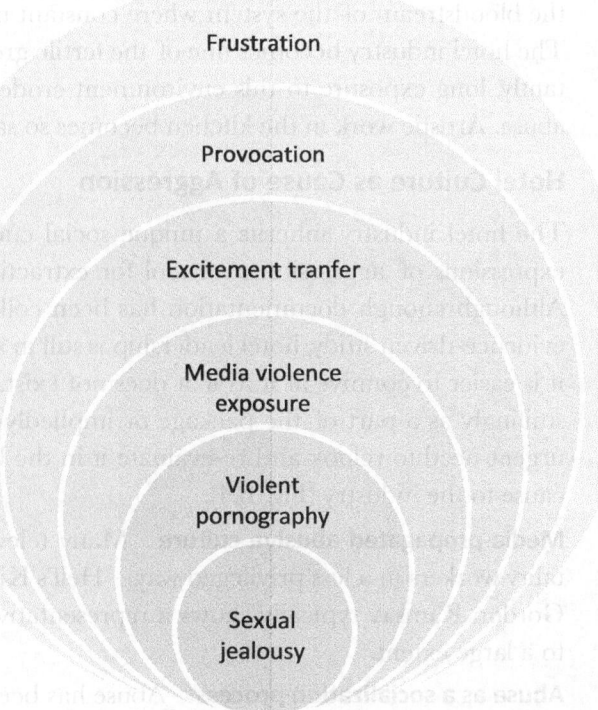

Figure B.3   Social explanation of aggression

Sexual jealousy This also potentially generates the likelihood of aggressive behaviour; this primitive gene has never been dormant in human civilization, no matter what height we achieve.

Personal Causes of Aggression

Narcissistic supervisor A narcissistic supervisor holds a glorified belief about self and encourages people to contribute to and nourish the glorified belief. Similarly, if there is any attack on the structure of this glorified belief of a narcissistic boss, there is high likelihood of violent reciprocation.

Demographics dynamics Young and weak trainees are often abused and harassed. Women employees are often denied social access to the inner core group of chefs who often drink in the early morning till the sun rises in the east. Women often become the target of derogatory remarks. Sexual exploitation is rampant; subsequently, floating stories about sexual exploitation leave the victim open for further exploitation and denial of tenured service. Women's progression in the kitchen is often surmised as an underground act of sexual satisfaction rather than as an act of merit. Often recasting the female self into the male infrastructure of kitchen provides greater acceptance and credibility. Noisy, aggressive, and foul mouth individuality helps frame a macho image of kitchen infrastructure. Abuse, thus, is in the bloodstream of the system where constant nourishment is available all across. The hotel industry becomes one of the fertile grounds for practising abuse. Importantly, long exposure to this environment erodes sensibility and interpretation of abuse. Artistic work in the kitchen becomes so satisfying that abuse is tolerated.

Hotel Culture as Cause of Aggression

The hotel industry inherits a unique social culture, which fosters and facilitates expressions of aggression as a tool for extracting performance from employees. Although enough documentation has been collected on this with the help of an evidence-driven study, hotel leadership is still in a denial mode. Quite conveniently, it is easier to connive at it as if it does not exist. Or, some of them accept it quite smilingly as a part of the package or impliedly accepted way of life. There is an urgent need to relook and re-evaluate it in the light of the immense harm it may cause to the industry (Fig. B.4).

Media-propagated abusive culture Many television programmes portray hospitality workers in a less privileged way—Hell's Kitchen Programme of British Chef Gordon Ramsay typically shows a representative kitchen culture quite accurately to a large extent.

Abuse as a socialization process Abuse has been embedded in the organizational infrastructure of hotels (especially in the kitchen) so intimately that residents and patrons of the system will find life meaningless and empty without it. Exchange of

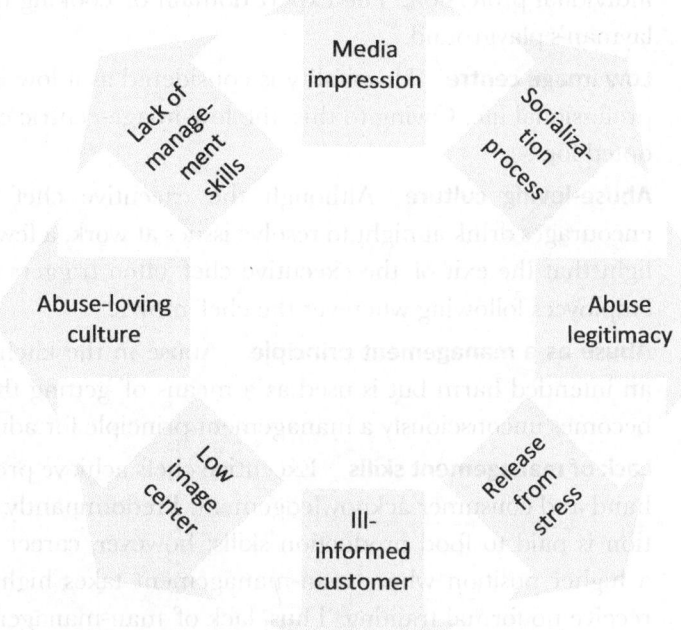

Figure B.4 Social infrastructure in hotels

abuse predominantly has been seen as a conduit of socialization process. Abuse is the means of forming a close community in the kitchen. Abuse has been labelled as affectionate glue, which creates bonds. A number of aspirants migrate to other streams of business because of the hostile environment. Abuse is also used as a socialization phase so intensely that most of the accepted members in the kitchen get immune and lose sensitivity to abuse. A number of studies have recorded relevant evidence to substantiate these statements.

Abuse as a release from stress   Abuse also works as a release from the stressful situation. The kitchen is often a victim of poor design and maintenance. Completion of long shifts in the early hours of the day often ushered in a new underground lifestyle, which often causes health hazards for the employees. This untimely drink and food habits also cause immense family and financial crisis. Thus, abusive supervision is the right match for each other.

Ill-informed customers   Kitchen job is often considered as an artist's factory. Artful creation of food is what makes a chef proud. In the game of superiority, ill-informed customers claim to possess authentic knowledge on the specific method of cooking, and whenever opportunity arrives, ill-informed customers discredit the very self that each chef stands for. This requires considerable denial of self and acceptance of what is not right. This is equivalent to disrobing the dignity of the individual profession. The expert domain of cooking often becomes an arena of layman's playground.

Low image centre   Hospitality is considered as a low image centre for practising professional life. Owing to this, the low-image-centric career format is not readily opted for.

Abuse-loving culture   Although the executive chef abuses subordinates and encourages drink at night to resolve issues at work, a few documented studies highlight that the exit of the executive chef often triggers mass resignation, with the employees following wherever the chef moves.

Abuse as a management principle   Abuse in the kitchen is often not necessarily an intended harm but is used as a means of getting the work done. Thus, abuse becomes unconsciously a management principle for administration of the kitchen.

Lack of management skills   Executive chefs achieve promotion because of a good hand and consumer acknowledgement. Predominantly, considerably higher attention is paid to food production skills; however, career progression leads them to a higher position where man-management takes higher priority, for which they receive no formal training. Thus, lack of man-management skills often may move them to utilize abuse as a means of achievement of results.

Situational Causes of Aggression

High temperature   There is a curvilinear relationship between high temperature and aggression. This signifies that with increase in temperature, aggression goes up; however, after reaching a certain point, the likelihood of aggression goes down. Therefore, in the kitchen of a five-star hotel, there is a high likelihood that employees will be vulnerable to aggressive behaviour (Fig. B.5).

Alcohol consumption   Research indicates that there is a close relationship between alcohol consumption and aggressive behaviour. This makes the hospitality industry relatively vulnerable as it deals with various types of alcohols. This proximity makes aggression an occupational hazard for the employees who are exposed. The underlying relationship between alcohol consumption and aggression could be explained in the following manner:

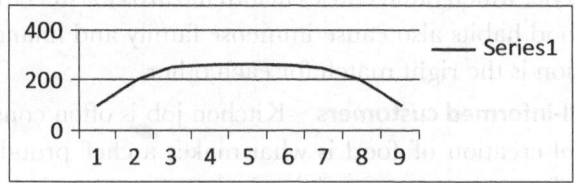

Figure B.5   Relationship between temperature and aggression

1. Alcohol consumption reduces the capacity to interpret the situation in an objective manner.
2. Alcohol consumption misdirects individuals to pay attention to the matters that otherwise individuals are not interested in usually.
3. Alcohol consumption reduces internal inhibitions and lets the individual loose for unlikely activities.

Lifestyle exposures   Individuals working in five-star hotels get exposure to luxurious lifestyles. Owing to long duty hours, although most of the employees are exposed to lurid consumption, human enjoyment, and horrible display of wealth, women, and wines, the personal lives of most of the employees are not financially robust, and many of them are deprived of basic ingredients of life. Thus, apparent paradox of lifestyle exposure potentially generates expectation for consummating lifestyle, which is practically not possible; thus, individuals experience frustration. Accompanied by long duty hours, extreme time pressure for production of quality services, life dissonance, and aggressiveness are displayed in a muted and transformed manner.

Process view   In case of violation of personal rights, privileges, identity, and control, the individual experiences injustice, anger, and negative emotions. It is argued that the individual follows the expectation-accountability-anger framework to process the perceived violation (Fig. B.6). As per the process, when individuals once experience violations of rights, privileges, and workplace incivility (Andersson and Pearson 1999), it creates an unjust experience. Subsequently, while ruminating on the issue, the individual evaluates whether the transgressor could be held accountable for the violations. If the individual successfully assigns the responsibility to the specific transgressor, he or she experiences anger and will be vulnerable to taking revenge. Bradfield and Aquino (1999) examined this process with the help of empirical data. They found that blame attribution (to the transgressor) positively influences generation of revenge cognition, which subsequently leads to revenge behaviour.

Regarding blame attribution, Bradfield and Aquino reported that offence severity significantly predicts blame attribution. Pertaining to achieving forgiveness behaviour, they examined the role of offender likableness. Offender likableness

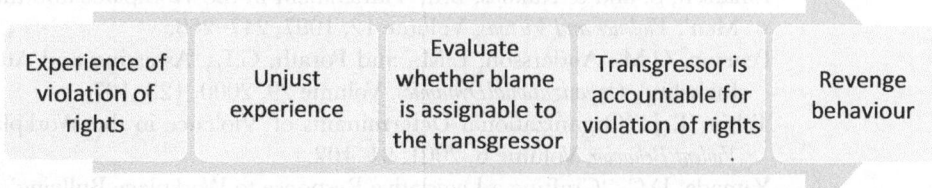

Figure B.6   Expectation-accountability-anger framework

significantly predicts forgiveness cognition, which results in forgiveness behaviour. One of the interesting elements of the research was that revenge cognition is significantly related to both revenge and forgiveness behaviour; however, forgiveness cognition is significantly related with only forgiveness cognition. They argued that rumination on revenge does not mean engaging in revenge behaviour. This could be due to the operation of power differentials (fear of counter-retaliation), which may prevent from engaging in revenge. Aquino, Tripp, and Bies (2006) advanced the arguments by examining the role of power position in organizational hierarchy and offence type in relation to revenge and forgiveness behaviour. Using Bies' and Tripp's (2004) typology of offenses (goal obstruction, rule violation, and status derogation), they reported that victims are more likely to engage in revenge-seeking behaviour in case of rule violation or derogation offences than goal-obstruction offences only, while experiencing unjust experience.

REFERENCES

Andersson, L., and Pearson, C., 'Tit for Tat? The Spiraling Effect of Incivility in the Workplace', *Academy of Management Review*, Volume 24, 1999, p.452–471.

Aquino, K. and Bradfield, M., 'Perceived Victimization in the Workplace: The Role of Situational Factors and Victim Characteristics', *Organization Science*, Volume 11, 2000, 525–537.

Aquino, K., and Byron, K., 'Dominating Interpersonal Behavior and Perceived Victimization in Groups: Evidence for a Curvilinear Relationship', *Journal of Organizational Behavior*, Volume 23, 2002, 267–285.

Aquino, K., Tripp, T.M., and Bies, R.J., 'Getting Even or Moving on: Power, Procedural Justice, and Types of Offense as Predictors of Revenge, Forgiveness, Reconciliation, and Avoidance in Organizations', *Journal of Applied Psychology*, Volume 91, 2006, 653–668.

Ashforth, B.E., 'Petty Tyranny in Organizations', *Human Relations*, Volume 47, 1994, 755–778.

Tepper, B.J., 'Consequences of Abusive Supervision', *Academy of Management Journal*, Volume 43, 178–190, 2000.

INTERESTING READINGS

Duffy, M.K., Ganster, D., and Pagon, M., 'Social Undermining in the Workplace', *Academy of Management Journal*, Volume 45, 2002, 331–351.

Einarsen, S. and & Raknes, B.I., 'Harassment in the Workplace and the Victimization of Men', *Violence and Victims*, Volume 12, 1997, 247–263.

Pearson, C.M., Andersson, L.M., and Porath, C.L., 'Assessing and Attacking Workplace Incivility', *OrganizationalDynamics*, Volume 29, 2000, 123–137.

Tobin, T. J., 'Organizational Determinants of Violence in the Workplace', *Aggression and Violent Behavior*, Volume 6, 2001, 91–102.

Yamada, D.C., 'Crafting a Legislative Response to Workplace Bullying', *Employee Rights and Responsibilities Journal*, Volume 8, 2004, 475–521.

Index

360-degree feedback system   99
   content   102
   feedback partners   104
   individual benefit   99
   organizational benefit   101
   prerequisites   101

Abusive supervision   327
   antecedents   328
   generalized hierarchical
      abuse   327
   hotel culture   331
   petty tyranny   327
   supervisor undermining   328
   theories   329
   workplace bullying   328
   workplace victimization   328

Balanced scorecard   95
   customer   96
   difficulties   97
   employee's learning and
      growth   96
   finance   96
   internal process   96

Collective bargaining   218
   process   219
Compensation   135
   basic pay   136
   brand-based pay   148
   business boom   145
   business strategy   145
   competency-based pay   147
   determinants   139
   effective   139
   equity   144
   limitations   154
   objectives   138

philosophical   146
policy   135, 139
psychological theories   143
recession   145
seniority-based pay   146
skill-based pay   148
tipping   154
variable pay   136, 147
Counterproductive
   behaviour   319
   causes   320
   implications   324
   personal aggression   320
   political deviance   319
   production deviance   319
   property deviance   319

Disciplinary action   255
   charge sheet   263
   disciplining   258
   employee misconduct   255
   equity   261
   guidelines   260
   natural justice   257
   positive discipline   258
   process   261
   promptness   261
   transparency   261
Dissatisfaction   169
   exit-voice-loyalty-neglect
      typology   170
   express   169

Employee motivation   115
   benchmarking   130
   crafting an interesting
      job   127
   employee recognition
      programme   125

employee training   127
empowerment   128
good remuneration   126
good supervision   127
job enrichment   125
joy at work   125
motivating group   130
offsite fun activities   129
participative work
   processes   129
positive organizational
   support   128
stock option   129
welfare initiatives   128
work–life balance   127
Employee performance   105
   deadwoods   108
   demotivated performers   107
   excellent performers   107
   motivated learners   107
   theoretical underpin-
      ning   106
Employment tests   60
   aptitude test   60
   group discussion   60
   psychometric test   60
   skill test   60
Executive compensation   148
   chronological age of the
      executive   149
   employee stock options
      plan   151
   executive benefit   152
   public shareholding   150
   shareholding   149
Expatriate management   308
   adjustment   308
External recruitment   52
   methods   52

Forecasting methods 39

HRIS 275
  compensation management
    module 281
  employee exit manage-
    ment 285
  e-recruitment solutions 281
  e-service 286
  payroll management 280
  time office management 279
HRM 1
  definition 1
  importance 9
  managing 9
  organizational/firm
    performance 18
HR managers 25
  challenges 18
  competency 25
  functions 22
  roles 16
Hospitality industry 12
  characteristics 12
  implications of the
    characteristics 15
  training in India 72
Human resource management 1

Indian multinationals 293
  accelerated growth 293
  acquisition 294
  competition 293
  late comer 293
  liabilities of foreignness 294
Indian service sector 5–8
  growth drivers 5
Internal recruitment 50
  advantages 50
  disadvantages 51
  methods 51
International HR manage-
  ment 291
  compensation 312

development 303
ethnocentric approach 299
host country nationals 302
manpower planning 301
masculinity versus
  femininity 298
national culture 294
need 291
parent country
  nationals 302
polycentric approach 300
power distance 296
recruitment 299
third country nationals 302
training 303
types of training 306
uncertainty avoidance 295

Job satisfaction 159
  correlates 161
  different cultures 166
  gender 163
  implications 170
  importance 165
  job descriptive index 168
  length of service 163
  measurement 167
  Minnesota satisfaction
    questionnaire 168
  organizational culture 162
  organizational status 163

Labour laws 223
  collective bargaining 234
  contract workers 240
  industrial dispute 234
Labour legislations 226
  Contract Labour (Regula-
    tion and Abolitions) Act,
    1971 242
  debate 246
  Employees State Insurance
    Act, 1948 237
  Equal Remuneration Act,
    1976 245

Gratuity Act 226
Industrial Dispute Act,
  1947 235
Payment of Bonus Act,
  1965 239
provident fund 237
rate of gratuity 227
Sexual Harassment at Work-
  place Bill, 2010 245
Shops and Establishment
  Act 239
Minimum Wages Act,
  1948 243
Payment of Wages Act,
  1936 244
Trade Union Act, 1926 230
Workmen Compensation Act,
  1923 228

Management by objectives 92
  underlying theories 94
Manpower planning 33
  effective 36
  importance 34
  introduction 33
  managing workforce 41
  offer 43
  planning process 40
  shortfall in workforce 42
  workforce surplus 42
Motivation 115, 160
  Adams' equity theory 119
  competitive edge 116
  creative tension 122
  employee satisfaction
    survey 121
  fair work process 123
  goal-setting theory 121
  Herzberg's theory 161
  Herzberg's two-factor
    theory 118
  how to 123
  job characteristics
    models 164
  job rotation 123

management by
    objectives 122
Maslow's theory   117, 160
measurement 120
reinforcement theory 120
theories 117
turnover rate 121
walk the talk 121

Organizational conflict 211
    conflict resolution 214
    desirable 211
    labour laws 214
    minimize 217
    types 213
Organizational culture 177
    communicate 202
    competing value frame-
        work 192
    cultural models 184
    cultural web 184
    diagnosing 194
    embed 202
    functions 179

leaders nurture 202
managing and changing 205
negative 198
observable aspect 178
OCTAPACE model 186
positive 198
shadow liability 180
strategic resource 180
transmit 201

Performance appraisal 85
    appraising what 87
    difficulties 88
    effective 108
    fail 91
    process 87
    purpose 85
    usage 88
Personal interview 61
    behavioural event
        interview 61
    how to prepare 63

Recruitment 49

communication 58
company brand 57
employee competency 55
legality 64
policy 56
sources 50
successful employees 54
when to recruit 56

The Indian Labour
    Movement 2
    union membership 4
Training 67
    cost or investment 78
    culture 79
    evaluation 75
    importance 67
    methods 75
    need identification
        process 70
    size of the hotel 69
    trainer 77
    training cycle 73

HUMAN RESOURCE MANAGEMENT | 9780198076681

Uday Kumar Haldar, Swami Vivekanand Institute of Management and Computer Science, Kokata, and **Juthika Sarkar**, HR practitioner

Comprehensive in its coverage of topics and with a lucid approach, the book provides various examples and case studies, which serve as a valuable guide for professionals.

Key Features

• Covers various facets of HR systems including acquiring, retaining, and developing talent
• Dedicates a chapter exclusively to the contemporary research findings in the field of HRM
• Discusses HR strategies in different sectors such as manufacturing, service, and knowledge industry

MANAGEMENT PRINCIPLES, PROCESSES AND PRACTICES | 9780195694451

Anil Bhat, BITS Pilani, and **Arya Kumar**, BITS Pilani

The book discusses both managerial (planning, organizing, leading, and controlling) as well as organizational functions (finance, marketing, operations management, MIS, strategy, and human resources) in detail. It acquaints readers with the entire gamut of terms, concepts, and processes of business and organizations.

Key Features

• Explains key concepts through numerous illustrations, examples, exhibits, tables, figures, and exercises
• Includes a detailed section on managerial competencies with separate chapters on motivation, team effectiveness, communication, conflict management, leadership, decision-making, emotional intelligence, stress management, and creativity and entrepreneurship

PERSONALITY DEVELOPMENT AND SOFT SKILLS (includes CD) | 9780198066217

Barun Mitra, Formerly Professor of English, Indian Institute of Technology, Kharagpur

The book addresses the requirements of students of any discipline who are on the threshold of starting their careers or young managers already working in the corporate world.

Key Features

• Provides inputs on avoiding common mistakes in speaking English
• Provides several case studies, examples, and illustrations to elucidate the concepts discussed
• Contains several classroom-based activities for students to develop their personalities and enhance their soft skills
• Provides PPTs on group discussions, job interviews, body language

COMMUNICATION SKILLS (includes CD) | 9780198069324

Sanjay Kumar, JK Lakshmipat University, Jaipur, and **Pushp Lata**, BITS Pilani

The aim of the book is to help students acquire the ability to speak and write English effectively in real-life situations.

Key Features

• Covers English grammar in detail with plenty of examples, practice tests, and exercises
• Contains numerous samples of business letters, reports, proposals, essays, and email correspondence

• 9780198061090 Hotel Housekeeping, 2/e
• 9780198065272 Food and Beverage Service
• 9780195699197 Hotel Front Office
• 9780198061816 Food Production Operations
• 9780198068495 Quantity Food Production Operations and Indian Cuisine
• 9780198073895 International Cuisine and Food Production Management

• 9780198064633 Hotel Facility Planning
• 9780198062912 Hotel Engineering
• 9780195694468 Hotel Finance
• 9780198078869 Food Science and Nutrition, 2/e
• 9780198072362 Tourism Principles and Practices
• 9780198060017 Tourism Operations and Management
• 9780198066309 Tourism Marketing

Visit us at www.oup.co.in and www.oupinheonline.com